España

Bilbao

S. Sebastián

Vasco

Pamplona

Rioja

Zaragoza

Cataluña

Penedés

Aragón

Barcelona

Tarragona

Teruel

Madrid

Valencia

Islas
Baleares

ancha

Valencia

Murcia

Alicante

Murcia

anada

Mar Mediterráneo

OCHOA

The Foods and Wines of Spain

THE FOODS
AND WINES
OF SPAIN

by *Penelope Casas*

Illustrated by
Oscar Ochoa

Alfred A. Knopf New York 1991

THIS IS A BORZOI BOOK
PUBLISHED BY ALFRED A. KNOPF, INC.

Copyright © 1979, 1980, 1981, 1982 by Penelope Casas

Some of the recipes in this book have been previously published in *Bon Appetit, Cuisine, Diversion, Food and Wine, The New York Times,* and *Vogue.*

Library of Congress Cataloging in Publication Data

Casas, Penelope.   The foods and wines of Spain

Includes index.
1. Cookery, Spanish.   2. Wine and wine making—
Spain.   I. Title.
TX723.5.S7C3574   1982   641.5946   82-47830
ISBN 0-394-51348-7

Manufactured in the United States of America

Published October 26, 1982
Reprinted Five Times
Seventh Printing, March 1991

Para Luis y Elisa —

Infatigables compañeros de viaje
y gastrónomos de primera clase

Contents

Acknowledgments

The Foods and Wines of Spain is the result of years of dogged, if often unfocused, research into the culinary and cultural heritage of Spain. It is also a consequence of chance circumstances that brought my interest in Spain and Spanish cooking to the attention of Craig Claiborne, food editor of *The New York Times*. Craig has been a good friend and advisor, and it was he who encouraged me to put my accumulated knowledge into a Spanish cookbook. My editor, Judith Jones, enthusiastically embraced the idea, and her editorial advice was an essential ingredient in the development of this book.

I am deeply appreciative of friends and relatives in Spain who took great interest in my book and contributed some exceptional recipes: my mother-in-law, Clara Orozco, who is unusually creative in the kitchen and taught me so much about Spanish cooking; Carmen and Pepe González, good friends and constant sources of information on Castilian cookery; Pepe and Paqui Delfín, who were enormously generous with their time and whose enthusiasm for their city of Cádiz knows no bounds; Sofía Pandiellas, who contributed many family recipes from her native Asturias; Lola and Chari Romero; Marilola and Enrique Torán; Dr. José Sanz Tobes; Chalo Peláez; Luis Gil Lus of Casa Fermín restaurant in Oviedo; Antonio and Simón Tomás of the Sol-Ric restaurant in Tarragona; Gonzalo Córdoba Gutiérrez of El Faro restaurant in Cádiz; Irene of Casa Irene in Artiés; and José Bárcena, native of Asturias and one of New York City's best chefs. The wineries of Pedro Domecq, R. López de Heredia, and Federico Paternina were most gracious in providing tours, tastings, and information, all of which expanded my knowledge and appreciation of Spanish wines.

Many thanks to Ramón San Martín, owner of the Café San Martín in New York City. While *The Foods and Wines of Spain* was being written, no one could have been more generous with his time and offers of assistance and professional advice.

I thank Antonia and Achilles Fexas, my parents, for their unfailing personal and professional encouragement and their constructive criticism on the many manuscripts I submitted to them for comments and suggestions. I am also ever grateful to my close friend, Marsha Stanton, who, in so many intangible ways, has given me support and encouragement over the years. And thanks to my daughter, Elisa, for enduring my long hours in the kitchen, tasting my creations, and tolerating the extremely late dinner hours that often resulted from my recipe testings.

The contributions of my husband, Luis, to *The Foods and Wines of Spain* are incalculable. He first introduced me to Spain many years ago and has accompanied me and my daughter on countless Spanish journeys of discovery. Luis has always been as persistent as I in tracking down the most exciting, most beautiful, and most delicious food and wine that Spain has to offer. His infectious love for his native land of Spain was a constant source of inspiration to me, and his unerring good taste in food and wine and his wide knowledge of Spain and Spanish cuisine were essential in the development and completion of this book.

Introduction
by Craig Claiborne

WHEN I once wrote, a few years ago, about a Spanish ingredient, I erred on the side of the angels. It was a minor point and had to do with those silvery, spaghettilike baby eels which are, to my taste, absolutely irresistible when cooked with garlic and oil and flecks of hot dried red peppers. One of the grandest appetizers in the total repertoire of Spanish cooking.

The trouble was, I referred to them in the column that appeared in *The New York Times* as *anguilas*. Within a day or so I had a letter from a reader, Penny Casas, informing me that the correct spelling was *angulas*, and, she added, if I would ever care to sample them in her own home, she would be happy to serve them to me. I was astonished to discover that she knew of a source in the city where she could purchase *angulas* freshly imported from Spain.

It was an invitation that I accepted with mouth-watering alacrity. To the best of my recollection I telephoned her on the day of receiving her note.

When I arrived at her address a few nights later, I met the author of the note and her husband, Luis, a Spanish-born physician, who, I shortly became aware, was a considerable authority on the wines of his country. And I was greeted by their daughter, Elisa (who was then 14 years old).

Prior to dining on those eels (they were to be served as first course to what turned out to be an elaborate Spanish feast), we had a fine conversation about Spanish cooking in general and *tapas*, the famed "small foods" or appetizers which number in the thousands in the Spanish bistros known as *tascas*.

It seems that *tapas* were one of the bonds that cemented the early relationship of Penny (Penelope) Casas and Luis.

In high school Penny studied Spanish and went to Spain when she was 19 as part of a student exchange program. The home to which she was assigned belonged to Luis's mother. His father had been killed during the Spanish Revolution.

Luis, she told me, "taught me very quickly how to adapt to the Spanish life. He was only 26 and each night we would go to all the *tascas* in the working-class section of Madrid. Those places catered to students and blue-collar workers. Like most Spaniards, Luis and I would spend most of the evening sampling *tapas*."

A *tasca*, the couple recounted, is a small bar, a gathering place for Spaniards who like to sip sherry or beer and exchange gossip. The *tapas* may range from foods like fresh sardines or squid in olive oil and vinegar to snails in sauce, *chorizos* (Spanish sausages), dried ham and a cold Spanish omelet. They explained that this version made with potatoes and eggs is the true Spanish omelet and not the American version made with a creole sauce.

Penny was so taken with these foods that she spent a good deal of her time in the kitchens of the *tascas* talking food with the owner and/or cook. And when she came back to this country she had accumulated a vast collection of recipes.

The true Spanish omelet, she noted, is "a national passion in Spain." "It is eaten," she added, "for breakfast, for lunch or dinner as well as in between as a snack. It is part of most picnics and included in every school child's lunch box." "In Spanish," she said, "the word for omelet is *tortilla* and the name of that potato omelet in Spain is *tortilla española.*"

At that point Penelope started to serve, as a preface to a sit-down dinner, a collection of *tapas*. They included an incredibly good stuffed-mussel dish and snails in a delectable oil-rich tomato and *chorizo* sauce.

As we sat at table we shared that famous eel dish, each portion served hot from the stove in individual ramekins. The eels were followed by another Iberian specialty, quails in *escabeche*, a marinade of oil, vinegar, saffron, garlic and white wine. The meal ended with three desserts: a formidably good lemon ice with cinnamon flavor, sand cookies lightly dusted with confectioners' sugar and *yemas* of St. Theresa—a rich dessert made with vigorously beaten egg yolks and a boiling syrup. With the meal we had consumed two excellent Spanish wines, a Gran Viña Sol, Reserva, 1976, and a Viña Tondonia Reserva, 1964. The evening ended with a glass of excellent Spanish brandy, Lepanto, González Byass.

To my mind that meal had been not only praiseworthy but prize-worthy. It was in fact one of the most memorable meals that I have experienced in nearly a quarter of a century with my newspaper.

As I rode home in a taxi, I mulled over the fact that of all the books in my fairly extensive library in my home in East Hampton, there is not a single, comprehensive volume on Spanish cooking in English that pretends to be all-embracing. The books that I own and that deal with the subject offer half-hearted (quarter-hearted would be more accurate) or terribly tailored versions of what the Spanish kitchen is really like.

As time progressed, and as I enjoyed meal after meal at the Casas table, I cajoled Penny into gathering all her recipes for what could and would be the definitive book on Spanish cooking. And she acquiesced. And, fortunately for those who care about such things, she shortly thereafter found a publisher, the distinguished house of Alfred A. Knopf, Inc.

And this is her book. It is all that I had hoped it would be and more. To my mind, she has produced a jewel to be added to the crown of culinary literature.

I am pleased beyond measure to think that I have played one ever-so-small role in the production of this book.

CRAIG CLAIBORNE
East Hampton, New York
April, 1982

Preface

I FIRST visited Spain some twenty years ago and immediately fell in love with the country's cuisine. Over the years, as I traveled to every region of Spain and delved into lesser-known regional cooking, my admiration for Spanish cooking became even greater. I am constantly amazed, however, to find how little the world knows about Spanish cuisine and how it has become confused with the cooking of the rest of the Spanish-speaking world. In Spain the food is not hot and spicy, as many assume it to be, nor does it include *tamales, tacos, enchiladas, frijoles,* or anything even vaguely resembling these traditional Latin American dishes. The cooking of Spain is subtle and refined, as well as simple and down-to-earth, and is the product of many centuries of fine eating.

The confusion between Latin American cooking and the cuisine of Spain stems from the all-inclusive term "Spanish" and the use of sometimes similar ingredients, some of which were carried to the New World by Spanish discoverers (for example, rice, bananas, wheat and sugar) as well as many other ingredients native to the New World that were brought back to Spain and rapidly incorporated into world cookery. Just think how impoverished the civilized world would be today without green and red peppers, chocolate, tomatoes, potatoes, and maize, all of which were introduced to Europe from America by way of Spain. Never do you find, however, a recipe in Spain's culinary repertoire that duplicates a dish from South America or Mexico. For at the time of the discovery of America, Spain already had a cuisine much admired and often copied by other European countries, including France. One strong influence was the more than seven-hundred-year Moorish occupation of Spain, which gave Spanish cooking a decidedly Middle Eastern flair that was missing from other European cuisines of the time. Sweet-sour sauces, sugar cane, almonds, citrus fruits, and seasonings such as cumin, saffron, and nutmeg all enriched Spanish cooking and helped to make it popular in Europe. The new products from the New World only enhanced an already flourishing cuisine.

Spain's culinary influence in Europe was most pronounced in the sixteenth and seventeenth centuries, when the Spanish crown ruled most of Europe and more than half of the American continent. The royal houses of Europe imported Spanish chefs, and Spain set the culinary standards among the well-to-do. In my collection of Spanish cookbooks is one dated 1525, written by Ruperto de Nola, chef to King Ferdinand of the Kingdom of Naples, Italy. His recipes were most sophisticated for his time and included all kinds of spices, as well as almonds, pine nuts, raisins, and fruits. However, exciting changes in European cooking came about with New World food imports.

For centuries Spain maintained the tradition of what is called _La Buena Mesa_ (The Good Table). As far back as the thirteenth century, King Alfonso "The Wise" wrote: "Spain is rich in honeys, abundant with fruits, teeming with fish, well provided with milk . . . filled with deer and hunt, covered with cattle, merry with good wine, happy with an abundance of bread and sugar . . . well stocked with oil and fragrant with saffron." This abundance of fresh produce naturally provided for some very good eating, such as the feast at the grand country wedding described in the sixteenth-century novel, _Don Quijote de la Mancha_. Cervantes speaks of whole sides of lamb and beef on the barbecue, each beef stomach filled with twelve suckling pigs to give added flavor, and enormous cauldrons for stewing hare, hens, and game. There were seventy wine skins, "pure white" breads, and whole cheeses, piled up like bricks to form a veritable wall. Pastries were fried, in two cauldrons of hot oil, then dipped in a huge vat of honey. More than fifty cooks were busy with the preparations.

THE SEARCH FOR THE FOODS AND WINES OF SPAIN

WHEN I first visited Spain, I never realized what an effect that visit, which promised to be little more than a student summer-study program, would have on my life. During the months I spent in Madrid, I found the city fascinating. Especially intriguing was Old Madrid, hardly changed since the sixteenth century, where the enticing aromas of roast lamb and suckling pig wafted through the cobbled streets. In the rustic bars and taverns, still operating much the same as they did in centuries past when these dark narrow streets were the hub of city life, I found the array of appetizers, or _tapas_, available everywhere, to be overwhelming. Many of these _tapas_ were completely new taste experiences for me, and equally new was the lively and colorful tavern atmosphere, the custom in Spain of gathering twice a day to meet friends, have a glass of wine or beer, sample _tapas_, and discuss the issues of the day (more on the _tapas_ tradition, p. 3). All this was so different from the life I had left behind on the other side of the Atlantic, and I found it enchanting and exciting.

Ever since that first trip to Spain I have been held captive by the country, its culture and its people. In Spain I met and married my husband, a native Madrileño, and lived there for several years before we moved to New York. Now we return to Spain without fail year after year, drawn by an irresistible urge to be joined to that wonderful country once more. It is partly our passion for Spanish food that attracts us, for there is nothing more enjoyable than sampling favorite foods once again, while at the same time anticipating the many pleasant culinary surprises that we know await us.

But our admiration and love for Spanish foods have not always been shared by Spaniards. For many years it was considered quite chic to emulate French cuisine. Then followed the enormous influx of tourists in the sixties, which turned the country toward a more international cuisine. Finally, in the past five years or so, Spain has once more begun to take pride and interest in its own culinary heritage, and none too soon, because those with firsthand knowledge of traditional Spanish cuisine are becoming rare. Today fine restaurants are sprouting up all over Spain, many devoted to classic Spanish cooking, including regional specialties, while others near the French border, in the Spanish Basque country, promote a "nouvelle" Spanish cuisine. At any social gathering now the main focus of conversation has changed dramatically from politics to food, and arguments rage for hours, in the typical Spanish manner, over which restaurant has the freshest fish, the tenderest lamb, the best *paella, fabada,* or *cocido.* Spaniards never discuss anything except in absolute terms.

Despite the renewed interest in Spanish cuisine and the wealth of new material coming to light, very little of the information about food, to say nothing of recipes that I needed to write *The Foods and Wines of Spain,* had as yet been put to paper. I found myself, along with Spaniards who have also become interested in expanding their knowledge of Spanish cuisine, groping in unexplored territory. Drawn into this challenging venture, I started collecting recipes; I pored over whatever Spanish food books were available, pressed Spanish friends and relatives for information and recipes, and sampled, of course, the foods at Spain's finest restaurants and interviewed their chefs and proprietors. But most important was my search covering over 25,000 miles in Spain, visiting isolated villages and towns, where twentieth-century products and eating habits have not yet arrived, where I came upon wonderful dishes that have survived the centuries. Authentic regional cooking, which in some cases goes back to Roman times, can still be found in these small, out-of-the-way places, often in ancient kitchens, where ladies dressed in black toil over woodburning stoves. Discovering such places has given me some of my most satisfying experiences and some of my finest recipes.

In writing this book, I envisioned the work to be as much an extensive collection of recipes and Spanish cooking techniques as a guide to travel and dining in Spain. Whenever possible I have included descriptions of unusual cities and villages I have visited and exceptional restaurants where I have dined, in the hope that the reader may wish to follow in my footsteps. For those who have already been to Spain, I hope I have included just about everything you've loved eating in Spain—such dishes as Tortilla Española, Gambas al Ajillo, Pincho Moruno, Calamares Fritos, *chorizo, paella, gazpacho,* and *churros.* I have worked out all the recipes so that they have the "taste" of Spain. I have also developed bread and sausage recipes, rarely found in Spanish cookbooks, much less prepared in the typical Spanish home. A host of other recipes, which most visitors and often Spaniards themselves never suspected were part of the enormously varied cuisine of Spain, are also part of this book.

Wine is an integral part of every Spanish meal, so I have included wine suggestions with all appropriate recipes. My purpose is to introduce you to the wonderful wines of Spain, still relatively unknown in this country. In the back of the book you will find charts that list Spanish wines and sherries that are imported in the United States. Depending on where you live, selection may be far more limited than these charts would suggest, in which case you can simply sample what is available and then try to persuade your wine merchant to order some of the others recommended. The wine charts will always be a helpful companion if you travel in Spain.

WHAT IS SPANISH CUISINE?

SPANISHtastes in foods have been molded over the centuries by availability of ingredients. Although Spain's mountainous terrain is generally poor dairy country and not spacious enough for cattle to graze, it is ideal for growing olive trees and grape vines and raising small animals, so the Spanish have naturally developed a taste for eggs, pork, lamb, and veal, using olive oil as a cooking base and wine as an accompaniment to all meals. Vegetables and fruits, then and now, are eaten when in season and according to region. In coastal areas, of course, a superabundance of fish makes the diet entirely different from that of inland areas. There are several other general characteristics of Spanish cuisine: Spaniards are inordinately fond of garlic, they love green and red peppers, sweet as well as hot, fresh as well as dried, and their beloved *jamón serrano*—cured ham—is not only eaten as an appetizer, but is incorporated into a wide variety of dishes. Seafood and meat are frequently found in combination. Ground almonds—in soups and sauces, as well as in desserts—lend a subtle savor to foods, while Spain's most famous wine—sherry—both dry and sweet, flavors main dishes and desserts alike. The paprika and garlic-scented *chorizo* sausage is commonly used to fill sandwiches or is sliced as an hors d'oeuvre, but it is also sometimes slowly simmered, lending its unique taste to a variety of soup and meat dishes. The golden aromatic spice, saffron, is added to many foods, most notably, *paella*.

Spanish cooking generally depends on basic, down-to-earth ingredients and should present few problems for the American cook. Most preparations are quite simple, and the flavors, although often quite new and exciting, are not so exotic that you can't enjoy these dishes on an everyday basis. And don't look only to the meat and fish sections for ideas for meals: one of the beauties of Spanish cooking is that many bean, rice, egg, and even some of the vegetable, *tapas*, pâté, and savory pie dishes make wonderful and very inexpensive meals. Just as in Spain a restaurant menu is not divided into appetizers and entrées—rather, it is broken into categories such as meats, poultry and game, fish, vegetables, eggs and rice, enabling the diner to choose what he pleases for each course—so too the reader should take this individualistic approach to planning a Spanish meal. Menu suggestions are given on pages 424–427, but there is ample opportunity, besides, to create meals that best suit your own taste.

SPANISH LIFE-STYLE

ALTHOUGH Spanish cooking adapts admirably to the American kitchen and to American eating habits, any visitor to Spain realizes immediately that the Spanish life-style is vastly different from ours. What is most impressive is the Spaniard's overpowering love for life, which carries over into all aspects of work and play. If it be true that a country's cuisine is a reflection of the character of its people, then Spanish cuisine should be the most colorful, lively, and exciting on earth! Spanish joie de vivre, however, does not allow for moderation in any area of life and definitely not when it comes to eating. A typical day usually involves the following breaks for food:

8 a.m.	- light breakfast
11 a.m.	- midmorning breakfast
1 p.m.	- *tapas*
2 p.m.	- three-course lunch
5–6 p.m.	- tea and pastries or snack (*merienda*)
8–10 p.m.	- evening *tapas*
10–11 p.m.	- three-course supper

It seems that the day never ends in Spain, beginning for most before 8 a.m. with hot coffee or chocolate, toast, or those wonderful strips of freshly fried dough called *churros*, and continuing well past midnight for many, especially in summer, when the cooler evening hours are the most inviting. For Spaniards, eating is a social occasion that often takes place outside the home, and their eating schedule reflects a large amount of time spent in cafeterias, bars, cafés, and restaurants. It seems that these establishments are overflowing at almost any hour, since one eating period moves right into the next; Spain is a nation of snackers (as well as serious food eaters), enjoying frequent bites in between meals. By 11 a.m. businesses have emptied into the cafeterias for coffee and a variety of delicious sweet buns. No one seems in a rush to return. At 1 p.m. and again at about 8 p.m. bars and taverns are filled with clients sipping beverages and sampling appetizers.

The two main meals of the day, *la comida*—lunch—and *la cena*—dinner, are no less opulent because of in-between snacks. Rather, lunchtime is observed religiously by Spaniards. At 2 p.m. the country comes to a halt, as everyone either returns home or heads toward a favorite restaurant to meet friends or family. Lunch is a serious meal, consisting of a substantial first course, a hefty main course, wine, dessert, and coffee. Spaniards never skimp. (Ernest Hemingway observed, "The first meal in Spain was always a shock with the hors d'oeuvres, an egg course . . . meat courses, vegetable, salad, dessert and fruit. You have to drink plenty of wine to get it all down.") For many, lunch is followed by the afternoon siesta, or at least a few hours' respite from work, since all stores and businesses customarily close from 1 to 4 p.m. Is it any wonder, with the day revolving around food, that "on time" performance and efficiency are not among Spain's shining glories?

The 10 o'clock dinner hour finds Spaniards either back home for a quiet evening or very often preparing for another round of eating and partying. Dinner at home may be relatively simple—including "lighter" dishes such as fish and eggs (but always with three courses)—or, if eating out is in order, dinner will be a repeat of the hearty lunch-hour menu.

REGIONAL COOKING

WHILE eating habits and hours are more or less uniform throughout Spain, cooking can be quite different. Spain by no means has a national cuisine. I can think of only a handful of dishes that are popular nationwide. (Chicken in Garlic Sauce, Potato Omelet, *paella*, Garlic Shrimp, *gazpacho*, and flan are a few that come to mind.) Rather, Spain is sharply divided by regions, each guarding its culinary traditions as jealously as its regional dialects and languages and its ancient cultures. Each region of Spain is therefore a cultural and gastronomic world in itself, defying generalization.

Spain's northwesternmost area, Galicia, is a land shrouded in legend and washed by fjordlike waterways. Besides its distinctive cuisine, Galicia is the only area that prominently displays its ancient Celtic heritage. As the Celts spread across Spain on their way to England and Scotland, they dwelled in this last Spanish outpost the longest, leaving indelible cultural traces. Visitors to Galicia are often startled by the strident sound of bagpipes and the colorful regional costumes, which include kilts and high socks for the men. In Galicia you will be sure to eat the savory meat and fish pies that will be found nowhere else in Spain. Seafood here is exquisite, and shellfish in particular comes in many unusual varieties, including the famed scallops, which are harvested only in this region and are baked and eaten in their shells. The misty and mountainous interior of Galicia is lushly grass-covered and ideal for grazing. For this reason, the finest veal in Spain is Galician. Also appropriate in this damp and often chilly climate is the robust Caldo Gallego soup, which has found its way into restaurants throughout the world.

A bit farther east along the coast is Asturias, with a climate and terrain similar to Galicia. Its mountainous, northern location made it an ideal retreat for Spanish Christians in the eighth century when the Moors overran Spain, and it was from here that the Christian reconquest of Spain began, under the watchful eye, it is said, of the Virgin of Covadonga, whose shrine is one of the most important tourist stops in Asturias. Asturias is best known in Spain for its legendary bean dish, *fabada*, and is famous also for its *Queso Cabrales*—a wonderful strong blue cheese. Because the climate is unsuitable for grape growing, hard cider—*sidra*—is the preferred drink with meals.

The Basque country (the only area referred to as a country rather than a region), a rich and rugged land of fiercely independent people who have a language unrelated to any other known tongue, has the reputation of Spain's gastronomic stronghold. There one finds principally fish dishes, such as the delicious *marmitako* fish soup, the stuffed king crab *shangurro*, garlicky baby eels (Angulas a la Bilbaína), squid in rich ink sauce, and a variety of dried cod and green-sauce dishes. Perhaps the culinary reputation of the Basque country stems partly from its much admired gastronomic societies. Hundreds of men-only gourmet clubs, curious in a region where women are fine cooks and often important restaurateurs, function throughout the region and pride them-selves on being classless—open to all social and economic levels. Members have access to the large club kitchens, buy food, invite their friends—men only—and treat them to their latest culinary creations, often in an atmosphere of uproari-ous gaiety. Cooking contests are held periodically and winners sometimes move on to become famous chefs. The long hours frequently spent away from home—some members eat at the club every evening—are a constant cause of marital friction and, I am told, have brought an end to many a Basque marriage.

Cataluña, where the Catalán language is spoken, is an area of diverse landscapes—the majestic Pyrenees, the port city of Barcelona, and the rugged Costa Brava coast are all located here. In my judgment Cataluña is the most gastronomically distinctive and exciting region of Spain. Catalán cuisine is equally inventive with fish—such dishes as Lobster with Chicken in a hazelnut sauce, *zarzuela* of mixed seafood in a spicy tomato sauce, and the incredibly delicious *romesco* fish sauce of ground almonds and dried sweet red peppers—as it is with meats and poultry, which are typically combined with local fruits—a combination quite foreign to Spaniards from other regions. Oca con Peras (Baby Goose with Pears) is perhaps the supreme creation of Catalán cookery.

Continuing down Spain's eastern coast (Spain has the longest coastline in Europe and some of the richest fishing grounds in the world), one reaches the heart of rice country, Valencia. This is an area of tidal flatlands, bright green as far as the eye can see, a marked contrast to the rest of Spain, which is second only to Switzerland in mountainous terrain. While in the Basque country fish is the food staple, in the Valencia region—often called the Levante (land of the sunrise)—rice in endless preparations is zestfully consumed on a daily basis. It may be combined with meat, fish, poultry, snails, or vegetables, or eaten by itself. In its most famous incarnation, *paella*, it is served in many parts of Spain, but only in Valencia is eating rice a way of life.

Arriving in Murcia, the rice paddies disappear and are replaced by fruit orchards and vegetable fields. The emphasis in this often forgotten region of Spain is naturally on foods prepared with the luscious tomatoes and peppers grown in the area.

Although Andalucía to the south is a parched and arid region whose land is best suited to grape vines and olive trees, its people are the gayest in Spain, enjoying life with a devil-may-care attitude that is light years away from that of the more sedate and business-oriented northerners. The Andalucian cuisine follows suit, and instead of the complex and cerebral art form that it often is in the Basque country and Cataluña, food is prepared in Andalucía with the same abandon and simplicity with which the people live their lives. The exquisite fish available along this southern coastline, coupled with the Andalucian's seemingly intuitive talent for frying fish exactly right—succulent within, crisp and golden without—is always a treat, and one does not feel the need to eat anything else, except, perhaps, a bright red chilled *gazpacho*, also native to Andalucía.

Spaniards demand freshness in food, which often means limiting themselves to locally produced ingredients. Consequently, in the interior areas—with the notable exception of Madrid—seafood falls into the background and is replaced by meat, beans, and sausage. The dry central *meseta* of Castilla, a noble and majestic land dotted with long-abandoned castles that silently speak of the greatness that once was Castile, is a palette of browns and ocres, where the wheat which is raised to produce the best bread in Spain, waves proudly in the wind. The baby roast meats of Castilla, especially mouth-melting suckling pig and tiny lambs, are simply incomparable. *Chorizo* sausage is found all over Spain, but undoubtedly is at its best here. And Castilla is the home of what is central Spain's most popular dish—*cocido*—an enticing mixture of meats, sausage, and chickpeas. Eggs with *chorizo* sausage and croutons, washed down with the powerful local red wines, can often be one of the most delicious meals imaginable. Keep in mind that Madrid, although in Castilla, is the country's capital and therefore open to many influences. Restaurants specializing in most of Spain's regional foods, as well as restaurants serving foreign cuisines, can be found in Madrid.

In the equally dry areas of Extremadura, land of the *conquistadores* and site of some of Spain's most beautiful villages with exotic names like Villanueva de la Vera, Trujillo, Cáceres, and Jerez de los Caballeros, there is a cuisine similar to that of Castilla. Poultry and meat stews take preference over other preparations, and simple pastries, often bathed in honey, are the order of the day.

Also landlocked are the northeastern areas of Aragón and Navarra, a varied landscape of plains, mountains, deep valleys, and rushing rivers. Here the emphasis is on game, including the excellent, locally caught trout. *Chilindrón* dishes—meat or poultry in combination with the region's red peppers—are at their best in these regions, although popular too in many other parts of Spain.

Remember that the Canary and Balearic Islands are also a part of Spain and lead their own culinary lives. In the sunny Canary Islands it is bananas, fish, and tiny tender potatoes that come to mind as the best produce, while the beautiful Balearic Islands, gastronomically more distinctive, are known for their fish stews, *sobrasada* sausage, and snail-shaped *ensaimada* pastries.

Although this book is not divided regionally, regional characteristics are easily seen in the recipe and chapter introductions, where I have described local holidays, ceremonies, and traditions associated with the eating of special foods. But the true flavor lies in the food itself, and I hope you will heartily partake of the dishes in this book, accompanied whenever possible by the superb wines of Spain. As the Spanish say, "¡*Que aproveche!*"—Good eating!

The Foods and Wines of Spain

Chapter 1

TAPAS

(*Appetizers*)

THE *tapas* tradition—that delightful Spanish custom of gathering before lunch and again before dinner for a glass of wine or beer and a sampling of appetizers—is so very popular in Spain as much for the Spaniard's overriding need for company and conversation as for the delicious food, which may range from the sophisticated to the most simple fare.

Conversation is a national pastime in Spain, and a Spaniard will enthusiastically discuss anything, even when his knowledge of a subject is less than adequate for the task. He will play the devil's advocate and passionately espouse his cause, even when his firm convictions lie with the opposing side. Now picture scores of Spaniards, packed into a bar or crowding tables at an outdoor café, all heartily and heatedly engaged in conversation while at the same time drinking and eating, and it is obvious that the *tapas* atmosphere is far from sober and sedate.

But what fun it is! There are no singles at such gatherings, for even if one arrives alone, joining a conversation is a matter of minutes; becoming fast friends with strangers takes only a few minutes more. Chances are one can even arrive penniless, for someone is always quick to treat, perhaps even to invite everyone in the house to a free round of drinks. My husband, a typically talkative Madrileño, has been known to treat in this fashion and rarely lasts more than five minutes in any bar without striking up a conversation with someone and ending on a first-name basis with everyone.

Every Spaniard has his favorite *tasca,* as such bars are called, where he goes regularly and where he can be sure to meet his friends or business acquaintances. (I use the masculine intentionally, for the majority of participants are men. Women are usually found in *tascas* in groups or in mixed company, but rarely alone.) A businessman may make or break a deal over *tapas.* A lucky client may purchase a million-*peseta* lottery ticket from vendors who make the rounds of the bars. Political gossip circulates. Roving shoeshine boys attend to your scuffed shoes, and *flamenco* singing often spontaneously bursts forth. In *tapas* bars on Victoria Street in Madrid, the topic of conversation is bound to be bullfights; at others, soccer aficionados will heatedly discuss the latest scores. Doctors, lawyers, politicians, actors—all have their favorite *tascas* to talk shop. In short, *tapas* are a way of life in Spain, and there is no better way for a visitor to Spain to savor life in that country than by joining in this lively ambience.

Tapas will be found in even the smallest bar in the tiniest village. The choice in such places will typically be limited to cured ham, *chorizo,* and cheese, unless there is someone unusually inventive in the kitchen. But it is in the big regional centers of Madrid, Barcelona, Santiago de Compostela, Sevilla, and Málaga where *tapas* often become inspired and are of an over-whelming variety. The Bar Gayango in Madrid was perhaps the epitome of a *tapas* bar, where no less than seventy-six *tapas* were available. Large demand for *tapas* in these urban areas also leads to specialization and *tasca*-hopping, the custom of visiting a half dozen or more establishments to eat the best each has to offer. In one bar in Madrid one sees nothing but armies of mush-rooms, sizzling on the grill. Another has nothing but grilled shrimp served with a robust house wine. In the Rastro, or flea market, a bar has cauldrons of spicy snails that everyone is sampling; there are grilled red peppers at another *tasca* and smoked fish at still another. In the more well-to-do neighborhoods around Serrano Street, the *tapas* may include, in addition to the usual fare, elegant puff pastries, pâtés, and caviar. *Tapas* are sometimes taken on the honor system, but in general are served by waiters, who miraculously keep track of everything everyone is eating, no matter how large and unwieldy the crowd may be.

Over the years I have become incurably addicted to *tapas,* and to this day it is not unusual for me to forgo conventional dining in Spain in favor of spending entire evenings *tasca*-hopping. In my student days in Madrid, when my husband, also a student at the time, seemed to live exclusively on *tapas* food, we would comb the streets of Madrid, always on the prowl for the ultimate in *tapas.* Many of my *tapas* recipes come straight from those bars and *tascas* I frequented over the years. In many cases owners have kindly and enthusiastically shared their recipes, while at other times I have come up with my own interpretations of *tapas* I have sampled.

The word *tapa,* meaning cover or lid, is thought to have originally referred to the complimentary plate of appetizers that many *tascas* would place on top of one's wineglass—like a "cover." Anything, however, served in small por-tions can be considered a *tapa.* A quail, for example, is a *tapa* when only one is served. Conversely, *tapas* served in larger amounts often make excellent main-course meals. *Tapas* and first course dishes are often interchangeable, and I have therefore included almost everything that may precede a main course under the heading of *tapas.* While it is obvious that canapés and tartlets would be served only as *tapas,* any of the clam or mussel dishes are also excellent as first-course offerings.

I heartily recommend a *tapas* party, ideas for which are given in the Menu Suggestions section. Every year I invite some sixty friends to my home and treat them to a wide array of *tapas,* accompanied by either wine, *sangría,* or sherry—the quintessential Spanish drink (see Sherry, p. 413)—and the evening is never less than a smashing success. Life in the United States may not be geared to leisurely afternoons and evenings spent with friends in taverns over *tapas,* but the camaraderie of the *tapas* tradition can easily be transposed to home entertaining. Bring out the *tapas,* perhaps play some *flamenco* music, and watch the Spanish spirit emerge!

GAMBAS AL AJILLO

(Garlic Shrimp)

IN SPAIN, garlic shrimp are nothing more than shrimp, dried red chili pepper, oil, and garlic and are a most popular appetizer. But since most of our shrimp are frozen, they lack the briny flavor of Spanish shrimp and taste quite bland in such a sauce. If you can obtain fresh shrimp, use the original recipe below. Otherwise, choose one of the delicious ways that two Spanish restaurants in New York City—Mesón Botín and Rincón de España—have devised to add more flavor to the shrimp.

Serves 1

1 clove garlic, peeled and sliced
½ dried red chili pepper, broken into
   3 pieces, seeds removed

½ bay leaf
5 tablespoons olive oil
2 ounces very small shrimp, shelled

In an individual flameproof ramekin, preferably earthenware, place the garlic, chili pepper, bay leaf, and oil. Heat over a medium-high flame until the garlic begins to sizzle and turn golden. Add the shrimp all at once. Cook, stirring, until the shrimp are done, about 2 minutes. Sprinkle with coarse salt if necessary. Serve in the same ramekin while still sizzling. Provide good crusty bread for dunking.

GAMBAS AL AJILLO
"MESÓN BOTÍN"

(Garlic Shrimp)

cowbells, wineskins, a full-size reproduction of *Los Borrachos*—"The Drunkards"—by Velázquez hung on a red wall, and even a suit of armor standing guard in one corner of the dining room—all combine to transport the diner from the city of concrete to the land of bullfights, chivalry, and *flamenco.* Besides holding the distinction of serving the best *paella* in the entire city, Mesón Botín, under the careful guidance of owner José Ruso, also has an excellent selection of *tapas,* one of the best being these garlic shrimp.

Serves 6

6 tablespoons olive oil
4 cloves garlic, sliced
1 dried red chili pepper, cut in 2
    pieces, seeds removed
¾ pound small or medium
    shrimp, shelled

2 tablespoons beef or veal broth
2 tablespoons lemon juice
Salt
2 tablespoons minced parsley

Heat the oil, garlic, and chili pepper in a large, shallow casserole, preferably earthenware (these shrimp may also be prepared in individual heatproof ramekins). When the garlic just begins to turn golden, add the shrimp and cook over high heat, about 3 minutes, stirring constantly. Add the broth and lemon juice. Sprinkle with salt and parsley and serve immediately, preferably in the same dish.

GAMBAS AL AJILLO
"RINCÓN DE ESPAÑA"

(Garlic Shrimp)

Serves 6

4 tablespoons olive oil
2 tablespoons butter
¾ pound small or medium shrimp,
    in their shells
4 cloves garlic, peeled and sliced
2 tablespoons lemon juice
2 tablespoons dry sherry

½ teaspoon paprika
1 dried red chili pepper, cut in 3
    pieces, seeds removed
Salt
Freshly ground pepper
1 tablespoon minced parsley

Heat the oil and butter in a shallow casserole. Add the shrimp and garlic and sauté over high heat about 3 minutes. Add the lemon juice, sherry, paprika, chili pepper, salt, and pepper. Sprinkle with parsley and serve immediately, preferably in the cooking dish.

TORTILLITAS DE CAMARONES

(Shrimp Pancakes)

SHRIMP pancakes are found only in Cádiz, where they are offered on all restaurant menus and are found frying at street stands. Their quality is gauged by the amount of shrimp they contain and by the type of shrimp used, which should ideally be the tiny *camarones.*

Makes 10 small pancakes

3 tablespoons olive oil
3 tablespoons finely chopped onion
2 tablespoons minced parsley
⅛ teaspoon paprika
3 tablespoons flour
7 tablespoons water

¾ teaspoon salt
½ teaspoon baking powder
¼ pound small shrimp, shelled and
    finely chopped
Oil for frying

Heat the 3 tablespoons of oil in a skillet. Add the onion and parsley and sauté very slowly, covered, until the onion is tender. Stir in the paprika.

In a bowl, mix together the flour, water, salt, and baking powder. Add the onion mixture and the shrimp. In a skillet, heat the frying oil, ¼ inch deep, until it reaches the smoking point. Drop the batter by the tablespoon into the oil, flattening the pancakes into 2½-inch rounds with the back of a spoon that has first been dipped in the hot oil. Fry until lightly golden, turning once. Drain and serve immediately.

GAMBAS CON SALSA PIPARRADA

(Shrimp in Piparrada Sauce)

"*Piparrada*" is a Basque word that refers to dishes having tomatoes and green peppers as principal ingredients. In this case the ingredients are finely minced and used as a dip for cold shellfish, but *piparrada* can also take the form of a salad (p. 115) and a scrambled egg dish (p. 161).

Serves 4–6

1½ pounds medium or large shrimp, in their shells	2 ripe tomatoes
	6 tablespoons olive oil
1 medium cucumber	3 tablespoons red wine vinegar
1 medium green pepper	Salt
1 small onion	Freshly ground pepper

COOKING LIQUID

6 cups water	5 peppercorns
1 cup fish broth (p. 13) or clam juice	1 slice onion
1 bay leaf	¼ teaspoon thyme
1 slice lemon	Salt
2 sprigs parsley	

In a large pot, mix together the cooking-liquid ingredients. Bring to a boil and simmer 15 minutes. Add the shrimp and cook very briefly, about 2–3 minutes, depending on the size of the shrimp. Drain, cool, and shell.

By hand or in a processor, finely mince the cucumber, green pepper, and onion; remove to a bowl. Chop the tomatoes finely by hand and add to the mixture. Stir in the oil, vinegar, salt, and pepper. Refrigerate until ready to use, but do not leave overnight—the tomato and pepper lose their bright colors. Serve the sauce in a small bowl with the shrimp arranged either around the rim or on a plate.

CÓCTEL DE GAMBAS

(Shrimp Cocktail, Spanish Style)

A SHRIMP cocktail in Spain is prepared with large numbers of tiny shrimp that are no bigger than thumbnails and are served in a tomato- and mayonnaise-based sauce. The cocktail is just as good, of course, with any size shrimp.

Serves 6

1½ pounds small shrimp, in
    their shells
Cooking Liquid (preceding recipe)

Shredded lettuce
Parsley for garnish

COCKTAIL SAUCE

1 cup mayonnaise, preferably
    homemade (p. 104)
5 teaspoons tomato paste
1 teaspoon brandy, preferably Spanish
    brandy, or Cognac
1 hard-boiled egg, finely chopped

¼ teaspoon tarragon
½ teaspoon caper or pickle juice
1 tablespoon minced parsley
Salt
Freshly ground pepper

Boil the shrimp in the cooking liquid according to the directions in the preceding recipe. Shell. Combine all the cocktail-sauce ingredients. Chill until ready to use. To serve, arrange the shrimp on a bed of shredded lettuce, pour on some sauce, and decorate with a sprig of parsley.

GAMBAS CON GARBARDINA

(Batter-Fried Shrimp)

LITERALLY, "shrimp in overcoats."

Serves 4–6

½ pound medium shrimp, in
    their shells
½ cup flour
1 teaspoon baking powder
⅛ teaspoon salt

1 tablespoon oil
½ cup beer
Oil for frying
1 clove garlic, peeled
Coarse salt

Shell the shrimp, leaving on the tails and the last joint of the shell.

In a bowl, mix the flour, baking powder, and salt. Add the oil and beer. Blend well, then cover and let sit in a warm spot for 20 minutes.

Place the frying oil, at least 1 inch deep, in a skillet with the garlic. Heat until the garlic browns, then discard the garlic. Dip the shrimp in the batter and fry over a medium flame until they are golden. Drain, then sprinkle with coarse salt and serve immediately.

LANGOSTINOS CON CLAVO

(Prawns in Clove-Scented Marinade)

PREPARE ONE DAY IN ADVANCE.

Serves 4

3 tablespoons olive oil	½ teaspoon thyme
4 cloves	1 bay leaf
3 cups water	½ dried red chili pepper, seeds removed
1 cup dry white wine	6 peppercorns
2 slices onion	Salt
½ carrot, scraped and sliced	1 pound medium or large shrimp, in their shells
1 slice lemon	
2 sprigs parsley	

Bring to a boil all the ingredients except the shrimp. Simmer 10 minutes. Add the shrimp and return the liquid to a boil; cook the shrimp briefly, about 2–3 minutes. Remove the shrimp, shell them, and place them in a bowl. Bring the liquid to a boil again and cook until it is reduced by half. Cool, then pour over the shrimp and refrigerate at least 24 hours. Serve cold.

GAMBAS VILLEROY

(Béchamel-Coated Fried Shrimp)

Serves 6–8

1 pound shrimp, medium or large, in their shells	2 eggs, beaten
Cooking Liquid (p. 8)	Bread crumbs
	Oil for frying

WHITE SAUCE

5 tablespoons butter	¼ teaspoon lemon juice
6 tablespoons flour	Salt
¾ cup milk	Freshly ground pepper

Boil the shrimp in the cooking liquid following the directions on page 8; reserve the cooking liquid. Once the shrimp are shelled, return the shells to the broth and continue cooking 15 minutes more. Strain and reserve ¾ cup. (Save the remaining broth for the next time you boil shellfish—it will immensely improve the flavor.)

To make the white sauce, melt the butter in a saucepan, add the flour and cook a minute. Stir in the reserved shrimp broth, milk, lemon juice, salt, and pepper. Cook until the sauce is thickened and smooth (it will be very thick). Cool, stirring occasionally.

Dip the shrimp in the sauce, coating well on all sides. Place the shrimp on a dish and refrigerate at least 1 hour, until the sauce has hardened. Dip the shrimp in the beaten eggs, coat with bread crumbs, and fry in hot oil, at least ½ inch deep. Drain.

ALMEJAS A LA MARINERA

(Clams in White Wine Sauce)

THIS is one of the most popular *tapas*. Clams tend to be of the tiny variety in Spain, and an order of these delicious clams will bring a dish with perhaps fifty *coquinas*, as they are called. Since clams like these rarely reach our markets, choose instead the very smallest ones available.

CLEANING CLAMS AND MUSSELS

When clams (or mussels) are cooked and opened in a sauce, there is always the danger that they will release some sand. To minimize this possibility, place them, for several hours or overnight, in the refrigerator in a bowl of salted water sprinkled with one tablespoon of cornmeal. The clams will release any foreign materials and at the same time will become quite plump.

Serves 4–6

7 tablespoons olive oil
2 tablespoons minced onion
4 cloves garlic, minced
2 dozen small clams, scrubbed,
   at room temperature
1 tablespoon flour
1 tablespoon paprika

2 tablespoons minced parsley
1 cup semisweet white wine
1 bay leaf
1 dried red chili pepper, cut in 3
   pieces, seeds removed
Freshly ground pepper
Salt

Heat the oil in a large, shallow casserole. Sauté the onion and garlic until the onion is wilted. Add the clams and cook, uncovered, over a medium-high flame until they open. (If some open much sooner than others, remove them so they do not toughen. Return to the pan when all have opened.) Sprinkle in the flour and stir, then add the paprika, parsley, wine, bay leaf, chili pepper, pepper, and salt, if necessary (the liquid the clams release may be salty). Continue cooking and stirring another 5 minutes. Serve in the cooking dish if possible, and let everyone help himself.

ALMEJAS ROMESCO

(Clams in Romesco Sauce)

IT IS said that only a handful of maestros in the region of Tarragona knows the secret of a proper *romesco* sauce and that these experts are the inheritors of a tradition that dates back almost one thousand years. *Romesco* is one of the most delicious and unusual sauces ever to season a seafood. I particularly like it with clams as an appetizer, although *romesco* is also served as an accompaniment to grilled shellfish (see p. 213) and is an extraordinary sauce for mixed seafood (p. 211).

One of the sauce ingredients, *aguardiente*, is a powerful Spanish liqueur made from the pressings of grape skins. Although only one teaspoon is required, it adds a special spark to the sauce and should not be eliminated. Its Italian equivalent, grappa, is available in most liquor stores.

Serves 4–6

2 dozen very small clams (see p. 11)
2 pimientos, homemade or imported,
   cut in strips
½ cup red wine vinegar
1 bay leaf

3 tablespoons olive oil
2 slices French-style bread, about ¼
   inch thick
3 cloves garlic, peeled
12 blanched almonds

¼ cup dry white wine
1 dried red chili pepper, seeds
    removed, crumbled
Salt

Freshly ground pepper
1 teaspoon *aguardiente* or grappa
1 tablespoon minced parsley

FISH BROTH

1 small whole fish, such as whiting,
    head on, cleaned
¼ cup dry white wine
1½ cups water
½ bay leaf

¼ teaspoon thyme
1 small onion
1 small carrot, scraped and cut in half
6 peppercorns
Salt

Scrub the clams well and soak overnight in water, salt, and cornmeal, as described in the previous recipe. Soak the pimientos in a bowl with the vinegar and bay leaf for 3–4 hours.

To make the broth, place all broth ingredients in a saucepan and bring to a boil. Cover and simmer 1 hour. Strain and reserve 1 cup. Drain the pimientos, and dry them on paper towels. Heat the oil in a large, shallow casserole. Sauté the pimientos about 2 minutes. Transfer them to a blender or processor, leaving the remaining oil in the pan; in it fry the bread slices and garlic until both are golden. Add them to the blender, along with the almonds. Beat until a paste forms. With the motor running, add ¼ cup of the fish broth. When it is well blended, add the remaining ¾ cup broth and the wine. Beat until smooth.

Heat the casserole again. Strain the contents of the blender into the pan and add the chili pepper, salt, and pepper. Arrange the clams in the pan, cover, and cook over a medium flame, removing the clams as they open. Correct the seasoning and remove the pan from the flame. Stir in the *aguardiente* and return the clams to the pan, making sure that the shell section with the clam meat is covered by the sauce. Cover and let sit 1–2 hours. Reheat and serve, sprinkled with the parsley.

ALMEJAS AL DIABLO

(Clams in Spicy Tomato Sauce)

Serves 4–6

1 onion
2 cloves garlic, minced
2 tablespoons olive oil
2 tomatoes, peeled and chopped
1 tablespoon tomato paste
1 teaspoon paprika
½ cup dry white wine

Salt
Freshly ground pepper
1 tablespoon minced parsley
½ dried red chili pepper, seeds
    removed, crumbled
18 very small clams (see p. 11)

In a shallow casserole, preferably Spanish earthenware, sauté the onion and garlic in the oil until the onion is wilted. Add the tomatoes, tomato paste, paprika, wine, salt, pepper, parsley, and chili pepper. Cover and cook 10 minutes. Add the clams, cover tightly, and cook over a high flame until the clams open. Serve in the same dish.

ALMEJAS AL HORNO

(Baked Stuffed Clams)

Serves 4–6

18 medium clams (see p. 11)
1 tablespoon olive oil
2 tablespoons minced onion
1 clove garlic, minced
6 tablespoons bread crumbs
2 tablespoons minced cured ham
1 teaspoon dry (*fino*) sherry

¼ teaspoon lemon juice
Salt
Freshly ground pepper
¼ teaspoon paprika
1 tablespoon minced parsley
Butter

Open the clams with a knife or place them in the oven briefly until they open. Chop the meat and reserve half of the shells.

    In a small skillet, heat the oil and sauté the onion and garlic until the onion is wilted. Stir in the bread crumbs, ham, sherry, lemon juice, a little salt (depending on how salty the ham is), pepper, paprika, and parsley. Mix in the clam meat, then stuff the reserved shells. Dot with butter. Bake at 350° F about 10 minutes, or until lightly browned.

MEJILLONES A LA VINAGRETA

(Marinated Mussels)

START PREPARATION ONE DAY IN ADVANCE.

MUSSELS as colorful as these are sure to be eye-catchers at any gathering. They are equally pleasing to the palate and will disappear rapidly — it is advisable to prepare at least a double recipe for large groups.

Serves 4–6

½ cup olive oil
3 tablespoons red wine vinegar
1 teaspoon small capers
1 tablespoon minced onion
1 tablespoon minced pimiento,
    homemade or imported

1 tablespoon minced parsley
Salt
Freshly ground pepper
2 dozen medium mussels
    (see p. 11)
1 slice lemon

Mix the oil, vinegar, capers, onion, pimiento, parsley, salt, and pepper in a bowl; set aside. Scrub the mussels well, removing the beards. Discard any that do not close tightly. Place 1 cup of water in a skillet with the lemon slice. Add the mussels and bring to a boil. Remove the mussels as they open; cool. Remove the mussel meat from the shells and add to the bowl with the marinade. Cover and refrigerate overnight. Reserve half the mussel shells, clean them well, and place them in a plastic bag in the refrigerator. Before serving, replace the mussels in their shells and spoon a small amount of the marinade over each.

MEJILLONES GAYANGO

(Stuffed Mussels)

THE Bar Gayango in Madrid (now closed but replaced by the equally good La Trucha) had perhaps the most extensive *tapas* menu in all of Spain. Not surprisingly, the small bar is, and continues to be enormously popular, with an array of *tapas* that boggles the mind.

Mejillones Gayango was one of the star *tapas* at Gayango and, in my experience, never fails to delight dinner guests.

Mejillones Gayango was one of the star *tapas* at Gayango and, in my experience, never fails to delight dinner guests.

Serves 6

18 medium mussels (see p. 11)
1 slice lemon
1 tablespoon olive oil
4 tablespoons minced onion
2 tablespoons minced cured ham
1 clove garlic, minced
1 teaspoon tomato sauce

1 tablespoon minced parsley
Salt
Freshly ground pepper
2 eggs
1 cup bread crumbs
1 tablespoon grated cheese
Oil for frying

WHITE SAUCE

3 tablespoons butter
4 tablespoons flour
½ cup milk

Salt
Freshly ground pepper

Scrub the mussels well and remove the beards. Place them in a pan with ¾ cup water and the lemon slice. Bring to a boil and remove the mussels as they open. Do not overcook. Reserve ½ cup of the cooking liquid.

Mince the mussel meat. Separate the shells and discard half of them. Heat the 1 tablespoon olive oil in a small skillet. Add the onion and sauté until it is wilted. Add the ham and garlic and sauté 1 minute more. Stir in the tomato sauce, the minced mussel meat, parsley, salt, and pepper. Cook 5 minutes. Half fill the mussel shells with this mixture.

To make the white sauce, melt the butter in a saucepan over moderate heat. Add the flour and stir a minute or two. Gradually pour in the reserved mussel broth and the milk. Cook, stirring constantly, until the sauce is thickened and smooth (it will be quite thick). Season with salt and pepper. Remove the pan from the heat and cool, stirring occasionally.

Using a teaspoon, cover the filled mussel shells with the white sauce, sealing the edges by smoothing with the cupped side of the spoon. Refrigerate 1 hour or more, until the sauce hardens.

Beat the eggs in a shallow bowl with 2 teaspoons of water. Mix together the crumbs and the cheese. Dip the mussels into the egg, then into the crumb mixture. Heat the oil, at least 1 inch deep, in a skillet. Fry the mussels, filled side down, until they are well browned. Drain. The mussels may be kept warm in a 200° F oven for up to 30 minutes.

MEJILLONES EN SALSA VERDE

(Mussels in Green Sauce)

MUSSELS in Green Sauce appear on almost every Spanish menu in the United States, although they are rarely found in restaurants in Spain, where other green-sauce dishes seem to be more popular. Nonetheless, mussels are fun to eat, and the sauce is great for bread dunking.

Serves 4

1 tablespoon olive oil
3 tablespoons finely chopped onion
3 cloves garlic, minced
2 tablespoons flour
¾ cup minced parsley
½ cup dry white wine
½ cup mussel broth (make with an

½ cup mussel broth (make with an
    extra ½ dozen mussels) or
    clam juice
Salt
Freshly ground pepper
2 dozen medium mussels, well
    scrubbed (see p. 11)

In a large casserole, sauté in the oil the onion and garlic until the onion is wilted. Add the flour and cook a minute. Stir in the parsley, wine, clam broth, salt, and pepper. Cover and simmer 15 minutes. Add the mussels and cook over a medium flame, covered, for 5 minutes. Uncover and continue cooking until all the mussels have opened. Serve in the same dish.

MEJILLONES GRATINADOS

(Baked Mussels and Mushrooms)

Serves 4

4 dozen medium mussels, well
    scrubbed (see p. 11)
1 cup water
1 slice lemon

½ pound mushrooms, sliced
4 tablespoons grated cheese
Butter

WHITE SAUCE

4 tablespoons butter
4 tablespoons flour
1 cup milk
1 tablespoon lemon juice

Pinch saffron
Freshly ground pepper
2 egg yolks

Place the mussels in a large skillet with the water and lemon slice; bring to a boil. Remove the mussels as they open. Reserve 1 cup of the cooking liquid. Discard the mussel shells.

To make the white sauce, melt the butter in a saucepan. Stir in the flour and cook briefly. Gradually pour in the reserved cooking liquid, milk, lemon juice, saffron, and pepper. Cook until thickened and smooth. Lightly beat the egg yolks in a small bowl. Stir in a small amount of the hot sauce, then add the yolks to the sauce and cook briefly over low heat until the sauce thickens.

Place the mussels and mushrooms in a baking dish, or divide into 4 individual casserole dishes or large scallop shells. Pour on the sauce, sprinkle with grated cheese, and dot with butter. Bake in a 450° F oven about 10 minutes, or until bubbly and lightly browned. Run under the broiler if further browning is necessary.

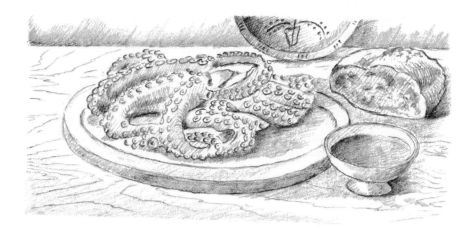

CALAMARES FRITOS A LA ROMANA

(Fried Squid, Spanish Style)

FRIED squid are a standby all over Spain and are always tender and delicious. Most prized are the tiny *chopitos*, which can be eaten in a single bite, tentacles and all. When buying squid, choose the smallest available, since the larger ones may be tough.

Serves 4–6

1 pound small squid
Flour for dusting
Oil for frying

2 eggs, lightly beaten
Salt
Lemon wedges

Clean the squid well (see p. 216), cutting the body into ½-inch–wide rings and leaving the tentacles in 1 piece. Dry well between paper towels, otherwise the squid will spatter when fried. Dust the pieces with flour.

Heat the oil, at least 1 inch deep, in a large skillet until it reaches the smoking point. Coat the squid rings and tentacles completely with the egg. Remove them one at a time and place directly in the hot oil. Cook *very* briefly, only until they are very lightly browned, about 2–3 minutes. Drain. Sprinkle with salt and serve immediately, garnished with lemon wedges.

CALAMARITOS RELLENOS

(Fried Stuffed Baby Squid)

ALTHOUGH the squid may be stuffed in advance, the frying must be done at the very last moment. However, it will take only a few minutes, and these tender, juicy baby squid are certainly worth the effort. Do not try to use larger squid—they are too thick and will toughen when fried in this manner.

Serves 4

1¼ pounds baby squid, bodies about 2 inches long, with tentacles
1 tablespoon olive oil
¼ cup finely chopped onion
1 clove garlic, minced
A ¼-pound piece cured ham, minced
⅛ teaspoon paprika
2 teaspoons minced parsley

Coarse salt
Freshly ground pepper
1 teaspoon dry white wine
4 teaspoons bread crumbs
Oil for frying
Flour for dusting
2 eggs, lightly beaten

Clean the squid thoroughly (see p. 216), leaving the bodies in 1 piece and reserving the tentacles. Dry the squid completely inside and out. Do the same with the tentacles—otherwise there may be a lot of spattering during frying.

Heat the 1 tablespoon of oil in a medium skillet. Sauté the onion and garlic until the onion is wilted. Mince the tentacles, adding them to the skillet along with the ham. Cook 2 minutes. Turn off the flame and add the paprika, parsley, salt, pepper, wine, and bread crumbs.

Fill the squid bodies ⅓–½ full with this mixture. Heat the frying oil, at least ½ inch deep, to the smoking point. Coat the squid with the flour, then dip in the egg and place immediately in the hot oil. Reduce the heat slightly and fry until the squid are lightly golden. This will take no more than a couple of minutes. Do not overcook or the squid will toughen. Sprinkle with coarse salt and serve immediately.

ANGULAS A LA BILBAÍNA

(Baby Eels in Garlic Sauce)

TO MY knowledge, baby eels (p. 222) can be found in the United States only at one New York restaurant, Café San Martín, which imports them privately from Spain. In the past few years, these *angulas* have received a good deal of publicity and have acquired quite a following. I include the recipe in the hope that soon this delicacy will be available for home consumption, or on the chance that *angulas*, native or imported, can be found elsewhere in this country.

Angulas are typically served in earthenware ramekins and eaten with small wooden forks that prevent transmission of heat and make the tiny eels easier to pick up.

Serves 1

3 tablespoons olive oil
1 large clove garlic, peeled
    and sliced

½ dried red chili pepper, cut in 3
    pieces, seeds removed
¼ pound baby eels

Put the oil, garlic, and chili pepper in an individual heatproof ramekin, preferably earthenware (about 5 inches in diameter). Heat over a high flame until the garlic begins to sizzle and just turns golden. Immediately add the baby eels, all at once. Do not stir. Remove the ramekin from the flame immediately and cover with a dish. Take the covered dish to the table, then uncover and stir the eels lightly.

BOQUERONES EN VINAGRE

(Marinated Anchovies)

PREPARE THREE DAYS IN ADVANCE.

JUST about every bar and cafeteria in Spain offers these tiny marinated fish. They are invariably tasty and refreshing.

Choose anchovies (or smelts) that are small—they must not be more than 5 inches long.

Serves 4–6

¾ pound very small fresh anchovies (or smelts), cleaned, heads, tails, and fins removed

Salt

¾ cup white wine vinegar
3 cloves garlic, minced
1 tablespoon minced parsley

Butterfly the anchovies, leaving the bone in. Soak 1 hour in cold water. Arrange in a shallow, flat-bottom bowl in 1 layer, skin side up. Sprinkle with salt and pour on ½ cup of the vinegar. Cover and refrigerate 2 days. (The fish will not be cooked, only marinated.)

Drain the anchovies, discarding the vinegar. Pull out the spine bone, split the anchovies in half, and return to the bowl. Pour on the remaining ¼ cup of the vinegar. Sprinkle with the garlic and parsley. Cover and refrigerate 1 day more. They will keep for many days.

BOQUERONES DON PEDRO

(Marinated and Fried Small Fish)

START PREPARATION SEVERAL HOURS IN ADVANCE.

ON THE dimly lit Don Pedro Street in Old Madrid is the Mesón de Don Pedro, a rustic tavern that goes back in its present form at least one hundred years and has been the site of taverns for the past four centuries. Local legend has it that at this very location the master painter Francisco de Goya, widely known in his times as a bon vivant, was stabbed by a jealous husband. In those early centuries this part of Madrid teemed with people and was often frequented by cloaked royalty seeking anonymity in the crowds. Night life in modern Madrid has shifted to other locations, but on Don Pedro Street the ambience of those times remains, especially at the Mesón de Don Pedro, where these tiny fish are a specialty.

A similar fish appetizer is served in Cádiz, using cubes of shark meat. Use ¾–1-pound shark or swordfish steaks (shark is delicious, but not commonly found here), cut in 1½-inch cubes, skin and bones removed. Marinate and fry in the same manner as for this recipe.

Serves 4–6

2 cloves garlic, minced
1 bay leaf, crumbled
4 peppercorns
Dash oregano
¼ teaspoon cumin, preferably
    freshly ground
4 tablespoons red wine vinegar
White pepper

Salt
2 tablespoons water
1 pound very small fish, such as
    smelts (about 20 to a pound),
    cleaned, heads on
Flour for dusting, preferably semolina
Oil for frying
Coarse salt

In a shallow bowl, mix the garlic, bay leaf, peppercorns, oregano, cumin, vinegar, white pepper, salt, and water. Add the fish, turning to coat, and marinate at least 4 hours, turning occasionally.

Drain the fish well, sprinkle with salt, dredge in flour, and fry in hot oil, at least ½ inch deep, until the fish is well browned and crisp. Drain and sprinkle with coarse salt. Serve immediately.

PULPO A LA VINAGRETA

(Marinated Octopus)

PREPARE ONE DAY IN ADVANCE.

OCTOPUS is most popular in Spain's northern provinces. In Galicia it always appears during fiestas, where it is boiled outdoors in huge metal drums.

Make sure to purchase small octopus, or they are apt to be tough. In any case, octopus tends to be chewy; if it's not to your taste, you might prefer to combine it with other seafood, adding it, for example, to Shellfish Vinaigrette (p. 24). I find it quite enjoyable, however, by itself.

Serves 4

1½ pounds octopus, preferably
    2 small ones, about ¾
    pound each

½ cup olive oil
3 tablespoons red wine vinegar
1 tablespoon minced onion

1 clove garlic, minced
1 tablespoon minced parsley

Salt
Freshly ground pepper

COOKING LIQUID

12 cups water
1 bay leaf
½ onion, peeled, in one piece

4 peppercorns
2 sprigs parsley
Salt

Clean the octopus by removing all waste material, including the eyes. Cut off the tips of the tentacles. Before cooking the octopus, tenderize it by throwing it with force into the kitchen sink. Repeat at least 10 times. Bring the 12 cups of water to a boil in a large pot. Submerge the octopus in the water and remove it immediately. Repeat 2 more times, then return the water to a boil. Add the bay leaf, onion, peppercorns, parsley, and salt. Return the octopus to the pot, cover, and simmer until tender. Depending on the size of the octopus, it will take 1¾–3 hours. Drain and cool, scraping off any loose skin. Cut the octopus body and tentacles into bite-size pieces with scissors.

To make the dressing, combine the oil, vinegar, onion, garlic, parsley, salt, and pepper. Add the octopus and refrigerate overnight. Serve cold or at room temperature.

PULPO A LA GALLEGA

(Octopus in Paprika and Oil)

ANY fish dish described as "*a la gallega*" denotes the presence of paprika and oil, sometimes in a sauce in which the fish is cooked or often, as in this recipe, as a dip or coating for fish that has been boiled or poached.

Serves 4

1½ pounds octopus, preferably
    2 small ones, about ¾
    pound each
Cooking Liquid (preceding recipe)
3 cloves garlic, crushed

½ cup olive oil
1 tablespoon paprika
Salt
Freshly ground pepper

Clean the octopus, boil in the cooking liquid, and cut it according to the directions in the preceding recipe. In a bowl mix together the garlic, oil, paprika, salt, and pepper. Add the octopus pieces and serve at room temperature.

ATÚN ESCABECHADO
(Marinated Tuna)

PREPARE ONE DAY IN ADVANCE.

USE this tuna as is on a salad plate, spread on bread, combine with mayonnaise, or use as a filling for an omelet (p. 171) or in a salad (Ensalada de San Isidro, p. 106; Pipirrana Jaenera, p. 115).

Makes 1 1/2 cups

7-ounce can light meat tuna, with
    its oil
2 teaspoons vinegar
2 teaspoons minced onion
1 teaspoon capers, chopped if they
    are large

2 teaspoons minced parsley
Salt
Freshly ground pepper

Place the tuna in a bowl and flake with a fork. Stir in the remaining ingredients and refrigerate overnight.

SALPICÓN DE MARISCOS
(Shellfish Vinaigrette)

PREPARE ONE DAY IN ADVANCE.

THIS delightful mixture of crab, lobster, and shrimp makes a cooling party or appetizer dish. In Spain it is particularly welcome in summer when the temperatures soar.

Serves 4–6

1½ pounds medium
    shrimp, in their shells
1–1½ pounds live lobster, or lobster
    tails

Cooking Liquid (p. 8); double the
    amount
½ pound cooked king crab meat, cut
    in chunks

SALPICÓN SAUCE

¾ cup olive oil
6 tablespoons tarragon vinegar
5 cornichon pickles, chopped
2 tablespoons capers
2 tablespoons minced onion

2 tablespoons chopped pimiento,
    homemade or imported
1 tablespoon chopped parsley
Salt
Freshly ground pepper

Boil the shrimp and lobster in the cooking liquid according to the directions on page 8. The shrimp will take 2–3 minutes; the lobster, about 15 minutes. Shell the shrimp and lobster and cut the lobster into chunks. Cool. Combine the Salpicón ingredients in a large bowl. Add the cooled shrimp and lobster and the crab meat, mixing carefully with a spatula. Chill overnight, mixing occasionally.

NOTE: Two or three small cooked mussels in their shells are a pleasant addition and an attractive contrast in color. Cooked octopus and squid may also be added.

    If this Salpicón is to be served as a first course instead of an appetizer, I prefer to leave the shrimp, lobster, and crab in their shells (crush the lobster and crab shells lightly for easy removal of the meat). The dish is then more colorful and much more fun to eat.

    Another variation is to drain the marinade and mix the shellfish with about 1 cup homemade mayonnaise (p. 104) and 1 tablespoon chopped capers.

ENSALADILLA RUSA

(Potato and Vegetable Salad)

START PREPARATION SEVERAL HOURS IN ADVANCE.

JUST about every place that serves *tapas* in Spain offers this appealing mayonnaise-coated salad. It is usually presented smoothed out in a small dish and decorated with pimiento strips. For party appetizers, you may prefer to use tiny unsweetened tartlet shells filled with the salad and decorated with pieces of pimiento.

In Madrid the place to eat Ensaladilla Rusa is the Cervecería Alemana on the Santa Ana plaza, which serves, besides, large mugs of cold beer (two excellent Spanish brands are Mahou and El Águila) and an excellent cured ham, all in a lively turn-of-the-century beer-hall atmosphere.

Serves 6–8

4 medium potatoes, preferably red
    waxy, boiled, peeled,
    and diced
¼ cup cooked carrots, diced
¼ cup cooked peas
2 tablespoons olive oil
1 tablespoon vinegar

Salt
Freshly ground pepper
Pinch sugar
¾ cup homemade
    mayonnaise (p. 104)
1 clove garlic, crushed
Pimiento strips for garnish

Gently mix together the potatoes, carrots, and peas. In a small bowl, mix the oil, vinegar, salt, pepper, and sugar. Fold into the potato mixture with a rubber spatula and let sit several hours.

Mix together the mayonnaise and garlic and fold into the potatoes. Refrigerate until ready to use, then leave at room temperature for a while before serving. Decorate with pimiento strips.

PINCHO MORUNO

(Miniature Kabobs, Moorish Style)

START PREPARATION SEVERAL HOURS
OR ONE DAY IN ADVANCE.

THE eight-hundred-year occupation by the Arabs introduced Spain to a new variety of foods and seasonings. Pincho Moruno, highly seasoned with cumin and paprika, is a favorite on the *tapas* circuit. It is commonly found throughout Spain.

THE eight-hundred-year occupation by the Arabs introduced Spain to a new variety of foods and seasonings. Pincho Moruno, highly seasoned with cumin and paprika, is a favorite on the *tapas* circuit. It is commonly found throughout Spain.

Serves 6

6 tablespoons olive oil
½ teaspoon thyme

¾ teaspoon ground cumin
½ teaspoon paprika

1 teaspoon crushed red pepper
1 bay leaf, crumbled
1 tablespoon minced parsley
Salt
Freshly ground pepper

Freshly ground pepper
1 pound lean pork, cut in
  ¾–1-inch cubes

Mix together in a large bowl all the ingredients except the pork. Add the meat cubes and stir to coat well. Cover and refrigerate several hours, or, for more flavor, leave the meat overnight, stirring occasionally. Thread the meat onto small skewers. Broil or, better still, grill over coals, until well browned but still juicy, basting with the marinade.

Pincho Moruno is also excellent as a main course. Cut the meat in larger cubes (increasing cooking time) and serve with mashed potatoes and a green vegetable, such as Peas with Cured Ham (p. 79).

FLAMENQUINES

(Pork and Ham Rolls)

THE Bar Lo Güeno, in the heart of Málaga's pedestrian shopping and dining district, has an excellent selection of *tapas*, including Flamenquines, a name of unknown origin, but related to the term "*flamenco*," which in cooking has come to mean any colorful dish native to Andalucía.

On a typical summer's ve, when every resident of Málaga seems to be out on parade, my family and I usually pass up a restaurant in favor of Bar Lo Güeno, where our *tapas* selection might include Flamenquines, Sautéed Lima Beans and Ham (p. 81), Braised Quail (p. 271), and *angulas*, incredibly delicate baby eels, no wider than spaghetti strands (see p. 20 and p. 222).

Serves 6–8

Béchamel Sauce (p. 254), omitting
  the nutmeg and adding
  ¾ cup chicken broth
1 pound pork loin, sliced very thin
  and cut in pieces
  about 2½ × 2 inches
¼ pound cured ham, sliced
  paper thin

2 eggs, lightly beaten
Bread crumbs
2 cloves garlic, crushed
2 tablespoons minced parsley
Oil for frying

Prepare the béchamel sauce according to directions and cool. Cover each pork slice with a slice of ham. Roll and secure with a toothpick. Dip the rolls in the white sauce, coating them completely, but not heavily. Place the rolls on a dish and refrigerate at least 1 hour, until the béchamel sauce hardens.

Dip the pork rolls in the beaten egg, then into the bread crumbs that have been seasoned with the garlic and parsley. Heat the oil, at least 1 inch deep, in a skillet. Over a medium-high flame, fry the pork rolls until they are golden. Drain. Transfer to a platter and keep in a 200° F oven while the others are frying.

REPOLLO RELLENO DE SALCHICHA
(Sausage Rolled in Cabbage Leaf)

Makes 16 wrapped sausages

1 pound sausage links (about
    8 sausages)
8 cabbage leaves

2 eggs, lightly beaten
Flour for dusting
Oil for frying

Sauté the sausages in a skillet until brown, but not overcooked. Cut each link in half. Boil the cabbage leaves in water until they are tender; drain. Cut each leaf in half. Wrap each sausage piece in cabbage, folding in the ends, then rolling up. Dip in egg, roll in flour, and fry in hot oil, at least ½ inch deep, until golden. Drain and serve immediately.

ALBÓNDIGAS
(Pork Balls)

Makes 20 small meatballs

½ pound ground pork loin
7 tablespoons minced parsley
2 cloves garlic, minced
1 tablespoon minced onion
3 tablespoons bread crumbs

2 eggs, lightly beaten
Salt
Freshly ground pepper
Flour for dusting
Oil for frying

Combine the pork, parsley, garlic, onion, bread crumbs, 1 of the eggs, salt, and pepper. Form into 1-inch balls, then roll them in flour. Heat the oil, at least ½ inch deep, to the smoking point. Dip the meatballs in the remaining beaten egg and place directly in the hot oil. Lower the flame and fry slowly until well browned on both sides and cooked through. These meatballs are excellent served with a quick *alioli* dip of at least 2 cloves crushed garlic to ½ cup mayonnaise.

CARACOLES A LA MADRILEÑA
(Snails, Madrid Style)

Los Caracoles on 15 de Cascorro street, is in the heart of the Rastro, Madrid's bustling flea market, where legendary stories abound of unknown paintings by Goya and Velázquez picked up for pennies and later sold for millions. Such treasures—and prices—no longer exist here, but it is still fun to browse, especially on a Sunday morning. There is no better place for a *tapa* in the Rastro than at the famous Los Caracoles bar, which specializes in snails with *chorizo*.

Although fresh snails are prized in Spain, they seem to have disappeared from the United States markets. I have found that live periwinkles are a delicious substitute. Sometimes frozen snails (unseasoned) are available in fish markets, and they are quite good. Canned snails may also be used, but they are less satisfactory.

Serves 4–6

1 pound live periwinkles, 1½ pounds frozen (unseasoned) snails, thawed, or 2 dozen canned snails, in their shells
3 tablespoons olive oil
1 medium onion, chopped
1–2 dried red chili peppers, each cut in 3 pieces, seeds removed
4 cloves garlic, minced

¼ pound *chorizo* sausage, sliced
A ¼-pound piece cured ham, diced
2 teaspoons flour
4 teaspoons paprika
½ cup tomato sauce, preferably homemade (p. 190)
2 cups dry white wine
Salt
4 tablespoons chopped parsley

Refrigerate the periwinkles in an open bowl until ready to use. Before cooking, rinse them under cold running water for 30 minutes. Drain.

In a shallow casserole, preferably earthenware, heat the oil. Add the onion and sauté until it is wilted. Add the chili peppers, garlic, *chorizo*, and ham. Cook 5 minutes. Sprinkle with the flour and the paprika. Stir to coat. Add the tomato sauce, wine, periwinkles or snails, salt, and 2 tablespoons of the parsley. Bring to a boil, then simmer 30 minutes more, uncovered, stirring occasionally. Sprinkle with the remaining parsley and serve in the cooking dish. The snails taste best the following day, reheated.

CHORIZO CAFÉ SAN MARTÍN

(Chorizo with Wine and Pimientos)

Chorizo is usually served as a *tapa* in a simple and straightforward manner. Either it is sliced and eaten cold with pieces of good crusty bread or, if the tiny *choricitos* are available, they are fried.

A fine Spanish restaurant in New York City, Café San Martín, has added a touch of elegance to this unpretentious *tapa* by including a few more ingredients and baking the *chorizo* in a large puff of foil. The presentation is impressive and the *chorizo* tender and flavorful.

For a quick preparation, which is always popular at a party, simply slice and fry some *chorizo* and spear the pieces onto cubes of bread (the bread may be fried or toasted if so desired). Otherwise, try the San Martín method.

Serves 6

1 pound *chorizo* sausage, in
    ¼-inch slices
4 tablespoons dry red wine
2 medium pimientos, homemade (p.
    430) or imported, cut in strips

2 tablespoons chopped parsley
2 cloves garlic, minced

Place the *chorizo* slices in a large skillet and sauté until lightly browned. Pour off some of the fat. Deglaze the pan with the wine, then add the pimiento, parsley, and garlic. Arrange this mixture in the center of a large, wide piece of foil. Place in a baking dish of an appropriate size and tightly close the foil, leaving a large air pocket above the *chorizo*. Place in a 350° F oven and bake 15 minutes. Present at the table in the foil, then slit the foil to serve. This may also be made in individual portions if it is to be served as a first course.

CHORIZO A LA SIDRA

(Chorizo and Apples in Hard Cider Sauce)

Serves 4

4 *chorizo* sausages (½ pound)   1 cup hard cider (see glossary)
2 apples, peeled, cored, and cut in
    ½-inch slices

In a skillet place the *chorizo* and apple slices in ½ cup of the cider. Cover and cook 15 minutes, adding the rest of the cider a little at a time as the liquid evaporates. Slice the *chorizo* and serve with the apples and sauce.

BUÑUELOS DE CHORIZO

(Chorizo Puffs)

Makes 25 puffs

1 cup flour   Salt
2 eggs, separated   3 *chorizo* sausages (6 ounces),
2 tablespoons salad oil   finely chopped
½ cup water   Oil for frying

Place the flour in a bowl and mix in the egg yolks, salad oil, water, and salt. In a separate bowl beat the egg whites until they are stiff but not dry. Fold them into the flour mixture, then let the batter sit 15 minutes.

    Fold the *chorizo* into the batter. Take the batter by the teaspoonful and drop into hot oil, at least ½ inch deep. Turn the puffs occasionally until they are golden. Drain and serve immediately.

HOJALDRADOS DE CHORIZO
(Chorizo in Puff Pastry)

THESE delicious appetizers are perfect for cocktail parties. They may be made in advance and frozen. Defrost before baking.

Makes 16 bite-size appetizers

½ pound puff pastry, homemade   ¼ pound *chorizo*, in ¼-inch slices
   (p. 336) or frozen   1 egg yolk, beaten

Roll the puff pastry to a thickness of ⅛ inch. Cut into circles ¼ inch larger than the *chorizo* slices. Center a slice of *chorizo* on each circle, paint the edges of the dough with the egg, and cover with another circle of pastry. Seal the edges well with a fork. Refrigerate each puff as it is made so that the pastry does not soften too much. Place the puffs on a cookie sheet and bake at 450° F on the upper rack of the oven for about 7 minutes, or until lightly browned and puffed.

HUEVOS RELLENOS DE SALMÓN
(Salmon-Stuffed Eggs)

START PREPARATION SEVERAL HOURS IN ADVANCE.

SALMON-STUFFED EGGS are to be found at the incredible Mallorca shop on Velázquez Street in Madrid. This small store is a pastry shop, bakery, delicatessen, wine store, cheese shop, *tapas* bar, and caterer all rolled into one, with top-quality items in all departments. If you can maneuver through the fashionable crowds that throng there at all hours, you will have a unique opportunity to sample an enormous assortment of foods served at Madrid's most elegant gatherings—such delicacies as crab salad in tiny tartlet shells; canapés of caviar, smoked trout, and sturgeon; shrimp aspic; *Chorizo* in Puff Pastry (above), Puff Pastry with Salmon Filling (p. 74), and Veal in Puff Pastry (p. 71). The pastry selection is equally overwhelming, and the wine section stocks an exceptional collection of brands and vintages. Early afternoon is the time to be there— when traveling to Madrid, don't miss it.

These delicious and unusual eggs are hard boiled, stuffed with a salmon mixture, coated with a béchamel sauce, then fried. There are several steps involved in their preparation, but everything can and should be done in advance, except the final frying.

Makes 10 stuffed egg halves

Half a 7¾-ounce can salmon
3 tablespoons tomato sauce
5 hard-boiled eggs, cut in
     half lengthwise
Salt
Freshly ground pepper
2 teaspoons minced parsley

Béchamel Sauce (p. 254), omitting
    the nutmeg and adding
    ¾ cup chicken broth
2 eggs, lightly beaten
Bread crumbs
Oil for frying

Flake the salmon and combine it in a bowl with the tomato sauce, 2 of the hard-boiled egg yolks, salt, pepper, and parsley. Remove the remaining egg yolks from the egg halves—these yolks will not be used in this recipe. Stuff the egg whites with the salmon mixture, forming a slight mound. Refrigerate the stuffed eggs, then prepare the béchamel sauce. Cool, stirring occasionally.

Carefully dip the stuffed eggs in the béchamel sauce, coating on all sides. Place the eggs on a platter and refrigerate until the sauce hardens, at least 1 hour. Dip the coated eggs in the beaten eggs, then cover with bread crumbs. Fry immediately in hot oil, at least 1 inch deep, until the eggs are brown on all sides. Drain.

TARTALETAS DE SALMÓN

(Salmon Tartlets)

Makes 30 tartlets

7¾-ounce can salmon
½ cup tomato sauce, preferably
    homemade (p. 190)
4 tablespoons minced hard-boiled egg
½ teaspoon anchovy paste
Salt
Freshly ground pepper

2 tablespoons minced radish
1½ teaspoons red wine vinegar
2 tablespoons minced pimiento,
    homemade or imported
30 miniature unsweetened
    tartlet shells
Parsley for garnish

Flake the salmon. Mix in the remaining ingredients except the shells and parsley. Fill the tartlet shells and decorate with parsley.

TARTALETAS DE CHAMPIÑÓN

(Mushroom Tartlets)

Makes 20 tartlets

5 tablespoons mayonnaise,
    preferably homemade
1 clove garlic, crushed
1 tablespoon chopped parsley
1 teaspoon lemon juice
Salt

Freshly ground pepper
¼ pound mushrooms, finely chopped
20 miniature unsweetened
    tartlet shells
Pickles and pimiento for garnish

Mix the mayonnaise, garlic, parsley, lemon juice, salt, and pepper. Stir in the mushrooms and refrigerate 1 hour. Fill the tartlet shells and decorate with pieces of pickle and pimiento.

NOTE: Do not prepare more than an hour in advance or the mushrooms may begin to give off liquid and thin the sauce.

CHAMPIÑONES RELLENOS

(Pork-Stuffed Mushrooms)

STUFFED mushrooms are a pleasant addition to any *tapas* selection, and these mushrooms, filled with an interesting mixture of pork and pine nuts, are particularly appealing.

Serves 4

¾ pound medium-size mushrooms
Lemon juice
5 tablespoons butter
3 tablespoons minced onion
1 clove garlic, crushed
¼ pound lean ground pork
Salt

Freshly ground pepper
3 tablespoons bread crumbs
½ teaspoon brandy, preferably
    Spanish brandy, or Cognac
1 tablespoon minced parsley
1 tablespoon chopped pine nuts

Separate the mushroom stems and chop finely, reserving ⅓ cup for this recipe and the rest for future use. Sprinkle the caps with lemon juice. Heat 4 tablespoons of the butter in a medium skillet and sauté the onion and garlic slowly until the onion is wilted. Add the meat and cook, sprinkling with salt and pepper, until it loses its color. Add the chopped stems and cook 3 minutes more. Turn off the heat. Stir in the bread crumbs, brandy, parsley, pine nuts, and more salt and pepper if necessary. Pile this mixture into the mushroom caps and dot with the remaining tablespoon of butter. Bake at 350° F for 15 minutes.

CHAMPIÑONES A LA SEGOVIANA

(Mushrooms, Segovia Style)

Serves 4

¼ cup diced slab bacon
1 clove garlic, minced
1 tablespoon minced parsley
½ pound mushrooms, halved
    or quartered

¼ cup dry white wine
Salt
Freshly ground pepper

Sauté the bacon in a flameproof casserole or in a skillet. When it begins to brown, add the garlic and parsley. Stir in the mushrooms and sauté 2 minutes. Add the wine, salt, and pepper. Cook over a high flame until the liquid evaporates. Serve immediately.

CHAMPIÑONES AL AJILLO

(Mushrooms in Garlic Sauce)

SPANIARDS adore garlic sauces, be they on chicken, seafood, or vegetables.

Serves 4–6

3 cloves garlic, minced
3 tablespoons olive oil
1½ tablespoons flour
1 cup beef broth,
    preferably homemade
½ dried red chili pepper, cut in 3
    pieces, seeds removed

2 tablespoons chopped parsley
2 teaspoons lemon juice
½ pound mushrooms, whole
    or halved

In a skillet heat the garlic in 2 tablespoons of the oil until the garlic starts to color. Turn off the heat immediately—the garlic should not turn brown. Stir in the flour and cook a minute. Gradually pour in the beef broth, then add the chili pepper, 1 tablespoon of the parsley, and the lemon juice. Stir until smooth and thickened.

In a separate skillet, heat the remaining tablespoon of the oil until it is very hot. Add the mushrooms and stir fry briefly until the mushrooms are lightly browned. Add the mushrooms to the sauce and simmer 5 minutes. Sprinkle with the remaining tablespoon of parsley and serve.

EMPANADILLAS

THE suffix *"illa"* means small and distinguishes these appetizer turnovers from *empanadas* (pp. 64–69), which are pie size. So popular are turnovers in Spain that the dough, prerolled and cut into small circles, is commonly sold in groceries. *Empanadillas* are particularly good with a tuna or veal filling, such as in the two recipes that follow.

EMPANADILLAS DE ATÚN

(Tuna Turnovers)

Makes about 40 turnovers

Empanadilla dough (p. 337)
1 tablespoon olive oil
1 medium onion, chopped
7-ounce can tuna, preferably light
    meat, drained and flaked
4 tablespoons chopped tomato, fresh
    or canned
5 tablespoons tomato sauce or diluted
    tomato paste

1 pimiento, homemade or
    imported, chopped
1 tablespoon minced parsley
Salt
Freshly ground pepper
1 hard-boiled egg, finely chopped
Oil for frying

Prepare the dough. While it is resting, heat the oil in a skillet. Sauté the onion until it is wilted. Add the tuna, tomato, tomato sauce, pimiento, parsley, salt, and pepper, and cook, uncovered, 10 minutes. Sprinkle in the egg and remove immediately from the flame.

Roll and cut the dough according to instructions. Place about 1 tablespoon of the filling in the center of each *empanadilla* circle. Fold over and seal by pressing the edges with a fork. Fry in hot oil, at least 1 inch deep, until the turnovers are well browned. Drain.

EMPANADILLAS DE TERNERA

(Spicy Veal and Tomato Turnovers)

Makes about 40 turnovers

Empanadilla dough (p. 337)
1 tablespoon olive oil
1 medium onion, chopped
1 clove garlic, minced
2 *chorizo* sausages (4 ounces),
    finely chopped
1 pound ground veal
3 tablespoons tomato paste
¼ cup dry white wine

1 pimiento, homemade or
    imported, diced
1 tablespoon chopped parsley
1 tablespoon chopped green
    Spanish olives
Salt
Freshly ground pepper
Oil for frying

While the dough is resting, heat the oil in a skillet and sauté the onion and garlic until the onion is wilted. Add the *chorizo* and cook, stirring, 5 minutes, then add the veal and brown over high heat. Stir in the tomato paste, wine, pimiento, parsley, olives, salt, and pepper. Simmer, uncovered, 20 minutes. To form and fry the Empanadillas, see the preceding recipe for Empanadillas de Atún.

NOTE: The same filling is excellent in a puff pastry roll—see Veal in Puff Pastry (p. 71).

EMPANADILLAS DE CARNE

(Mini Meat Pies)

START PREPARATION
AN HOUR AND A HALF IN ADVANCE.

AT THE busy Bar Coruña in Santiago de Compostela, trays of these spherical meat pies are constantly emerging from the kitchen and are devoured by the two- and three-deep crowds at the bar. The favorite accompaniment is the thick raspberry-colored Ribeiro wine of Galicia.

The pies are made with a light yeast dough and are filled with a spicy meat mixture. They are excellent hot or cold.

Makes 32 mini meat pies

DOUGH

1 package dry yeast	1 egg, lightly beaten
¼ cup warm water	1 cup warm milk
3½ cups flour	2 tablespoons melted butter
½ teaspoon salt	

FILLING

1 tablespoon olive oil	3 tablespoons tomato paste
1 large onion, finely chopped	½ cup water
3 cloves garlic, minced	1½ tablespoons dry red wine
4 tablespoons minced green pepper	¼ teaspoon crushed dried red
1 pound ground beef	chili pepper
Salt	Oil for frying
Freshly ground pepper	

To make the dough, dissolve the yeast in the warm water. Mix together in a bowl the flour and salt. Add the egg, then stir in the warm milk, butter, and the yeast mixture. Turn onto a working surface and knead a minute or two, just until the dough is smooth and no longer sticky, adding more flour as necessary. Place the dough in a bowl greased with oil, turning to coat with the oil. Cover with a towel and leave in a warm spot until doubled in bulk, about 1½ hours.

Meanwhile, prepare the filling. Heat the olive oil in a large skillet and sauté the onion, garlic, and green pepper until the green pepper is tender. Add the meat and cook over a high flame until it begins to brown. Season with salt and pepper. Add the tomato paste, water, wine, and red pepper. Cover and cook 10 minutes.

Divide the dough into thirty-two 1½-inch balls. Roll each into a 3-inch circle. Place 1 tablespoon of the filling in the center of each circle, pull up the sides, and pinch to seal.

Heat the frying oil, at least 1 inch deep, in a skillet. Lower the heat to medium and fry the meat pies slowly, turning frequently, until they are golden. Drain.

EMPAREDADOS DE JAMÓN Y QUESO

(Fried Ham and Cheese Sandwiches)

ONE of my husband's favorites, especially as part of a "mixed fry" that might include, besides, Croquetas de Lhardy (p. 40), *empanadillas* (pp. 36–39), and Chorizo in Puff Pastry (p. 32).

Makes 8 small sandwiches

¼ pound cured ham, sliced
    very thin
¼ pound cheese, such as Tetilla
    (p. 432) or Fontina, in thin slices
16 slices French-style bread,
    ⅜–½-inch thick,
    preferably day old and
    not airy (Pan de Pueblo,
    p. 324, is ideal)

½ cup milk
2 eggs
Oil for frying

Fit the ham in several layers, then the cheese, onto half of the bread slices. Cover with the remaining bread slices. Pour the milk into a flat dish and dip the sandwiches quickly into it, moistening both sides. Place on a dry dish and let sit 20 minutes.

Beat the eggs lightly in a shallow bowl. Heat the oil, at least ½ inch deep, to the smoking point. Dip the sandwiches in the egg, then place immediately in the hot oil. Fry until golden on both sides. Drain and serve immediately.

CROQUETAS DE LHARDY

(Chicken and Cured Ham Croquettes)

START PREPARATION SEVERAL HOURS
OR ONE DAY IN ADVANCE.

LHARDY is an institution in Madrid. Having survived over eight decades of changing times, it is the grande dame of Spanish food establishments, with its elegant chandeliers, mirrored walls, and antique display cases. The second floor is a restaurant, but Lhardy's main interest lies in its first-floor *tapas* and takeout service. *Tapas* are on the honor system, and sherried consommé is available, also self-served, from an ornate silver tureen. And to accompany the soup, these outstanding croquettes.

The chicken may be chopped in a processor, but the ham must be minced by hand or it will become stringy. Since the recipe also calls for chicken broth, it makes sense to boil your own chicken (you will need a whole breast) and reserve the broth.

Makes about 35 croquettes

3 tablespoons butter	Dash nutmeg
5 tablespoons olive oil	1 cup very finely chopped boiled
¾ cup flour	chicken breast
1½ cups milk	½ cup very finely minced cured ham
½ cup chicken broth,	Flour for dusting
preferably homemade	2 eggs, lightly beaten
Salt	Bread crumbs
Freshly ground pepper	Oil for frying

Heat the butter and olive oil in a saucepan until the butter melts. Add the flour and cook 3 minutes, stirring constantly. Gradually add the milk and the broth, salt (very little if the ham is salty), pepper, and nutmeg, and cook over a medium flame, stirring constantly, until the sauce is thickened and smooth. Add the chicken and ham and continue cooking and stirring 10 minutes more, until the sauce reaches the boiling point. Check the seasoning, adding more salt if necessary, then cool. Refrigerate until cold, at least 3 hours. (The croquettes may be made up to this point the day before.)

Flour a work surface and divide the mixture into balls of about 1 tablespoon each, rolling with floured hands. Dip the croquettes in the egg, and coat with crumbs. Chill for 30 minutes. Fry in hot oil, at least 1 inch deep, turning several times, until golden. Drain.

NOTE: The croquettes may be kept warm in a 200° F oven for about 30 minutes. They can also be reheated, although they are at their best when served immediately.

CROQUETAS DE PAELLA

(Paella Croquettes)

A NICE way to use leftovers from a *paella*, or any other mixed rice dish in Chapter 7.

Makes 10 croquettes

1 cup leftover *paella* rice
½ cup chopped chicken, fish, or meat
     from a *paella*
2 eggs, beaten

2 teaspoons flour
Flour for dusting
Bread crumbs for coating
Oil for frying

In a bowl mix together the rice and meat or fish. Add one of the eggs and the 2 teaspoons of flour. With floured hands, shape the mixture into 2-inch balls. Dip them in the other beaten egg, then in bread crumbs.

Heat the oil, at least 1 inch deep, and fry the croquettes until golden. Drain.

CROQUETAS DE GAMBAS

(Shrimp Croquettes)

START PREPARATION SEVERAL HOURS
OR ONE DAY IN ADVANCE.

Makes 35–40 croquettes

3 tablespoons butter
5 tablespoons olive oil
¾ cup flour
1¼ cups milk
¼ cup dry white wine
½ cup fish broth (p. 13) or
    clam juice
Salt
Freshly ground pepper
Dash cayenne
¼ pound shelled and uncooked
    shrimp, ground

½ pound shelled and uncooked
    shrimp, chopped
½ cup finely chopped
    mushrooms (optional)
1 tablespoon minced parsley
¼ teaspoon thyme or tarragon
Flour for dusting
2 eggs, beaten
Bread crumbs
Oil for frying

Heat the butter and oil in a saucepan until the butter is melted. Add the flour and cook 3 minutes, stirring constantly. Gradually add the milk, wine, broth, salt, pepper, and cayenne. Cook over a medium flame until the sauce is thickened and smooth. Add the shrimp, optional mushrooms, parsley, and thyme and continue cooking and stirring 10 minutes more, until the sauce reaches the boiling point. Cool. Refrigerate until cold and easy to handle, several hours or overnight.

    Take the dough by the tablespoon and form into balls, using floured hands. Dip in the egg, then roll in bread crumbs. Fry in at least 1 inch of oil until golden. Drain. The croquettes may be kept warm in a 200° F oven for up to 30 minutes, but are best when eaten immediately.

DELICIAS DE QUESO

(Cheese Balls)

Makes 26 cheese balls

2 eggs, separated
½ cup milk
½ cup flour
Salt
Freshly ground pepper
Dash nutmeg

½ pound cheese, such as Tetilla
    (p. 432) or Gouda, grated
2 tablespoons granted Manchego
    (p. 431) or Parmesan cheese
3 tablespoons minced cured ham
1 teaspoon grated onion
Oil for frying

In a bowl beat the egg yolks with a wire whisk until light colored. Stir in the milk, then gradually add the flour and beat until smooth. In a separate bowl beat the egg whites until stiff but not dry. Fold the yolk mixture into the whites, adding the salt, pepper, nutmeg, cheeses, ham, and onion. Drop by the teaspoonful into hot oil, at least ½ inch deep, and fry, turning once, until just golden—do not overcook. Drain and serve immediately.

BUÑUELOS DE BACALAO

(Cod Puffs)

ALTHOUGH the taste of dried codfish can sometimes be powerful, these puffs are only mildly flavored with cod and are unusually crunchy. An *alioli* dip is an ideal accompaniment.

Makes about 40 puffs

½ pound skinned and boned dried
    salt cod
1 pound medium potatoes, scrubbed
    and quartered
2 cloves garlic, crushed

1 tablespoon chopped parsley
Salt
Freshly ground pepper
2 egg yolks
Oil for frying

Soak the cod in cold water to cover for 24–36 hours, changing the water occasionally. Drain.
    Leaving the skin on the potatoes, place them with the cod in a pot, cover

with water, then bring to a boil. Cover and simmer 30 minutes, or until the potatoes are tender. Drain. Skin the potatoes and pass them through a sieve into a bowl. Crumble the cod with the fingers, being sure no bones remain. Mix with the potatoes. Add the garlic, parsley, salt, and pepper. Stir in the egg yolks. Refrigerate 1 hour.

Take teaspoons of the cod mixture and drop them in hot oil, at least 1 inch deep, until the puffs are well browned on all sides. Keep them warm in a 200° F oven until ready to use. Serve with an *alioli* dip of at least 2 crushed garlic cloves to each ½ cup of mayonnaise.

CANAPÉ DE ANCHOA Y PIMIENTO
(Anchovy and Pimiento Spread)

PREPARE SEVERAL HOURS
OR ONE DAY IN ADVANCE.

THIS always proves a popular appetizer.

Makes 12–16 bread triangles

One and a half 2-ounce cans flat
    fillet of anchovy, drained
    and finely chopped
2 pimientos, homemade or imported,
    finely chopped
½ cup finely chopped Spanish onion

1 tablespoon minced parsley
Freshly ground pepper
1 tablespoon olive oil
1¼ teaspoons red wine vinegar
Sandwich bread, crusts removed

In a small bowl mix together the anchovy, pimiento, onion, parsley, and pepper. Add the olive oil and vinegar. Refrigerate. To serve, spread on the bread and cut into triangles.

CANAPÉ DE CABRALES Y PIÑONES
(Blue Cheese and Pine Nut Canapé)

CABRALES cheese is from Asturias (see Spanish Cheese, p. 431).

Makes 20 triangles

10 tablespoons strong blue cheese,
    such as Cabrales (p. 431)
    or Gorgonzola
5 slices sandwich bread,
    crusts removed

5 tablespoons pine nuts
5 strong black olives, sliced

Bring the cheese to room temperature, then mash with a fork until it is smooth enough to spread. Cover each slice of bread with cheese and cut into triangles. Sprinkle with the pine nuts, pressing them down lightly so that they adhere to the cheese. Decorate each triangle with a slice or two of black olive.

CANAPÉ DE ANCHOA
(Anchovy, Chicken, and Tomato Canapé)

Makes 10 canapés

10 slices French-style bread,
    ¼ inch thick
Mayonnaise
20 anchovy fillets
2 pimientos, homemade or imported
4 tablespoons tomato sauce or diluted
    tomato paste

Dash cayenne
4 tablespoons finely chopped
    boiled chicken
Chopped parsley for garnish

Toast the bread slices in a 450° F oven for 5 minutes. Spread them with mayonnaise. Cut the anchovy fillets in pieces to fit on the toast and arrange them on the top. Spread on another layer of mayonnaise and cover with a piece of pimiento the size of the toast. Mix the tomato sauce with the cayenne. Spread 1 teaspoon of the tomato sauce on each canapé, sprinkle with the chicken, and garnish with parsley.

CANAPÉ DE ATÚN Y TOMATE
(Marinated Tuna and Tomato on Bread)

START PREPARATION ONE DAY IN ADVANCE.

IN THE Basque fishing town of Bermeo, where hundreds of brightly painted green, red, and blue boats decorate the harbor, this tuna *tapa* is a popular offering. The fish is canned; nevertheless the mixture has the strong taste of the sea.

Makes about 15–20 canapes

7-ounce can light meat tuna
1½ teaspoons red wine vinegar
2 tablespoons minced onion
1 tablespoon minced parsley
2 tablespoons minced pimiento, homemade or imported
5 tablespoons tomato sauce or diluted tomato paste

2 tablespoons minced hard-boiled egg
Salt
Freshly ground pepper
French-style bread, in ¼-inch slices
Hard-boiled egg, sliced, for garnish

Drain the tuna, place in a bowl, and break up the pieces with a fork. Add the vinegar, onion, parsley, and pimiento and mix well. Stir in the tomato sauce, chopped egg, salt, and pepper and let the mixture marinate overnight. To serve, spread thickly on the bread slices and top with a slice of egg.

NOTE: White meat tuna should not be substituted. A stronger-flavored tuna is necessary.

CANAPÉ DE LECHUGA A LA VINAGRETA
(Marinated Lettuce Canapés)

START PREPARATION ONE DAY IN ADVANCE.

I ALWAYS associate these miniature lettuce sandwiches with the elegance of Lhardy in Madrid, where I have often nibbled on such canapés while sipping sherried consommé. The turn-of-the-century surroundings of Lhardy take one back to a more gracious era and provide the ideal ambience for the enjoyment of the dainty finger foods available there (more on Lhardy, p. 40).

Makes about 25 triangles

3 teaspoons mayonnaise
6 tablespoons olive oil
3 tablespoons vinegar
Pinch sugar
Salt

Freshly ground pepper
1 medium head romaine lettuce,
    green part only, shredded
Sandwich bread, crusts removed
    and thinly sliced

Place the mayonnaise in a small bowl. Gradually beat in the oil with a wire whisk, then add the vinegar, sugar, salt, and pepper and beat well. Pour this mixture over the shredded lettuce and mix well. Cover and refrigerate overnight.

Spread the lettuce mixture between the bread slices. Cut into triangles. Wrap the canapés in a damp towel until ready to serve.

PINCHO DE HUEVO

(Egg Tapa)

Pinchos—small appetizers meant to be picked up with toothpicks—come in uncountable varieties. This one has a particularly pleasing mixture of tastes, although you may prefer to concoct your own combinations.

Makes 2 appetizers

2 teaspoons mayonnaise
1 hard-boiled egg, cut in
    half lengthwise

2 cooked shrimp
2 pimiento-stuffed olives
2 rolled anchovies

Place 1 teaspoon of mayonnaise on top of each egg half. Insert a toothpick in the center of the egg halves. Spear a shrimp, an olive, and an anchovy on top of each.

PEPINILLO RELLENO

(Tuna-Filled Pickle)

MAKE as many as you wish—the recipe describes how to make one.

1 teaspoon light meat tuna, flaked	1 baby dill pickle
Salt	1 teaspoon minced onion
Freshly ground pepper	1 pimiento-stuffed green olive

Mix the tuna with the salt and pepper. Slit the pickle lengthwise without passing all the way through. Fill the pickle with the tuna, sprinkle with the onion, and secure with a toothpick. Spear an olive onto the toothpick.

ACEITUNAS NEGRAS ALIÑADAS

(Marinated Black Olives)

THE olives take on more flavor the longer they marinate. Serve preferably after several weeks, at room temperature. They will keep for several months.

1 pound black olives, preferably Italian or Greek style	Salt (omit if the olives are salty)
2 cloves garlic, peeled and lightly crushed	1 teaspoon paprika
	2 tablespoons red wine vinegar
	1 slice lemon

Mix together all ingredients and refrigerate in a jar, mixing occasionally.

ACEITUNAS VERDES ALIÑADAS
(Marinated Green Olives)

PREPARE MANY DAYS IN ADVANCE.

13-ounce jar large Spanish green
    olives with pits, drained
    and very lightly crushed

8 cloves garlic, lightly crushed
    and peeled
¼ cup olive oil

Combine the olives, garlic, and oil in a glass jar. Cover tightly and refrigerate, the longer, the better the flavor becomes. Bring to room temperature before serving.

Chapter 2

EMBUTIDOS, PASTELES Y EMPANADAS

(Sausages, Pâtés, and Savory Pies)

THIS chapter is a potpourri of related categories. Almost all the recipes included are meats or fish in combination with spices and/or vegetables, either stuffed into skins to form sausages, placed between dough to make pies, or shaped into loaves as pâtés. They serve many different purposes, from appetizers to main courses. Some are eaten hot and others cold. The sausages may stand alone or enter into many recipes found in other chapters.

Spain is incredibly rich in sausages, a legacy from prerefrigeration times, when meats were cured in cool places in winter, then consumed over the rest of the year. To this day, the tradition of the winter *matanza*, or slaughter, continues in small villages, where it is always a treat to eat the locally dried and earthy-tasting sausages and hams that are a result of this yearly ritual. Of course, most sausages are now commercially produced, but the variety remains astounding—just about every bar in Spain will have dozens of cured meats and sausages hanging from the rafters; a count at Mallorca, a specialty food shop in Madrid, turned up twenty-five different kinds of *embutidos*, as they are called, falling into four general categories: the red paprika sausages; the so-called "white" sausages; the black blood sausages; and the cured solid meats, such as ham and loin of pork.

Chorizo, a rusty red sausage, is by far the best-loved Spanish sausage, found in endless varieties, lengths, and thicknesses, although *chorizo* from Cantimpalos and Villarcayo are the most highly regarded. The heavy paprika and garlic flavoring in *chorizo* makes it distinct from the sausage of any other country and equally appealing hot, cold, fresh, cured, or in combination with a wide variety of other foods. It is a mystery to me why *chorizo* has not become immensely popular in this country.

White sausage—what we might call breakfast or Italian style—is the favorite in Asturias and Cataluña. It lacks the paprika seasoning of *chorizo*, but includes other spices—from thyme and parsley to cinnamon and cloves. It is often eaten freshly made and enters into many regional recipes.

Blood sausage—*morcilla*—is particularly famous in León, but eaten all over Spain, especially the version that includes rice. Always fried or boiled before eating, it is popular as an accompaniment to fried eggs and is used in the Castilian boiled dinner, *cocido*. When it is of good quality, it is one of my favorites, and it enters into many recipes in this book.

The cured meats are usually pork products, but in some areas they also include beef. Cured ham, similar to Italian prosciutto (which is not smoked), has a following that the very high price fails to deter—it continues to be eaten as an appetizer, in slices or cubes, and to be included in all types of recipes, from vegetables to fish. There is never any skimping. Jabugo ham is regarded with special reverence, for it is cured in mountain snow and made from the meat of pigs that have eaten nothing but acorns, giving the ham a wonderfully nutty flavor. Ham from Trevélez in the Alpujarra mountain range is equally revered. Another exquisite pork product is cured pork loin, and in several beef-producing areas, *cecina*, also called *jamón de toro*—cured beef—is found.

Many of these sausage types are represented in this chapter, especially those frequently used in cooking. Don't be put off by sausage making—it is quite simple and requires no elaborate equipment. And the sausage you make is most likely to be a purer product than similar sausages commercially produced. There is only one catch: and that is, drying meats so that they do not spoil and so that all harmful organisms are destroyed requires special conditions that most homes cannot meet. Therefore, all sausages made at home should be cooked before eating and, unfortunately, cannot be eaten as cold cuts, uncooked, as one would eat a commercial salami or a cured ham. There are many delicious alternative ways, however, to eat the sausage you make. Sausage making is great fun, definitely worth trying.

Pâtés are as popular in Spain as in the rest of the world. Since Spain has an abundance of game birds and wild rabbit, pâtés are usually made with such meats; partridge is particularly popular because of its wonderfully strong flavor. What are called in Spanish *pudin*—a bastardization of the English word—are delicious meat or fish loaves that are eaten cold with mayonnaise or warm with a sauce.

Empanadas, meat and fish pies from Galicia, are rarely found elsewhere in Spain. One explanation for the popularity of *empanadas* in Galicia is that they suit the character of these northern peoples, for the pies hide their contents from public view, just as the Gallegos often remain aloof and secretive. The idea may be a bit farfetched, but there is little doubt that Gallegos make better meat pies than anyone else, using fillings as varied as the produce of Galicia. Most *empanadas* contain lots of onion and green or red pepper, in combination with meat or fish. The doughs take many different forms, from puff pastry to those made with cornmeal. There are other areas of Spain known for their pies, but these are called *pasteles* instead of *empanadas*. Murcia in particular has an excellent veal and *chorizo* pie represented in this chapter.

Meat and fish pies are extremely versatile—they may be eaten hot or cold, cut up into appetizer or first-course portions, or eaten as a light supper. They also travel well and are ideal for picnics. Try the whole range, for each is different and delicious.

BASIC SAUSAGE INSTRUCTIONS

To MAKE sausages you will need pork sausage skins, found in some supermarkets, but otherwise available through your butcher. A funnel, about 7/8-inch wide at the tube end, is necessary for stuffing, and you will need a food processor or meat grinder to chop the meats, a job that may also be done by the butcher. Some sausage recipes call for saltpeter, potassium nitrate, which has been used for centuries to preserve meat and to help retain its color. It may be purchased in drugstores.

1. Soak the sausage skins in water for about 20 minutes, rinsing occasionally to remove salt. Drain.

2. Make a knot at one end of the sausage casing. Blow through the other end to make sure it inflates—otherwise it has a hole and cannot be used. Squeeze out all of the air. An alternate method is to feed the sausage casing onto a faucet and fill with water to test for leaks.

3. Starting at the open end, feed all of the casing onto the tube of the funnel. Force the sausage meat through the funnel with your fingers, releasing the casing from the funnel as it fills. Do not pack the meat too tightly, or the casing may burst when cooked. If any air pockets form, prick with a pin to release the air.

4. If the sausage is to be left in one long piece, tie off the other end after filling. Otherwise, to make individual sausages, start at the tied end and twist the sausage at desired lengths. Tie with a string so that they will not untwist. Leave long strings on the ends to aid in hanging.

5. Hang the sausages for the amount of time specified in the recipe (salt and spice content prevents spoilage). Make sure the sausages hang free and do not touch one another. After drying, refrigerate, lightly wrapped in wax paper, until ready to use. (Homemade sausage must be cooked before eating.)

CHORIZO

(Spanish Sausage)

PREPARE SEVERAL DAYS IN ADVANCE.

SPANISH cuisine would be unthinkable without *chorizo*, a sausage heavily spiced with paprika and garlic. It is used as an appetizer—cold, fried, or baked (p. 30)—or as an ingredient in omelet, tripe, soup, meat, and vegetable dishes, to which it imparts a special flavor. There are recipes scattered throughout this book that need *chorizo* in their preparation.

Chorizo is cured but eaten uncooked, like salami, or used in cooking like sausage. However, it is not advisable to consume homemade *chorizo* uncooked. If you wish to eat it as a cold cut, the commercially made product must be used.

Makes 6–8 sausage links

¾ pound lean pork loin, cut in
    ½-inch cubes
¼ pound pork fat or
    unsalted fatback, cut in
    ¼-inch cubes
¼ pound pork fat or
    unsalted fatback, ground
2 teaspoons coarse salt
¼ teaspoon freshly ground pepper
2 tablespoons paprika

¼ teaspoon ground cumin
½ teaspoon ground or crushed
    coriander seeds
½ teaspoon sugar
3 tablespoons dry red wine
2 cloves garlic, crushed
1 teaspoon crushed dried red
    chili pepper
½ teaspoon saltpeter
Sausage casings

Mix together the cubed pork and the cubed and ground fat. Add the remaining ingredients except the sausage casings. Cover and refrigerate overnight.

Stuff the sausage casings, twisting and tying every 4 inches. Hang to dry at room temperature for 3 days, then refrigerate, loosely covered with wax paper, and continue to dry several more days before using. They will keep for a few weeks in the refrigerator.

NOTE: Miniature *chorizos*, called *choricitos*, are popular as appetizers, fried. To make them, twist and tie the sausage every 1½ inches (makes about 16–20).

SOBRASADA

(Mallorcan Chorizo Spread)

Sobrasada comes from the island of Mallorca, but it is quite popular all over Spain. It is basically a soft *chorizo* with some additional seasoning and is usually used as a spread—grilled *sobrasada* sandwiches are particularly well liked.

Because this sausage will not be cooked, it is imperative to use commercially produced *chorizo*, not homemade. Similarly, the pork fat used must not be fresh—use the trimmings from cured ham (your store will be glad to give them to you) or from other similarly processed products.

About 1 1/2 cups

½ pound commercial *chorizo* sausage, casing removed
½ cup chopped fat from cured ham or other cured meat

¼ teaspoon ground nutmeg
1 teaspoon lemon juice

Place all ingredients in a processor and blend until smooth. Pack into a crock and serve at room temperature as a spread on bread or crackers, hot or cold. Or use as a filling for puff pastry appetizers (p. 32).

BUTIFARRA CATALANA

(Catalán Sausage)

PREPARE AT LEAST ONE DAY IN ADVANCE.

A SPICY sausage native to Cataluña, *butifarra* enters into many regional dishes, such as Baked Sausage and Mushrooms (p. 313), Catalán-Style Beef Stew (p. 298) and Pork and Sausage Casserole (p. 310).

Makes one 40-inch sausage

½ pound lean pork, finely chopped (by hand)
½ pound ground lean pork
½ pound ground fresh pork fat
1 tablespoon salt
2 cloves garlic, crushed

⅛ teaspoon cinnamon
¼ teaspoon pepper
⅛ teaspoon ground nutmeg
1 tablespoon white wine
1 clove, crushed
Sausage casings

Combine all ingredients. Stuff a sausage casing in one continuous piece, tying off the ends. Hang to dry for 2 hours, then refrigerate, loosely wrapped in wax paper, at least overnight before using. This sausage will keep for many days in the refrigerator.

BUTIFARRÓN DULCE

(Catalán Sausage in Caramelized Sugar)

THIS unusual sausage, all solid meat with no addition of fat, is best served in slices as an appetizer.

Makes one 26-inch sausage

1 pound ground lean pork
2 teaspoons salt
¼ teaspoon grated lemon rind
Sausage casings

¼ cup water
2 tablespoons sugar
Juice of 1 lemon

Season the pork with salt and lemon rind. Stuff the meat into a sausage casing, making one long sausage. Hang to dry for 2 hours.

Put the sausage in a skillet with the water, sugar, and lemon juice. Cook very slowly, turning the sausage frequently, until the sugar is caramelized and all the liquid is absorbed. Serve cut into pieces and speared to small thick squares of fried or toasted bread.

SALCHICHA BLANCA ASTURIANA

(Asturian-Style Sausage)

PREPARE ONE DAY IN ADVANCE.

THIS basic "breakfast-style" sausage is particularly good in Sausages with Sweet-Sour Figs (p. 311)

Makes ten 4-inch sausages

1 pound lean pork, cubed
6 ounces fresh pork fat, preferably unsalted fatback, cubed
2½ teaspoons salt
1½ teaspoons freshly ground pepper
5 tablespoons minced parsley
½ teaspoon thyme
Sausage casings

In a processor, chop the pork and pork fat to medium-coarse. Remove to a bowl. Season with salt, pepper, parsley, and thyme and mix well. Stuff into sausage casings, twist, and tie off in 4-inch lengths. Hang to dry for 24 hours. Refrigerate, loosely covered in wax paper. The sausages will keep for many days in the refrigerator.

LONGANIZA

(Rosemary-Flavored Sausage)

PREPARE ONE DAY IN ADVANCE.

I ALWAYS associate *longaniza* with the famous sixteenth-century picaresque novel, *Lazarillo de Tormes*, which relates the struggle for existence and the constant fight against hunger of its young antihero, Lazarillo. Ir one unforgettable episode he takes up employment with a blind man, who preys on the sympathies of people and makes a good amount of money by begging—none of which goes to feed Lazarillo. One day, the story relates, the blind man is grilling a succulent *longaniza* sausage for himself. Lazarillo's hunger gets the best of him, and, not thinking of the consequences, he seizes the sausage, replaces it with a long thin turnip, and greedily devours the tasty *longaniza*. When the blind man takes a bite of what he thinks is sausage, the deception is, of course, discovered, and the pungent and spicy aroma that the *longaniza* has left behind on Lazarillo's breath makes it impossible for him to deny the theft. He is severely thrashed for his treachery.

Longaniza receives its name because of its long length. It is a well-flavored and meaty sausage, ideal for frying and a good accompaniment to fried eggs.

Makes one 30-inch sausage

¾ pound ground loin pork, with some fat on it
1½ teaspoons salt
1½ teaspoons paprika

¾ teaspoon crushed rosemary
Freshly ground pepper
⅜ teaspoon saltpeter
Sausage casings

Mix together all ingredients. Stuff into sausage casing in one long sausage. Tie off the end. Hang to dry for 1 day, then refrigerate, loosely wrapped in wax paper.

BLANQUETS VALENCIANOS

(Valencian Boiled Sausage)

PREPARE AT LEAST FIVE DAYS IN ADVANCE.

THE cold cuts from the eastern region of Spain, such as the *butifarra* of Cataluña and this *blanquet* from Valencia, are quite different from the sausages of other areas, mainly because they rely on such aromatic spices as cloves, cinnamon, and nutmeg. Since this sausage has been precooked, it is delicious to eat as is, at room temperature, and is appropriate for *tapas*, sandwiches, and in salads. I also like it sliced and fried.

Makes 10 sausages

½ pound lean pork
½ pound fresh pork fat
½ beaten egg
½ teaspoon pepper
2 cloves, crushed

¾ teaspoon fine salt
¼ teaspoon cinnamon
¼ teaspoon grated nutmeg
Sausage casings

Grind the pork and the fat in a processor until medium-fine. Place in a bowl and mix in, by hand, the remaining ingredients. Feed into sausage casings, being sure not to pack too tightly. Twist and tie every 3½ inches. Prick the sausage skins all over with a pin to prevent bursting.

Bring a pot of water to a boil. Add the sausages, return to the boil, and continue cooking 5 minutes. Drain on paper towels and hang to dry for 3 days. Wrap loosely in foil and refrigerate at least 2 more days.

PUDIN DE MERLUZA

(Cold Fish Timbale with Mayonnaise Dressing)

THIS is one of my favorite hot-weather fish recipes, from the files of my mother-in-law. It makes an excellent first-course serving.

Note that the "bain-marie" cooking of this fish loaf is done on top of the stove rather than in the oven.

Serves 6–8

2 tablespoons butter
1 medium onion, chopped
1 carrot, scraped and chopped
1 cup dry white wine
1 pound fish steak, such as hake or
    fresh cod
1 bay leaf
2 sprigs parsley
Salt

1½ slices white bread, crusts removed
2 tablespoons tomato sauce
1 pimiento, imported or
    homemade, chopped
5 eggs
3 tablespoons heavy cream
Freshly ground pepper
Dash nutmeg
Homemade mayonnaise (p. 104)

Heat the butter in a shallow casserole. Add the onion and carrot and sauté until the onion is wilted. Add the wine and cook over a high flame until the liquid is reduced by half. Add the fish, cover with water, and add the bay leaf, parsley, and salt. Bring to a boil, reduce the heat, cover and simmer 20 minutes. Transfer the fish to a dish, remove any skin and bones and shred with your fingers. Strain the cooking liquid into a bowl and reserve ¾ cup (if there is more you may want to boil it down for added strength and flavor).

Soak the bread in the ¾ cup cooking liquid until it falls apart. Add the shredded fish, tomato sauce and pimiento. In a separate bowl beat the eggs lightly with the cream and add to the fish mixture. Season with salt and pepper and sprinkle with nutmeg.

Pour the fish mixture into a very well-greased ring mold or loaf pan. Cover tightly with foil and place in a pan of hot water on top of the stove. Cook over a medium flame, about 1½ hours. Remove the mold from the water, loosen the foil and cool. Refrigerate until cold. Unmold and serve chilled and sliced, passing separately a bowl of homemade mayonnaise.

PASTEL DE PUERROS Y GAMBAS
(Shrimp and Leek Custard)

START PREPARATION ONE DAY IN ADVANCE.

THIS delicate dish will serve from one to four people, depending on whether it is a luncheon meal, a first course, or, cut in small wedges, an appetizer.

Serves 1–4

2 small, well-cleaned leeks (a total of 6 ounces) or
    6 medium scallions
¼ pound medium-large shrimp, in their shells
2 eggs

½ cup heavy cream
Salt
Freshly ground pepper
Minced parsley for garnish

Clean the leeks and discard most of the green part (or save for some other use). Cook the leeks in salted water until tender, about 5 minutes. Cut into 1-inch lengths. Cook the shrimp in the water from the leeks until just tender, about 1 or 2 minutes. Shell and cut each shrimp into about 1-inch lengths.

    In a bowl, mix together with a fork the eggs, cream, salt, and pepper. Mix in the shrimp and leeks. Grease well a small round mold, about 5½ inches across. Pour in the egg mixture. Place in a pan of hot water and bake at 350° F for 30 minutes. Remove from the water and cool. Unmold and refrigerate overnight. To serve, flip the custard over onto an ovenproof serving dish. Heat at 350° F for about 10 minutes, or until heated through. Leave whole or cut in wedges and sprinkle with parsley.

GRANADINA
(Eggplant and Cured Ham Loaf)

GRANADINA combines meats and vegetables into a loaf bound with eggs. Accompanied by a salad, it makes a nice luncheon dish, or it could be served, perhaps with potatoes, for dinner.

Serves 6

2 tablespoons olive oil
1 large onion, minced
½ red pepper, chopped
½ pound ground pork
1 medium eggplant (about ¾ pound), skinned and cut in small cubes
3 medium tomatoes, skinned and chopped
1 clove garlic, minced
1 tablespoon minced parsley
A ¼-pound piece cured ham, chopped
Salt
Freshly ground pepper
¼ cup bread crumbs
4 eggs
Pimiento strips for garnish

Heat the oil in a skillet. Sauté the onion and red pepper until the onion is wilted. Add the ground pork and sauté until it loses its color. Add the eggplant and cook 5 minutes more. Stir in the tomatoes, garlic, parsley, ham, salt, and pepper. Simmer 10 minutes, uncovered. If there is still liquid at the end of this time, turn up the flame to evaporate it. Stir in the bread crumbs. Beat the eggs in a large bowl. Add the mixture from the pan and mix well. Pour into a well-greased mold, such as a loaf pan, and place the mold in a pan of hot water. Bake at 350° F for about 45 minutes, or until a knife inserted comes out clean. Remove from the hot water. Cool 5 minutes, then unmold. Slice into serving portions and decorate with pimiento strips.

This can also be made in individual molds, in which case the cooking time will be reduced to 20–30 minutes.

TERRINA DE CONEJO
(Rabbit Pâté)

PREPARE SEVERAL DAYS IN ADVANCE.

RABBIT makes an excellent pâté that is full of flavor and well textured. It is one of my favorites.

Makes 1 pâté loaf

A 2½-pound rabbit
A ¼-pound piece cured ham, diced
2 tablespoons minced parsley
½ teaspoon thyme
3 cloves garlic, minced
4 bay leaves
2 tablespoons salt
Freshly ground pepper
⅛ teaspoon crushed rosemary
4 tablespoons olive oil
¾ cup brandy, preferably Spanish
    brandy, or Cognac

½ pound veal, cut in pieces
½ pound lean pork, cut in pieces
½ pound chicken livers, gristle
    removed, chopped
1 pound fresh pork fat (not
    salted), cubed
2 eggs, lightly beaten
Pork fatback, in thin slices
¾ cup flour
½ cup water

Remove the large meaty pieces from the rabbit and cut in ½-inch cubes. Scrape all the smaller pieces of meat from the bones and place them in a processor. In a bowl mix the cubed rabbit and the diced ham. Add the parsley, thyme, garlic, 1 of the bay leaves, salt, pepper, rosemary, oil, and brandy. Let this marinate a few minutes while preparing the rest of the pâté.

In the processor grind together the small pieces of rabbit, the veal, pork, liver, and fresh pork fat until medium-fine. Mix these meats with the cubed meat mixture. Discard the bay leaf. Stir in the eggs. Line a 9¼ × 5¼-inch loaf pan with the strips of fatback, letting them overhang the sides. Pour in the meat mixture, place the 3 remaining bay leaves along the top, and cover with the overhanging fatback, adding more if the pâté isn't completely enclosed.

Mix together the flour and water into a smooth paste. Seal the top of the pâté mold with this paste. Place the loaf pan in a larger pan of water. Bring the water to a boil on top of the stove, then place in a 350° F oven for 2 hours.

Remove from the hot water. Pour off any fat from around the sides of the pâté. Discard the flour crust. Cover the pâté with foil and place a weight on top—a brick is ideal. Let sit until cool. Remove the weight and then refrigerate several days. To serve, bring to room temperature.

TERRINA DE PERDIZ
(Partridge and Liver Pâté)

THIS pâté is delicious spread on a strong dark bread such as Pan de Cebada (p. 328) or a pumpernickel. The flavor is best when prepared several days in advance.

Makes 1 pâté loaf

¼ pound slab bacon, chopped
Meat from a 1-pound partridge or
    pheasant, coarsely chopped
1 partridge liver (optional)
1 pound chicken livers, cut in pieces
1 small can truffles (optional)
¼ cup flour
¼ cup dry (*fino*) sherry

2 tablespoons brandy, preferably
    Spanish brandy, or Cognac
6 tablespoons heavy cream
2 eggs
4 teaspoons salt
¼ teaspoon freshly ground pepper
½ teaspoon ground nutmeg

In a processor or blender place the bacon, partridge meat, partridge and chicken livers. Blend until finely chopped. Add the flour and blend until smooth. With the motor running, pour in the sherry, brandy, cream, eggs, salt, pepper, and nutmeg. Chop truffles and add to mixture.

Pour into a well-greased loaf pan, cover tightly with foil, and place in a pan of hot water. Bake at 325° F for 2 hours. Remove from the hot water, loosen the foil, and cool 20 minutes. Place a weight (a brick wrapped in foil is excellent) on the pâté and let sit about 1 hour. Remove the weight and refrigerate for several days, then serve at room temperature.

PASTEL DE PERDIZ

(Pâté of Partridge)

PREPARE SEVERAL DAYS IN ADVANCE.

THIS is a layered pâté, meant to be sliced rather than spread.

Makes 1 pâté loaf

A 1-pound partridge or pheasant
    (chicken or turkey slices
    may be substituted)
1 small can truffles (optional)
½ cup dry (*fino*) sherry
Salt
Freshly ground pepper
Thyme
1 pound veal
¾ pound pork
½ pound pork fat

2 eggs
2 tablespoons salt
¼ teaspoon pepper
1 medium onion, coarsely chopped
1 clove garlic, coarsely chopped
½ teaspoon thyme
¼ teaspoon allspice
Pork fatback, in thin slices
A ¼-pound piece cured ham, sliced
    very thin
3 bay leaves

Allow the whole partridge to sit in the refrigerator, uncovered, for 2–3 days to tenderize. Bone, skin, and cut the partridge into long, thin slices (save the scraps to add to the veal and pork mixture). Drain the truffles and slice. Reserve the liquid. Marinate the partridge slices in ¼ cup of the sherry, the liquid from the truffles, and a sprinkling of salt, pepper, and thyme for 30 minutes. Remove the meat and reserve the marinade.

In a processor, grind the veal, pork, pork fat, and scraps of partridge, in 2 operations if necessary. Do not overblend—the mixture should have texture. Transfer the ground meat to a bowl. In the processor beat the eggs, remaining sherry, salt, pepper, onion, garlic, thyme, allspice, and partridge marinade until quite smooth. Combine this mixture with the ground meats.

Line a loaf pan with the strips of fatback. Let the slices overhang the sides of the pan. Spoon ⅓ of the chopped meat mixture into the pan. Cover with half of the ham, partridge, and sliced truffles. Repeat with another layer of meat mixture and another of ham, partridge, and truffles, ending with a third layer of the meat mixture. Arrange the bay leaves over the top. Cover with overhanging fatback, adding more if needed to cover the meat.

Cover tightly with foil and bake in a pan of hot water in a 350° F oven for 1½ hours. Remove from the hot water and weigh down with a heavy object (a brick wrapped in foil is excellent). Cool. Remove the weight and refrigerate 1–2 days. Serve at room temperature.

EMPANADA DE LOMO

(Pork Pie)

START DOUGH PREPARATION ONE DAY IN ADVANCE.

THIS is the most commonly prepared Galician pie, known for its tasty pork filling.

Makes 4 dinner or 6 appetizer portions

Empanada dough (2) (p. 338)
4 tablespoons reserved oil (from dough recipe)
2 green peppers, cut in strips
¾ pound pork loin, cut in thin strips (⅛ inch thick)
¾ pound veal, cut in thin strips
Salt
Freshly ground pepper

½ cup dry white wine
Reserved onion, garlic, and bacon mixture (from dough recipe)
¼ teaspoon thyme
¼ teaspoon oregano
2 teaspoons paprika
Few strands saffron
1 egg, lightly beaten

Prepare the dough the day before according to instructions. Heat 2 tablespoons of the reserved oil and sauté the peppers, covered, until they are tender. Remove. Add the remaining 2 tablespoons reserved oil and stir fry the pork and veal over high heat until lightly browned. Season with salt and pepper. Add ¼ cup of the wine and cook until almost completely evaporated. Add the green peppers and the reserved onion mixture to the pan, along with the thyme, oregano, paprika, and saffron. Add the remaining ¼ cup wine and cook until little liquid remains. Taste for salt and pepper.

Divide the dough into 2 equal pieces. Roll each to 10 × 15 inches. Place 1 piece on a greased cookie sheet of the same size. Spread on the filling, then cover with the other piece of dough, rolling up the edges to seal. Make several slits. Let sit 20 minutes in a warm place. Brush with beaten egg, then bake at 350° F for 20–30 minutes, or until golden. To serve, cut in squares.

EMPANADA ASTURIANA

(Asturian Chorizo Pie)

START DOUGH PREPARATION
A FEW HOURS IN ADVANCE.

THE *chorizo* in this meat pie makes it exceptionally aromatic and delicious—one of my favorites. Eat hot or at room temperature.

Makes 6 dinner or 8 appetizer portions

Empanada dough (1) (p. 338)
2 tablespoons olive oil
2 large onions, chopped
2 cloves garlic, minced
½ pound lean pork, cut in thin
    strips, about ⅛ inch thick
½ pound *chorizo*, skinned and cut in
    ⅛-inch slices
1 ripe tomato, skinned and diced

2 pimientos, homemade or imported,
    cut in strips
Pinch saffron
Salt
Freshly ground pepper
2 hard-boiled eggs, chopped
¼ cup warm water
1 egg, lightly beaten
1 tablespoon milk

Prepare the dough according to instructions. While the dough is rising, make the filling. Heat the oil in a large skillet. Sauté the onion and garlic until the onion is wilted. Add the pork strips and the *chorizo;* cook over medium heat for 10 minutes. Add the tomato, pimientos, saffron, salt, and pepper. Continue cooking, uncovered, another 10 minutes over a low flame. Sprinkle in the hard-boiled eggs and turn off the heat immediately. Thin the mixture with the warm water and cool before filling the pie.

Divide the dough into 2 equal parts. Roll each part into a circle about ⅛ inch thick and 12 inches across. Place 1 circle in an ungreased 11-inch pie plate, extending the edges over the sides of the plate. Add the filling and cover the pie with the other dough circle. Curl the bottom dough over the top dough, pressing to seal. Make decorative slits in the center. Brush with the beaten egg mixed with the milk. Bake at 350° F until the pie is nicely browned, about 30 minutes. Let it sit about 15 minutes before cutting it into serving wedges.

EMPANADA DE SARDINAS

(Fresh Sardine Pie)

START DOUGH PREPARATION
SEVERAL HOURS IN ADVANCE.

SARDINE pies are prepared with a special dough made from cornmeal, which is the perfect complement for the strong taste of the sardines.

Makes 4 dinner or 8 appetizer portions

Empanada dough (3) (p. 339)	1 tomato, chopped
4 tablespoons olive oil	Salt
½ pound fresh sardines, cleaned	Freshly ground pepper
(canned sardines may also	Few strands saffron
be used, drained)	1 egg, lightly beaten
2 medium onions, sliced	1 teaspoon water
2 pimientos, homemade or	
imported, chopped	

Prepare the dough according to instructions. While the dough is resting, prepare the filling. Heat 2 tablespoons of the oil in a skillet and lightly fry the sardines on both sides until they are golden. Fillet them, leaving the skin on.

Wipe out the skillet and heat the remaining 2 tablespoons of oil. Sauté the onions until wilted. Add the pimientos, tomato, salt, pepper, and saffron. Cover and cook 15 minutes.

Separate the dough into 2 equal parts. Roll each piece into a circle less than ⅛ inch thick and about 9 inches across. Place 1 circle on a greased cookie sheet, then arrange the sardine fillets on top of the dough in a pinwheel pattern. Cover with the onion mixture. Cover the pie with the other dough circle, rolling up the sides to seal. Make decorative slits on the top. Brush with the beaten egg mixed with the water. Bake at 350° F until golden, about 20 minutes. Serve hot or at room temperature.

EMPANADA DE BONITO
(Tuna Pie)

START DOUGH PREPARATION ONE DAY IN ADVANCE.

TUNA and peppers make a very tasty filling for another popular Galician pie.

Makes 4 dinner or 6 appetizer portions

Empanada dough (2) (p. 338),
    omitting bacon
2 green peppers, cut in strips
2 tablespoons reserved oil (from
    dough recipe)
Reserved onion and garlic (from
    dough recipe)

7-ounce can light meat tuna
4 tablespoons tomato sauce
2 tablespoons water
Salt
Freshly ground pepper
1 egg, lightly beaten

Prepare the dough the day before according to instructions. In a skillet sauté the green peppers in the reserved oil, covered, until tender. Add the reserved onion and garlic, the tuna, and the tomato sauce and cook, uncovered, 5 minutes. Stir in the water. Taste for salt and pepper.

Divide the dough into 2 equal pieces. Roll each to 10 × 15 inches. Place 1 piece on a greased cookie sheet of the same size. Spread on the filling, then cover with the other piece of dough, rolling up the edges to seal. Make several slits. Let sit 20 minutes in a warm place. Brush with the egg, then bake at 350° F for 20–30 minutes, or until golden. To serve, cut in squares.

EMPANADA DE BERBERECHO

(Clam Pie)

START DOUGH PREPARATION ONE DAY IN ADVANCE.

Berberechos are tiny clams—actually cockles—that are found in Galicia and make a delicious pie filling.

Makes 4 dinner or 6 appetizer portions

Empanada dough (2) (p. 338), omitting bacon
Reserved onion and garlic (from dough recipe)
2 tablespoons reserved oil (from dough recipe)
¾ cup minced pimiento, homemade or imported
12 ounces shelled fresh (see p. 11) or canned clams, drained, reserving 3 tablespoons of juice—if very small, leave whole; otherwise chop coarsely
¼ cup tomato sauce or diluted tomato paste
½ teaspoon paprika
Salt
Freshly ground pepper
1 egg, lightly beaten

Prepare the dough the day before according to instructions. Heat in a skillet the reserved onion, garlic, and oil. Add the pimiento, clams, tomato sauce, paprika and cook, uncovered, 10 minutes. Turn off the heat and stir in the reserved clam juice. Add pepper and salt, if necessary.

Divide the dough into 2 equal pieces. Roll each to 10 × 15 inches. Place 1 piece on a greased cookie sheet of the same size, spread on the filling, then cover with the other piece of dough, rolling up the edges to seal. Make several slits. Let sit 20 minutes in a warm place. Brush with the egg, then bake at 350° F for 20–30 minutes, or until golden.

EMPANADA DE ESPINACAS

(Spinach Pie)

START DOUGH PREPARATION A FEW HOURS IN ADVANCE.

Although *empanadas* usually have meat or fish fillings, this one is mainly vegetable and is eaten at Lenten time.

Makes 4 dinner or 6 appetizer portions

Empanada dough (1) (p. 338)
1 pound spinach leaves, washed
Salt
3 tablespoons olive oil
1 clove garlic, minced

2 anchovies, chopped
2 tablespoons pine nuts
4 tablespoons raisins
Freshly ground pepper

Make the dough according to instructions. Prepare the filling while the dough is rising. Leave the spinach leaves wet after washing, then place them in a pot with no additional water. Sprinkle with salt, cover, and cook until barely tender, about 5 minutes. Drain and chop coarsely.

Heat the oil in a skillet. Add the garlic, anchovy, spinach, pine nuts, and raisins. Season with salt and pepper and cook, uncovered, 5 minutes.

Divide the dough into 2 equal parts. Roll out each piece to a 10 × 15-inch rectangle. Place 1 piece on a cookie sheet and spread on the spinach filling. Cover with the remaining dough and roll up the edges to seal. Slit the dough in several places. Bake at 350° F for 25 minutes. This spinach mixture also makes a good filling for fried turnovers, using the *empanadilla* dough (p. 337).

PASTEL MURCIANO

(Veal Pie of Murcia)

THE province of Murcia lies along the southeastern coast of Spain and is often called the "Orchard of Spain" because the climate is ideal for the growth of luscious fruits and vegetables. The peppers and tomatoes from Murcia are particularly well regarded and enter into almost all the cuisine of the area. These tasty and attractive meat pies, covered with puff pastry, are specialties of Murcia and are ideal for snacks and light dinners, served hot or at room temperature.

Makes 6 individual pies

1 onion, chopped
1 clove garlic, minced
2 green peppers, finely chopped
2 tablespoons olive oil
2 *chorizo* sausages (¼ pound), in
     ⅛-inch slices
A ¼-pound piece cured ham, diced
½ pound veal, in ½-inch cubes

½ pound tomatoes, skinned
     and chopped
Salt
Freshly ground pepper
1 hard-boiled egg, chopped
Puff pastry, homemade (p. 336)
     or frozen

DOUGH

3 cups flour	½ cup plus 1 tablespoon salad oil
¾ teaspoon salt	½ cup water

To make the dough, mix together the flour and salt. Stir in the oil and water. Turn out onto a working surface and knead until the dough holds together. Wrap and let sit 30 minutes.

Meanwhile, sauté the onion, garlic, and peppers in 1 tablespoon of the olive oil until the onion and peppers are tender. Remove and reserve the vegetables. Add the remaining 1 tablespoon of olive oil to the pan. Sauté the *chorizo*, ham, and veal over high heat until the veal loses its color. Return the pepper-and-onion mixture to the pan. Add the tomato, salt, and pepper and simmer 10 minutes, uncovered. Remove from the heat and stir in the chopped egg.

Roll the dough on a lightly floured surface into a rectangle. Fold lengthwise in thirds, business-letter fashion. Roll again, then fold and roll twice more, rolling finally to ⅛-inch thickness. Cut into six 6-inch circles. Divide the filling onto the circles, not reaching the edges.

Roll the puff pastry to ⅛ inch. Cut it into 1-inch strips and cut also six 2-inch circles. Arrange a strip (piecing if necessary) in a circle over the outer edges of the filling, pinching the ends of the puff pastry together. Repeat with a second slightly overlapping concentric circle. Plug the center of the pie with one of the puff pastry rounds, also overlapping the edges a bit. Fold up the sides of the bottom pastry and squeeze to attach it well to the puff pastry. Bake at 350° F for 25–30 minutes, or until the puff pastry is golden.

COCA "LA PLANA"

(Tomato and Green Pepper Pie)

Cocas come from Cataluña and the Levante region and refer to any round, thin breadlike dough, either sweetened and embedded with candied fruits or pine nuts, or unsweetened with a vegetable or meat topping. This version was found near Jávea, province of Alicante, at Merendero La Plana, an unpretentious family-run restaurant where, besides these delicious *cocas*, we ate an excellent shoulder of baby lamb and what can only be described as the best fried potatoes in the world.

The ingredients for *coca* are absolutely simple and therefore must be of top quality—the tomatoes especially should be fresh and well flavored. *Cocas* can be eaten as snacks or cut into appetizer wedges.

Makes 5 small pies

½ recipe Pan de Pueblo (p. 325), pizza
    dough, or pita bread
1 tablespoon oil
½ pound firm ripe tomatoes, in
    ¹⁄₁₆-inch slices
2 green peppers, sliced extremely
    thin, seeds removed

1 small onion, slivered
2 cloves garlic, minced
Salt
Freshly ground pepper
15 teaspoons fruity olive oil

If using the bread dough, prepare it through the first 3-hour rising. Punch down and knead in the 1 tablespoon of oil, adding some flour if necessary. Divide into 5 balls and roll out into 6-inch circles, about ⅛ inch thick. Curl up the edges to make a rim. Place on a cookie sheet.

Arrange tomato slices in overlapping circles on the dough. Cover each pie with 3 green pepper rings and then sprinkle with the onion slivers, garlic, salt, and pepper. Drizzle 3 teaspoons of oil over each pie. Bake at 350° F for about 20 minutes, or until the vegetables are tender and the crust very lightly golden.

AGUJA DE TERNERA

(Veal in Puff Pastry)

Makes about 10 pastries

Veal turnover filling (p. 37)

Puff Pastry (p. 336)

Prepare the veal filling according to instructions. Roll the puff pastry to ⅛ inch. Cut into 5 × 3-inch pieces. Place 3 tablespoons of the filling along the length of the pastry. Fold up the sides and ends and press to seal. Place seam side down on a baking sheet. Bake at 425° F on the upper rack of the oven until golden, about 15 minutes.

PEPITOS DE TERNERA

(Veal Sandwiches)

Pepitos could not be more simple—sautéed veal cutlets on rolls—but we are inordinately fond of them and often order these sandwiches for lunch in

Spain. Although found all over, they are most deliciously prepared at the bar of the Parador Nacional de Nerja, a charmingly decorated and architecturally beautiful hotel facing a patio overflowing with cactus, ferns, and flowers. The *parador* is in the village of Nerja, a delightful town with a decidedly Arab flavor. Nerja has managed to retain all its small-town charms despite the influx of tourism and has been christened the "Balcony of Europe" because of its spectacular views of this area's rugged Mediterranean coastline.

The excellence of *pepitos* depends on three factors: the texture of the bread, the quality of the veal, and the final frying of the bread. You may use commercial rolls or hero bread for these sandwiches, but the results will not be the same.

Serves 4 (8 sandwiches)

Pan de Pueblo (p. 325)
Cornmeal or bread crumbs
1½ pounds veal cutlet, in
　　¼-inch slices

Coarse salt
At least 5 tablespoons olive oil

Prepare the bread recipe through the 3-hour rising. Punch down and knead 5 minutes. Divide the dough into 8 equal parts. Roll each out into an oval about 6½ × 5½ inches. Starting with a long side, roll up tightly, jelly-roll fashion. Pinch to seal well. Taper the ends. Place the rolls, seam side down, on a baking sheet that has been sprinkled with cornmeal or bread crumbs. Slash the tops diagonally 2 or 3 times. Place in a warm spot to rise about 1 hour more, or until double in bulk. Bake according to the bread recipe instructions.

Sprinkle the veal with salt. Heat 5 tablespoons of the oil in a large skillet and quick-fry the meat, browning lightly on each side. Remove to a warm platter.

Slice open the rolls. Pierce the crust of one piece of bread with a fork and rest the soft side of the bread on the surface of the hot oil. Fry quickly until lightly browned. Repeat for the rest of the bread pieces, adding more oil to the pan if necessary. Place the meat on the rolls and pour any meat juices remaining on the platter onto the soft side of the bread. Serve with a French-style grain mustard.

CARACOLES DE CARNE

(Meat Spirals)

START PREPARATION THREE HOURS IN ADVANCE.

THESE are suitable for light suppers or snacks.

Serves 6 (12 rolls)

2 tablespoons olive oil
2 medium onions, finely chopped
½ green pepper, finely chopped
1¼ pounds ground veal
6 tablespoons tomato sauce or
    diluted tomato paste

Salt
Freshly ground pepper
1 cup chopped mushrooms
1 tablespoon chopped parsley
1 cup grated Parmesan cheese

DOUGH

½ package dry yeast
½ cup warm water
2 cups flour

1 teaspoon salt
1 egg
1½ tablespoons oil

To make the dough, in a small bowl dissolve the yeast in ¼ cup of the warm water. Add ½ cup of the flour and turn out onto a board. Knead lightly, adding flour if necessary, until a ball forms and the dough is smooth. Slit the top, wrap in a towel, and let sit in a warm place while preparing the rest of the dough.

In a bowl mix the remaining ¼ cup of water with the salt and the egg. Add the remaining 1½ cups of flour and turn out onto a board, kneading until all the flour is incorporated. Knead together the 2 balls of dough, gradually incorporating the oil and adding a little flour if necessary. Knead until smooth and elastic. Wrap in a towel and let sit in a warm place while preparing the filling.

To make the filling, heat the olive oil in a skillet and sauté the onion and pepper until they are tender. Add the veal and cook until it loses its color. Add the tomato sauce, salt, pepper, mushrooms, and parsley. Cook, uncovered, for 15 minutes. Remove from the heat and stir in the cheese. Cool.

Roll the dough to 19 × 15 inches. Fold lengthwise in thirds, business-letter fashion. Gently roll again, making the length the width, to 19 × 9 inches. Spread with the filling, then roll, jelly-roll fashion, starting with a short end. Pinch to seal the roll. Cut into ¾-inch slices and place them on their sides on a greased cookie sheet. Leave in a warm spot for 3 hours. Heat the oven to 400° F and bake on the middle-upper rack for 10–15 minutes, until the rolls are brown.

BOLLO PREÑADO

(Sausage Buns)

START DOUGH PREPARATION
SEVERAL HOURS IN ADVANCE.

A TERRIBLY unappealing title ("Pregnant Bun") for a very nice snack or lunchtime offering. In smaller sizes, these bread-wrapped sausages make tasty appetizers.

Makes 8 sausage buns

½ recipe Pan de Pueblo (p. 325)
8 pieces *chorizo*, each about 3 inches long
8 thick slices bacon, each 3 inches long

Cornmeal or bread crumbs
1 egg, lightly beaten

Prepare the bread dough recipe up to the end of the 3-hour rising period. Punch down and knead 5 minutes. Divide the dough into 8 balls. Roll each into a rectangle large enough to enclose the *chorizo*, about 5 × 3 inches. Place a piece of *chorizo* covered by 1 slice of bacon in the center of each dough rectangle. Fold up the sides and ends and pinch to seal. Place the rolls, pinched side down, on a cookie sheet that has been sprinkled with cornmeal or bread crumbs. Place in a warm spot for 30 minutes.

Heat the oven to 450° F. Brush the rolls with the egg and bake 15 minutes, or until they are golden. They may be eaten hot or cold.

SALMÓN EN HOJALDRE

(Puff Pastry with Salmon Filling)

Serves about 6

1 medium onion, chopped
1 tablespoon olive oil

¾ pound cooked fresh or canned salmon, flaked

10 tablespoons tomato sauce,
    preferably homemade (p. 190)
1 hard-boiled egg, minced
1 anchovy, chopped
4 tablespoons chopped pimiento
1 teaspoon Worcestershire sauce

3 tablespoons dry white wine
Salt
Freshly ground pepper
Puff Pastry (p. 336)—you will only
    need part of the recipe
    (freeze the rest)

Sauté the onion in the oil until wilted. Add the remaining ingredients and cook 5 minutes.

Roll the puff pastry to a thickness of ¼ inch. Cut into twenty-four 4 × 3-inch rectangles. Place about 2 tablespoons of the salmon filling down the middle of 12 pastry pieces. Cover with the other 12 and press to seal the edges. Place on a cookie sheet and bake at 425° F on the upper rack for 15–20 minutes, or until well browned. These may be made instead into smaller rectangles to serve as appetizers.

Chapter 3

VERDURAS Y LEGUMBRES

(Vegetables)

VEGETABLES, unadorned, are not generally among the most popular foods in Spain. In fact, many Spaniards seem to have an absolute aversion to any sustenance green in color. Combined with eggs, meat, or fish, however, vegetables—usually not of the green variety—are considered much more palatable and are important ingredients in some of Spain's most popular dishes—the Basque *piparrada,* combining eggs, sweet peppers, and tomato; the Catalán *samfaina,* a mixture of eggplant, sweet peppers, and tomato used with meat or fish; and the Riojan *chilindrón* dishes, using red peppers with almost anything.

Since most vegetables tend to be quite seasonal in Spain and are not otherwise always of top quality, fresh vegetables often play second fiddle to dried vegetables of the bean family, one of the country's favorite foods. (Most bean recipes appear in Chapter 5, "Soups and Meals-in-a-Pot.") But in spring and summer, the vegetables can be spectacular—rare white asparagus and tiny artichokes from Rioja, glowingly red sweet peppers from Murcia, tiny emerald green peppers from Galicia, and tasty fresh limas from Andalucía.

Potatoes, of course, are in a class by themselves, and ever since they were introduced from South America in the sixteenth century, they have been a staple of the Spanish diet. A main-course dish would appear naked in Spanish eyes without its fried potatoes, and I doubt there is any self-respecting restaurant in Spain that does not include them with every dinner. (I can't help but suppose that the Spaniards, having introduced the potato, must have been the first also to make so-called "French" fries.) The passion for potatoes seems limitless, and they are the key ingredient in what has to be considered Spain's national dish: the potato omelet.

A country's cooking is always closely related to climate, and in the case of vegetables, the historic lack of fresh water in many areas of Spain meant that vegetables were rarely boiled—rather, they were slowly sautéed in oil until tender or else quick-fried. They were also combined in casseroles, such as the

popular Castillian *pisto,* which relied on slow stewing with juicy vegetables, such as zucchini and tomato, making additional liquid unnecessary. Spaniards today, although no longer lacking for water, still prefer their vegetables prepared by these traditional methods.

A visit to a vegetable store in Spain will provide few surprises: most vegetables are familiar ones, commonly found in the United States, although their different preparations can give them new excitement. *Acelgas,* greens similar to our Swiss chard or collard greens, are much more popular there than here and were a revelation to me. When interestingly prepared—for example, with raisins and pine nuts (p. 87)—they are among the tastiest in the vegetable family.

Vegetables do not appear in great variety on restaurant menus, but when they do, they are served as a separate course before the main dish, in which case the portions are often enormous. Some of the recipes I have included are hearty enough to make meals. Others can, of course, be served as accompaniments to main courses, American style.

JUDÍAS VERDES CON AJO
(Garlic Green Beans)

I MAKE these green beans regularly, so popular are they in my household. They are prepared in the Spanish way: without liquid.

Serves 4

¾ pound fresh green beans
1 tablespoon butter

1 clove garlic, crushed
Coarse salt

Snap off the ends of the beans. Melt the butter in a skillet, add the beans, and cook over a medium flame, stirring, until they begin to brown. Lower the flame, cover, and cook about 20 minutes, or until the beans are the desired tenderness, stirring occasionally. Mix in the crushed garlic, sprinkle with salt, and serve immediately.

JUDÍAS VERDES "BÁRCENA"
(Green Beans and Cured Ham)

I FIND these green beans exceptionally flavorful and a tasty addition to almost any meal.

Serves 4

¾ pound fresh green beans
1 tablespoon white wine vinegar
2 tablespoons olive oil
4 tablespoons finely chopped onion
2 cloves garlic, minced

½ cup thinly sliced cured ham, cut in ½-inch pieces
Salt
Freshly ground pepper

Snap off the ends of the green beans. Plunge them into boiling water to which the vinegar has been added. Boil 5 minutes. Drain and plunge into cold water. Dry on towels. (This preliminary blanching may be done in advance.)

Heat the oil in a skillet, then add the beans and cook over a medium-high flame, about 5 minutes, to brown lightly. Add the onion, garlic, and ham, lower the flame, and cook 2 minutes more. Cover the pan and cook about 10 minutes, stirring occasionally, until the beans are tender, but still slightly crunchy. Season with salt and pepper.

GUISANTES A LA ESPAÑOLA
(Peas with Cured Ham)

Serves 4

2 tablespoons olive oil
4 tablespoons minced onion
4 tablespoons minced carrot
4 tablespoons minced cured ham

½ pound fresh or frozen peas
Salt
Freshly ground pepper

Heat the oil in a medium casserole and sauté the onion and carrot until the onion is wilted. Add the ham and cook a minute. Stir in the peas, salt, and pepper, eliminating the salt if the ham is salty. Cover tightly and cook about 20 minutes, or until the peas are tender.

GUISANTES CON SALCHICHAS
(Peas with Sausage)

Serves 4

2 breakfast or sweet Italian sausages
   —for homemade, use
   Salchicha Blanca (p. 57)
   or *Butifarra* (p. 55)
1 tablespoon olive oil
1 tablespoon lard

4 tablespoons minced onion
½ medium tomato, chopped
½ pound fresh or frozen peas
⅛ teaspoon mint
5 blanched almonds
1 clove garlic, peeled

Fry the sausages in the oil and lard until cooked through. Slice and remove to a warm plate. In the remaining oil, sauté the onion until it is wilted. Add the tomato and cook 15 minutes. Pour this mixture into a blender or processor and purée, adding enough water to make a sauce. Return to the pan and add the peas, sausage, and mint. Cover, and cook until the peas are almost tender.

In the blender or processor (the bowl should be clean and dry), grind the almonds and garlic. Add to the peas and cook a few minutes more, until the peas are tender.

MICHIRONES PICANTICOS
(Spicy Lima Beans)

A SPECIALTY of the southern province of Murcia, where lima beans are grown.

Serves 4

10 ounces lima beans
1 *chorizo* sausage (2 ounces), cut in
   ½-inch slices
½ dried red chili pepper,
   seeds removed

Salt
Freshly ground pepper
1 bay leaf
1 ham bone (optional)

Place all ingredients in a saucepan. Add about ½ cup water, cover, and cook slowly until the beans are done and the liquid is absorbed. Remove the bone before serving.

HABAS CON JAMÓN
(Sautéed Lima Beans and Ham)

IN ANDALUCÍA, lima beans are the preferred food for raising strong, brave fighting bulls for the bullring. Sautéed with ham, they are one of my favorite *tapas* at the Bar Lo Güeno in Málaga, a place I never fail to visit on my yearly trips to Spain.

Serves 6

3 tablespoons olive oil
1¼ pounds baby lima beans
2 cloves garlic, minced
2 tablespoons dry white wine
A ¼-pound piece cured ham,
    finely diced

1 tablespoon minced parsley
Salt
Freshly ground pepper

Heat the oil in a medium-size skillet or casserole. Add the lima beans and the garlic and cook 5 minutes. Stir in the wine and continue cooking over a low flame, covered, about 15 minutes. Add the ham and parsley, season with salt (lightly) and pepper, and cook another 15 minutes, or until the lima beans are tender.

ALCACHOFAS SALTEADAS CON JAMÓN
(Sautéed Artichokes and Cured Ham)

Serves 4

1 pound artichoke hearts
2 tablespoons olive oil
4 tablespoons finely diced cured ham

Freshly ground pepper
2 tablespoons minced parsley

Boil the artichoke hearts in salted water until barely tender; drain. Heat the oil in a skillet and add the ham, artichokes, and pepper. Sauté 10 minutes. Sprinkle with parsley and serve.

CHAMPIÑONES SALTEADOS

(Sautéed Mushrooms)

Serves 4

1 pound mushrooms, stems trimmed
2 teaspoons butter
6 cloves garlic, minced

2 tablespoons minced parsley
2 tablespoons bread crumbs
Salt

Wash the mushrooms and dry well. If they are very large, cut in halves. Melt the butter in a large skillet and add the mushrooms, garlic, and parsley. Sauté over high heat very briefly, until the mushrooms are lightly browned. Stir in the bread crumbs and salt to taste.

CHAMPIÑONES AL JEREZ

(Mushrooms in Sherry Sauce)

Serves 4

1 pound mushrooms, whole or cut
    in halves
Lemon juice
1 tablespoon olive oil
2 tablespoons finely chopped onion
2 teaspoons flour

¼ cup dry (*fino*) sherry
¼ cup chicken or beef broth
Salt
Freshly ground pepper
1 tablespoon chopped parsley

Wash the mushrooms and dry well. Sprinkle them with lemon juice. Heat the oil in a skillet and sauté the onion until it is wilted. Stir in the mushrooms and sauté 3 minutes more. Remove the mushrooms to a warm plate. Sprinkle the flour into the skillet. Cook a minute, stirring, then add the sherry, broth, salt, pepper, and parsley. Stir until thickened and smooth. Return the mushrooms to the pan and cook 2 minutes more.

PIMIENTOS FRITOS

(Fried Green Peppers)

IN SPRING and summer, *pimientos de Padrón*—tiny bright green peppers from the village of Padrón in Galicia—are on the market and are unrivaled for sweetness and flavor. They are always found fried, heaped on platters, and sprinkled with coarse salt. To eat, pick them up by the stems and eat around the seeds.

Serves 4

6 tablespoons olive oil
1 pound Italian-style green frying
    peppers, smallest available

Coarse salt

Heat the oil in a large skillet. Add the whole peppers, reduce the heat to medium, and fry, turning occasionally, until the peppers are browned on all sides. Remove from the pan and sprinkle with coarse salt.

PIMIENTOS MORRONES SALTEADOS

(Sautéed Pimientos)

Serves 4

1 tablespoon olive oil
4 pimientos, homemade (p. 430), cut
    in strips

2 cloves garlic, sliced
Salt
Freshly ground pepper

Heat the oil in a skillet and sauté the pimientos over high heat until they begin to brown. Lower the heat, add the garlic, salt, and pepper. Cover and cook slowly about 10 minutes.

PIMIENTOS DE BIERZO
(Sautéed Green Peppers and Pimientos)

Serves 4

2 tablespoons olive oil
6 Italian-style green frying peppers,
    cut in strips
3 pimientos, homemade (p. 430), cut
    in strips

2 cloves garlic, minced
2 tablespoons minced onion
2 thin slices cured ham, cut in pieces
Salt
Freshly ground pepper

Heat the oil and sauté the green peppers and pimientos over high heat for 5 minutes. Add the garlic, onion, ham, salt, and pepper. Lower the heat, cover, and simmer until the green peppers are tender, about 15 minutes.

BERENGENA CON QUESO
(Eggplant with Cheese)

Tres cosas me tienen preso
de amores el corazón:
la bella Inés, el jamón
y berengenas con queso

Baltasar del Alcázar
(1530–1606)

THIS amusing sixteenth-century poem ("Three things have my heart/ imprisoned by love:/ the beautiful lady Inés, ham/ and eggplant with cheese") sent me scurrying to my Spanish cookbooks to find a recipe for Berengena (old spelling for eggplant) con Queso. I was unsuccessful until I consulted a sixteenth-century cookbook, *Libro de Cozina,* by Ruperto de Nola. The following adaptation is a delicious and unusual preparation of eggplant.

Serves 4

1 pound eggplant, peeled and cut
    crosswise in ½-inch slices
1 cup beef or chicken broth
2 slices onion
12 blanched almonds, lightly toasted
Salt

2 slices mild cheese, such as Tetilla
    (p. 432) or Muenster
1 tablespoon grated Manchego
    (p. 431) or Parmesan cheese
Freshly ground pepper
Nutmeg

Place the eggplant slices in a pan with the broth and the onion slices. Simmer until the eggplant is just tender. Remove the eggplant to an ovenproof dish, reserving the broth.

In a processor or blender chop the almonds as fine as possible. With the motor running, pour in ½ cup of the reserved broth, adding water if necessary to make ½ cup. Salt to taste. Pour the liquid over the eggplant, cover with the slices of cheese, sprinkle with the grated cheese, pepper, and nutmeg. Bake in a 350° F oven for 20 minutes.

BERENJENAS "RINCÓN DE PEPE"

(Eggplant with Shrimp and Ham)

THE Rincón de Pepe in Murcia, one of the finest restaurants in the southeast region of Spain, offers this taste sensation that joins the mild flavor of eggplant with shrimp and pungent cured ham. This dish has a variety of uses—it may act as an accompaniment to simple meat courses, it is wonderful for a first course and exceptional as a luncheon dish.

Serves 4

2 eggplants (½ pound each), skinned
    and sliced crosswise in
    ¾-inch thicknesses
Coarse salt
Flour for dusting
Oil for frying
2 cloves garlic, peeled
8 medium-large shrimp, uncooked
    and shelled

¼ cup julienne strips of cured ham
2 tablespoons minced onion
2 tablespoons flour
1 cup milk
¼ cup beef broth
Freshly ground pepper
2 tablespoons grated Swiss cheese

Sprinkle the eggplant slices with salt and dredge in flour. In a large skillet heat the oil, ½ inch deep, and fry the garlic until it is golden. Discard the garlic. Fry the eggplant in the oil over a medium-high flame until golden; do not overcook. Drain on paper towels. Reserve 2 tablespoons of the oil. Arrange the eggplant in overlapping lengthwise rows on a greased metal platter. Place the shrimp and ham strips on top.

In the 2 tablespoons of oil left in the skillet, sauté the onion very slowly until it is tender. Stir in the 2 tablespoons of flour, cook a minute, then gradually add the milk, broth, salt, and pepper. Cook until smooth and thickened. Strain the sauce over the eggplant. Sprinkle with the grated cheese and place under the broiler until golden.

BERENJENA FRITA
(Fried Eggplant)

Serves 4

1 large eggplant
Coarse salt
Flour for dusting

Oil for frying (a mixture of olive and
  salad oils)

Peel the eggplant and cut in thin lengthwise strips, less than ⅛ inch thick. Place the strips in layers in a colander, sprinkling salt between each layer. Let stand 1 hour to drain.

Dry the eggplant slices on paper towels. Dust with flour. Fry in hot oil, at least ½ inch deep, until golden. Drain. Sprinkle with salt and serve immediately.

CALABACÍN AL HORNO
(Baked Zucchini)

Serves 4

2 medium zucchini (about 1 pound)
4 tablespoons olive oil
Salt
Freshly ground pepper

1 tablespoon bread crumbs
1 clove garlic, minced
1 tablespoon minced parsley

Lightly scrape the zucchini, removing only part of the green. Cut off the ends, then slice in half lengthwise, then crosswise. Grease a baking pan with 1 tablespoon of the oil. Arrange the zucchini and spoon the remaining 3 tablespoons of oil over them. Sprinkle with salt and pepper. Bake at 350° F, brushing occasionally with the oil and pan juices. When tender, after about 20 minutes, sprinkle with bread crumbs, garlic, and parsley. Spoon the pan juices over the zucchini and run under the broiler until the top is golden.

ACELGAS CON PASAS Y PIÑONES
(Greens with Raisins and Pine Nuts)

I HAVE recently become quite fond of greens served as a vegetable, and the intriguing additions of raisins and pine nuts in this recipe—a Catalán specialty—make these greens an uncommon taste treat.

Serves 4

3 tablespoons raisins
1 pound collard greens or Swiss
    chard, thick stems
    removed (weight
    after trimming)
Salt

3 tablespoons olive oil
2 cloves garlic, minced
2 tablespoons minced onion
3 tablespoons pine nuts
Freshly ground pepper

Soak the raisins in warm water while preparing the greens. Place the greens in boiling water for 5 minutes; drain. Return the greens to the pot, cover with water, add the salt and 1 tablespoon of the oil. Return to a boil and cook 10 minutes, or until tender. Drain and chop coarsely.

    Heat the remaining 2 tablespoons of oil in a skillet. Sauté the garlic and onion until the onion is wilted. Add the greens and the raisins, drained, the pine nuts, salt, and pepper. Cook 5 minutes. The greens may be eaten right away, but gain in flavor when left several hours and then reheated.

ACELGAS SALTEADAS CON MIGAS
(Sautéed Greens with Croutons)

Serves 4

½ pound collard greens or Swiss
    chard, thick stems removed
    (weight after trimming)
Salt
3 tablespoons olive oil

1 teaspoon vinegar
2 teaspoons minced onion
¾ cup garlic croutons (p. 131)
Freshly ground pepper

Place the greens in a pot of boiling water and cook 5 minutes. Drain, cover with water again, add salt and 1 tablespoon of the oil. Bring to a boil, cover, and cook until tender, about 10 minutes. Drain and chop coarsely.

Heat the remaining 2 tablespoons of oil in a skillet. Add the greens and sauté 5 minutes. Mix in the vinegar, onion, croutons, salt, and pepper and serve.

ESPÁRRAGOS TRIGUEROS

(Sautéed Asparagus)

Serves 4

2 tablespoons olive oil   ¾ pound thin asparagus
1 clove garlic, peeled   Coarse salt

Snap off the ends of the asparagus. Heat the oil in a skillet. Add the garlic and asparagus and cook, uncovered, over a low flame, turning occasionally, until the asparagus is tender, about 20 minutes. Sprinkle with salt.

ESPÁRRAGOS AMARGUEROS

(Asparagus with Garlic and Paprika)

Serves 4

1 pound thin asparagus   ½ cup water
2 tablespoons olive oil   1 tablespoon vinegar
1 slice French-style bread   Salt
1 clove garlic, peeled   1 tablespoon minced parsley
¼ teaspoon paprika

Snap off the ends of the asparagus. Heat the oil in a skillet and fry the bread slice until it is golden. Remove to a blender or processor. Sauté the garlic clove in the oil until it is golden and remove it to the blender also. In the same oil sauté the asparagus for 3 minutes. Add the paprika and stir to coat. Pour in the water, cover, and cook until the asparagus is almost tender. Meanwhile, beat the bread and garlic in the processor. Gradually add the vinegar and a few tablespoons of the cooking liquid from the asparagus. Pour this mixture over the asparagus. Salt to taste and continue cooking 5 minutes more, or until the asparagus is tender. Sprinkle with parsley and serve.

ESPÁRRAGOS ESTILO MANCHEGO
(Asparagus, Manchego Style)

A SAUCE of egg yolk and cumin makes this asparagus preparation distinctive.

Serves 4

¾ pound thin asparagus
2 tablespoons olive oil
2 cloves garlic, peeled
2 egg yolks

¼ teaspoon ground cumin
4 teaspoons water
Salt
Freshly ground pepper

Snap off the ends of the asparagus. Heat the oil in a skillet with the garlic cloves, until the cloves turn slightly brown. Add the asparagus and cook slowly, uncovered, until the asparagus is tender, about 20 minutes or more, depending on size.

In a small saucepan mix together the egg yolks, cumin, water, salt, and pepper. Heat very gently (to avoid curdling), only until warm. Serve the asparagus with the sauce poured over it.

LOMBARDA NAVIDEÑA
(Baked Red Cabbage and Apples)

A POPULAR part of every Spanish Christmas Eve dinner (see Christmas Eve menu, p. 425).

Serves 4–6

2 tablespoons lard or olive oil
1 medium onion, finely chopped
1 pound red cabbage, tough outer
    leaves removed,
    coarsely chopped
1 large apple, peeled, cored, and cut
    in ½-inch pieces
¼ pound slab bacon, diced

2 tablespoons red wine vinegar
1 bay leaf
Salt
Freshly ground pepper
1 tablespoon minced parsley
½ cup warm water
2 medium potatoes, cooked and cut
    in cubes (optional)

In an ovenproof casserole, melt the lard and sauté the onion until it is wilted. Stir in the cabbage, apple pieces, and bacon; cook a minute or so. Add the vinegar, bay leaf, salt, pepper, parsley, and warm water. Bring to a boil, cover, and place in a 325° F oven for 45 minutes. Add the potatoes if desired and cook 10 minutes more.

COLES DE BRUSELAS SALTEADOS

(Sautéed Brussels Sprouts)

Serves 4

¾ pound Brussels sprouts
1 tablespoon olive oil
2 cloves garlic, peeled and
   lightly crushed

Salt
Freshly ground pepper
2 teaspoons red wine vinegar

Cut off the ends of the Brussels sprouts and remove any old leaves. Place the sprouts in salted boiling water and cook 10–15 minutes, or until tender.

Heat the oil in a skillet. Add the garlic cloves and sauté until they are golden on all sides. Discard. Add the sprouts and sauté them over medium-high heat for several minutes. Sprinkle with the salt and pepper and add the vinegar. Cook until the vinegar evaporates, stirring constantly.

COLIFLOR AL AJO ARRIERO

(Cauliflower in Garlic and Paprika Sauce)

Serves 4

1 head cauliflower
2 cloves garlic
1 tablespoon chopped parsley
Salt

5 tablespoons olive oil
2 tablespoons red wine vinegar
1 tablespoon paprika

Separate the cauliflower into individual flowers. Boil in salted water until tender. Drain, reserving the cooking liquid. Keep the cauliflower warm. In a processor or blender, finely mince 1 of the garlic cloves, the parsley, and the salt. With the motor running, gradually add 3 tablespoons of the oil and 3 tablespoons of the cooking liquid.

In a skillet heat the remaining 2 tablespoons of oil and sauté the remaining garlic clove until brown on all sides. Discard the garlic. Turn off the flame and add the vinegar and paprika. Add the mixture from the processor and simmer 5 minutes. Pour over the cauliflower and serve immediately.

GARBANZOS A LA CATALANA
(Chickpeas with Tomato and Sausage)

Serves 4 as a main course
or 6–8 as a side dish

1 pound chickpeas
Salt
1 bay leaf
1 tablespoon olive oil
1 large onion, chopped
¼ pound sweet Italian or breakfast
    sausage, sliced

2 tablespoons diced cured ham
4 fresh or canned tomatoes, chopped
Freshly ground pepper
1 tablespoon minced parsley

Soak the chickpeas overnight. Cover and cook in the same water, adding more if necessary and seasoning with salt and the bay leaf, for about 1½–2 hours, or until the chickpeas are tender. Drain.

In a large casserole, heat the oil, then sauté the onion, sausage, and ham until the onion is wilted. Add the tomato, salt, and pepper and cook slowly, covered, about 15 minutes. Add the drained chickpeas, cover, and cook 20 minutes more. Sprinkle with the parsley and serve.

GARBANZOS REFRITOS
(Refried Chickpeas)

REFRIED chickpeas are commonly prepared in the evening or the next day after a *cocido* (p. 138) has been served, utilizing the leftover chickpeas.

Serves 1

1 tablespoon olive oil
3 tablespoons minced onion
1 clove garlic, minced
1 *chorizo* sausage (2 ounces), sliced or
    cut in pieces

2 cups cooked chickpeas, well drained
1 pimiento, homemade or imported,
    cut in strips

Heat the oil in a skillet. Add the onion and garlic and sauté until the onion is wilted. Add the *chorizo* and chickpeas and cook over a medium-high flame until the *chorizo* and chickpeas are lightly browned. Stir in the pimiento and serve.

NOTE: If leftover *cocido* is served as well, this recipe is adequate for 3 or 4 servings.

MENESTRA A LA RIOJANA
(Mixed Vegetables, Rioja Style)

IN THE lush region of Rioja, heart of wine-producing country (see Wines, p. 399), the fertile soil yields some of Spain's best vegetables, which grow side by side with the grape vines. When I recently visited the area in spring, the crops of artichokes, peas, string beans, leeks, and cauliflower had just been harvested, and the resulting mixture, or *menestra*, was the specialty on all the restaurant menus in the area. In the town of Haro, hub of this prosperous region, at the curiously named Beethoven Restaurant (tradition has it that the owner's grandfather was deaf and therefore was given this nickname), the *menestra* is done to perfection. A hearty dish, combining boiled and fried vegetables with the added punch of cured ham, a *menestra* can easily be a complete meal for vegetable lovers.

Serves 4

2 carrots, scraped
½ pound green beans
½ head cauliflower, broken
    into flowers
2 well-cleaned leeks, white part only
4 small artichoke hearts
¼ pound peas
2 tablespoons olive oil
4 thin slices cured ham, cut in
    small pieces

1 small onion, finely chopped
1 clove garlic, minced
Oil for frying
Flour for dusting
1 egg, lightly beaten
2 hard-boiled eggs, cut in wedges
1 pimiento, homemade or imported,
    cut in strips
Salt

In a large, shallow pan (more than one pan may be necessary) bring ½ inch of salted water to a boil. Add the carrots, green beans, cauliflower, leeks, and artichokes. Cover and cook, removing the vegetables with a slotted spoon as they become tender. Do not overcook. Meanwhile, cook the peas in a separate pot. Drain all the vegetables well. Cut the carrots and leeks into 1½-inch slices.
    Heat the 2 tablespoons of oil in a shallow ovenproof casserole (preferably earthenware). Add the ham and sauté a minute, then add the onion and garlic

and cook until the onion is wilted. Stir in the carrots, green beans, and peas and sauté 2 minutes. Remove from the heat.

Heat the frying oil, about 1 inch deep, in a skillet. Dip the cauliflower, leeks, and artichokes in the flour, then in the beaten egg, and fry them very briefly, only until they are lightly browned. Drain. Place them on top of the other vegetables already in the casserole. Decorate with the egg wedges and pimiento strips. Sprinkle with salt. Bake in a 350° F oven for 10 minutes. The Menestra may also be baked and served in 4 individual casserole dishes.

MENESTRA DE ACELGAS A LA EXTREMEÑA

(Greens and Potato Casserole)

BE SURE to try this one, appealing even to those who normally dislike green vegetables. It can be prepared in advance, except for the final browning, and is an exceptionally tasty accompaniment for simple meat or chicken dishes.

Serves 6

1 cup olive oil, or a mixture of olive and salad oils, for frying
3 medium potatoes, peeled and cut in ⅛-inch slices
1 large onion, half of it thinly sliced, the other half chopped
Coarse salt
1¼ pounds collard greens or Swiss chard, thick stems removed (weight after trimming)

3 tablespoons olive oil
2 cloves garlic, crushed
1 tablespoon minced parsley
Freshly ground pepper
Dash paprika
3 eggs, lightly beaten

Heat the 1 cup of frying oil in a skillet. Add the potatoes, one at a time to prevent sticking. Alternate potato layers with the thinly sliced onion. Salt each layer lightly. Cook over a medium flame, uncovered, until the potatoes are just tender, lifting and turning them occasionally. (The potatoes should remain separated — not in a "cake" — and should not brown.)

Meanwhile, place the greens in boiling water for 5 minutes, then drain. Cover with water again, adding salt and 1 tablespoon of the olive oil. Return to a boil, cover, and cook 10 minutes more, or until just tender. Drain and chop coarsely.

In a skillet, heat the remaining 2 tablespoons of olive oil. Sauté the chopped onion until wilted. Add the greens and sauté 5 minutes. Add the garlic, parsley, salt, pepper, 1 tablespoon warm water, and paprika. When the potatoes are done, drain them and mix them with the greens (the potatoes will break up a bit in stirring). Transfer this mixture to a shallow casserole dish, preferably Spanish earthenware. (The dish may be made in advance up to this point.) Pour the eggs over the casserole and place under a broiler for about 5 minutes, or until the eggs have formed a golden crust.

PISTO MANCHEGO

(Zucchini, Green Pepper, and Tomato Medley)

PISTO MANCHEGO hails from the land of Don Quijote—La Mancha—in central Spain. The addition of bacon and potatoes to this traditional vegetable dish makes it a satisfying light supper. Fried or poached eggs and slices of fried bread are common accompaniments.

Serves 4–6

¼ cup diced slab bacon
1 large onion, chopped
1 clove garlic, minced
1 medium potato, peeled and diced
2 green peppers, seeded and cut
    in strips

2 large tomatoes, chopped
2 medium zucchini, sliced
1 tablespoon chopped parsley
¼ cup chicken broth
Salt
Freshly ground pepper

Sauté the bacon in a large, deep casserole until it is transparent. Add the onion and garlic and cook until the onion is wilted. Add the potato and peppers and cook 10 minutes. Mix in the tomato, zucchini, parsley, broth, salt, and pepper. Cover and cook until the vegetables are tender, about 20 minutes.

HABAS A LA ANDALUZA

(Limas with Artichoke and Cumin)

THE Arab occupation of Spain lasted almost eight hundred years and left its traces on Spanish history and on Spanish cuisine. The presence of saffron and cumin in this vegetable casserole attests to its Moorish origin.

Serves 4

1 tablespoon olive oil
2 tablespoons chopped onion
2 cloves garlic, minced
1 small tomato (about 2
    ounces), chopped
1 pound lima beans
4 artichoke hearts, halved
¾ cup water

1 bay leaf
2 tablespoons minced parsley
Large pinch saffron
½ teaspoon ground cumin
Salt
Freshly ground pepper
4 eggs (optional)

Heat the oil in a skillet. Sauté the onion and garlic until the onion is wilted. Add the tomato and cook 5 minutes. Stir in the limas, artichokes, water, bay leaf, parsley, saffron, cumin, salt, and pepper. Cover and cook about 10 minutes, or until the vegetables are tender.

This dish becomes a luncheon or light dinner when eggs are added. When the vegetables are almost tender, crack the eggs and slide them whole into the pan over the vegetables. Cover and continue cooking until the eggs are set, about 5 minutes.

JUDÍAS VERDES A LA GALLEGA

(Green Beans and Potatoes, Galician Style)

Serves 4

4 small new potatoes
¾ pound flat green beans
2 tablespoons olive oil
1 medium onion, chopped

2 cloves garlic, coarsely chopped
Salt
Freshly ground pepper
2 hard-boiled eggs, cut in wedges

Boil the potatoes in salted water until tender, then peel and halve. Meanwhile, boil the green beans in salted water until just tender. Drain.

Heat the oil in a large, shallow casserole. Sauté the onion until it is wilted. Add the garlic, then the beans, and sauté them 5 minutes. Add the potatoes, salt, and pepper. Place the egg wedges on top. Cover and continue cooking 10 minutes. Serve in the same dish.

POTATOES

SPANISH potato dishes, except for the standard fried potatoes, or my favorite, Patatas Pobres, tend to be casserole-style preparations that may be the first course of a meal or, in some cases, a meal in itself. Some are also served as *tapas*. If the following recipes are to accompany a main course, I suggest, in general, serving with simple meat, fish, or poultry dishes.

PATATAS Y JUDÍAS
VERDES A LA EXTREMEÑA

(Potatoes and Green Beans, Extremadura Style)

Serves 4

½ pound green beans
2 medium–large all-purpose
    potatoes (about ¾
    pound), peeled and cubed
1 medium onion, finely chopped
1 medium tomato, chopped
1 green pepper, cut in strips

1 bay leaf
1 clove garlic, minced
1 tablespoon minced parsley
Salt
Freshly ground pepper
¼ cup olive oil

In a medium-size casserole, preferably earthenware, place the green beans, potatoes, onion, tomato, and green pepper. Add the bay leaf, garlic, parsley, salt, and pepper. Mix in the oil. Cover tightly and cook 1 hour, or until the vegetables are tender.

PATATAS POBRES

(Poor Man's Potatoes)

Poor Man's Potatoes are a misnomer, to be sure, for their enjoyment knows no economic boundaries. They are the potatoes most often served at my house.

Serves 4

3 tablespoons olive oil	Salt
4 medium all-purpose potatoes, in ⅛-inch slices	1 clove garlic, minced
	1 tablespoon minced parsley

Heat the oil in a 9- or 10-inch skillet. Add the potato slices in layers, and sprinkle each layer with salt. Turn the potatoes to coat with the oil. Lower the heat and cook the potatoes, covered, until they are tender, about 20 minutes, lifting and turning occasionally. (The potatoes will be separated, not in a "cake.") Turn up the flame so that some of the potatoes brown. Sprinkle in the garlic and parsley and serve immediately.

NOTE: These potatoes become a meal by using this recipe to serve 2 instead of 4, breaking 4 eggs over the potatoes when they are done, then covering the pan and letting the eggs cook about 5 minutes until set.

PATATAS A LA BRAVA

(Piquant Potatoes)

A COMMON *tapa* in Madrid, these spicy potatoes are also excellent with simple meat or chicken dishes.

Serves 4

3 tablespoons olive oil
3 medium all-purpose potatoes, peeled
    and cubed
Salt
Freshly ground pepper
2 tablespoons finely chopped onion
1 clove garlic, minced

1 cup tomato sauce, preferably
    homemade (p. 218)
¼ cup dry white wine
1 tablespoon chopped parsley
½ dried red chili pepper, seeds
    removed, crushed
Dash Tabasco

Heat 2 tablespoons of the oil in a large skillet. Brown the potatoes well on all sides over a medium flame. Season with salt and pepper, then cover and reduce the heat. Cook until the potatoes are tender, about 20 minutes.

Meanwhile, heat the remaining 1 tablespoon of oil in a saucepan. Sauté the onion and garlic until the onion is wilted. Add the tomato sauce, wine, parsley, chili pepper, Tabasco, salt, and pepper. Cook, uncovered, about 20 minutes. The sauce should be thick.

You may serve the potatoes and the sauce separately or pour some of the sauce over the potatoes. In either case, the potatoes should be only lightly coated with the sauce.

PATATAS CON CHORIZO

(Potatoes with Chorizo)

Serves 4

1 tablespoon olive oil
10 thin slices (about ⅛ inch) *chorizo*
3 thin slices bacon, chopped
4 medium all-purpose potatoes,
    peeled and cut in large
    cubes (or use small new
    potatoes, about 1 dozen)

Salt
1 tablespoon chopped parsley
1 clove garlic, minced

Heat the oil in a large skillet, then sauté the *chorizo* and bacon until they begin to give off their oils. Add the potatoes, sprinkle with salt, cover, and sauté slowly until the potatoes are golden and tender. Sprinkle with the parsley and garlic and cook 5 minutes more, uncovered, over a moderately high flame to further brown the potatoes.

PATATAS EN SALSA VERDE
(Potatoes in Green Sauce)

GREEN sauce is usually associated with seafood, but it is equally good on potatoes.

Serves 4

3 tablespoons olive oil
1 clove garlic, peeled
1 tablespoon minced onion
4 medium all-purpose potatoes,
    peeled and cut in
    ⅛-inch slices

¾ cup hot chicken broth or water
Salt
Freshly ground pepper
3 tablespoons minced parsley

Heat the oil in a skillet or shallow casserole, add the garlic clove, and cook until it is lightly browned. Remove the garlic, mash it, and reserve. Add the onion to the skillet and sauté until it is wilted. Add the potato slices and brown lightly. Stir in the broth, salt, pepper, the reserved garlic, and the parsley. Cook over low heat, uncovered, about 10 minutes. Turn the potatoes, cover, and cook about 10 minutes more, or until the potatoes are tender.

PATATAS PICANTES
(Spicy Potatoes)

Serves 4

3 medium all-purpose potatoes
3 tablespoons olive oil
⅛ teaspoon paprika
⅛ teaspoon crushed dried red chili
    pepper, seeds removed

2 cloves garlic, minced
Salt

Bring the potatoes to a boil in salted water to cover and cook until tender. Peel, then cut in ¼-inch slices.

Heat the oil in a large skillet. Sauté the potatoes until lightly browned. Sprinkle on the paprika, chili pepper, garlic, and salt. Cook 5 minutes more, turning occasionally.

PATATAS ASADAS RELLENAS

(Baked Stuffed Potatoes with Cured Ham)

Serves 4

4 large baking potatoes
3 tablespoons butter
Hot milk
Salt
Freshly ground pepper

A ¼-pound piece cured ham,
    finely diced
4 teaspoons bread crumbs
Butter

Bake the potatoes at 400° F about 1 hour, or until tender. Cut an oval piece from the tops of the potatoes and scoop out the potato, leaving the skins intact. Place the potato in a bowl and beat with the 3 tablespoons of butter, enough milk for the desired consistency, salt, and pepper. Stir in the ham. Fill the potato shells with the purée, sprinkle with bread crumbs, and dot with butter. Return to the oven for 10 minutes.

PATATAS CASTELLANAS

(Castilian-Style Potatoes)

Serves 4

3 tablespoons olive oil
3 tablespoons minced onion
1 clove garlic, minced
3 large all-purpose potatoes, cubed
1 tablespoon flour

1 teaspoon paprika
Salt
Freshly ground pepper
1 bay leaf

Heat the oil in a shallow casserole. Sauté the onion and garlic until the onion is wilted. Add the potatoes and sauté 5 minutes more. Sprinkle in the flour and paprika, stirring to coat the potatoes. Barely cover the potatoes with hot water. Add salt, pepper, and bay leaf and cook, covered, until the potatoes are tender and most of the liquid absorbed, about 20 minutes.

PATATAS FRITAS A LA VINAGRETA

(Potatoes Vinaigrette)

THIS is a popular *tapa* in Rioja country, although I find it more suitable with a cold summer meal.

Serves 4

4 medium red waxy potatoes, peeled   ¼ cup vinegar
    and cut in ⅛-inch slices   2 cloves garlic, sliced
½ cup plus 3 tablespoons olive oil   ¼ teaspoon freshly ground pepper
Salt

In a heavy skillet, fry the potatoes slowly in 3 tablespoons of the oil, salting lightly, until they are cooked but not brown. Transfer to a shallow casserole and arrange in layers.

In a saucepan, heat the vinegar, garlic, and pepper until it reaches a boil. Simmer 2 minutes. Remove from the heat and mix in the remaining ½ cup of oil. Pour this mixture over the potatoes and let them sit in a warm place for 10 minutes. Pour off the excess oil and serve the potatoes slightly warm or at room temperature.

PATATAS EN AJOPOLLO

(Potatoes in Garlic and Almond Sauce)

Serves 6

½ cup olive oil   White pepper
1 slice French-style bread, about   1 cup water
    ¼-inch thick   5 medium all-purpose potatoes,
12 blanched almonds   peeled and cubed
2 cloves garlic, peeled   1 cup chicken broth
1 sprig parsley   Salt
¼ teaspoon saffron

Heat the oil in a medium skillet. Fry the bread, almonds, garlic, and parsley until golden (if the almonds brown quickly, remove them first). Place in a processor or blender, reserving the oil. Add the saffron and pepper to the processor and beat until a paste forms. With the motor running, gradually add the water.

Place the potatoes in a saucepan. Pour the mixture from the processor over them, adding the reserved cooking oil and the broth. Season with salt and stir. Cook over a medium flame, uncovered, until the potatoes are tender.

Chapter 4

ENSALADAS
(Salads)

SPAIN'S summers tend to be long and very warm, and, perhaps for this reason, Spaniards are inordinately fond of foods bathed in cooling vinaigrettes. Especially in the south, where temperatures are as fiery as the temperaments of the people who inhabit these lands, there is nothing more appealing in the summer than a refreshing salad. It is not by chance that the world-renowned "liquid" salad—*gazpacho*—comes from this area.

Visit any restaurant in Spain and you will probably find exactly two salads listed on the menu: a simple lettuce and tomato combination and the more complex *ensalada mixta,* or *Ensalada de San Isidro,* which may have additions of tuna, asparagus, onion, egg, and olives. Both are usually first rate, the tomatoes sweet and vine ripened, and the lettuce a flavorful romaine (iceberg is unknown in Spain), and both make excellent accompaniments to any meal. However, it would be wrong to conclude that this is the extent of the Spanish salad repertoire, for delicious bean, vegetable, rice, and seafood salads abound. Many are regional specialties that rely on local seasonal produce and are most likely to be tasted in private homes or in a handful of restaurants. Some of these salads may take the form of *tapas.*

Salads in Spain are most often eaten as first courses and are invariably served undressed, accompanied by cruets of oil and vinegar. More involved salad dressings are rarely found—Spaniards subscribe to the idea that the fresh taste of top-quality produce must never be masked. For casual meals, salads are sometimes served with the main course, in which case enough salad for all diners is placed in the center of the table for everyone to taste, *tapas* style.

EL ALIÑO

(Salad Dressing with Cheese and Herbs)

MOST salads in this chapter come with their own dressings. El Aliño is used when a more forceful dressing is required, such as in the Mushroom and Cured Ham Salad and Catalán-Style Salad. It is, of course, excellent also on any simple green or mixed salad.

Makes about 1 1/2 cups

1 cup olive oil, or a mixture of olive
    and salad oils
1/3 cup red wine vinegar
1 teaspoon Dijon-style mustard
1 clove garlic, minced
1/4 teaspoon sugar
1/4 teaspoon basil

1/4 teaspoon thyme
1/8 teaspoon marjoram
1 tablespoon grated cheese
1/4 teaspoon horseradish
1 tablespoon minced parsley
Salt
Freshly ground pepper

Beat together all ingredients, preferably in a blender or processor, until smooth and creamy.

MAYONESA

(Mayonnaise)

SPANIARDS claim mayonnaise as their own creation, and although there is some dispute over the origin of the word, the commonly accepted derivation is that the sauce and the name come from Mahón, the principal city of the Balearic island of Menorca.

    There is absolutely no excuse for not making homemade mayonnaise when it is this simple and tastes so immeasurably better than the bottled variety.

Makes about 1 1/2 cups

1 whole egg
1 egg yolk
1/4 teaspoon Dijon-style mustard
1 teaspoon salt

2 tablespoons lemon juice
1 cup olive oil, or a mixture of
    olive oil and salad oil

Place in the bowl of a blender or processor the whole egg, egg yolk, mustard, salt, and lemon juice. Blend a few seconds. With the motor running, very gradually pour in the oil and continue beating until thickened and silky.

PICADILLA

(Creamy Almond Salad Dressing)

IN VALENCIA this dressing is typically used as an accompaniment to boiled fish. I prefer it as a dressing for a green salad.

Makes about 1 cup

½ cup blanched almonds
4 cloves garlic, chopped
1 cup olive oil
4 teaspoons vinegar

4 teaspoons lemon juice
½ teaspoon salt
Freshly ground pepper

Grind the almonds with the garlic in a blender or processor. Gradually pour in the oil, then add the vinegar, lemon juice, salt, and pepper. Beat until creamy and smooth. This dressing is best on a mixed green salad.

PEPINILLOS EN VINAGRE

(Pickled Cucumbers)

PREPARE SEVERAL HOURS IN ADVANCE.

Small green cucumbers, preferably
    Kirbies, peeled and sliced in
    quarters lengthwise

Coarse salt
Tarragon vinegar
Peppercorns, crushed

Sprinkle the cucumber slices with salt. Let them sit 1 hour in a colander to drain. Place the cucumbers in a glass jar with liquid to cover in the proportion of 1 part vinegar to 2 parts water. Season with salt and a few peppercorns. Cover and let stand at room temperature for several hours—better still, refrigerate and leave a day or more. Use in salads, or for Salsa Picante (p. 307).

ENSALADA DE SAN ISIDRO

(Mixed Salad, San Isidro Style)

THIS basic salad is found all over Spain. Obviously it has its variations—asparagus may be omitted, cucumber added, proportions changed. But the onion, tomato, lettuce, and tuna are essential ingredients.

Serves 4

4 tablespoons olive oil
2 tablespoons red wine vinegar
Salt
Freshly ground pepper
1/2 head romaine lettuce, torn
   in pieces
2 tomatoes, cut in eighths
3 thin slices onion

Half a 7-ounce can light meat tuna,
   drained and separated, or
   1/2 recipe Atún
   Escabechado (p. 24)
6 white asparagus, cut in
   half crosswise
1 dozen small green Spanish olives,
   without pimiento

In a small bowl blend the oil, vinegar, salt, and pepper. In a salad bowl, gently mix together the lettuce, tomato, onion, tuna, asparagus, and olives. Pour on the vinaigrette and toss.

ENSALADA DE PIPARRADA

(Cucumber, Tomato, and Pepper Salad)

A WONDERFULLY refreshing salad of Basque origin.

Serves 4–6

1 cucumber, peeled and cut in
   1-inch cubes
2 tomatoes, cut in eighths,
   then halved
1 green pepper, in 1-inch pieces
1 small onion, chopped

6 tablespoons olive oil
3 tablespoons red wine vinegar
1/2 teaspoon sugar
Salt
Freshly ground pepper

Mix together all ingredients. Refrigerate at least 30 minutes before serving.

ENSALADA DE TOMATE Y HUEVO
(Tomato and Egg Salad)

A SUMMER favorite, often served by my Spanish mother-in-law, who, I believe, originally devised the recipe. Notice there is no oil—only vinegar tempered by the addition of sugar.

Serves 4

¼ cup red wine vinegar	2 hard-boiled eggs, cut in wedges
4 teaspoons sugar	3 tomatoes, cut in wedges
Salt	1 small onion, sliced
Freshly ground pepper	1 tablespoon minced parsley

Combine the vinegar, sugar, salt, and pepper in a salad bowl. Gently fold in the egg, tomato, and onion. Refrigerate. Sprinkle with the parsley before serving.

ENSALADA A LA ALMORAINA
(Escarole Salad with Tomato and Cumin Dressing)

THE Moorish influence on this Andalucian salad is noted in its name (any word beginning with "al" is of Arab origin) and in the use of cumin in the dressing, which lends a distinctive and very pleasant flavor to the salad.

Serves 4–6

2 ripe tomatoes, skinned and chopped
½ teaspoon crushed or ground cumin
1 clove garlic, crushed
1 teaspoon paprika
6 tablespoons olive oil
3 tablespoons red wine vinegar

Salt
Freshly ground pepper
1 escarole, cut in pieces
Cured black olives and hard-boiled
    egg slices or wedges
    for garnish

In a blender or processor beat the tomato, cumin, garlic, paprika, and 2 tablespoons of the oil. Blend until smooth. Gradually pour in the remaining 4 tablespoons of oil, the vinegar, salt, and pepper.

Arrange the escarole on individual salad plates. Spoon on the dressing and decorate with the olives and eggs.

ENSALADA DE BERROS CON VINAGRETA DE ANCHOA

(Watercress and Carrot Salad in Anchovy Dressing)

AN ELEGANT salad created by the talented chef José Bárcena at New York's San Martín Restaurant, using typically Spanish ingredients.

Serves 4

1 bunch watercress, thick
    stems trimmed

2 carrots, in very fine julienne strips

SALAD DRESSING

½ cup olive oil
3 tablespoons red wine vinegar
¼ teaspoon Dijon-style mustard
3 anchovy fillets, minced
½ teaspoon minced capers
4 teaspoons minced onion

Salt
Freshly ground pepper
1 tablespoon minced sour pickle
1 tablespoon minced fresh tomato
2 teaspoons minced parsley

In a small bowl beat together with a fork all the salad dressing ingredients (this may be done several hours in advance). Arrange on salad plates first the watercress, covering half the plate, with the stems toward the center, then, on the other half of the dish the carrot strips, covering the watercress stems and fanning out from the center. Beat the dressing again, pour it on the salad, and serve.

NOTE: Endives, chopped or in julienne strips and attractively arranged, are a nice addition to this salad. The same dressing is excellent over cold white asparagus.

ENSALADA DE PIMIENTO Y TOMATE
(Pimiento and Tomato Salad)

PREPARE SEVERAL HOURS IN ADVANCE.

COLORFUL and delicious.

Serves 4–6

2 pimientos, preferably homemade, cut in strips
4 onion rings, thinly sliced
4 medium tomatoes, cut in eighths
Salt
Freshly ground pepper

2 tablespoons olive oil
2 tablespoons red wine vinegar
½ teaspoon sugar
3 anchovies, chopped
1 tablespoon minced parsley
12 or more cured black olives

Arrange the pimiento strips in layers in a shallow, flat-bottom bowl. Separate the onion rings and place them over the pimientos. Arrange the tomato wedges in an attractive design over the onions. Sprinkle with salt and pepper.

In a small bowl, mix the oil, vinegar, sugar, salt, pepper, and anchovy. Pour over the salad. Sprinkle with parsley and decorate with the olives. Refrigerate several hours before serving.

ENDIVIAS CON QUESO CABRALES
(Endives with Blue Cheese)

THE blue cheese fills the cuplike leaves of the endives, making an extremely attractive and very tasty salad. Serve with any simple meat preparations, such as steak or Breaded Beefsteak (p. 296). Since the endive leaves are easy to pick up, this salad is also suitable as a *tapa*.

Serves 4–6

2 endives (about 24 leaves)
12 tablespoons blue cheese, such as
    Cabrales (p. 431) or
    Gorgonzola, at room
    temperature

8 tablespoons mayonnaise
2 tablespoons minced parsley

Separate the endives into individual leaves. Mash the blue cheese until smooth. Mix in the mayonnaise. Spread 2 teaspoons of the cheese mixture on the green ends of the endive leaves. Arrange 4–6 leaves on individual salad plates, green tips facing outward. Sprinkle with parsley.

ENSALADA MURCIANA

(Salad, Murcia Style)

Serves 4

½ head escarole
Coarse salt
½ pound tomatoes, sliced
6 tablespoons olive oil
3 tablespoons red wine vinegar

Freshly ground pepper
Dash paprika
Dash sugar
½ bunch watercress, leaves only

Wash and dry the escarole, then tear into pieces and place in a salad bowl. Sprinkle with salt. Arrange the slices of tomato on top of the lettuce and sprinkle with more salt.

In a small bowl mix the oil, vinegar, salt, pepper, paprika, and sugar. Pour the dressing slowly over the tomato and lettuce, distributing evenly. Cover with the watercress leaves and serve. Do not mix — try to keep the layers intact.

EMPEDRAT TARRAGONI

(Codfish Salad)

START PREPARATION TWO DAYS IN ADVANCE.

WHEN I saw this codfish salad on the menu of the charming Agut d'Avignón restaurant in the old quarter of Barcelona, I thought it sounded singularly unappealing. But at the urging of our waiter, I ordered it and found it perfectly delightful. Serve as a salad (it is not at all strong tasting) or a first course.

Serves 6

1 pound dried salt cod
1 onion, peeled
1 medium tomato, in thin slices, each slice cut in half
20 small cured black olives
1 cup cooked white beans, preferably homemade

2 hard-boiled eggs, sliced
2 tablespoons minced parsley
8 tablespoons olive oil
4 tablespoons red wine vinegar
Salt
Freshly ground pepper

Soak the dried cod in water to cover for about 36 hours, changing the water occasionally. Drain and shred the cod with your fingers. (The cod will not be cooked.)

Bake the onion in a 350° F oven for 30 minutes. Sliver. In a bowl, combine the cod, onion, tomato, olives, beans, egg slices, and parsley. In a small bowl, beat together the oil and vinegar. Combine with the cod mixture, season with salt and pepper, then chill the salad for a few hours—don't leave it overnight or it will lose some of its flavor.

SALPICÓN DE LANGOSTINO Y TOMATE

(Shrimp and Tomato in Sherry Vinaigrette)

SHERRY is a cooking ingredient in almost all parts of Spain, but vinegar made from sherry is rarely used except in the southwestern area around Jerez. This is a lovely salad in which sliced shrimp are attractively arranged over a bed of chopped tomato, all in a wonderfully fragrant sherry vinaigrette. It is found at the Anteojo Restaurant in Cádiz, my favorite Spanish city. (More on Cádiz, p. 223.)

Serves 6

1 pound medium or large shrimp, in their shells
Cooking Liquid (p. 8)
4 tablespoons sherry vinegar
8 tablespoons olive oil
Salt

Freshly ground pepper
Pinch sugar
6 tablespoons finely chopped Spanish onion
4 tablespoons minced parsley
4 medium tomatoes, diced

Boil the shrimp in the cooking liquid according to the instructions on page 8. Shell. In a large bowl mix together the vinegar, oil, salt, pepper, sugar, onion, and 2 tablespoons of the parsley. Slice the cooked shrimp down the middle (and devein, if you wish) and place them, along with the diced tomato, in the dressing. Stir to coat well. Cover and refrigerate, preferably for several hours, stirring occasionally. Separate the shrimp and the tomatoes. Spread the tomatoes in the bottom of a wide, shallow serving bowl. Arrange the shrimp halves in overlapping rows over the tomatoes. Pour on the dressing and sprinkle with the remaining 2 tablespoons of parsley. When serving, try to keep the tomato and shrimp layers intact.

ENSALADA CATALANA
(Catalán-Style Salad)

PREPARE SEVERAL HOURS IN ADVANCE.

ALTHOUGH this salad often goes by the name "Catalana," I first ate it in southern Spain, far from Cataluña, in a unique village near Ronda called Setenil. Here the homes are hollowed out from the gray brown cliffs. From the street the houses appear to be ordinary dwellings, but inside, the rooms are irregularly shaped and undulating, giving the appearance of igloos. The residents manage to make charming homes of their "caves," whitewashing the walls, covering them with cascading ivy, and filling the rooms with rustic furnishings.

The bar where we sampled Ensalada Catalana was housed in a cave on the village's main plaza. Our elderly waiter, who was also the town barber, regaled us with stories of Setenil's history—"According to our forefathers, these houses have been here centuries upon centuries. . . . They say a queen once had a son here named Sebastián"—all the while rushing about arranging the table and bringing our food.

In southern Spain, where the temperatures in summer often top 100 degrees, a cooling salad such as this one is ideal. It is my favorite for a light summer meal.

Serves 4–6

4 large potatoes, preferably red waxy
El Aliño salad dressing (p. 104)
3-ounce jar small green olives, preferably unstuffed
1 red onion, sliced thin
1 green pepper, sliced in rings

7-ounce can white or light meat tuna, drained
Salt
Freshly ground pepper
2 hard-boiled eggs, quartered
2 ripe tomatoes, cut in eighths

Boil the potatoes in salted water until they are tender. Cool them slightly, peel, and cut into ⅛-inch slices. Spread 2 tablespoons of the salad dressing in a large, flat-bottom bowl. Add one layer of the potatoes, some of the olives, some sliced onion and peppers, and a part of the tuna, separated into chunks. Sprinkle with salt and pepper. Coat this layer with some of the dressing. Continue layering and coating each layer until all ingredients have been used, except 3 tablespoons of the dressing. Arrange the egg and tomato wedges on top of the salad. Coat them with the remaining dressing. Refrigerate the salad several hours but not overnight: the potatoes change texture. Serve by cutting through all the layers with a large serving spoon. Provide plenty of good crusty bread.

ENSALADA VALENCIANA
(Potato and Orange Salad)

POTATOES and oranges make a wonderfully refreshing combination. This salad may accompany a simple meal as a salad or may be used as a *tapa*.

Serves 4

3 medium-size red waxy potatoes, boiled, skinned, and cut in 1-inch chunks
½ cup slivered Spanish onion
1 orange, peeled and cut in ¼-inch slices, each slice cut in quarters

1 pimiento, homemade or imported, cut in thin strips
2 tablespoons red wine vinegar
4 tablespoons salad oil
Salt
Freshly ground pepper

In a bowl, combine with a rubber spatula the potatoes, onion, orange pieces, and pimiento. In a small bowl beat together the vinegar and oil. Gently fold into the salad. Season with salt and pepper. Refrigerate until well chilled.

ENSALADILLA ESPARTERO
(Tuna, Egg, and Potato Salad)

ON ALCALÁ STREET in Madrid, right across from the beautiful Retiro Park, was the old-fashioned and very popular Espartero café. Especially prized were the outdoor tables, always packed at *tapas* time in summer with people eating one of the famous Espartero salads—either the following version, which contains potatoes and is coated with mayonnaise, or others that are strictly seafood and are served in a spicy vinaigrette.

Homemade mayonnaise (see p. 104) will produce a far superior salad, but if bottled mayonnaise is to be used, thin it with a little lemon juice for easier blending.

Serves 4–6

3 medium potatoes, preferably
    red waxy
7-ounce can tuna, white or
    light, drained
1½ teaspoons vinegar
1½ teaspoons grated onion
1 tablespoon minced parsley

1 teaspoon capers
1 hard-boiled egg, finely chopped
Salt
¾ cup mayonnaise,
    preferably homemade
1 pimiento, homemade or imported,
    cut in strips

Boil the potatoes in salted water until they are tender. Cool them slightly, then peel and cube them. Place the tuna in a large bowl, separating it into large chunks. Stir in the vinegar, onion, parsley, and capers. Add the potatoes and the chopped egg and blend gently with a rubber spatula. Salt to taste. Let this mixture sit 30 minutes or more.

Gently fold in the mayonnaise. Shape the salad into a dome on a flat plate and decorate with pimiento strips. This mixture may also be used as a filling for tiny unsweetened tartlet shells, in which case the potatoes and tuna should be cut in smaller pieces.

ENSALADA KOSHKERA

(Fish and Lobster Salad)

A SPECIALTY of the Basque region.

Serves 4

1 pound fresh cod or porgy
1¾ pounds live lobster, cooked
    and shelled (about ¾ pound
    lobster meat)
2 pimientos, homemade or imported,
    cut in strips

3-ounce jar small green Spanish
    olives, pitted
1 teaspoon vinegar
3 tablespoons olive oil
Salt
4 hard-boiled eggs, cut in wedges

MARINADE

2 tablespoons olive oil   Salt
2 tablespoons vinegar   Freshly ground pepper

Place the cod in a pan with water to cover that has been seasoned according to directions on page 8; here you will use less water, but use the same amount of seasoning and eliminate the clam juice. Cover and cook 15 minutes. Drain, cool, then shred. In a small bowl mix together the marinade ingredients. Pour over the fish and let sit 30 minutes.

Cut the lobster into thin slices. Combine with the shredded fish, pimiento, olives, 1 teaspoon vinegar, 3 tablespoons oil, and salt. Refrigerate until cold. To serve, decorate with the egg wedges.

PIPIRRANA JAENERA

(Tomato, Green Pepper, Ham, and Tuna Salad)

PREPARE SEVERAL HOURS IN ADVANCE.

THIS cold crisp salad is delicious as a summer dinner.

Serves 4

2 hard-boiled eggs   1½ tablespoons red wine vinegar
2 cloves garlic, crushed   1 pound tomatoes, cut in salad pieces
3 tablespoons olive oil   ¼ pound green pepper,
½ slice bread, soaked and   finely chopped
    squeezed dry   ¾ cup Marinated Tuna (p. 24) or
Salt   plain canned tuna, drained
Freshly ground pepper   ¼ cup julienne strips of cured ham

Separate the egg yolks and whites; mash the yolks and finely chop the whites. Mix the yolks with the garlic, oil, and bread until smooth. Add the salt, pepper, and vinegar.

In a separate bowl, mix together the tomatoes, green pepper, egg white, salt, pepper, tuna, and ham. Gently stir in the dressing. Refrigerate several hours and serve very cold.

ENSALADA DE REMOLACHA

(Fresh Beet Salad)

Serves 4

4 medium-size fresh beets,
    stems removed
2 tablespoons olive oil
1 tablespoon red wine vinegar

Salt
Freshly ground pepper
½ Spanish onion, slivered

Simmer the unpeeled beets in water, covered, for 1 hour, or until tender, being sure to replenish the water if necessary. Cool, peel, and slice ¼ inch thick.

In a small bowl combine the oil, vinegar, salt, and pepper. Arrange a layer of beets in a serving dish. Sprinkle with salt, pepper, and onion slivers and pour on part of the dressing. Repeat. Refrigerate briefly before serving—the salad should not be too cold. Serve on a bed of lettuce.

ENSALADA DE PATATA Y REMOLACHA

(Potato and Beet Salad)

Serves 6

4 medium-size fresh beets, stems
    removed, or 9-ounce can
    or jar of beets
4 tablespoons vinegar
4 medium potatoes, preferably red
    waxy, boiled and cubed

Salt
Freshly ground pepper
¾ cup homemade
    mayonnaise (p. 104)
2 hard-boiled eggs, sliced

For fresh beets, follow the cooking instructions in the previous recipe. If the beets are canned, drain and dry on paper towels. Cube the beets and mix them in a bowl with the vinegar. Let sit 1 hour. Arrange the beets in a serving dish or in individual dishes. Cover with the cubed potatoes. Season with salt and pepper, coat with the mayonnaise, and decorate with the egg slices.

ENSALADA DE ESCALIBADA

(Eggplant, Artichoke, Pepper, and Tomato Salad)

A WONDERFUL mixture of fresh and cooked vegetables that is a refreshing accompaniment to any cold meat or fish dish and is great with a potato omelet (p. 163).

Serves 4–6

½ pound small Italian eggplants
1 green pepper
1 red pepper
2 medium onions, peeled
3 artichoke hearts, cooked and sliced
½ pound tomatoes, cut in salad pieces
¼ cup olive oil

3 tablespoons lemon juice
1 clove garlic, crushed
1 tablespoon minced parsley
1 teaspoon small capers
Salt
White pepper
2 hard-boiled eggs, cut in wedges

In a roasting pan place the eggplant, green and red peppers, and onions, and bake at 350° F for about 30 minutes, turning occasionally (the onions will still be slightly crunchy). Peel the eggplant and peppers and cut in thin strips. Slice the onions. Place these vegetables in a serving dish and add the cooked artichoke hearts and the tomato.

In a small bowl, beat together the oil, lemon juice, garlic, parsley, capers, salt, and white pepper. Pour over the vegetables and mix gently. Chill. To serve, decorate with the egg wedges.

ENSALADA DE CHAMPIÑÓN

(Mushroom and Cured Ham Salad)

MUSHROOMS and cured ham produce a beautiful blend of flavors. This salad is also suitable as a *tapa*.

Serves 4–6

½ pound mushrooms, cut in halves
    or quarters or sliced
Lemon juice
¼ cup of 1-inch long julienne strips
    of cured ham

½ cup El Aliño salad
    dressing (p. 104)
1 tablespoon minced parsley

Sprinkle the mushrooms with lemon juice. Gently fold in the ham, then the salad dressing and parsley. Refrigerate until ready to serve (don't keep too long or the mushrooms may discolor).

JUDÍAS VERDES A LA VINAGRETA

(Green Bean Salad)

PREPARE SEVERAL HOURS IN ADVANCE.

A VERSATILE salad that goes well with almost anything.

Serves 4

¾ pound fresh green beans
4 tablespoons olive oil
2 tablespoons red wine vinegar
Salt
Freshly ground pepper
⅛ teaspoon sugar

2 tablespoons minced onion
1 tablespoon chopped parsley
2 tablespoons chopped pimiento,
    homemade or imported
1 hard-boiled egg, finely chopped

Cook the green beans in boiling salted water, covered, until they are just tender, about 15 minutes. Drain, cool, and transfer to a bowl.

In a small bowl, mix the oil, vinegar, salt, pepper, and sugar. Pour over the beans. Add the onion, parsley, and pimiento and toss gently with a rubber spatula. Taste for salt. Cover and refrigerate several hours or overnight. Before serving, sprinkle the beans with the chopped egg.

BERENJENA DE ALMAGRO

(Pickled Eggplant, Almagro Style)

PREPARE SEVERAL DAYS IN ADVANCE.

THE lovely village of Almagro in Castilla is well known for four reasons: the beautiful lace its women create, its elegant and unusual main plaza, its recently discovered sixteenth-century theater—and its pickled eggplants.

Makes 4 small eggplants

4 very small Italian eggplants (about ¾ pound), stems on
1 cup red wine vinegar
2 cups water
⅓ cup olive oil
1½ teaspoons salt

Freshly ground pepper
1 dried red chili pepper
2 cloves garlic, minced
1 teaspoon ground cumin
¼ teaspoon oregano

Make a 1-inch lengthwise slit in each eggplant. Place in boiling salted water and cook 10–12 minutes, until barely tender. Cool and place in a glass jar or ceramic crock.

In a bowl, mix together the vinegar, water, oil, salt, pepper, chili pepper, garlic, cumin, and oregano. Pour this marinade over the eggplants, cover, and let sit at room temperature for several days.

To serve, arrange the eggplants on a serving dish whole, or sliced lengthwise into quarters, leaving a piece of stem on each. They may be served as a salad or a *tapa*.

TRIGUEROS EN VINAGRILLO

(Marinated Asparagus)

PREPARE SEVERAL HOURS IN ADVANCE.

Serves 4

¾ pound very thin green asparagus
6 tablespoons olive oil
3 tablespoons red wine vinegar
3 cloves garlic, crushed

½ teaspoon paprika
Salt
Freshly ground pepper

Snap off the hard ends of the asparagus and discard or reserve for future use. Place the asparagus spears in a skillet with water barely to cover. Simmer, covered, until they are just tender, about 5–10 minutes. Drain and reserve the cooking liquid.

In a shallow bowl, mix the oil, vinegar, garlic, paprika, salt, pepper, and 1½ tablespoons of the reserved cooking liquid. Add the asparagus, turn to coat, cover, and marinate at room temperature for about 4 hours (if you leave them longer they will start to lose their color). Serve at room temperature.

GARBANZOS ALIÑADOS

(Marinated Chickpeas)

PREPARE ONE DAY IN ADVANCE.

Serves 4

2 cups freshly cooked (about ½ pound when dry) or canned chickpeas
1 hard-boiled egg yolk
4 tablespoons olive oil

2 tablespoons red wine vinegar
1 tablespoon finely chopped onion
1 clove garlic, minced
2 tablespoons chopped parsley
1 tablespoon small capers

Cook the dried chickpeas according to directions for Garbanzos a la Catalana (p. 91). Wash and drain canned chickpeas. Pass the egg yolk through a sieve into a bowl. Beat in the oil and vinegar with a wire whisk, then stir in the onion, garlic, 1 tablespoon of the parsley, capers, and chickpeas. Refrigerate overnight. Bring to room temperature before serving and sprinkle with the remaining tablespoon of parsley.

ENSALADA DE LENTEJAS

(Lentil Salad)

Serves 4

½ pound uncooked lentils
½ onion, peeled
1 clove
1 bay leaf
½ carrot, scraped
1 clove garlic, peeled
Salt

Freshly ground pepper
¼ cup olive oil
1 tablespoon red wine vinegar
2 tablespoons minced onion
1 clove garlic, crushed
2 tablespoons minced pimiento

Wash the lentils, then place them in a pot with water to cover. Add the onion, clove, bay leaf, carrot, peeled garlic, salt, and pepper. Bring to a boil, cover, and simmer about 35 minutes, or until the lentils are barely tender. Rinse well under cold water. Drain. Discard the onion, bay leaf, clove, and garlic. Dice the carrot and place it in a bowl with the lentils. Mix in gently with a rubber spatula the oil, vinegar, salt, pepper, minced onion, crushed garlic, and pimiento. Let sit at least 1 hour. Serve cold or at room temperature.

ENSALADA DE JUDÍAS BLANCAS

(White Bean Salad)

Serves 4

½ pound dried kidney beans
1 onion, peeled and halved
1 bay leaf

Salt
Freshly ground pepper

MARINADE

2 tablespoons olive oil
1 tablespoon vinegar
Salt
Freshly ground pepper

Pinch sugar
1 tablespoon minced onion
1 tablespoon minced green pepper
1 tablespoon minced parsley

Place the beans in a pot with cold water to cover. Bring to a boil, drain the water, and cover the beans again with cold water. Simmer, covered, for 1 hour. Add the onion, bay leaf, salt, and pepper. Cook about 1 hour more, or until the beans are just tender. Rinse, drain, and cool.

Prepare the marinade by mixing together all the marinade ingredients. Gently fold into the beans. Chill and serve on a bed of lettuce.

ENSALADA DE ARROZ

(Rice Salad)

PREPARE SEVERAL HOURS IN ADVANCE.

Serves 4–6

Turbante de Arroz (pp. 191–192),
    substituting 2 tablespoons
    olive oil for the butter

¼ pound mushrooms
1 tablespoon lemon juice
3 tablespoons olive oil

1 tablespoon vinegar	1 clove garlic, crushed
¼ teaspoon sugar	1 tablespoon minced parsley
Salt	1 anchovy, finely chopped
Freshly ground pepper	½ teaspoon anchovy oil (from
¼ teaspoon Dijon-style mustard	the can)
¼ teaspoon thyme	1 pimiento, diced

Make the rice as for Turbante de Arroz. Bake according to instructions, then remove from the oven, discard the parsley, cover, and let sit 5–10 minutes. Cool. Combine the mushrooms with the lemon juice and let them sit while preparing the dressing.

To make the dressing, in a small bowl mix together the oil, vinegar, sugar, salt, pepper, mustard, thyme, garlic, parsley, anchovy, and anchovy oil. Pour this over the rice, then fold in the pimiento and mushrooms, sliced or chopped, along with the lemon juice in which they have soaked. Let the salad sit several hours before serving. It may be eaten cold or at room temperature.

ENSALADA DE ANGULAS

(Baby Eel Salad)

Angulas (see p. 20 and p. 222) are the ultimate Spanish delicacy, most commonly prepared by plunging the baby eels into hot olive oil well seasoned with garlic and chili pepper. I always thought that no dish could be more exquisite until I sampled somewhere in Castile a salad made with these same tiny elvers. Nothing that I have ever eaten has given me more pleasure.

Serves 2

¼ pound fresh or frozen and defrosted baby eels	½ dried red chili pepper, seeds removed, crushed
2½ tablespoons virgin olive oil	1 teaspoon minced parsley
1½ teaspoons red wine vinegar	Salt
2 cloves garlic, crushed	Freshly ground pepper

Dry the *angulas* well and place them in a salad bowl. In a small bowl combine the olive oil, vinegar, garlic, chili pepper, parsley, salt, and pepper with a wire whisk. Gradually toss together the *angulas* and the dressing. Transfer to a serving platter lined with lettuce leaves. This salad should be served cool, not cold.

Chapter 5

SOPAS Y POTAJES

(Soups and Meals-in-a-Pot)

I N EVALUATING Spanish soups, it soon became evident to me that there would have to be a division between those soups light enough for first courses and those that most of us would consider meals-in-a-pot. Let me not speak for the Spaniard, however—he will consume a huge bowl of lentil or chickpea soup and then go on to a main course of meat and potatoes without batting an eyelash.

Traditionally, Spanish soups were of the robust variety, providing inexpensive eating that was filling and nutritious. Such soups utilized cheap and easily obtainable ingredients of each region of Spain. Like so many other eating habits that began for economic reasons, the Spanish love for hearty soups continues, even though their raison d'être is not as compelling as it once was.

Certain Spanish soups are as much a way of life as a means of satisfying hunger. The *cocido* of Castilla, the *fabada* of Asturias, the *caldo gallego* from Galicia, and the Basque *marmitako* come close to being code words for regional pride, love of country, and respect for tradition. A Madrileño will surely boast of some small restaurant in Old Madrid where the cook still prepares a "real" *cocido*, carefully simmering the meats and chickpeas for hours on end. An Asturiano speaks reverentially of his bean and sausage *fabada* and will go to great pains to explain its "authentic" preparation (it *must* use the beans grown in Asturias). A Galician will claim that nowhere else in the world can a really top-notch *caldo gallego* be made, for it will lack the tender young potatoes and the typical greens of the area that make this soup so outstanding. And Basque purists will claim that the best *marmitako* fish soup can be made only on board the fishing vessels that have just caught the bonito needed in its preparation. Everyone is an expert when it comes to analyzing these soups, and a native of one of these four regions will accept neither discussion nor innovative recipe suggestions that may alter the character of his beloved soup. Only he and he alone knows just how that soup must be made and exactly how it should taste when done.

Because of their long tradition and the enthusiasm they arouse, Spanish soups are at their best when they are of this hearty peasant variety. Rarely will you find a soup mellowed with cream and butter, for Spaniards are clearly uninterested in such refinements. Even the most worldly city dweller, when given a choice, will invariably elect a soup that reminds him of his family roots, and the most exclusive restaurants will usually present a selection of regional, down-to-earth Spanish dishes alongside their offerings of sophisticated French fare.

There are, nevertheless, a limited number of Spanish soups that fall into a "first course" category, most notably, the consommés, some garlic soups, and several of the simpler fish soups. Included in this "lighter" category also are the enormously popular cold summer soups; when temperatures rise, even a Spaniard with the most robust appetite will reject his favorite rib-sticking soups in favor of a refreshing, icy *gazpacho*—either the standard red version native to Andalucía, the white type from Extremadura in west-central Spain, or the creamy cold almond *gazpacho* of Málaga.

In the final analysis, there are Spanish soups to satisfy all tastes. Try the light as well as the hearty, but take care to select the type of soup that best suits the season and best complements your menu plans.

CONSOMÉ AL JEREZ

(Sherried Consommé)

Serves 6

3 pounds beef bones such as shin, with meat on them
10 cups water
1 large carrot, scraped and cut in half crosswise
1 medium onion, peeled and cut in half
2 sprigs parsley
Salt
4 peppercorns

½ teaspoon thyme
2 scallions or 1 leek
½ turnip, peeled
1 stalk celery
1 bay leaf
2 egg whites
2 tablespoons dry (*fino*) sherry
Chopped scallions for garnish, green part only

Brown the bones in a 350° F oven for 30 minutes, turning once. In a large pot place the bones and all remaining ingredients, except the egg whites, sherry, and garnish. Salt sparingly. Bring to a boil, skim off the foam. Simmer 5 hours, uncovered, skimming off the foam as necessary. The broth should be reduced by about half.

Strain the broth and return it to the pot. In a large bowl beat the egg whites until firm but not stiff. Gradually pour in the soup. Return to the pot and cook gently 20 minutes, stirring frequently (this clarifies the soup). Strain the broth through cheesecloth. Add the sherry and more salt if necessary. To serve, sprinkle with scallions.

To make a more substantial soup, add julienne strips of cooked chicken breast and cured ham, in which case the broth is known as "Sopa Real." An *amontillado* sherry such as Hartley & Gibson is an elegant accompaniment.

SOPA DE AJO CASTELLANO

(Garlic Soup, Castilian Style)

GARLIC soup is one of the simplest soups imaginable, and it has nourished generation upon generation of Spaniards. Traditionally it is made with water rather than broth, so its only ingredients are the most basic ones possible—oil, garlic, bread, and eggs.

Serves 4

2 tablespoons olive oil
4 cloves garlic, peeled
4 slices French-style bread, in
    ¼-inch slices
1 tablespoon paprika
4 cups beef broth,
    preferably homemade

¼ teaspoon ground cumin
Few strands saffron
Salt
4 eggs

Heat the oil in a shallow ovenproof casserole suitable for soup—Spanish earthenware is the best. Add the garlic cloves and cook until they are golden on all sides. Reserve them. In the oil fry the bread slices slowly until golden on both sides. Reserve. Cool the oil slightly, then stir in the paprika. Add the broth, cumin, and saffron. Return the garlic cloves to the soup, lightly crushing them with a fork. Salt to taste and cook 5 minutes. Crack 4 whole eggs and slide them into the soup. Arrange the bread slices on top of the soup. Place in a 450° F oven until the eggs are set, about 3–4 minutes. Be careful not to overcook. Instead of whole eggs, it is also common to cover the top of the soup with beaten eggs and run the casserole under the broiler. In this case, reduce the number of eggs to 2. This soup may also be be made in individual soup dishes. A robust Valdepeñas Red is a proper choice as an accompaniment.

SOPA DE AJO "CASA IRENE"
(Garlic Soup, "Casa Irene")

HIGH in the Pyrenees in Artiés, a tiny village of a handful of slate-roofed houses on the banks of the rushing river Garona, is one of the finest restaurants in Spain. Irene, the gracious owner, cook, hostess, and sometime waitress, is responsible for this unlikely situation. Native to this village, Irene likes the peace and tranquility of her hometown and would not dream of trading it for big-city life. There seems no need to; Spaniards are beating a path to the door of her tastefully decorated restaurant in ever-increasing numbers.

Irene presents no menu. Each day she goes to market, decides what is best, and then determines what will be offered that evening. For a surprisingly low prix fixe, course after course is brought to the diner, beginning with an aperitif of champagne and walnut-flavored wine, continuing with pâtés, salads, marinated fish, soup, meat, dessert, and cheeses, and ending with a carafe of coffee liqueur and another of orange liqueur, homemade as well, by Irene.

Irene's garlic soup is an old village recipe going back hundreds of years. Somehow, Irene found time to sit with us over coffee and describe its preparation.

Serves 8

2 tablespoons olive oil
6 cloves garlic, peeled
8 slices day-old French-style bread, ⅛ inch thick
8 cups strong chicken stock, preferably homemade and well seasoned with peppercorns, bay leaf, thyme, onion, and parsley

3 tablespoons dry (*fino*) sherry
3 eggs, at room temperature
2 tablespoons heavy cream
Minced parsley for garnish

In a skillet, heat the oil and sauté the garlic cloves slowly until they are golden on all sides. Reserve. Sauté the bread slices in the remaining oil until they are golden and very crusty. Keep them warm. Add the reserved garlic to the chicken stock (it should be warm), crushing them lightly with a fork. Stir in the sherry and let the stock sit about 1 hour, stirring occasionally. Strain the chicken stock, pressing the garlic pieces through the strainer with a wooden spoon so that most of the pieces pass through.

Right before serving, heat the broth to the boiling point. In a large bowl beat the eggs with an electric beater or wire whisk until they are light and foamy. Stir in the cream. Gradually beat in the hot broth. (If it is necessary to reheat the soup once the cream has been added, do so only in a double boiler, to prevent curdling.) Serve with the fried bread and minced parsley decorating the soup bowls. A *fino* sherry such as Tío Pepe makes an interesting wine selection.

CEBOLLADA CON ALMENDRAS
(Onion and Almond Soup)

A SIXTEENTH-CENTURY cookbook, the first in the Spanish language, written by Ruperto de Nola, chef to King Fernando, Spanish ruler of Naples, has a recipe for onion soup that is remarkably similar to what we today refer to as "French Onion Soup." This 460-year-old version contains ground almonds, but I have eliminated the sprinkling of sugar and cinnamon the recipe calls for. Spices, perhaps because of their novelty, were grossly overused in the sixteenth century—and best excluded from this otherwise delicious recipe.

Serves 6

2 tablespoons olive oil
2 large onions, sliced thin
6 cups chicken broth,
    preferably homemade
1 cup dry white wine
1 bay leaf
2 sprigs parsley
Salt
White pepper

2 ounces blanched almonds (about
    40 almonds)
¼ teaspoon ground cumin
6 slices French-style bread, about ¼
    inch thick, lightly toasted in
    the oven
½ cup grated Parmesan cheese
Sliced toasted almonds

In a large pot, heat the olive oil and sauté the onion slices until they are wilted but not brown. Add the broth, wine, bay leaf, parsley, salt, and pepper. Cover and simmer 30 minutes.

Grind the almonds in a food processor or blender until they are as fine as possible. While the motor is running, gradually add ½ cup of the broth to the almonds and beat until the liquid is milky white and no pieces remain. Strain. (If a lot of almond remains in the strainer, return the pieces to the processor with a little broth and beat again.) Return the almond mixture to the pot and add the cumin. Cover and simmer another 30 minutes.

Remove the parsley and bay leaf from the broth. Transfer the soup to a large, shallow casserole or 6 individual shallow ovenproof bowls. Cover with the 6 slices of toast and sprinkle with the cheese. Run the soup under the broiler until the bread and cheese are golden. Serve immediately, sprinkled with the toasted almonds. A light dry white wine, perhaps a Monopole, is suitable.

CREMA DE PERDIZ

(Cream of Partridge Soup)

I SUGGEST preparing this rich and flavorful soup in a more economical fashion by using only the carcasses of two or more partridges (perhaps partridges that have been boned to make one of the partridge pâtés, p. 62 and p. 63). The bones should, of course, have some meat on them.

Serves 4

1 partridge (about 1 pound)	Salt
1 small carrot, scraped and cut in pieces	4 peppercorns
	1 bay leaf
1 onion, peeled	10 medium mushrooms
1 sprig parsley	3 tablespoons butter
¼ teaspoon thyme	3 tablespoons flour
1 clove	½ cup milk
3 cups water	½ cup heavy cream
1 cup dry white wine	1 tablespoon dry (*fino*) sherry

In a deep pot, place the partridge with the carrot, onion, parsley, thyme, clove, water, wine, salt, peppercorns, and bay leaf. Bring to a boil. Cover and simmer 1½ hours. Discard the parsley, peppercorns, bay leaf, and clove. Remove the partridge from the pot, bone and skin it, reserving the meat.

Sauté the mushrooms in 1 tablespoon of the butter for about 5 minutes. Place the mushrooms in a processor or blender with the partridge meat and the carrot and onion from the broth. Blend until smooth. Gradually add at least 6 tablespoons of the soup broth.

In a saucepan, melt the remaining 2 tablespoons of butter, add the flour, and cook a minute. Stir in the broth (there should be about 3½ cups), then the purée from the blender. Cook 15 minutes, covered. Strain. Place the milk and cream in a bowl. Slowly add the hot soup, beating with a wire whisk. Stir in the sherry and correct the seasoning. Keep warm in a double boiler (direct heat might curdle the soup). Try a light red wine such as Lan with this soup.

CALDO DE PERRO GADITANO
(Cádiz-Style Fish Broth)

FISH broth "Gaditano"—the adjective describing anything or anyone from Cádiz—is easy and quick to prepare and is commonly found simmering in the bars and restaurants frequented by the fishermen of Cádiz and of nearby Puerto de Santa María. Highly unusual is the astringent taste of the juice of the Seville orange (the type of orange used to make marmalade), which gives the soup its captivating flavor. The orange is difficult to find in America, but a mixture of sweet orange juice with lemon or lime juice can produce the proper acidity.

Serves 4

A 1-pound whiting, cleaned and
    sliced into ½-inch-thick rounds
Coarse salt
4 tablespoons olive oil
2 cloves garlic, peeled
1 onion, finely chopped
4 cups fish broth (p. 13; make about
    double the recipe) or
    clam juice

Juice of 1 orange (if Seville orange is
    available, use 1½ oranges
    and eliminate the lime juice)
Juice of 1 lime or lemon

Sprinkle the fish slices with coarse salt. Let them sit 1 hour (this helps to firm the fish). In a deep casserole, heat the oil; add the garlic and cook until it is golden on all sides. Discard the garlic and add the onion to the pot. Sauté until it is wilted. Pour in 2 cups of the fish broth, cover, and simmer 10 minutes. Add the remaining 2 cups of the fish broth and the fish. Cover and cook 15 minutes more.

    Transfer the fish pieces from the broth to a dish. Remove all skin and bones and break the fish into small pieces. Return to the broth. Add the orange and lime juices and serve very hot.

SOPA AL CUARTO DE HORA
(Quick Fish Soup)

A COMMON entry on restaurant menus, this soup derives its name from the fact that cooking time is 15 minutes, or *"un cuarto de hora."* The soup varies greatly from place to place depending on what the cook has on hand at the last minute.

Serves 6

6 medium clams (see p. 11)
4 tablespoons olive oil
2 tablespoons minced onion
⅓ cup diced ham
2 medium tomatoes, skinned and
    finely chopped
⅛ teaspoon paprika
5 cups water
1 cup clam juice or fish stock
¾ pound fresh cod, skin and
    bone removed, cut in
    ¾-inch pieces

½ pound medium shrimp, shelled
    and cut in 3 pieces each
1 cup peas
2 tablespoons raw rice
1 tablespoon minced parsley
Salt
Freshly ground pepper
1 hard-boiled egg, minced

Pour ¾ cup water into a skillet and add the clams. Bring to a boil, then remove the clams as they open. Coarsely chop the clam meat and reserve, along with the cooking liquid.

In a deep casserole, heat the oil. Add the onion and ham, cover, and cook slowly until the onion is tender. Add the tomato, cover, and cook 5 minutes more. Mix in the paprika, then gradually add the rest of the water, clam juice or fish stock, the reserved liquid from the clams, the cod, shrimp, peas, rice, and parsley. Season with salt and pepper. Bring to a boil, cover, and simmer 15 minutes. Add the reserved clam meat and the minced egg and serve.

GAZPACHO ANDALUZ

(Cold Tomato Soup)

ALTHOUGH *gazpacho* originated in the southern lands of Andalucía, it is today one of the most universally loved soups in the world. There is absolutely nothing like it during the hot summer months, although it seems to be just as popular when the weather turns cold.

This *gazpacho* recipe comes from the files of my Spanish mother-in-law, who claims that most *gazpachos* contain too much bread and oil and consequently are unnecessarily heavy and fattening. She has eliminated both of these ingredients entirely, producing a bright red and truly refreshing version of this famous soup, which has often been referred to as a "liquid salad." Even my mother-in-law makes her *gazpacho* today in a blender, although traditionally the *gazpacho* ingredients were painstakingly pushed through a metal cone-shaped sieve with a pestle. Purists still insist that this method produces a superior *gazpacho*.

It is customary to serve the *gazpacho* and then pass small bowls containing croutons, cucumbers, green pepper, tomato, and onion for the diner to sprinkle on his soup as he pleases.

Gazpacho is at its best, of course, when made with juicy red vine-ripened tomatoes. If they are not available, I find it preferable to use good-quality canned tomatoes and skip the awful mushy tomatoes found in markets most of the year. A mixture of canned and fresh tomatoes, even when the fresh tomatoes are not of top quality, also produces good results.

Serves 6

1½ pounds fresh or canned
    ripe tomatoes
1 medium green pepper, cut in pieces
1 small onion, cut in pieces
2 small Kirby cucumbers, or 1 small
    cucumber, peeled and cut
    in pieces
4 tablespoons red wine vinegar
¼ teaspoon tarragon

¼ teaspoon sugar
1 clove garlic, chopped
1 cup tomato juice or ice water (if
    the tomatoes are very
    flavorful, use ice water)
Salt
Diced cucumber, green pepper,
    tomato, and onion
    for garnish

CROUTONS

2 tablespoons butter
1 clove garlic, crushed

6 slices white bread, crusts removed,
    cut in small cubes

To make the soup, place all ingredients except the garnish in the bowl of a processor or blender, in several steps if necessary. Blend until no large pieces remain. Strain, pressing with the back of a wooden spoon to extract as much liquid as possible. Correct the seasoning, adding more salt and vinegar if desired. Chill very well, preferably overnight.

To make the croutons, melt the butter in a heavy skillet. Add the crushed garlic, then stir in the bread cubes, coating them with the butter and garlic. Cook over a very low flame, stirring occasionally, for about 30 minutes, or until the bread cubes are golden and very crunchy. Cool.

Serve the soup and pass the garnishes and the croutons. *Gazpacho* keeps for many days in the refrigerator.

AJO BLANCO CON UVAS
(White Gazpacho with Grapes, Málaga Style)

ALL the world is familiar with cooling *gazpachos* made with tomatoes. However, there are two other types of *gazpacho*—both white, containing no tomato—that I find more interesting than the popular red versions. This white gazpacho has a lovely milky color imparted by the almonds, and the garnish of sweet grapes adds an interesting counterpoint of flavor.

Serves 6

4 ounces blanched almonds
2 cloves garlic, peeled
1½ teaspoons salt
4 slices day-old bread, crusts removed
6 tablespoons olive oil

3 tablespoons red wine vinegar
4 cups ice water
Croutons (see preceding recipe)
Seedless grapes, peeled, about 8
    per portion

Place in the bowl of a processor or blender the almonds, garlic, and salt. Beat until the almonds are very finely ground. Soak the bread in cold water. Squeeze to extract most of the moisture.

With the motor running, gradually add the bread to the almond mixture. Pour in the oil in a thin stream, then add the vinegar, scraping the bowl occasionally with a rubber spatula. Beat in 1 cup of the ice water. Transfer the soup to a large bowl and stir in the remaining 3 cups of ice water. Add more salt and vinegar if desired. Strain, pressing with the back of a wooden spoon to extract as much liquid as possible. Chill. Serve very cold, garnished with the croutons and the grapes (the grapes are not merely decorative; they are essential to the soup's flavor). Serve with a medium-dry white wine such as Viña Esmeralda.

GAZPACHO EXTREMEÑO
(White Gazpacho)

THIS version of white *gazpacho* hails from the arid lands of the *conquistadores*—Extremadura—and is a refreshing change of pace from the traditional *gazpacho* whose main ingredient is tomato.

Serves 6

1 egg
4 slices white bread, crusts removed
7 tablespoons olive oil
2 cloves garlic, peeled and cut
    in halves
1 green pepper, seeded and cut
    in strips
2 small Kirby cucumbers, or
    1 cucumber, peeled and
    cut in chunks

¼ teaspoon sugar
2 tablespoons red wine vinegar
2 tablespoons white tarragon vinegar
Salt
Freshly ground pepper
½ cup ice water
Chopped cucumber and green
    pepper for garnish
Croutons (optional) (p. 131)

VEGETABLE BROTH

2 tablespoons olive oil
1 onion, chopped
3 parsnips, scraped and cut in
    1-inch lengths
3 carrots, scraped and cut in
    1-inch lengths
3 small turnips, scraped and quartered
2 stalks celery, cut in 1-inch lengths

2 sprigs parsley
¼ teaspoon thyme
1 bay leaf
Dash cayenne
Salt
Freshly ground pepper
3 cups water

To make the broth, heat the oil in a large saucepan. Add the onion and sauté until it is wilted. Add the parsnips, carrots, turnips, celery, parsley, thyme, bay leaf, cayenne, salt, and pepper. Stir. Add the water, cover, and simmer 1 hour. Strain and chill well. (There should be 3 cups of broth.)

To make the *gazpacho*, place the egg in the bowl of a processor or blender; beat until light colored. Soak the bread slices in cold water. Squeeze thoroughly to extract most of the moisture. With the motor running, add the oil to the processor in a thin stream, then add the bread, garlic, green pepper, cucumber, sugar, red and white vinegars, salt, and pepper. Blend until no large pieces remain.

Beat in 1 cup of the broth. Strain the mixture into a large bowl, forcing through as much as possible by pressing with the back of a wooden spoon. Stir in the remaining 2 cups of the broth and the ice water. Add more vinegar and salt if desired. Refrigerate several hours or overnight, then serve very cold, garnished with chopped cucumber, green pepper, and croutons.

MEALS-IN-A-POT

CALDO GALLEGO

(Beef, Beans, and Greens Soup,
Galician Style)

EVERY region of Spain has its favorite meal-in-a-pot. This one from Galicia has become famous worldwide, although only in Galicia will one find the delicious new potatoes (*cachelos*), the fresh cut greens (*grelos*), and the excellent beans that go into this soup. Caldo Gallego is often served in cups as a first course or appetizer in taverns and restaurants in Spain. In larger portions, it is a meal in itself.

Serves 6–8

12 cups water
½ pound dried white beans
¼ pound salt pork or slab bacon
¼ pound cured ham, in a
    thick chunk
½ pound beef chuck
1 ham or beef bone
1 small onion, peeled
1 leek or 2 large scallions,
    well-cleaned

Salt
Freshly ground pepper
3 medium new potatoes, peeled
    and quartered
2 turnips, scraped and halved
2 cups coarsely chopped kale, collard
    greens, or Swiss chard,
    thick stems removed

In a large pot, bring to a boil the water, beans, salt pork, ham, beef, ham bone, onion, leek, a little salt, and pepper. Skim off the foam. Cover and simmer over a very low flame about 2 hours, or until the beans are almost tender.

Add the potatoes, turnips, greens, and more salt if necessary. Continue cooking about 30 minutes more, or until the potatoes are done. Serve in large soup bowls. Include pieces of the meats, potato, turnip, beans, leeks, and greens in each portion. A full-bodied red wine such as a Galician Tres Ríos is suitable.

ARROZ CON ACELGAS

(Rice, Bean, and Greens Soup)

A SPECIALTY of Valencia, this soup sometimes includes small snails found in the Valencian marshlands.

Serves 6

½ pound large dried white beans
8 cups water
¾ pound collard greens or Swiss
    chard, thick stems removed
    (weight after trimming),
    coarsely chopped
½ teaspoon paprika

Few strands saffron
1 turnip, scraped and thinly sliced
7 cups chicken broth,
        preferably homemade
Salt
1 cup rice, preferably short grain

Place the beans and water in a large pot, bring to a boil, and simmer, covered, 1 hour. Add the greens, paprika, saffron, turnip, chicken broth, and salt. Cook about 30 minutes more, or until the beans are almost tender. Add the rice, cover, and cook about 20 minutes, until the rice is done. Add more liquid if necessary—the soup should be thick but should also have some broth.

FABADA ASTURIANA

(Asturian Bean Stew)

START PREPARATION ONE DAY IN ADVANCE.

So RENOWNED is Asturias for its delicious *fabada* that, according to Luis Gil Lus, owner of Casa Fermín, the excellent restaurant in Oviedo, much of the region's other fine dishes have gone unnoticed. Mr. Gil Lus relishes the apocryphal story that tells of the conquering Moors in the eighth century, arriving in Asturias and feasting on *fabada* provided by their Christian hosts. By late afternoon, so the story goes, they were so sated that the Christians regained control of Asturias with little resistance.

Beans are universally considered robust fare and are best eaten on a cold winter's eve.

Serves 6–8

2 pounds very large dried
    white beans
¾ pound *morcilla* (blood sausage)
    (see glossary)
¾ pound *chorizo* sausage
1 pound smoked or salted pork
    hocks, cut in several pieces
    (if hocks are salted, soak
    several hours before using)

¾ pound slab bacon, cut in chunks
Salt
2 tablespoons olive oil
2 cloves garlic, crushed
1 tablespoon paprika

The night before, soak the beans in water to cover. Using the same water in which they have soaked, place the beans on the stove, adding the blood sausage, *chorizo*, hocks, and bacon. Bring to a boil, then add ½ cup cold water to cut the boil. Cover and simmer very slowly—the beans will probably take over 2 hours to become tender. Test frequently to avoid overcooking and remove from the flame immediately when they are done. Taste for salt.

In a small saucepan, heat the oil, garlic, and paprika until the garlic begins to sizzle. Add this to the beans, stir gently, cover, and let sit at least 1 hour.

To serve, reheat and transfer to a large, shallow casserole, arranging the meats on the top. Once you have presented the dish to your guests, cut the meats into serving pieces and serve with the beans. Guests should then proceed to cut up the meats so that they mix with the beans. Viña Pomal, a full-bodied red wine, is an appropriate choice.

JUDIONES DE LA GRANJA

(Broad Beans with Sausage and Pig's Foot)

A SPECIALTY of the province of Segovia, where these broad beans, prized for their flavor and texture, are grown. This is a most flavorful and satisfying bean dish.

Serves 4–6

1 pound very large dried lima beans
¼ pound *chorizo*, cut in 1-inch pieces
A ¼-pound piece cured ham, cut in
    1-inch cubes
1 pig's foot, split in half
1 pig's ear (optional)

2 tablespoons olive oil
1 onion, chopped
2 cloves garlic, minced
1 teaspoon paprika
1 pimiento, homemade or
    imported, chopped

| ¼ pound fresh tomatoes, chopped | 2 bay leaves |
| 1 tablespoon chopped parsley | Salt |

Rinse the beans, then place them in water to cover with the *chorizo*, ham, pig's foot, and pig's ear. Bring to a boil. Cover and simmer until the beans are almost tender, about 1½–2 hours. Heat the oil in a skillet and sauté the onion and garlic until the onion is wilted. Stir in the paprika. Add the pimiento, tomato, parsley, and bay leaves. Cook 10 minutes. Add this mixture to the beans, salt to taste, and cook about 30 minutes more. To serve, discard the bone and chop the meat from the pig's foot and pig's ear. Add to the beans. Viña Bosconia, a full-bodied red wine, will stand up to this hearty bean dish.

FABES CON ALMEJAS

(Beans with Clams)

START PREPARATION ONE DAY IN ADVANCE.

THE combination of beans and clams, a specialty of Asturias, sounds unlikely, but you will be surprised to find how beautifully these tastes blend and how very delicious this dish is.

Serves 4–6

1 pound large white dried beans	2 sprigs parsley
2 onions, peeled and cut in halves	2 bay leaves
4 cloves garlic, peeled	Few strands saffron
2 carrots, scraped and cut in halves crosswise	Salt

CLAMS

6 tablespoons olive oil	2 tablespoons minced parsley
2 tablespoons minced onion	½ cup white wine
4 cloves garlic, minced	½ dried red chili pepper, crumbled
2 dozen very small clams, at room temperature (see p. 11)	Salt
1 tablespoon paprika	Freshly ground pepper

Soak the beans overnight. The following day, drain them and cover with cold water. Add the onions, garlic, carrot, parsley sprigs, and bay leaves. Bring to a boil, add 1 cup cold water to cut the boil, then return to a boil, cover, and simmer very slowly 1½–2 hours, or until the beans are tender.

When the beans are almost tender, start preparing the clams. Heat the oil in a skillet and sauté the onion and garlic until the onion is wilted. Add the clams and cook over a medium-high heat, stirring frequently, until they open. Sprinkle in the paprika and parsley. Add the wine, chili pepper, salt (if necessary), and pepper. Cook 5 minutes more.

Stir the saffron and salt into the beans, then add the clams with all the liquid in the pan. Shake the pot to mix in the clams and the liquid. Cover and cook 5 minutes.

Serve the beans in soup bowls with the clams arranged on top. Good crusty bread and a white wine with body, such as Viña Tondonia, should accompany this dish.

COCIDO MADRILEÑO

(Boiled Beef and Chickpea Dinner)

START PREPARATION ONE DAY IN ADVANCE.

IN SPAIN the popularity of *cocido* rivals that of *paella* and *gazpacho*. *Cocido* means "boiled" and is the Spanish equivalent (or precursor, some will say) of a French pot-au-feu. It is thought that the Sephardic Jews introduced *cocido* to Spain many centuries ago, and in its original preparation it admitted no pork products and cooked for a long period of time in heat-retaining containers, allowing the meal to continue cooking on the Sabbath without the aid of human hands. When the Jews were expelled from Spain in 1492, many remained behind as converts, and in order to prove their religious sincerity, they added pork to the pot. Today the dish survives among Jews as "Adafina."

Over the years, *cocido* became a staple meal in central Spain because of its inexpensive and easy-to-obtain ingredients. Wives would bring a lunchtime *cocido* to their husbands laboring in the fields or in the cities, while in well-to-do households the broth from the *cocido* was served to the family and the rest of

the pot went to feed the servants. *Cocido* is no longer the inexpensive dish it once was, and for this reason, it has become a "special occasion" meal, dear to the heart of every Spaniard.

Although this recipe comes from Madrid, every region of Spain has its own version, adapted to locally available produce. The Catalán "Escudella" uses *butifarra* sausage (p. 55) instead of *chorizo*. "Pote Gallego" from Galicia eliminates the *pelotas*, quenelle-like meatballs, and adds the locally popular *lacón*, salted pork hocks. Andalucian *cocidos* naturally utilize the many vegetables grown in the south of Spain.

An ancestor of *cocido*, "Olla Podrida" (literally "rotten pot"), is still found in some villages of Castilla and was immortalized in an amusing episode in *Don Quijote de la Mancha*. In the latter part of this classic, Don Quijote's squire, Sancho Panza, is appointed governor of an island and is treated as royalty, a situation that ill suits this clever and down-to-earth villager. In one scene he is ravenously hungry and sits down to a feast. Sumptuous dishes are brought before him—such robust fare as roast partridge and veal and stewed rabbit—only to be whisked away by his personal physician as "dangerous to his health." Sancho can no longer contain himself and suggests that perhaps an "Olla Podrida" would be an appropriate meal:

"By the diversity of ingredients to be found in this dish, surely I can find some that I will enjoy and that will be to my benefit," he hopefully remarks to his doctor.

"Quite the contrary," responds his doctor. "Olla Podrida is the worst thing you could eat. It's all right for priests, school masters and peasant weddings, but not for you who should eat only first class ingredients. Simple things are always better than mixtures."

Sancho, beside himself with hunger, summarily dismisses his doctor, threatening to break a chair over his head if he does not leave immediately, and then orders that some food be brought to him forthwith.

Centuries ago, I am sure "Olla Podrida" and *cocido* were clever disguises for low-quality ingredients, but today such mixed pots are a delight to eat, especially when excellent products have been used. *Cocido* is not difficult to make, but needs some organization to assemble and serve. Start the day before by soaking the chickpeas and cooking the meats. The following day, complete the operation and serve in two stages: first the soup, which is the cooking liquid with the addition of fine noodles, then the meats and vegetables, attractively arranged on one or two platters.

Serves 6–8

1 pound chickpeas	Salt
2 chicken thighs	Freshly ground pepper
2½ pounds beef chuck	1 onion, peeled and halved
¼ pound slab bacon, in 1 piece	1 leek or 2 large scallions,
½ pound *chorizo* sausage	well cleaned
¼ pound *morcilla* (blood sausage)	2 cloves garlic, peeled
(optional) (see glossary)	2 large carrots, scraped
¼ pound cured ham, in a thick piece	4 medium new potatoes, peeled
2 ham or beef bones	4 ounces very fine noodles (optional)
18 cups cold water	

PELOTAS (*Meatballs*)

1 cup shredded beef chuck (from	2 tablespoons soup broth (from
the pot)	the pot)
½ cup chopped bacon (from the pot)	Salt
2 eggs	Freshly ground pepper
1 clove garlic, minced	Bread crumbs
1 tablespoon minced parsley	1 tablespoon olive oil

REPOLLO (*Sautéed Cabbage*)

2 tablespoons olive oil	½ head cabbage, coarsely chopped
2 tablespoons chopped onion	Salt
1 clove garlic, minced	Freshly ground pepper

The day before, soak the chickpeas in salted water. Place the chicken, beef, bacon, *chorizo, morcilla,* ham, and the bones in a large soup pot with the 18 cups of water. Add salt and pepper and bring to a boil. Skim off any foam. Cover and simmer 1½ hours. Cool, then refrigerate. Remove the fat that solidifies on the top of the pot.

The following day, drain the chickpeas and add them to the meats, preferably enclosed in a net bag or cheesecloth for easy removal. Add the onion, leek, garlic, carrots, and potatoes. Adjust the seasoning, cover, and simmer 1 hour.

To make the meatballs, place the beef, bacon, and eggs in the bowl of a processor or blender. Beat until smooth. Transfer to another bowl and add the garlic, parsley, broth, salt, pepper, and enough bread crumbs so that the mixture can be handled. Form into sausage shapes, at least 2 inches long and 1 inch wide. Heat the oil in a skillet and fry the meatballs until they are golden. Add them to the soup pot and continue cooking the *cocido,* covered, about 2½ hours more, or until the chickpeas are tender and the soup slightly thickened.

To make the cabbage, heat the oil in a skillet. Sauté the onion and garlic until the onion is wilted. Add the cabbage, salt, and pepper and continue cooking over a medium flame until the cabbage is tender.

If noodles are desired for the soup, boil them in salted water until tender. Drain.

To serve the *cocido*, strain the broth, leaving some liquid to cover the meats. Mix the broth with the noodles—this will be the soup, which is served first.

Arrange the meats and vegetables on one or two platters, cutting the *chorizo* and *morcilla* into thick slices; the leek, carrots, potatoes, beef, ham, bacon, and chicken into serving portions; and leaving the *pelotas* whole. Place the cabbage on one of the platters. Serve with a hearty red wine from the Valdepeñas area of central Castilla.

CALLOS A LA GALLEGA

(Tripe and Chickpeas, Galician Style)

START PREPARATION ONE DAY IN ADVANCE.

THE flavors of tripe and chickpeas are a perfect match in this hearty one-dish meal from Galicia. It will have to simmer most of the day on the stove.

Serves 4

½ pound chickpeas
1 pound beef tripe, preferably both smooth and honeycombed
1 pig's foot, split in half
1 meaty ham or beef bone
4 cups water
5 peppercorns
Salt
2 bay leaves
5 cloves garlic, unpeeled

1 onion, peeled
2 tablespoons olive oil
2 cloves garlic, peeled
1 tablespoon minced parsley
½ cup white wine
1 onion, finely chopped
1 *chorizo* (2 ounces), chopped
1 tablespoon flour
1 tablespoon paprika
½ –1 teaspoon freshly ground cumin

Soak the chickpeas overnight. Drain and reserve.

Rinse the tripe well. Place in a pot and cover with water. Bring to a boil, then drain immediately. Cut the tripe into 1½-inch squares and return to the pot. Add the pig's foot, the bone, water, peppercorns, salt, and 1 of the bay leaves. Bring to a boil, cover, and simmer slowly about 4 hours.

When the tripe has been cooking for 2 hours, start the chickpeas. Place them in a large pot with water to cover. Add the unpeeled garlic cloves, the other bay leaf, the whole onion, and salt. Bring to a boil. Cover and simmer until the chickpeas are just tender, about 1½–2 hours. Discard the garlic and onion. Drain the chickpeas.

In a small skillet, heat the oil. Fry the 2 peeled garlic cloves until they start to brown. Transfer them to a processor and leave the remaining oil in the skillet. Add the parsley to the processor and blend until the garlic and parsley are finely chopped. Gradually pour in the wine and beat until smooth.

In the skillet, sauté the chopped onion until it is wilted. Add the *chorizo* and cook slowly about 3 minutes. Stir in the flour, cook a minute, add the paprika, and turn off the flame.

Combine the tripe and the drained chickpeas. Add the mixture from the processor plus the *chorizo*-and-onion mixture. Correct the seasoning. Cover and cook about 2–3 hours more, or until the tripe is very tender. Serve with good crusty bread and a full-bodied red wine such as Campo Viejo or a Galician Tres Rios.

SOPA DE GARBANZOS Y CHORIZO

(Chickpea and Chorizo Soup)

START PREPARATION ONE DAY IN ADVANCE.

IF TIME doesn't permit the preparation of a *cocido*, this soup is a delicious alternative, but by no means a substitute.

Serves 4

¾ pound chickpeas	Salt
3 cloves garlic, peeled	Freshly ground pepper
½ onion, peeled	6 *chorizo* sausages (about ¾ pound)
2 sprigs parsley	¼ pound slab bacon, in 1 piece
1 bay leaf	

Soak the chickpeas overnight in water to cover. Drain, cover with cold water, and add all the other ingredients. Bring to a boil, cover, and simmer until the chickpeas are tender, about 2 hours. Skim off the fat, cut the *chorizo* in thick slices, and cut the bacon into 4 pieces. Serve in bowls with the chickpeas, sausage slices, and a piece of bacon each. Parboiled potatoes may be added for the last 30 minutes of cooking. Serve with a hearty red wine, such as Zapardiel from Valdepeñas.

POTAJE DE ESPINACAS Y GARBANZOS

(Spinach and Chickpea Soup)

START PREPARATION ONE DAY IN ADVANCE.

THIS is often prepared as a Lenten dish, sometimes with the addition of salt cod. It is easy to assemble and a wonderful meatless meal, if the ham is omitted.

Serves 6

1 pound chickpeas
½ head garlic, unpeeled, in 1 piece
1 bay leaf
1 whole onion, peeled
Salt
1 pound spinach
2 tablespoons olive oil

2 slices French-style bread, ¼ inch thick
1 clove garlic, peeled
Few strands saffron
4 tablespoons diced cured ham
2 tablespoons minced parsley

Soak the chickpeas overnight in water to cover. Drain and place in a pot with water to cover. Add the ½ head garlic, bay leaf, the whole onion, and salt. Bring to a boil, cover, and simmer until the chickpeas are tender, about 1½–2 hours. Discard the garlic and onion.

Wash the spinach well, remove the stems, and coarsely chop the leaves. Do not dry. Place the still-wet spinach in a pot, add salt, and cover and cook slowly until tender, about 5 minutes or less.

In a skillet, heat the oil and fry the bread and garlic clove until both are golden. Transfer them to a processor or blender, leaving the remaining oil in the skillet. Blend the garlic and bread in the processor with the saffron. Gradually pour in about 1 cup of the cooking liquid from the chickpeas and blend until smooth. Add this mixture to the chickpeas and salt to taste. Stir.

Reheat the reserved oil in the skillet, add the spinach, ham, and parsley and sauté lightly for a minute. Add this mixture to the chickpeas, stirring so that the spinach separates and mixes in well. Cover and cook 10 minutes more. Serve in soup bowls—there should be some liquid, but the *potaje* should not be thin. Potatoes may be boiled with the chickpeas for the last 30–40 minutes of cooking. A white or light red wine may accompany this dish, according to your preference.

NOTE: To make the soup with salt cod, eliminate the ham and use ½ pound salt cod, which has been soaked 36 hours (changing the water occasionally) to remove the salt. Add the cod, cut in serving pieces or chunks, to the chickpeas during the last half hour that the chickpeas cook by themselves. Cook the spinach and continue cooking the soup as indicated.

SOPA DE LENTEJAS

(Lentil Soup, Spanish Style)

LENTILS have been a staple of Western man's diet for millenniums. Literary references to lentils appear at least as far back as the Bible, in which the tale is told of Esau, who sold his birthright to his twin brother Jacob—all for a bowl of lentil soup. In Spain today, lentil soup is still common fare in most households, not only for its nutritional value, but because it makes a delicious and satisfying cold-weather meal.

Serves 6

1 pound lentils
2 bay leaves
2 sprigs parsley
¼ pound salt pork or slab bacon, cut in chunks
3 tablespoons olive oil
3 medium onions, chopped
2 carrots, scraped and finely chopped
4 cloves garlic, chopped

2 teaspoons paprika
Salt
Freshly ground pepper
½ pound *morcilla* (blood sausage) (optional) (see glossary)
3 tablespoons red wine vinegar
2 all-purpose potatoes, peeled and quartered (optional)

Wash the lentils. Place them in a large pot and cover with water. Add the bay leaves, parsley sprigs, and salt pork. Bring to a boil, cover, and simmer 45 minutes.

Meanwhile, in a skillet heat the oil. Sauté the onion, carrot, and garlic until the onion is wilted. Turn off the heat.

Stir in the paprika. Add this mixture to the lentils, then add the salt, pepper, *morcilla* (pinched with a fork), vinegar, and potatoes. Cover and cook 45 minutes more, or until the lentils and potatoes are done. Serve with a good crusty bread and a full-bodied red wine—Sangre de Toro would be a good choice. Crunchy Piparrana Jaenera (p. 115) is a nice contrast of texture and taste.

CALDERETA DE CODORNICES
(Potted Quail)

QUITE by chance—there was no other place to eat for miles around—my husband, daughter, and I stopped at an unprepossessing restaurant, El Galán, in the town of Santa María at the cross of the Huesca and Pamplona roads in northern Spain. The dining room was filled with locals, rapturously viewing a TV screen. The *"plato del día"* was Potted Quail, a simple but delicious dish of quail and onions in broth. Consumed by giggles, the waitresses, all daughters of the cook, took us to meet their mother in the kitchen; she, in turn, was astounded that visitors from New York were praising her cooking and requesting her recipe. "Nothing to it," she stated flatly. "Anyone can make it."

Serves 4

2 tablespoons olive oil
3 medium onions, coarsely chopped
3 cloves garlic, peeled
8 quail
2 tablespoons red wine vinegar
1 bay leaf

3 sprigs parsley
6 peppercorns
4 cups water
3 cups chicken broth
Salt
Fine noodles (optional)

Heat the oil in a soup pot. Add the onion and garlic and sauté until the onion is wilted. Add all the remaining ingredients except the noodles. Cover and simmer slowly 1½ hours. Ladle off most of the broth and strain, leaving the onions in the pot with the quail. Serve the broth first, with fine noodles if desired. Then serve the quail and onions as the main course. A light red wine, perhaps an elegant Claret Fino Reserva, would be a nice accompaniment.

LACÓN CON GRELOS

(Boiled Dinner with Greens)

LACÓN CON GRELOS, along with *caldo gallego*, are the two most typical dishes from the region of Galicia. Although the recipe sounds almost too simple, this dish is an extremely tasty and satisfying winter meal.

Serves 4

1½ pounds *lacón* (smoked or salted pork hocks—if salted, soak several hours in cold water before using)
Salt
Freshly ground pepper

1 pound collard greens or Swiss chard, thick stems removed
4 *chorizo* sausages (about ½ pound)
4 new potatoes, peeled and halved or whole, depending on size

Place the *lacón* in a deep casserole with water to cover and salt and pepper to taste. Bring to a boil, reduce heat, and simmer 1 hour. Add the greens and *chorizo* and cook 1 hour more. Add the potatoes and continue cooking until the potatoes are tender. This dish is usually served without the liquid—only a little bit poured over to moisten the meat and vegetables. However, the broth is very flavorful, so you might wish to serve it first, perhaps with noodles, as a soup. Otherwise, save the liquid for some future use. If available, Tres Ríos red wine from Galicia would be an authentic regional accompaniment.

SOPA DE ALBÓNDIGA

(Meatball Soup)

*Makes 6 first-course
or 4 supper portions*

¼ pound veal, cut in pieces
¼ pound uncooked, boned, and skinned chicken breast
A ¼-pound piece cured ham
4 tablespoons bread crumbs
1 tablespoon minced parsley
1 clove garlic, minced
¼ teaspoon pepper

Few strands saffron, crushed
Salt
½ teaspoon lemon juice
1 egg, lightly beaten
1 tablespoon olive oil
6 cups chicken broth, preferably homemade
½ onion, peeled

Grind together the veal, chicken, and half of the ham in a meat grinder or food processor (or have the butcher do it). Combine these meats with the bread crumbs, parsley, garlic, pepper, saffron, salt, lemon juice, and egg. Form into bite-size (about ½-inch) meatballs. Heat the oil in a skillet and lightly sauté the meatballs.

Heat the chicken broth with the onion and remaining ham (in 1 piece). Add the meatballs, cover, and simmer 1 hour. Remove the ham from the soup and finely chop. Return it to the pot, stir, and serve. The soup may be accompanied by a light red wine such as Diamante.

CALDERETA DE LANGOSTA MENORQUINA

(Lobster Stew, Menorca Style)

THIS two-part dish of soup and lobster is not overly appropriate for a formal dinner—guests must dig in and shell lobster pieces that have been cooked in tomato. However, it is great fun to eat and produces an extraordinarily tender and tasty lobster. The recipe was provided by our good friend, Dr. Sanz Tobes, who had dined on this dish many times at the Casa Burdó Restaurant in the village of Fornells on the island of Menorca.

Menorcan lobster stew is oddly similar to the mysterious "Lobster à l'americaine" or "Lobster à l'armoricaine," a dish over which experts have quibbled for years in their effort to determine its origins. I can only add to the confusion with yet another theory, i.e., that the dish originated here on the isle of Menorca and should be called "Lobster a la menorquina."

Serves 4

4 live lobsters, about 1 pound each
1 cup olive oil
5 cloves garlic, peeled
4 medium onions,
    coarsely chopped
2 pounds tomatoes, skinned
    and seeded
3 green peppers, coarsely chopped

2 tablespoons chopped parsley
6 cups fish broth (p. 13; make about
    triple the recipe), clam
    juice, or water
Salt
8 slices French-style bread, ⅛ inch
    thick, lightly toasted (optional)

Holding the lobster firmly by the head with a towel, sever the spinal cord with a knife at the place where the tail joins the body. (Have your fish man do this, if you prefer.) Cut up the lobster with scissors or a knife, separating the tail into pieces at the rings, and cutting off the large and small claws. Reserve. Slice the head down the middle, discard the stomach sack, and scoop out the tomalley (green matter) and the coral, if any. Reserve. Partially crush the large claws for easy removal of the meat when serving.

Heat the oil in a large, shallow casserole, preferably earthenware, with 1 clove of the garlic until the oil is very hot. Discard the garlic clove. Add the lobster pieces a few at a time and fry them only a few seconds, turning them once. Remove to a warm platter. Repeat until all the pieces are done. Pour off all but 4 tablespoons of the oil.

Place in a processor or blender the onion, tomato, green pepper, parsley, and the 4 remaining garlic cloves. Blend well, in several stages if necessary. Add this mixture to the casserole, pour in the fish stock, and cook over a low flame, about 15 minutes. Add more liquid if the soup thickens too much—it is, however, a thick soup. Salt to taste. In the processor blend the reserved tomalley and the coral, if any, until smooth. Add it to the casserole and continue cooking 15 minutes more. (Everything may be made in advance up to this point.)

When ready to serve, add the lobster pieces to the soup and cook over a low flame 10 minutes. To serve, bring the casserole to the table. Place 2 slices of the toasted French bread (this may be omitted) in each soup dish and pour in the soup. Let guests serve themselves the lobster, either in the soup or after the soup. A dry, full-bodied white wine is best with this dish—try Campo Viejo.

MARMITAKO

(Bonito and Tomato Soup, Basque Style)

MARMITAKO, from the French word for "metal soup kettle," is one of the most popular items of Basque cuisine and is found on just about every menu in the region. It is said that the best *marmitakos* are those prepared on board the local fishing boats with freshly caught bonito. Some *marmitako* lovers would never dream of using tomato or green pepper in their soup, and others will invariably add pimiento. As is usually the case in Spanish cooking, there are as many recipes as cooks, and each will insist that his version is the only correct one.

Serves 4

1 medium onion, finely chopped	½ teaspoon brandy, preferably
5 tablespoons olive oil	Spanish brandy, or Cognac
2 medium tomatoes, skinned, seeded, and diced	½ dried red chili pepper, seeds removed, crushed
1 tablespoon minced parsley	Salt

Freshly ground pepper
3 cloves garlic, minced
2 medium red waxy potatoes, peeled
   and cubed

1 green pepper, minced
1½ pounds fresh tuna (bonito) or
   mackerel steaks

Sauté 1 tablespoon of the onion in 1 tablespoon of the oil until the onion is wilted. Add the tomatoes, parsley, brandy, chili pepper, salt, and pepper. Cover and cook 20 minutes. Purée this mixture in a blender or processor, then thin with water to the consistency of tomato soup. Reserve.

While the tomato mixture is cooking, in a large, shallow casserole heat the remaining 4 tablespoons of olive oil and sauté the remaining onion and the garlic over very low heat, covered, until the onion is tender, about 10 minutes. Stir in the potatoes and green pepper and cook 5 minutes more. Cover the potatoes with boiling water (about 1½ cups), add salt and pepper. Return to a boil, then add the fish, arranging it in 1 or 2 layers over the potatoes. When the fish turns white on both sides (about 5 minutes), remove to a warm platter while continuing to cook the potatoes until they are tender, another 15 minutes or so.

Cut the fish into chunks, removing any skin or bone. Season with salt. Arrange the fish over the cooked potatoes, then pour on the reserved tomato sauce. Stir gently and simmer 5 minutes more. Cover and let sit 5 minutes and serve, if possible, in the cooking dish. Eat with good crunchy bread and a fruity white wine such as Diamante.

PURRUSALDA

(Codfish Soup)

START PREPARATION AT LEAST ONE DAY IN ADVANCE.

A FAVORITE in the northern Basque provinces, where dried salt cod is enormously popular, even though fresh seafood is available in abundance.

Serves 8

1 pound boned and skinned dried
   salt codfish
2 tablespoons olive oil
3 cloves garlic, peeled
½ pound cleaned leeks (white and
   green part), chopped

1 pound all-purpose potatoes, peeled
   and cubed
10 cups water
Salt
2 tablespoons chopped parsley
Freshly ground pepper

Soak the codfish in cold water for 36 hours, changing the water occasionally. Drain and shred.

Heat the oil in a soup pot. Mince 1 of the garlic cloves and sauté it lightly in the oil. Stir in the leeks, shredded cod, and potatoes. Cook 5 minutes. Add the water and salt, bring to a boil, then reduce the heat. In a processor or blender place the other 2 cloves of garlic, the parsley, and the pepper. Blend to form a paste. Add ½ cup of the cooking liquid, beat, and return the mixture to the pot. Simmer about 1¼ hours. Viña Paceta, a full-bodied white wine, goes well with this soup.

SUQUET

(Catalán Fish Stew)

TOASTED almonds give an unusual and very compatible nutty flavor to this fish stew. It is one of my favorites.

Serves 4

1½ cups fish broth (p. 13) or clam juice	Salt
8 large clams (see p. 11)	¾ teaspoon paprika
1 dozen medium mussels (see p. 11)	1½ tablespoons flour
1 slice lemon	2½ pounds fish steaks, preferably of
5 tablespoons olive oil	2 different types—choose
6 cloves garlic, peeled	from halibut, striped
4 slices French-style bread, ¼ inch thick	bass, tile fish, or fresh cod—cut in 1½-inch pieces,
12 blanched almonds, lightly toasted	bone and skin removed
2 tablespoons minced parsley	6 tablespoons dry white wine
Few strands saffron	2 tablespoons peas
	Freshly ground pepper

Prepare the fish broth as directed, increasing the water to 1½ cups. Meanwhile, place the clams and mussels in a skillet with ¾ cup water and the lemon slice. Bring to a boil and remove the clams and mussels as they open. Take the clam and mussel meat from the shells and cut the meat in halves. Reserve. Strain the cooking liquid and add to the fish broth.

Place the oil and garlic in a shallow casserole, preferably Spanish earthenware. Heat over a medium flame until the garlic is golden on all sides. Transfer the garlic to a processor or blender. Fry the bread slices in the same oil until golden on both sides and transfer the bread to the processor. Add to the processor the almonds, parsley, saffron, and salt. Grind until a paste forms. Add the paprika, flour, and ¼ cup of the fish broth and beat until smooth.

Gradually pour in the remaining fish broth. Return this mixture to the casserole. Bring to a boil. Add the fish pieces, wine, peas, salt, and pepper. Cover and simmer about 12 minutes. Stir in the clam and mussel pieces. Serve in soup bowls, and accompany with a Catalán white wine such as René Barbier.

GAZPACHUELO
(Vinegared Fish Soup)

DERIVED from the word "*gazpacho*," this soup actually has little connection with the famed cold tomato soup except for the addition of vinegar. Use any firm white fish that will not crumble in cooking. Halibut is ideal, but tile fish and fresh cod are also very good.

Serves 4

1 pound fish steak, such as halibut
4 cups cold water
2 tablespoons dry white wine
½ cup clam juice or fish stock
1 bay leaf
½ small onion
Salt

Freshly ground pepper
1 pound red waxy potatoes, peeled
    and cut in ¼-inch slices
1½ cups mayonnaise, preferably
    homemade (p. 104)
2 tablespoons red wine vinegar

Place the fish in a pot with the water, wine, clam juice, bay leaf, onion, salt, and pepper. Bring to a boil, then simmer 2 minutes. Remove from the heat, cover, and let sit until cool.

Take out the fish and remove any skin and bone. Cut into chunks. Place in a shallow bowl and pour on enough of the cooking liquid to cover the fish. Add the potato slices to the cooking liquid remaining in the pot, cover, and cook until the potatoes are barely tender. Remove the potatoes and keep them warm. Strain the liquid.

Place the mayonnaise in a warm soup tureen. Mix in the vinegar. With a wire whisk slowly beat in the hot broth. Add the potatoes and the fish, stir gently and serve. If the soup needs reheating, do so in a double boiler, or the soup could curdle.

Chapter 6

HUEVOS Y TORTILLAS

(Eggs and Egg Dishes)

IF A Spaniard were exiled to a far-off island and allowed only one food, I have little doubt that he would choose eggs. Nothing is more basic to Spanish cuisine than eggs, and it is hard to imagine a Spanish meal that does not include eggs in several guises. Not only are they used in their more or less international modes—for desserts, omelets, and as a coating for frying—but here they take many interesting and unusual forms as well. Whole eggs are cooked in garlic soup; they are baked into bread; a covering of beaten egg forms a crust on a well-known *paella* variation; minced hard-boiled egg or egg wedges garnish a variety of meat, fish, and vegetable dishes; raw egg is a part of cold white *gazpacho;* and egg yolks combined with sugar make the popular *yema* candies.

As all-purpose as the egg is in Spanish cooking, there is no doubt that Spain's real love affair is with the Tortilla Española—potato omelet—and with fried eggs. Both dishes are eaten at any time of the day or night and transcend any conventional meal categories—Spaniards will eat them as first courses or main courses, as light suppers or snacks. Although not usually a breakfast food (the continental breakfast is standard fare), eggs will be favored on particularly hungry mornings. Fried eggs and *tortilla* may be ordered in the most elegant of restaurants as well as in the most run-down establishments, and they will invariably be delicious and wholly satisfying. A picnic would be unheard of without a *tortilla*, and a *tapas* bar will always have appetizing wedges of *tortilla* on display.

Along with the ever-present fried eggs and potato omelet, Huevos a la Flamenca—baked with vegetables and *chorizo*—have acquired national appeal and commonly appear on restaurant menus. Scrambled eggs evoke little interest, except in the Basque country, and the remaining entries are usually omelet varieties, which are generally flat, not folded. Perhaps the most delicious omelet I have ever eaten is *Tortilla de Angulas*, an omelet of tiny eels (read about these eels, p. 222), which has a flavor so delicate that it is difficult to put into words. Although rarely appearing on a menu, any restaurant serving *angulas* will be glad to prepare a *Tortilla de Angulas.*

Eggs in Spain are rarely meant as dainty dishes for those on diets or with delicate stomachs. Almost all the recipes included here are hearty and robust, and unless eaten in small portions, they are not appropriate as first courses (although Spaniards, accustomed to large meals, would eat them as such). However, they adapt beautifully to brunches and suppers, and I recommend that they be used for these types of meals.

HUEVOS FRITOS A LA ESPAÑOLA

(Fried Eggs, Spanish Style)

A FRIED egg, in a Spaniard's opinion, does not deserve its name unless it is truly fried—in sizzling olive oil. Butter will not do, for it produces a flat and rubbery egg a Spaniard hardly finds edible. Spanish-style fried eggs are cracked into very hot oil and emerge light and crunchy—*"vestidos de torero,"* dressed like a bullfighter, as Spaniards like to describe the golden edges of the fried eggs. I have come to prefer eggs prepared in this manner, especially when they are to be served for lunch or dinner. Accompanied by *chorizo* sausage, fried potatoes, *migas* (see following recipe), a good country bread, and a strong red wine, there is nothing quite so satisfying when you have spent a long day outdoors and are ravenously hungry. This is my husband's very favorite meal, which he invariably requests when asked for dinner suggestions.

Eggs, any number desired   Coarse salt
Olive oil, or a mixture of olive and
    salad oils

In a skillet heat the oil, at least ½ inch deep, until it reaches the smoking point. Break no more than 2 eggs at a time into the oil and, working quickly with a large spoon, fold the edges of the egg whites, which will have spread, up over the yolks, forming a circle. Spoon the hot oil over the eggs until they begin to be crunchy around the edges and the yolks have set. This whole process will take only about a minute. Remove the eggs with a slotted pancake turner and rest the pancake turner on paper towels to drain the eggs lightly. Repeat for as many eggs as desired. Sprinkle with coarse salt and serve immediately, accompanied by a strong red wine from the Valdepeñas or Valencia region (see wine chart).

MIGAS

(Fried Bread)

START PREPARATION SEVERAL HOURS IN ADVANCE.

Migas, the word for crumbs or small bread pieces, are extremely popular in Spain, primarily as an accompaniment to fried eggs. The combination is of rustic origin and is particularly common in the villages of Castilla, where the coarse country bread is ideal for preparing *migas*. *Migas* may consist of bread only, but are much tastier when bacon and ham are added, as in this recipe. When the flavor and texture of the bread pieces blend with the fried eggs, a Spaniard will tell you it is the grandest dish in the world, non plus ultra.

Serves 4

1 loaf bread, not airy and at least 1 day old (either of the white breads, pp. 325–326, are perfect)	Salt Freshly ground pepper ¼ teaspoon ground cumin ½ teaspoon paprika
2 tablespoons finely diced slab bacon	2 tablespoons minced onion
3 tablespoons olive oil	2 tablespoons minced cured ham
2 cloves garlic, peeled	

Remove the crusts from the bread and rip the bread into crouton-size pieces by hand (or cut into cubes with a knife, if you prefer). Dampen the bread pieces by wetting your hands and shaking them over the bread. Repeat several times. Wrap the bread in a towel or foil and let sit several hours or overnight.

In a skillet, heat the bacon slowly until it gives off its oil. Remove and reserve the bacon pieces. Add 2 tablespoons of the olive oil to the bacon fat in the skillet, add 1 clove of the garlic, and cook until the garlic is well browned. Discard the garlic. Add the bread pieces to the pan and stir to coat with the oil.

Sprinkle with salt, pepper, cumin, and paprika. Cook very slowly, stirring occasionally, about 30 minutes. The bread should be crisp but not brown.

Meanwhile, in a separate skillet, heat the remaining tablespoon of oil and sauté the onion and the remaining clove of garlic, minced, until the onion is wilted. Stir in the ham and the reserved bacon and cook a minute. Add this mixture to the bread pieces. At this point, if you wish your bread a little less crisp, you may sprinkle in another tablespoon of oil or a little water. Serve with Spanish-style fried eggs.

HUEVOS FRITOS AL AJILLO

(Fried Eggs with Garlic and Paprika)

Serves 2

Oil for frying
4 eggs
2 tablespoons olive oil
2 pimientos, homemade or imported,
    cut in strips

2 cloves garlic, sliced
1 teaspoon vinegar
½ teaspoon paprika
Coarse salt

Heat the oil, at least ½ inch deep, to the smoking point and fry the eggs, following the directions for preparing Huevos Fritos a la Española (p. 153). Place the eggs on a warm platter or on individual dishes. Pour off all the frying oil from the skillet and add the 2 tablespoons of fresh olive oil. Lightly sauté the pimientos and arrange them around the eggs. Add the garlic to the pan and when it starts to turn golden, turn off the flame. Cool 2 minutes. Add the vinegar and paprika and cook 2 minutes more, adding a little water if the pan dries out. Sprinkle the eggs and pimientos with salt. Pour the garlic sauce over them and serve immediately with a good loaf of bread.

HUEVOS AL NIDO

(Eggs in a Nest)

MY SPANISH mother-in-law, one of the most inventive cooks in Spain, introduced me to these most unusual "puffed" eggs. They begin with hollowed-out rolls filled with tomato sauce and egg yolk and are capped with beaten egg whites that puff in cooking. By themselves, Huevos al Nido make an elegant first course. With a salad, they make a meal.

Serves 6

2 tablespoons olive oil
1 small onion, finely chopped
½ cup diced bacon
6 tablespoons tomato paste
¾ cup water
Salt

Freshly ground pepper
6 large rolls (hard rolls, challah rolls, etc., but not hamburger rolls—they are too soft)
6 eggs
Salad oil for frying

Heat the olive oil in a saucepan and sauté the onion until it is wilted. Add the bacon and cook until the bacon is transparent. Stir in the tomato paste, water, salt, and pepper. Simmer, uncovered, for 20 minutes, adding more water if necessary (the sauce should have the consistency of a thick spaghetti sauce). Cool.

Meanwhile, cut out a plug, about 1½ inches in diameter, from the center of each roll. Through that opening, hollow out the rolls with a small spoon (espresso size is best) until only a ¼-inch thickness of bread remains on the bottom and ½ inch on the sides of the rolls. Be careful not to pierce the rolls. Spoon 3 tablespoons of sauce into each of the hollowed rolls. Separate the eggs, placing the whites in a bowl for beating and slipping 1 yolk into each of the rolls. The yolks should remain intact, but if they break, no dire consequences will result. Beat the egg whites until stiff but not dry. Using a large spoon, cover each roll with egg white, forming a smooth dome about 2 inches high in the center. There may be some egg white left over, depending on the size of the eggs.

Heat the salad oil in a medium skillet to the depth of about ½ inch. When it reaches the smoking point, reduce the heat slightly. Place 1 of the rolls on a slotted pancake turner. Hold it over—not in—the hot oil. With a large spoon, pour oil over the top of the roll, letting the excess oil run down into the pan. Continue doing this until the whites are puffed and golden and the roll is crisp (it will take only a minute or two). Slip the roll onto a paper towel to drain, then place on a warm platter. Repeat this process for each roll. Serve immediately, for the egg whites deflate quite rapidly. Try a slightly sweet white wine like Viña Esmeralda with this.

HUEVOS A LA FLAMENCA

(Baked Eggs with Ham, Sausage, and Asparagus)

THIS dish originated in the gypsy lands of Andalucía and has all the color and gaiety of that most vivacious area of Spain. More specifically, Huevos a la

Flamenca is said to have been created in Sevilla, an elegant city of cool patios, wide boulevards, orange trees, and festive horse-drawn buggies. El Burladero in Sevilla is a fine place to taste these eggs, not only because they are very well prepared there, but because the quiet sophistication and taurine ambience of the restaurant perfectly capture the mood of the city. Bullfight mementos are everywhere—a wooden bullring barricade, or *burladero*, discreetly separates the kitchen from the dining room. Paintings and tiles of bullfighting themes decorate the walls, and numerous autographed bullfight photographs are the pride of the restaurant. It is not at all unusual to find a famous bullfighting figure dining or drinking at El Burladero.

Huevos a la Flamenca are excellent as a light supper or first course and are thoroughly appealing for brunch.

Serves 4

2 tablespoons olive oil
1 medium onion, finely chopped
1 clove garlic, minced
6 fresh or canned plum
    tomatoes, chopped
½ cup chicken broth
¼ teaspoon paprika
Salt
Freshly ground pepper

A ¼-pound piece cured ham, cubed
¼ pound *chorizo* sausage, in
    ¼-inch slices
8 eggs
12 cooked asparagus spears
6 tablespoons cooked peas
2 pimientos, homemade or imported,
    cut in strips
2 tablespoons chopped parsley

To make the tomato sauce, heat the oil in a skillet and sauté the onion and garlic until the onion is wilted. Add the chopped tomato, broth, paprika, salt, and pepper. Cover and cook 10 minutes.

Meanwhile, in another skillet, slowly sauté the ham and *chorizo* about 5 minutes.

Pour the tomato sauce into 4 individual ovenproof ramekins, preferably Spanish earthenware. Break 2 eggs into each dish. Arrange the ham-and-*chorizo* mixture, asparagus and peas, and pimiento attractively around the eggs. Sprinkle the eggs with salt and pepper and sprinkle the entire dish with parsley. Place the ramekins in a 450° F oven and cook until the egg whites are set, but the yolks are still soft, about 5–6 minutes. Serve in the same dish. A light red wine—Preferido, for example—is appropriate.

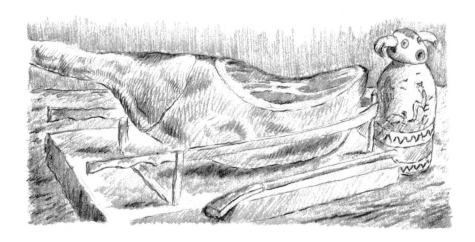

HUEVOS A LA MADRILEÑA

(Baked Eggs with
Sliced Tomato and Sausage)

THESE tasty eggs are good as a first course or for lunch.

Serves 1

1 medium tomato, in ¼-inch slices
Salt
Freshly ground pepper
1 large clove garlic, crushed
1 tablespoon minced parsley
1 tablespoon olive oil
4 slices (¼ inch) rice-filled *morcilla*
    (blood sausage) (see glossary)

    or any breakfast or sweet
    Italian sausage
1 or 2 eggs
1 tablespoon grated Parmesan cheese

Season the tomato slices with salt, pepper, garlic, and parsley. Heat the oil in a medium skillet and sauté the tomato slices lightly on each side. Arrange them in an individual ovenproof casserole. Deglaze the skillet with 1 tablespoon of water and pour this liquid over the tomatoes. Wipe out the pan, grease lightly, and sauté the sausage slices until lightly browned on each side. Break the egg(s) into the middle of the casserole. Place the sausage slices around the sides and sprinkle all over with the grated cheese. Bake at 450° F until the egg whites are set, but the yolks are still soft, about 6–7 minutes. Serve a light red wine like Olarra.

HUEVOS CON PICADILLA
DE CHAMPIÑÓN

(Baked Mushrooms and Eggs)

THIS dish, excellent for a luncheon or light supper, is incredibly easy and quick to prepare. It proves that simple need not mean dull.

Serves 4

4 tablespoons olive oil
½ pounds mushrooms, quartered
    (if the mushrooms are large,
    cut into still smaller pieces)
4 cloves garlic, minced

8 eggs
Salt
Freshly ground pepper
2 tablespoons minced parsley

Heat the oil in a large skillet until it is very hot. Add the mushrooms and garlic and fry, stirring constantly, over high heat—2 or 3 minutes should be enough. Transfer the mushrooms to 4 individual casserole dishes, preferably Spanish earthenware, making 2 depressions for the eggs. Slide 2 raw eggs into each dish, sprinkle all over with salt, pepper, and parsley, and bake at 450° F for about 5 minutes, or until the egg whites are barely set and the yolks are still soft. Rioja Bordón, a light red wine, is a fitting accompaniment or you may prefer a white wine such as Monopole.

HUEVOS RELLENOS DE GAMBAS

(Shrimp-Stuffed Eggs)

IDEAL for luncheon or a light dinner are these hard-boiled eggs, stuffed with a mixture of egg yolk and shrimp and coated with a light wine sauce.

Serves 2

4 teaspoons olive oil
4 tablespoons minced onion
4 teaspoons flour
2 tablespoons dry white wine
6 tablespoons fish broth (p. 13) or
    clam juice
½ pound cooked shrimp, chopped

4 hard-boiled eggs
Salt
Freshly ground pepper
2 teaspoons minced parsley
    for garnish

To make the white sauce, heat the oil in a small saucepan and sauté the onion until it is wilted. Stir in the flour and cook a minute. Add the wine and the broth and cook, stirring constantly, until thickened and smooth.

Place the chopped shrimp in a small bowl. Split the eggs lengthwise, remove the yolks, and mix them with the shrimp. Add 2 tablespoons of the white sauce, salt, and pepper. Fill the egg whites with this mixture and place the stuffed eggs in a greased baking dish. Cover with the remaining sauce and bake at 350° F for 10 minutes. Sprinkle with parsley before serving.

REVUELTO DE LANGOSTINO
Y ESPINACAS

(Soft-Set Eggs with Shrimp and Spinach)

OCCUPYING the second floor of an apartment house in the heart of the lovely seaside city of San Sebastián, Casa Nicolasa has been catering to well-to-do Basques and summer residents of this traditional and conservative resort for the past seven decades. Its reputation as one of Spain's finest restaurants is well deserved, for one dines here in quiet elegance, as if in a private home, on a variety of Basque and continental specialties. The dish that most impressed me, for its delicacy and subtle flavor, was the soft-set eggs, gently mixed with spinach and large pieces of Spanish prawns, fresh from the sea. It is an excellent luncheon or first-course serving.

Serves 1

¼ pound spinach, stems removed
Salt
3 tablespoons butter
1 slice bread, crust removed, cut into
    4 triangles (use a good
    solid loaf)

6 medium–large shrimp, shelled and
    cut in halves
2 eggs
1 tablespoon milk
Freshly ground pepper

Wash the spinach well and drain in a colander. Place in a saucepan with salt (no water), cover, and cook over medium heat about 5 minutes. Drain. In a small skillet, heat 2 tablespoons of the butter. Sauté the bread triangles over a low flame until they are golden and crisp. Remove and keep the bread warm. Wipe out the pan.

Half fill a large skillet with water, for use as a double boiler. Bring to a boil, then reduce to a simmer.

Melt the remaining tablespoon of the butter in the small skillet used to sauté the bread. Add the shrimp and sauté lightly until they turn pink, about 2 minutes. Remove the pan from the flame. Beat the eggs in a small bowl with the milk, salt, and pepper. Add the eggs to the pan with the shrimp and place the pan inside the larger skillet of water, double-boiler fashion. Stir constantly with a wooden spoon until the eggs just begin to set. Mix the spinach in gently and continue cooking and stirring gently until the eggs are set but are still quite soft (the spinach should remain a separate entity, not completely mixed with the eggs). Serve with the bread triangles standing on end around the sides of the dish. A fine white wine, such as the Paternina Reserva, would be very appropriate.

PIPARRADA

(Eggs Scrambled with Tomato and Peppers)

Piparrada is a Basque specialty that may be served by itself as a lunch or breakfast egg dish or as an accompaniment to simple meats, such as grilled lamb chops.

Serves 1

2 tablespoons olive oil
3 tablespoons finely chopped onion
1 clove garlic, minced
3 tablespoons finely chopped
    green pepper
3 tablespoons finely chopped
    red pepper

2 tablespoons finely chopped
    cured ham
1 small tomato, finely chopped
Salt
Freshly ground pepper
2 eggs

Heat 1 tablespoon of the oil in a medium skillet and sauté the onion, garlic, green pepper, and red pepper slowly until the peppers are tender. Add the ham and cook another minute. Mix in the tomato, salt, and pepper. Cover and cook 10 minutes.

In a bowl, lightly beat the eggs with a fork. Stir the tomato mixture into the eggs. Wipe out the skillet and heat the remaining tablespoon of oil. Add the contents of the bowl and stir constantly with a fork until the eggs are set, but not dry. Serve, if desired, with triangles of bread sautéed in butter (see instructions in preceding recipe). In the Basque country a very young dry white wine called Chacolí might be served, but it is not imported into this country, so serve any of the dry white wines listed.

REVUELTO DE AJETES
(Soft-Set Eggs and Scallions)

A DELICATE and light preparation that is an oddity among robust Spanish egg dishes.

Serves 1

1 tablespoon butter	2 eggs
5 very thin scallions, cut in	1 tablespoon milk
2-inch lengths	Salt

Melt the butter in a medium skillet and sauté the scallions slowly until they are tender. Meanwhile, half fill a large skillet with water and bring to a boil. Reduce to a simmer.

Beat the eggs in a bowl with the milk and salt. Add the eggs to the pan with the scallions, remove immediately from the flame, and place the pan in the large skillet of water, double-boiler fashion. Stir the eggs gently with a wooden spoon and remove when the eggs are no longer liquid but are still quite soft. Decorate with wedges of bread sautéed in butter. (Directions for the bread appear in Soft-Set Eggs with Shrimp and Spinach, p. 160.)

DUELOS Y QUEBRANTOS
(Eggs Scrambled with Bacon and Chorizo)

THE literary masterpiece, *Don Quijote de la Mancha*, opens with the following paragraph:

> In a place in La Mancha, whose name I do not wish to recall, lived a gentleman who owned a lance, an old shield, a weak horse and a racing hound. Three parts of his income were consumed in food—a stewpot of beef, leftover ground meat on other nights, "duelos y quebrantos" on Saturdays, lentils for Fridays and perhaps a pigeon on Sundays.

Duelos y Quebrantos, literally "sorrow and suffering" but in reality eggs and bacon, were standard fare in Castilla in the sixteenth and seventeenth centuries, when little else was available, and continue to be a favorite in modern times.

Serves 1

1 tablespoon olive oil	2 tablespoons *chorizo*, in ¼-inch pieces
¼ cup slab bacon, in ¼-inch cubes	2 eggs

Heat the oil in a medium skillet. Add the bacon and fry slowly until the pieces are brown and crisp. Add the *chorizo* and cook 1 minute more. Beat the eggs in a bowl with a fork. Add the bacon and *chorizo* to the eggs and discard all but 1 tablespoon of the oil from the skillet. Heat the skillet again, scraping to make sure no particles of bacon are stuck to the bottom. Pour in the egg mixture and cook over high heat, very briefly, stirring constantly, until the eggs are set but not dry. Obviously, this makes an excellent breakfast or brunch dish.

TORTILLA ESPAÑOLA

(Potato Omelet)

THE *tortilla* is a way of life in Spain (see introduction, p. 152) and is loved by all, natives and tourists alike. A Spanish *tortilla* has nothing in common with its Mexican counterpart except its Latin root—*torte*, meaning a round cake. Although a Spanish *tortilla* is simply a potato omelet, it is not as simple to prepare as you might expect, unless you know the technique involved. And it is much more delicious than you might think a dish of such limited ingredients could be.

Tortilla is a great favorite with my family and friends. We often have it, cut in wedges, for dinner, accompanied by fried peppers and sausages. For large parties, I cut the *tortilla* into 1-inch squares to be picked up with toothpicks. It is good hot, but usually preferred at room temperature.

Serves 4–6

1 cup olive oil, or a mixture of olive and salad oils	Coarse salt
	1 large onion, thinly sliced
4 large potatoes, peeled and cut in ⅛-inch slices	4 large eggs

Heat the oil in an 8- or 9-inch skillet and add the potato slices one at a time to prevent sticking. Alternate potato layers with the onion slices and salt the layers lightly. Cook slowly, over a medium flame, lifting and turning the potatoes occasionally, until they are tender but not brown. (The potatoes will remain separated, not in a "cake.")

Meanwhile, in a large bowl beat the eggs with a fork until they are slightly foamy. Salt to taste. Remove the potatoes from the skillet and drain them in a colander, reserving about 3 tablespoons of the oil. (The potatoes give the oil a delicious flavor, so reserve the rest for future use.) Add the potatoes to the beaten eggs, pressing the potatoes down so that they are completely covered by the egg. Let the mixture sit 15 minutes.

Heat 2 tablespoons of the reserved oil in a large skillet until very hot (you may use the same skillet as long as absolutely nothing is stuck on the bottom). Add the potato-and-egg mixture, rapidly spreading it out in the skillet with the aid of a pancake turner. Lower the heat to medium-high and shake the pan often to prevent sticking. When the potatoes begin to brown underneath, invert a plate of the same size over the skillet. Flip the omelet onto the plate. Add about 1 tablespoon more of oil to the pan, then slide the omelet back into the skillet to brown on the other side. (If your skillet was not hot enough, some of the omelet may stick to the pan. If this happens, don't despair—scrape off the pieces and fit them into their places on the omelet. With subsequent flips, the pieces will mesh with the omelet.)

Lower the heat to medium. Flip the omelet 2 or 3 more times (this helps to give it a good shape) cooking briefly on each side. It should be slightly juicy within. Transfer to a platter and serve hot or at room temperature. I prefer it after it has been sitting for several hours. Serve with a Valdepeñas or Valencia wine (see wine chart).

TORTILLA A LA GALLEGA

(Potato, Chorizo, and Pimiento Omelet)

THIS is a variation of the basic Tortilla Española and is commonly found in Galicia.

Serves 4–6

4 medium potatoes, peeled, in
    ⅛-inch slices
1 medium onion, thinly sliced
Salt
1 cup olive oil, or a mixture of olive
    and salad oils

5 eggs
1 *chorizo* (2 ounces), diced
3 tablespoons diced pimiento,
    homemade or imported

Fry the potatoes and onion with salt in the oil in the same manner as in the preceding recipe. Meanwhile, beat the eggs with salt in a bowl. In a small skillet lightly sauté the *chorizo*. Add it to the beaten egg along with the pimiento. Drain the potatoes and add them to the egg mixture, pushing them down with a pancake turner so that the egg covers the potatoes. Let sit 15 minutes.

Proceed to cook the omelet as in Tortilla Española. Serve with a strong everyday wine such as Burgella.

TORTILLA PAISANA

(Country-Style Omelet)

TORTILLA PAISANA is one of my favorite omelets, good hot or at room temperature and ideal in the summer.

Serves 6–8

4 tablespoons olive oil
1 medium onion, chopped
¼ pound *chorizo*, diced
A ¼-pound piece cured ham, diced
2 medium potatoes, cooked, skinned, and diced
2 pimientos, homemade or imported, cut in strips

½ cup cooked string beans, cut in halves
½ cup cooked peas
6 cooked asparagus spears, each cut in 3 parts
8 eggs
Salt

Heat 2 tablespoons of the oil in a 10-inch skillet. Add the onion and sauté until it is wilted. Add the *chorizo*, ham, and potatoes and cook 5 minutes. Stir in the pimiento, cooked string beans, peas, and asparagus and cook 5 minutes more.

Lightly beat the eggs in a large bowl. Add the contents of the skillet to the eggs and salt to taste. Stir. Clean the skillet thoroughly, then heat the remaining 2 tablespoons of the oil until very hot. Add the egg mixture and cook over low-medium heat until the eggs are set enough to turn. Invert a plate over the skillet. Flip the omelet onto the plate, then slide the omelet back into the skillet, adding more oil if necessary. Cook until brown. Flip once more and cook briefly again on the other side. Serve cut in wedges. A hearty red wine from the Valdepeñas or Valencia region is appropriate.

TORTILLA CORUÑESA

(Potato and Cured Ham Omelet)

THE city of La Coruña and the town of Betanzos nearby are known all over Spain for their excellent omelets. I couldn't imagine what could make an omelet so special until I tried this one at the then famous Viuda de Alfredín Restaurant in La Coruña (it has since closed), a casual and unpretentious place frequented by soccer players and fans alike from the nearby stadium. This omelet is cooked on only one side, leaving it juicy and delicious. It is good for a light supper.

Makes 2 large portions

½ cup olive oil, or a mixture of olive
    and salad oils
2 medium potatoes, finely cubed
Salt

5 eggs
¼ pound cured ham, in thin slices
    (about ¹⁄₁₆ inch)

Heat the oil in a 9-inch skillet. Add the potatoes, one at a time to prevent sticking, and season with salt. Cook slowly until the potatoes are tender, lifting and turning occasionally. The potatoes remain separated, not in a "cake," and should not brown, but don't worry if a few do. Drain the potatoes in a colander, reserving 1 tablespoon of the oil to make the omelet.

In a large bowl, beat the eggs with a fork. Season with salt and add the potatoes. Let this mixture sit 5 minutes. In a 10- or 11-inch skillet, heat the reserved 1 tablespoon of oil until very hot. Cover the bottom of the pan with the ham slices and add the egg mixture immediately. Shake the pan to avoid sticking. Reduce the heat to medium. When the bottom of the omelet is set and brown (the top will still have some liquid), place a dish over the skillet and flip out the omelet.

To serve, cut into wedges, spooning on any remaining liquid. This omelet may also be prepared in individual portions. A light red wine, such as Domecq Domain, goes very nicely.

TORTILLA ASTURIANA

(Onion, Tuna, and Tomato Omelet)

The large quantity of onion in this recipe makes this omelet extremely flavorful. The recipe was supplied to me by a good friend, Sofía Pandiellas, who is a native of Asturias in northern Spain and an expert cook.

Serves 1

2 tablespoons olive oil
1 medium onion, thinly sliced
1 small ripe tomato, chopped
2 eggs

Half a 7-ounce can white or light
    meat tuna, drained and flaked
Salt
Freshly ground pepper

Heat 1 tablespoon of the oil in a medium skillet and sauté the onion very slowly, covered, until it is tender but not brown. Add the tomato and cook 10 minutes more, uncovered.

Beat the eggs in a bowl. Add the tuna, salt, pepper, and the onion-and-tomato mixture from the skillet. Mix well. Wipe out the skillet. Heat the remaining tablespoon of the oil, and when it is very hot, pour in the egg mixture. Lower the heat slightly and cook until the omelet is brown underneath, shaking the pan constantly. Flip to the other side, adding more oil if necessary, and continue cooking. The omelet should remain juicy within. Serve a hard, dry apple cider (see glossary), as they would in Asturias, or a dry white wine.

TORTILLA DE GARBANZOS

(Chickpea Omelet)

Serves 1

2 tablespoons olive oil
2 tablespoons minced onion
1 clove garlic, minced
½ cup cooked chickpeas, fresh
    or canned
2 eggs

Salt
Freshly ground pepper
1 tablespoon chopped pimiento,
    homemade or imported
1 tablespoon minced parsley

Heat 1 tablespoon of the oil in a medium skillet and sauté the onion and garlic until the onion is wilted. Add the chickpeas and sauté 5 minutes more.

Meanwhile, beat the eggs in a small bowl. Add the salt, pepper, pimiento, and parsley, then the chickpea mixture from the pan. Wipe out the pan. Heat the remaining tablespoon of oil until very hot and proceed as in the preceding recipe.

TORTILLA DE HABAS

(Lima Bean Omelet)

Serves 1

½ medium onion, chopped
3 tablespoons olive oil
¼ pound lima beans

1 tablespoon minced cured ham
2 eggs
Salt

Sauté the onion in 2 tablespoons of the oil in a medium skillet until wilted. Stir in the lima beans, cover, and cook slowly, about 30 minutes, or until the beans are tender. Add the ham and cook 5 minutes more.

Beat the eggs in a bowl. Mix in the contents of the skillet and salt. Wipe out the skillet and add the remaining tablespoon of oil. Heat to the smoking point, then add the lima-and-egg mixture and cook as for Tortilla Asturiana (p. 166). The limas, typical of the south of Spain, suggest that a dry sherry such as La Ina would be an interesting accompaniment.

TORTILLA ALICANTINA

(Alicante-Style Omelet)

Serves 1

2 eggs
Salt
Freshly ground pepper
2 tablespoons olive oil
2 tablespoons minced onion
2 ounces shrimp (about 8 small
    shrimp), shelled and cut
    in half crosswise

3 cooked asparagus spears, in
    1-inch pieces
2 tablespoons chopped boiled ham
2 tablespoons flaked light meat tuna
2 tablespoons chopped tomato

Beat the eggs in a bowl and season with salt and pepper. Heat 1 tablespoon of the oil in a medium skillet. Sauté the onion until wilted, then add the shrimp and cook about 2 minutes, until they turn pink. Add the cooked asparagus, ham, tuna, tomato, salt, and pepper. Cook 2 minutes more. Stir this mixture into the eggs. Wipe out the pan. Heat the remaining tablespoon of oil until very hot and add the egg mixture. Cook according to instructions for Tortilla Asturiana (p. 166). Try a dry white wine such as Viña Sol.

TORTILLA DE DÁTILES

(Date Omelet)

IT IS only fitting that this date omelet should come from Elche, the city with the largest date palm forest in Europe, planted by the Phoenicians many hundreds of years ago. Nestled in the midst of the vast palm groves is the pretty Huerto del Cura Hotel and Els Capellans restaurant with its excellent regional specialties, one of which is this unusual omelet.

Serves 1

2 eggs
2 tablespoons butter
4 medium shrimp, shelled and cut in
 half crosswise
1 tablespoon diced cured ham
2 dried dates, chopped

Salt
Freshly ground pepper
3 tablespoons tomato sauce, seasoned
 with salt and pepper
 (homemade, p. 190)

In a bowl, beat the eggs lightly with a fork. Heat 1 tablespoon of the butter in a medium skillet. Sauté the shrimp until they turn pink—a minute or two will suffice. Add them to the beaten eggs along with the ham, dates, salt, and pepper. Stir.

Wipe out the skillet. Heat the remaining tablespoon of butter and, when hot, pour in the egg mixture. Let it set slightly on the bottom; then, with the aid of a pancake turner, gently roll up the omelet. Transfer to a serving plate, heat the tomato sauce, and dribble a thin line of the sauce across each end of the omelet.

TORTILLA CATALANA

(Sausage and Bean Omelet)

A CATALÁN specialty, succulent and very satisfying.

Serves 1

1 teaspoon lard
1½ tablespoons olive oil
¼ cup slivered onion
5 slices *butifarra* sausage (p. 55), ½ inch
    thick; or Italian sweet sausage,
    cut in pieces
5 tablespoons chopped fresh tomato

¼ cup cooked dried white beans,
    freshly made or canned
Salt
Freshly ground pepper
2 eggs
1 tablespoon minced parsley
    for garnish

Heat the lard and ½ tablespoon of the oil in a medium skillet. Sauté the onion
very slowly until it is softened. Add the sausage and cook until it loses its color.
Stir in the tomato, cover, and cook about 3 minutes. Add the beans, salt, and
pepper and cook 3 minutes more.

    Beat the eggs with a fork in a bowl. Season with salt and pepper. Heat the
remaining tablespoon of oil in a clean medium-size skillet. Pour in the eggs
and cook until they are set underneath. Add the sausage mixture to the center
and fold the omelet in half. Continue cooking to taste. Sprinkle with parsley.
A light red wine, such as the Cabernet Sauvignon, which comes from the
Catalán region, would be most appropriate.

TORTILLA DE CHAMPIÑÓN

(Mushroom Omelet)

Serves 1

2 tablespoons olive oil
½ pound mushrooms, chopped or
    sliced, stems trimmed
1 small clove garlic, minced
1 tablespoon minced parsley

1 tablespoon minced cured ham
2 eggs
Salt
Freshly ground pepper

Heat 1 tablespoon of the oil in a medium skillet. Add the mushrooms, garlic,
parsley, and ham and cook over high heat briefly—a couple of minutes will
suffice.

Beat the eggs in a small bowl. Add salt and pepper and the mushroom mixture. Heat the remaining tablespoon of oil in a clean skillet until very hot, and prepare the omelet as for Tortilla Asturiana (p. 166).

TORTILLA DE ATÚN ESCABECHADO

(Marinated Tuna Omelet)

Makes 1 large portion

2 tablespoons olive oil
2 tablespoons minced onion
¾ cup Marinated Tuna (p. 24), or
    light meat tuna, drained
    and flaked

2 eggs
Salt
Freshly ground pepper

TOMATO SAUCE

1 tablespoon olive oil
1 tablespoon minced onion
½ cup tomato sauce, preferably
    homemade (p. 218)

Salt
Freshly ground pepper

To make the tomato sauce, heat the 1 tablespoon olive oil in a small skillet and sauté the onion until it is wilted. Add the tomato sauce, salt, and pepper. Cover and simmer 15 minutes.

To make the omelet, in a medium skillet heat 1 tablespoon of the oil and sauté the onion until wilted. Add the tuna and cook 5 minutes.

Beat the eggs in a small bowl. Season with salt and pepper. In another skillet, heat the remaining tablespoon of oil. Pour in the eggs and cook until the bottom is set. Add the tuna mixture to the center and fold the omelet in half. Continue cooking until done to taste. Serve with the tomato sauce. A dry white wine such as Cepa de Oro is appropriate.

TORTILLA DE BACALAO

(Cod Omelet)

START PREPARATION AT LEAST ONE DAY IN ADVANCE.

Makes 1 large portion

¼ pound dried salt cod, skinned
   and boned
2 tablespoons olive oil
1 clove garlic, minced
1 tablespoon chopped onion

2 eggs
Salt
Freshly ground pepper
1 tablespoon minced parsley

Soak the cod in cold water for 24–36 hours, changing the water occasionally. Drain. Place in a pot of water over high heat, and when the water comes to a boil, remove the cod. Shred.

Heat 1 tablespoon of the oil in a medium skillet and sauté the garlic and onion until the onion is wilted. Add the cod and cook slowly 10 minutes.

Beat the eggs in a bowl. Add the cod mixture, salt (if necessary), pepper, and the parsley. Let sit 5 minutes. Heat the remaining tablespoon of oil in a medium skillet until very hot and add the egg mixture. Cook as for Tortilla Asturiana (p. 166). A dry white wine—Blanco Seco, for example—goes well with this omelet.

Chapter 7

ARROCES

(Rice Dishes)

I APPROACH this chapter with a sense of mission: to introduce readers to Spanish rice as it should be made, but never is, in this country. We have become so accustomed to what passes for "*paella*" and "saffron rice" in restaurants that few realize how glorious the genuine article can be.

I recently tasted *paellas* all over New York City for a New York newspaper, and the results were appalling—some restaurants used food coloring instead of saffron, none used Spanish-style short-grain rice, many *paellas* were watery and tasteless, and some were grossly overpriced. The unknowing diner has come to believe that *paella* is basically a seafood dish accompanied by quite ordinary rice when, in fact, it is just the opposite. "When the rice is good, the rest is superfluous," my husband, a dyed-in-the-wool Spaniard, is wont to say, and until you have tasted Spanish rice as it should be prepared, it is difficult to imagine what he means. When I prepare real Spanish rice for guests at home, more often than not the luscious fresh lobster atop the rice is ignored, but few will pass up seconds on rice.

Paella is a word that has come worldwide to mean a Spanish rice dish with a variety of seafood and usually some chicken. However, the word originally referred only to the pan in which the food was cooked—the *paella* or *paellera*, from the Latin word for pan, *patella. Paellas* actually come in endless varieties, depending on the chef and on regional specialties. Those rice dishes that are made in *paella* pans, whatever the ingredients, are often referred to as *paellas*, although just as often the name of a rice dish is a description of its ingredients— Rice with Rabbit, Seafood Rice, Vegetable Rice, etc. All names, however, basically refer to the same kinds of rice dishes.

Although variations on *paella* abound, no one will dispute that the home of *paella*, and of most Spanish rice dishes, is Valencia. Rice growing in Valencia was made possible when, more than a thousand years ago, the Romans introduced irrigation, a system later perfected by the Arab invaders. It is thought that these same Arab conquerors brought rice to Valencia in the eighth century. Many centuries would pass, however, before rice would become the staple of the Valencian diet that it is today and become a basic crop of the Valencian economy. The visitor to Valencia can't help but be aware that he is in rice country. Located on the Mediterranean in a unique area of marshlands, Valencia is ideal for rice production. In spring and early summer, the bright green rice shoots cover the land as far as the eye can see; stooped laborers, pants rolled to the knee, sloshing through the rice fields tending to the crops, are a common sight. In the excellent restaurants in the center of Valencia, and in others in El Palmar, outside the city in the middle of the rice fields, everyone—tourist and native alike—is eating rice. Valencians, you see, eat rice all the time, just as Gaditanos in Cádiz exist mainly on fish. The rice may be fairly plain peasant fare, containing little more than rice, water, and a few vegetables, or it can be used to create meals of pure luxury, which include the most expensive seafood available. The whole range is found in Valencia, although the people are particularly fond of what is considered the "original" *paella*, based on easy-to-obtain local ingredients like green vegetables, land snails, and eels from the beautiful Albufera lagoon. Rice is used in such a variety of dishes in Valencia and is prepared with such expertise that it is easy to see how one could eat it on an everyday basis. The Spanish food writer Luis Antonio de Vega describes Valencia rice creations thusly:

> Valencia took rice and with it created one of the best dishes of world cookery. Imagine—with rice! That white grain on which the impoverished of the world depend for sustenance. It is impossible to take culinary science much farther. Paella is not just another dish among the many that form the glorious Spanish cuisine: it is a gastronomic miracle.

Purists insist that, indeed, Valencia is the only place in the world to eat a properly prepared *paella*. The short, stubby grain grown in the vast Valencian wetlands has a quality all its own, the local water supply—dreadful for drinking—seems to have a unique chemical composition that is perfect for rice cookery, and the local cooks are especially skilled in preparing and timing the rice to perfection. I have eaten *paellas* all over Spain, as well as in London and New York, but I must admit there is nothing quite like a *paella* eaten in Valencia, especially if the setting is sunset at El Palmar's Racó de l'Olla Restaurant, which overlooks the vast Albufera lagoon in the heart of the Valencian rice fields. Or if it is at the *paella* mecca of the world, La Pepica, on the Levante Beach next to the port of El Grao, where dozens of chefs deftly handle huge *paella* pans that may reach up to six feet across, depending on the number of portions being cooked in one pan.

Ask a Spaniard what makes a perfect *paella* and never expect two opinions to coincide. The arguments may become heated as one insists that meat and seafood should not be mixed, another asserts that the "real" *paella* should contain only the "original" ingredients of rice, snails, and green beans, and yet a third denies the existence of a decent *paella* that has not been cooked over a woodburning fire in the out-of-doors, a method that produces the *socarrat*, a golden crust of rice that forms on the bottom of the pan and is considered the most desirable part of the *paella*. I remain apart from all such controversies, for

I love Spanish rice in all its guises and believe that once one has tasted the full range of these delicious and unusual dishes, it is difficult to pick a favorite. Rice cookery is a very special category of Spanish cuisine—a world in itself that is fascinating to explore.

Spanish rice dishes are all crowd pleasers and could not be more elegant and colorful to serve to guests. They are a boon, besides, to the harried host or hostess, for they are meals in themselves—no need to make vegetables, potatoes, or the like. They are also great fun to eat because of the surprise ingredients each one contains—there may be tiny meatballs, spareribs, pea pods, rabbit, quail, almonds, dried cod, or sausage, not to mention the more widely used shrimp, lobster, clams, and mussels. Pungent garlic sauces also sometimes accompany rice dishes and add an extra touch I find irresistible. So diverse are the ingredients in *paellas* that *paella* is sometimes referred to as the most baroque dish ever invented. Try all of the rice variations included here for rice more delicious and satisfying than you ever imagined it could be.

Be sure to note the following tips for perfect rice results:

1. Use only short-grain rice. It may be imported from Valencia, or short-grain pearl rice grown in California (Spanish or Japanese style), or imported Italian rice. Do not rinse before using, unless indicated in the recipe. Long-grain rice produces rice dishes entirely different in character, flavor, and texture from those made with short-grain rice. I discourage such a substitution, but in the case that short-grain rice is absolutely unavailable, use the long-grain rice in the proportion of 1 cup rice to 2½ cups liquid.

2. For most rice recipes, it is important that the dish be wide and shallow and that the rice cooks *uncovered*—this prevents it from steaming, which is undesirable in a *paella*. Recipes in this chapter call for two basic types of pans:

   a. *Paella* pans, the inexpensive thin metal types imported from Spain with handles on either side are the best. Recipes in this chapter are geared for pans with about a 15–15½-inch base and about 17 inches across the top, excluding handles (be sure to measure your oven width and depth before purchasing a pan of this size).

   b. Earthenware casseroles, 12 inches across and about 2 inches deep, are perfect for other rice dishes.

3. The broth in which the rice is cooked is extremely important to the flavor of the finished dish. Therefore, when cooking other kinds of meals, always be thinking of leftovers that might make great broth for rices—such things as chicken carcasses, lobster and shrimp shells, or fish heads. When boiling shellfish, always save the cooking liquid.

4. Home stove burners are not large enough to accommodate a *paella* pan; therefore, it should be placed over 2 burners and turned frequently to equalize the heat. Stirring the rice, frowned upon by purists, becomes necessary when the heat is uneven.

5. Never wait until the rice tastes "done" before removing it from the stove or oven. The rice must finish cooking away from the heat; otherwise, the rice grains will burst and turn mushy.

6. Most rice dishes can be partially prepared in advance. However, the final

cooking must be done at the last minute. The dish never quite tastes the same when reheated, although I must admit I enjoy leftover *paella*. When cooking for company, it is advisable to do some of the cooking in advance—recipes will indicate up to what point this may be done. (Materials cooked in advance should *not* be refrigerated—they will keep with no problem for several hours.) Since *paella* pans are shallow, there is quite a bit of spattering at the beginning, which can be cleaned up earlier in the day. The final stages are easy and no problem to handle after guests have arrived.

7. Saffron is not included in all rice dishes, but when it is called for, it should be the real thing—imported from Spain and in strands, not powdered. It is fantastically expensive—in fact, the most expensive spice in the world at about $2,000 a pound. Fortunately, only small amounts are needed, and a small container goes a long way. Many people are under the misconception that saffron is merely a colorant, when actually it imparts a very definite flavor and aroma to the rice. Therefore, accept no substitutes—Mexican marigold petals, tumeric, or artificial coloring will not do.

PAELLA A LA VALENCIANA
(TRADICIONAL)

(Traditional Valencian Paella)

THIS is the original Valencian *paella*, not the one that has become famous worldwide under the same name. It utilizes all the produce of the Valencian inland *huertas* (orchards), easy-to-obtain ingredients such as rabbit, land snails, green vegetables, and, of course, the renowned Valencian rice. The custom is to eat this rice accompanied by crunchy scallions instead of bread. The taste combination is, I must say, inspired.

Serves 6

2 dozen small snails, either live periwinkles (sea snails), frozen unseasoned snails, thawed, or canned snails, in their shells
6½ cups strong chicken broth, preferably homemade
1 small onion, peeled
1 bay leaf
½ teaspoon thyme

2 sprigs parsley
5 peppercorns
A 2½–3-pound rabbit or chicken, cut in small serving pieces
Salt
½ cup olive oil
½ green pepper, finely chopped
1 medium tomato, finely chopped
3 cloves garlic, minced
3 cups short-grain rice (see p. 175)

2 teaspoons paprika
¼ pound large lima beans

½ pound wide, flat string beans
12 scallions

If periwinkles are being used, see page 29 for washing instructions. Mix the chicken broth with the onion, bay leaf, thyme, parsley, and peppercorns. Bring to a boil, cover, then simmer 30 minutes. Reserve 6 cups.

Sprinkle the rabbit pieces with salt. Heat the oil in a metal *paella* pan with about a 15-inch base. Fry the rabbit over high heat until golden on all sides. Remove to a warm platter. Add the green pepper and cook over medium heat until wilted. Add the tomato and the garlic, turn up the flame, and cook until the liquid from the tomato evaporates. (Make in advance up to this point.)

Stir in the rice and cook 5 minutes until the rice is transparent. Sprinkle in the paprika, then add the broth, boiling hot, the limas, and string beans. Bring to a boil, add salt to taste, and boil, uncovered and stirring occasionally, 7–10 minutes, or until the rice is no longer soupy but some liquid remains. Return the rabbit to the rice. Bury the snails. Place in the oven and bake, uncovered, at 325° F for 20 minutes, or until the liquid is absorbed but the rice is not quite done. Remove from the oven, cover lightly with foil, and let sit 10 minutes before serving. Serve with 2 scallions decorating the edges of each individual plate. Take bites of scallion while eating the rice. Serve with a light red wine like Marqués de Murrieta.

PAELLA A LA VALENCIANA
(Chicken and Seafood Rice)

THIS is the rice dish that has achieved world renown—and justly so, for when it is well prepared it is truly a glorious dish. A medley of colors and tastes, this version has authentic flavor and is spectacularly beautiful. Although the list of ingredients is long, most of the work can be done in advance, and since *paella* is a meal in itself, it needs no accompaniment. Paella a la Valenciana never fails to delight guests, especially when preceded by a chilled red *gazpacho* (p. 130) and washed down with an icy *sangría* (p. 392).

Serves 8–10

6 cups very strong chicken broth, preferably homemade
½ teaspoon saffron
1 small onion, peeled
1–2 small chickens, about 2½ pounds each
Coarse salt
½ cup olive oil
¼ pound *chorizo* sausage, in ¼-inch slices
1 large pork chop, boned and diced
A ¼-pound piece cured ham, diced
1 medium onion, chopped
4 scallions, chopped
4 cloves garlic, minced
2 pimientos, homemade or imported, diced
1 pound small or medium shrimp, shelled

2 live lobsters, split and divided into tail sections and claws (discard or keep the head and small claws); or 4 lobster tails, split lengthwise; or 8 king crab claws; or 8 jumbo shrimp, in their shells
3 cups short-grain rice (see p. 175)
5 tablespoons chopped parsley
2 bay leaves, crumbled
½ cup dry white wine
1 tablespoon lemon juice
¼ pound fresh or frozen peas
18 clams, smallest available, at room temperature, scrubbed (see p. 11)
18 small mussels, scrubbed (see p. 11)
Lemon wedges for garnish
Chopped parsley for garnish

Heat the broth with the saffron and the whole onion. Cover and simmer 15 minutes. Remove the onion and measure the broth—you need exactly 5½ cups. Cut the chicken into small serving pieces—the whole breast in 4 parts, each thigh into 2 parts, the bony tip of the leg chopped off, the wing tip discarded, and the rest of the wing separated into 2 parts. Dry the pieces well and sprinkle with salt. In a metal *paella* pan, with about a 15-inch base, heat the oil. Add the chicken pieces and fry over high heat until golden. Remove to a warm platter. Add the *chorizo*, pork, and ham to the pan and stir fry about 10 minutes. Add the chopped onion, scallions, garlic, and pimientos and sauté until the onion is wilted. Add the shrimp and the lobster and sauté about 3 minutes more, or until the shrimp and lobster barely turn pink (the lobster will cook more in the oven). Remove the shrimp and lobster to the platter with the chicken. Add the rice to the pan and stir to coat it well with the oil. Sprinkle in the 5 tablespoons chopped parsley and the crumbled bay leaves. (Make in advance up to this point.)

Stir in the broth, boiling hot, the wine, lemon juice, and peas. Salt to taste. Bring to a boil and cook, uncovered and stirring occasionally, over medium-high heat about 7 minutes or until the rice is no longer soupy but some liquid remains. Bury the shrimp and chicken in the rice. Push the clams and mussels into the rice, with the edge that will open facing up. Decorate the *paella* with the lobster pieces, then bake at 325° F, uncovered, for 20 minutes. Remove from the oven and let sit on top of the stove, lightly covered with foil, for about 10 minutes. To serve, decorate with lemon wedges and chopped parsley.

ARROZ CON POLLO

(Rice and Chicken)

ARROZ CON POLLO is more or less a simplified version of *paella*, appropriate for those who don't or cannot eat seafood and good to prepare on a last-minute basis because its ingredients can all be found in the supermarket.

Serves 4–6

A 3-pound chicken, cut in small
    serving pieces
Salt
6 tablespoons olive oil
2 green peppers, chopped
1 onion, chopped
2 cloves garlic, minced
2 fresh tomatoes, skinned
    and chopped
2 pimientos, homemade or
    imported, chopped

3 teaspoons paprika
¼ teaspoon saffron
2 cups short-grain rice (see p. 175)
3½ cups strong chicken broth,
    preferably homemade
½ cup dry white wine
Freshly ground pepper
1 tablespoon minced parsley
    for garnish

Sprinkle the chicken pieces with salt. Heat the oil in a metal *paella* pan with about a 15-inch base and fry the chicken until golden on all sides. Remove to a warm platter. Add the green pepper, onion, and garlic and sauté until the green pepper is tender. Stir in the tomato and pimiento and cook, uncovered, 10 minutes more. Add the paprika and saffron, then add the rice and stir to coat well with the oil. Pour in the broth, boiling hot, the wine, salt, and pepper. Boil over medium heat, uncovered and stirring occasionally, for about 7 minutes, or until the rice is no longer soupy, but not yet dry. Arrange the chicken pieces over the rice and place in a 325° F oven, uncovered, for 15 minutes. The liquid should be absorbed, but the rice still "al dente." Remove and let sit, lightly covered with foil, for 10 minutes more. Sprinkle with the parsley. An Ensalada a la Almoraina (p. 107) and a light red wine like Diamante are the only accompaniments necessary.

ARROZ CON COSTRA ALICANTINO

(Egg-Crusted Rice
with Chickpeas and Meatballs)

A VERY distinctively flavored rice preparation that has no seafood and includes tiny meatballs and chickpeas, chicken, and sausage, all baked under a fluffy egg topping, which forms a crust and gives this dish its name. It is the special *paella* of the Alicante region, and nowhere is it more expertly prepared than at the excellent Els Capellans restaurant in Elche.

Serves 6

4 tablespoons olive oil
2 cloves garlic, peeled
1 dried sweet red pepper (see glossary), softened in warm water, stem and seeds removed, or 1 pimiento, homemade or imported
1 whole chicken breast, boned and cut in 1-inch cubes
¼ pound *butifarra* (p. 55), sweet Italian, or breakfast sausage, in ½-inch slices

¼ pound lean pork loin, cut in ½-inch cubes
2 cups short-grain rice (see p. 175)
Few strands saffron
4 cups strong chicken broth, preferably homemade
1 cup chickpeas, freshly cooked or canned
Salt
7 eggs
3 tablespoons milk

MEATBALLS

¼ pound ground pork
2 tablespoons beaten egg
¼ cup bread crumbs

1 tablespoon minced parsley
8 blanched almonds, ground
2 tablespoons lemon juice

To make the meatballs, mix together all the meatball ingredients except the lemon juice and shape into small balls, less than 1 inch in size. Dip the meatballs in the lemon juice.

To make the rice, heat the oil in a shallow 12-inch casserole, preferably earthenware, and fry the whole garlic cloves until they are tender. Remove the garlic to a processor. Add the dried pepper to the pan and sauté until golden, being careful not to burn; add it to the processor. Fry the chicken pieces in the same skillet until golden, then remove them to a warm platter. Add the sausage and pork and stir fry over high heat 2 or 3 minutes. Remove to the platter. Fry the meatballs until they are well browned and add them to the platter. Add the rice to the casserole and stir to coat well with the oil. (Make in advance up to this point.)

In the processor, blend the reserved red pepper and garlic along with the saffron. Gradually add ½ cup of the chicken broth. Add this mixture to the rice and the remaining 3½ cups of broth, boiling hot, the chickpeas, chicken, sausage, pork, and meatballs. Salt to taste. Bring to a boil, then reduce the heat and cook, uncovered, about 7 minutes, stirring frequently, until the rice is no longer soupy but some liquid remains. Place in a 325° F oven and bake, uncovered, 10 minutes. Beat the eggs and the milk in a bowl with a whisk. Cover the rice with the beaten egg and bake 5 minutes in a 500° F oven. Run briefly under the broiler if the eggs are not golden. Remove the rice from the oven, cover loosely with foil, and let sit 10 minutes before serving.

ARROZ A LA CATALANA

(Rabbit Paella, with Sausage, Pork Ribs, and Pea Pods)

THIS *paella* is Catalán style, using *butifarra*, the region's typical sausage, which, along with the interesting additions of pork ribs and pea pods, both common to Cataluña, give this rice dish a wonderful flavor.

Serves 6

A 3-pound rabbit or chicken, cut in small serving pieces
Salt
8 tablespoons olive oil
½ pound pork ribs, cut into individual ribs
1 medium onion, chopped
A 12-inch piece of *butifarra* (p. 55); or 3 sweet Italian sausages, cut in ¾-inch pieces

¼ pound cured ham, diced
1 tomato, chopped
2½ cups short-grain rice (see p. 175)
5 cups strong chicken broth, preferably homemade
2 cloves garlic, minced
2 tablespoons minced parsley
¼ pound Chinese-style pea pods
2 pimientos, homemade or imported, cut in strips

Sprinkle the rabbit pieces with salt. Heat the oil in a *paella* pan and brown quickly the rabbit with the pork ribs. Remove both to a roasting pan and bake at 350° F for 15 minutes. Meanwhile, in the *paella* pan sauté the onion, sausage, and ham until the onion is wilted. Add the tomato and cook 5 minutes. (Make in advance up to this point.) Mix in the rice and stir until well coated with the oil. Add the broth, boiling hot, garlic, parsley, and salt. Boil, uncovered, about

10 minutes, or until the rice is no longer soupy but some liquid remains. Stir frequently. Add the pea pods, then arrange the rabbit and ribs on top of the rice. Decorate with the pimiento strips and bake at 325° F, uncovered, for 20 minutes. The liquid should be absorbed and the rice still slightly underdone. Remove from the oven, cover loosely with foil, and let sit 10 minutes before serving. Ensalada a la Almoraina (p. 107) and a light red wine like Viña Lanciano are appropriate.

PAELLA MARINERA
(Seafood Paella)

VARY this recipe as you wish—the shellfish may be eliminated, other fish added. Just be sure to keep the basic proportions the same.

Serves 6–8

¾ pound halibut steak, or similar fish
Coarse salt
¾ pound small shrimp, in their shells
7 cups water
A ¾-pound whiting, cleaned, head on
1 bay leaf
½ teaspoon thyme
2 sprigs parsley
1 small onion, peeled
½ cup olive oil
2 lobsters, 1¼–1½ pounds each, split lengthwise (optional)
3 medium squid, cleaned (see p. 216) and cut in rings

1 medium onion, chopped
1 medium tomato, skinned and chopped
3 cups short-grain rice (see p. 175)
¼ cup peas
¼ teaspoon saffron, crumbled
2 cloves garlic, crushed
2 pimientos, homemade (p. 430) or imported, cut in strips
18 small mussels (see p. 11)
2 tablespoons minced parsley for garnish
Lemon wedges for garnish

Skin and bone the halibut, then cut into 1½-inch cubes. Reserve the scraps. Sprinkle the halibut pieces with coarse salt and let sit until ready to use. Shell the shrimp and reserve the shells. In a large pot place 7 cups water, the reserved shrimp shells, the halibut scraps, whiting, bay leaf, thyme, parsley sprigs, salt, and the peeled onion. Bring to a boil, cover, and simmer 1 hour. Strain and reserve 6 cups of the broth. Flake the whiting, removing the skin and bones, and add this fish to the broth.

Heat the oil in a metal *paella* pan with about a 15-inch base and sauté the shrimp and lobster until they turn pink (leave the lobster a little longer than the shrimp). Remove. Add the halibut pieces to the pan and sauté a minute.

Remove. In the remaining oil, sauté the squid rings quickly, then add the chopped onion and cook until it is wilted. Add the tomato and cook a minute or two until most of the tomato liquid has evaporated. Stir in the rice and coat well with the oil. Pour in the reserved fish broth, boiling hot, the peas, saffron, and salt. Boil, uncovered and stirring occasionally, about 10 minutes, or until the rice is no longer soupy but some liquid remains. Add the crushed garlic and stir in the shrimp, the halibut pieces, and the pimiento strips. Arrange the lobster on top and push the mussels into the rice. Place in a 325° F oven, uncovered, for 15–20 minutes, or until the liquid is absorbed but the rice is not quite done. Remove, cover lightly with foil, and let sit 10 minutes. Sprinkle with parsley and garnish with lemon wedges. Serve with a green salad and a chilled white wine like Marqués de Riscal. You may also pass a garlic sauce (p. 185).

ARROZ NEGRO

(Rice with Squid)

THE name "Black Rice" refers to the dark color this rice takes on from the squid ink sacs used in its preparation. The addition of an oil and garlic sauce lends a final touch of flavor. (If you prefer an *alioli* sauce, see page 186).

I urge you to try Arroz Negro, despite any misgivings you may have concerning squid or squid ink. It is one of the most delicious rice preparations ever invented.

Serves 4–6

2 pounds uncleaned squid, with tentacles	Large pinch saffron
4 tablespoons olive oil	1 teaspoon paprika
1 large onion, chopped	1/4 cup dry red wine
1 cup finely chopped green pepper	2 cups short-grain rice (see p. 175)
8 cloves garlic, minced	3¾ cups fish broth (p. 13; make about double the recipe) or clam juice
1 medium tomato, chopped	
1 tablespoon minced parsley	1/2 pound small shrimp, shelled
Salt	1 pimiento, cut in strips
Freshly ground pepper	

GARLIC SAUCE

3 cloves garlic, crushed	1/2 cup olive oil

Clean the squid (see p. 216), reserving the ink sacs and tentacles. Cut squid into 1/2-inch-wide rings or into pieces. Chop the tentacles. In a wide, shallow casserole, preferably earthenware (or a metal *paella* pan) and about 12 inches across, heat the oil and sauté the onion and green pepper until the onion is wilted. Add the squid rings and tentacles, sauté 5 minutes, then add the garlic, tomato, parsley, salt, pepper, saffron, and paprika. Cover and simmer 30 minutes.

Break the ink sacs in a cup and mix with the wine. Pass this mixture through a sieve several times until most of the ink is extracted. Reserve. Add the rice and broth, boiling hot, to the casserole and stir in the ink mixture and the shrimp. Season with salt and pepper. Bring to a boil and cook over medium-high heat, uncovered and stirring occasionally, for 10 minutes, until the rice is no longer soupy but some liquid remains. Decorate with the pimiento strips and transfer to a 325° F oven. Bake 15 minutes, uncovered, until the liquid is absorbed but the rice is not quite done. Remove from the oven, cover lightly with foil, and let sit 10 minutes.

While the rice is resting, make the garlic sauce. Place the crushed garlic in a processor or blender. Very gradually, with the motor running, pour in the oil (you may also do this with a mortar and pestle). Serve the rice with a salad and a dry white wine like Cepa de Oro. Pass the garlic sauce separately.

ARROZ CON BACALAO

(Rice with Codfish)

START PREPARATION AT LEAST ONE DAY IN ADVANCE.

MILD-TASTING dried cod and an unusual topping of thinly sliced potato give this rice dish its special character. Don't pass up the garlic sauce—it provides an added burst of flavor.

Serves 4–6

½ pound dried salt cod, boned and skinned
4 tablespoons olive oil
2 cloves garlic, minced
2 medium onions, chopped
1 medium tomato, chopped
1 tablespoon minced parsley
2 pimientos, homemade or imported, cut in strips
2 cups short-grain rice (see p. 175)
4 cups fish broth (p. 13; make about double the recipe) or clam juice

½ cup peas, fresh or frozen
Salt
½ teaspoon paprika
½ dried red chili pepper, seeds removed, crumbled
Few strands saffron
1 medium potato, peeled and cut in very thin slices (about ¹⁄₁₆ inch)

GARLIC SAUCE

3 cloves garlic, crushed   ½ cup olive oil

Soak the cod 36 hours in water to cover, changing the water several times. Drain the cod and chop. Heat the oil in a shallow 12-inch casserole, preferably earthenware. Sauté the garlic and onion until the onion is wilted. Add the tomato and parsley and cook 5 minutes. Stir in the pimiento and cod and cook 5 minutes more. Add the rice, stirring to coat well. (The dish may be prepared in advance up to this point.) Pour in the broth and add the peas. Season with salt, paprika, chili pepper, and saffron. Cook, uncovered, over a medium flame for 10 minutes, stirring, until the rice is no longer soupy but some liquid remains.

Arrange the potato slices over the casserole. Place in a 325° F oven for 15 minutes, until the liquid is absorbed but the rice is not yet done. Place under the broiler briefly to brown the potatoes. Let sit, lightly covered with foil, for about 10 minutes more.

While the rice is resting, place the crushed garlic in a processor or blender. Very gradually, with the motor running, pour in the oil (you may also do this with a mortar and pestle). Pass this garlic sauce separately. Serve the rice with Tomato and Egg Salad (p. 107) and a dry white wine like Campo Viejo.

ARROZ A BANDA

(Seafood-Flavored Rice, Alicante Style)

WE WERE at the beach near Denia in Alicante and stopped for lunch at what we thought was a casual beachside snack bar, but turned out to be *the* place to eat in the area. At El Pegolí every table was taken, and everyone dressed as if they had just arrived from the office. A large posted menu, which we perused with care, proved meaningless, for everyone was eating exactly the same meal—a large tray of glistening cold shrimp and crayfish, an artistically arranged salad, a platter of Arroz a Banda, accompanied by the strongest *alioli* sauce I had ever tasted, a light white Penedés wine (Masía Bach), and a beautiful bowl of exquisite local fruits for dessert. The rice, completely unadorned, looked like the poor cousin of the meal but proved to be the highlight. I always remember this lunch as the most wonderfully balanced and enjoyable menu ever conceived and would like nothing better than to return to that out-of-the-way restaurant at the first possible opportunity.

Arroz a Banda is the ultimate rice—it must stand on its own without a supporting cast of clams, shrimp, lobster, or other seafood usually found in rice dishes. Yet, when prepared with a well-flavored broth (the key to the success of this dish), all those traditional ingredients, although not present, seem to be there. "The meal is the rice," a dinner guest of mine mused, "yet I taste all the flavors of the sea, as if this were a seafood dinner."

To complete a meal centered on Arroz a Banda, I can think of nothing better than duplicating the menu at El Pegolí. Start with boiled and cooled shellfish—only if it is fresh, not frozen. Otherwise, a delicious alternative is Shellfish Vinaigrette on page 24 (save the cooking liquid from the shellfish to make the broth for the rice). Accompany the rice with garlic sauce (it adds a decisive touch to the rice) and a salad that includes lettuce, radish, onion, olives, hard-boiled egg wedges, green peppers, carrots, and some smoked or canned fish like mackerel or sardine—all separate and arranged attractively on a dish. Then end with the most beautiful fruit you can find.

Serves 6–8

¾ pound small or medium shrimp, in their shells
¾ cup olive oil
4 cloves garlic, peeled
1 dried sweet red pepper such as "New Mexico" style (see glossary), stems and seeds removed; or 1 pimiento, homemade or imported

(the dried pepper gives much more flavor)
Salt
Freshly ground pepper
2 tablespoons minced parsley
2 teaspoons paprika
⅛ teaspoon saffron
1 large tomato, finely chopped
3 cups short-grain rice (see p. 175)

FISH BROTH

1 pound whiting, or similar fish, cleaned, head on
1 cup clam juice
1 bay leaf
½ cup white wine

2 sprigs parsley
1 slice onion
1 slice lemon
Salt
6 peppercorns

ALIOLI SAUCE

10 cloves garlic, crushed
1 teaspoon salt
1 egg

3 teaspoons lemon juice
1 cup olive oil

Cook the shrimp in their shells in boiling salted water to cover for a minute or two, until just tender. Drain and reserve the cooking liquid. Shell the shrimp, reserve the shells, and finely chop the shrimp. Put aside.

To make the fish broth, use the reserved shrimp cooking liquid and add enough water to make 6 cups. Add the reserved shrimp shells and all the other broth ingredients. Bring to a boil, cover, then simmer 1½ hours or more—the broth must have a strong seafood flavor, but at the same time not be overly salty. Strain and reserve 6 cups. Clean the skin and bone from the whiting, then shred it and reserve.

While the broth is cooking, make the *alioli* sauce. In a processor or blender, mix the garlic and salt, add the egg and lemon juice, and beat until pale yellow. Gradually, with the motor running, incorporate the oil. Transfer the sauce to a serving bowl and leave at room temperature.

In a metal *paella* pan with about a 15-inch base, heat the ¾ cup olive oil and fry 2 of the garlic cloves until golden on all sides. Transfer them to a processor or blender, leaving the oil in the pan. Sauté the dried pepper until softened (careful not to burn) and add it, broken in pieces, to the processor. Add to the processor the salt, pepper, parsley, paprika, and saffron. Blend until finely chopped. Gradually pour in 1 cup of the broth. (The dish may be made in advance up to this point.)

Heat the oil in the *paella* pan again. Add the remaining 2 cloves of garlic, minced, then the tomato. Sauté 3 minutes. Stir in the rice and mix well to coat with the oil, for 3 minutes. Pour in the mixture from the processor, the remaining 5 cups of the broth, boiling hot, the chopped reserved shrimp, and the shredded whiting. Bring to a boil and cook over a medium-high flame, uncovered, for about 7 minutes, stirring until the rice is no longer soupy but some liquid remains. Transfer to a 325° F oven and bake, uncovered, 15 minutes, until the liquid is absorbed but the rice is not quite done. Remove from the oven and let sit, loosely covered with foil, for 10 minutes. Pass the *alioli* sauce and serve a dry white Catalán wine like Masía Bach.

PAELLA HUERTANA DE MURCIA
(Vegetable Paella)

THE province of Murcia is known for its tender, sweet vegetables, and therefore this dish most appropriately comes from that region. It is an excellent and colorful meatless meal that includes peas, limas, carrots, artichokes, red peppers, tomatoes, and a wonderful touch of ground almonds.

¼ pound green beans
½ cup peas, fresh or frozen
¾ cup lima beans
2 carrots, scraped and sliced
    ¼-inch thick
8 artichoke hearts
6 tablespoons olive oil
1 large onion, chopped
1 pimiento, homemade or
    imported, chopped
2 tomatoes, skinned and chopped

8 blanched almonds
2 cloves garlic, peeled and
    coarsely chopped
4 tablespoons minced parsley
2 cups short-grain rice (see p. 175)
3 cups strong chicken broth,
    preferably homemade
¼ teaspoon saffron
Salt
2 hard-boiled eggs, cut in wedges
1 lemon, cut in wedges

Cook the green beans, peas, limas, carrots, and artichokes in salted water until just tender. (The vegetables, of course, have different cooking times—you may want to cook some in separate pots.) Drain the vegetables and reserve 1 cup of the liquid.

In a metal *paella* pan with about a 15-inch base, heat the oil. Sauté the onion and pimiento until the onion is wilted. Add the tomato and cook 10 minutes, stirring. Meanwhile, in a processor or blender, mix the almonds, garlic, and 2 tablespoons of the parsley until they are very finely chopped (or use a mortar and pestle). Add the rice to the tomato mixture and stir to coat, then add the garlic mixture, the green beans, peas, lima beans, and carrots. Pour in the broth, boiling hot, and the reserved vegetable cooking liquid. Add the saffron and salt. Bring to a boil, lower the heat to medium, and cook 7 minutes on top of the stove, uncovered, stirring frequently, until the rice is no longer soupy but some liquid remains. Transfer to a 325° F oven and bake, uncovered, 10 minutes, until the liquid is absorbed but the rice is not quite done. Decorate with the egg wedges and artichokes, then bake 5 minutes more. Remove, cover loosely with foil, and let sit 10 minutes before serving. Decorate with lemon wedges and sprinkle with the remaining parsley. Serve with Ensalada de San Isidro (p. 106) and a light red wine like Marqués de Murrieta.

ARROZ EN CALDERO A LA MURCIANA

(Rice with Dried Red Peppers and Seafood)

LET'S reserve this rice for real garlic lovers—among whose ranks I count myself—for there is garlic everywhere: in the rice, over the fish that is served on the side, and in the powerful *alioli* sauce that accompanies the rice. In

Murcia this rice is typically cooked in an iron kettle hung by chains over a fire. The dried red peppers are essential to the flavor of Arroz en Caldero.

Serves 4–6

Alioli Sauce (p. 186)
2 pounds fish steaks, such as fresh cod, hake, or halibut
Coarse salt
6 tablespoons olive oil
2 dried sweet red peppers, such as "New Mexico" style (see glossary), stems and seeds removed
11 cloves garlic, peeled
2 tablespoons minced parsley

2 pimientos, homemade or imported
4 cups fish broth (p. 13; make about double the recipe) or clam juice
½ pound small shrimp, shelled
½ pound squid, cleaned (see p. 216) and cut in rings
2 medium tomatoes, skinned and chopped
2 cups short-grain rice (see p. 175), rinsed

Make the *alioli* sauce according to directions on page 186. Let it sit at room temperature while preparing the rice. Sprinkle the fish steaks heavily with coarse salt. Let sit 1 hour (this firms the flesh of the fish).

Heat 3 tablespoons of the oil in a skillet. Sauté the dried peppers over low heat until softened—be careful not to burn them. Break the peppers into pieces and transfer to a processor or blender, leaving the oil in the pan. Add all but 1 clove of the garlic, 1 teaspoon salt, 1 tablespoon of the parsley, and 1 of the pimientos. Beat until finely chopped. With the motor running, gradually pour in 1 cup of the fish broth and blend until smooth. Transfer to a kettle (typically earthenware) or deep casserole and stir in the remaining 3 cups of broth.

In the remaining oil in the skillet, sauté the shrimp and squid about 1 minute. Remove and reserve. Add the remaining 3 tablespoons of oil to the pan and sauté the tomato 3 minutes over high heat until most of the liquid has evaporated.

Heat the contents of the kettle, then add the tomato and oil from the skillet. Rinse the salt from the fish. Add the fish to the kettle and cook about 7 minutes. Remove the fish to a warm platter. Spoon on a tablespoon or 2 of the cooking sauce. Slice the remaining garlic clove over the fish and sprinkle with the remaining tablespoon of parsley. The fish will be served at room temperature. Add the rice to the kettle, the remaining pimiento, chopped, the shrimp, squid, and salt. Bring to a boil. Cover and simmer 10 minutes, stirring occasionally. Turn off the flame, cover lightly with foil, and let sit 10 minutes more. Serve the rice and the fish on separate plates. Pass the *alioli* sauce. Serve with a green salad and a dry white wine like Cepa de Oro.

ARROZ A LA CUBANA
(Rice with Fried Eggs and Bananas)

BANANAS grow in profusion in the Spanish Canary Islands and were first introduced to the New World by the Spanish in the sixteenth century. Nevertheless, it was left to Spanish America to use bananas in cooking. This tasty dish of bananas, rice, eggs, and tomato sauce is referred to in Spain as "Cuban Style Rice."

Serves 4

5 tablespoons butter
2 tablespoons diced slab bacon
2 cloves garlic, minced
1½ cups short-grain rice (see p. 175)
1½ cups chicken broth
1½ cups water
Salt
Freshly ground pepper

Oil for frying
3 bananas, peeled and cut in half
    lengthwise and crosswise
Flour
1 egg, lightly beaten
8 whole eggs
1 tablespoon minced parsley
    for garnish

TOMATO SAUCE

3 tablespoons olive oil
1 medium onion, finely chopped
2 cloves garlic, minced
1⅓ cups puréed fresh or
    canned tomato

Salt
Freshly ground pepper

To make the tomato sauce, heat the oil in a saucepan, add the onion and garlic, cover, and sauté over low heat for 10 minutes (the onion should not brown). Add the tomato purée, salt, pepper, and enough water to make a tomato-sauce consistency. Cover and cook slowly 30 minutes.

In a shallow 12-inch casserole, heat the butter, then sauté the bacon and garlic. When the bacon begins to brown, add the rice and stir to coat with the butter. Stir in the chicken broth and water, both boiling hot, salt, and pepper. Cover and transfer to a 350° F oven for 15 minutes. Remove and let sit 10 minutes, covered.

While the rice is resting, heat the oil, ¼ inch deep, in a skillet. Coat the banana pieces with flour and dip them in the beaten egg. Fry them lightly in the oil until just golden. Drain. Fry the eggs as for Fried Eggs, Spanish Style (p. 153).

Arrange the bananas and eggs decoratively over the rice. Sprinkle with parsley and serve in the same dish. Pass a bowl with the tomato sauce separately. Serve with a salad and a light red wine like Rioja Clarete.

MOROS Y CRISTIANOS
(Rice with Black Beans)

The name of this dish, "Moors and Christians," has its origins/ in Spanish history. For more than seven hundred years, Moorish invaders from North Africa ruled Spain and left indelible cultural and culinary marks. I have no idea how far back this dish can be traced, but the name, coupled with the contrast of black beans and white rice, obviously refers to the religious and racial strife of that period in Spanish history. You may serve Moros y Cristianos as a dinner or as an accompaniment to a simple meat dish.

Serves 4–6

½ pound black beans (*frijoles negros*)
½ onion, peeled
Freshly ground pepper
2 cloves garlic, peeled
2 tablespoons olive oil
1 medium onion, chopped

2 cloves garlic, minced
¼ cup diced slab bacon
½ teaspoon paprika
1 teaspoon flour
Salt
Parsley sprigs for garnish

TURBANTE DE ARROZ (*Rice Ring*)

6 tablespoons butter
1 tablespoon finely chopped onion
1 cup short-grain rice (see p. 175)
1 cup chicken broth
1 cup water

Salt
1 sprig parsley
¼ teaspoon thyme
⅛ teaspoon tarragon

Soak the beans for 1 hour in 2 cups cold water. Drain. Place the beans in a pot, cover with 2 cups water, add the ½ onion, pepper, and the whole garlic cloves. Cover and simmer 1 hour.

While the beans are cooking, heat the oil in a small skillet. Sauté the chopped onion, minced garlic, and bacon, until the bacon is lightly browned. Sprinkle on the paprika and flour. Add this mixture to the bean pot, along with the salt. Continue cooking until the beans are done, about 1 hour more, adding some water if necessary (the beans should have very little liquid when done). Discard the ½ onion.

To make the rice, melt 3 tablespoons of the butter in a deep ovenproof casserole. Add the onion and sauté until wilted. Add the rice, stir to coat with the butter, then stir in the broth and water, boiling hot, salt, parsley, thyme, and tarragon. Cover and bake at 400° F for 15 minutes. Remove from the oven, discard the parsley, and dot the rice with the remaining butter. Cover and let sit 5–10 minutes.

To mold the rice, grease well an 8-inch ring mold with butter. Fill with the rice and press down so the rice is well packed. Return to the oven for 2 minutes. Place the beans on a slightly concave round serving platter. Turn the rice out over the beans to form a crown. Decorate with parsley sprigs. If this is to be a main course, serve with Cucumber, Tomato, and Pepper Salad (p. 106) and a light red wine like Marqués de Cáceres.

ARROZ AL HORNO

(Rice and Chickpeas)

ALTHOUGH this rice is perhaps most appropriate as a side course, it may be a main dish as well. Arroz al Horno is decorated with a whole head of garlic in the center, which in the Valencian dialect is humorously called the *perdiu*, the partridge.

Serves 3–6

5 ounces dried or 1¼ cups
    canned chickpeas
¼ cup olive oil
½ medium onion, chopped
½ medium tomato, skinned and
    finely chopped
1 clove garlic, minced
½ medium potato, peeled, in
    ⅛-inch slices

¼ teaspoon paprika
1 cup short-grain rice (see p. 175)
Few strands saffron
Salt
1 head garlic, unpeeled, in one piece
2 ounces *morcilla* (blood sausage)
    in ¼-inch slices (optional)
    (see glossary)

If the chickpeas are dry, soak overnight, then cook 1½–2 hours in salted water until tender. Reserve 2 cups of the cooking liquid. If using canned chickpeas, drain the chickpeas and reserve the liquid. Add enough chicken broth to make 2 cups.

Heat the oil in an 8-inch shallow casserole, preferably earthenware, and sauté the onion until wilted. Add the tomato and cook 3 minutes. Add the garlic, then the potato slices and paprika and cook a couple of minutes more. Stir in the rice and cook, stirring, 5 minutes more. Add the chickpeas and reserved broth, season with saffron and salt. Bring to a boil and cook over a medium-high flame, uncovered and stirring occasionally, for 5 minutes, or until the rice is no longer soupy but some liquid remains.

Place the head of garlic in the center of the casserole (the garlic is decorative and not meant to be eaten). Arrange the *morcilla* slices on top and place in a 325° F oven for 20 minutes. Remove and cover lightly with foil. Let rest 5–10 minutes before serving.

ARROZ CON CORDERO

(Rice with Lamb and Chickpeas)

START PREPARATION ONE DAY IN ADVANCE.

ALTHOUGH lamb is not usually associated with Spanish rice dishes, this Valencian recipe proves that this need not be so, for lamb combines beautifully with rice, and when chickpeas, pig's foot, and sausage are added besides, the results are excellent.

Serves 4–6

½ pound dried chickpeas
9 tablespoons olive oil
½ pound boneless lamb such as
    shoulder, in ½-inch cubes
Coarse salt
1 medium tomato, finely chopped
6 cups water
2 pork bones
1 pig's foot, split in half
2 ounces slab bacon, in ½-inch cubes
    (about 8 cubes)
1 small onion, peeled and halved

Few strands saffron
2 cloves
Freshly ground pepper
1 head garlic, separated and peeled
2 cups short-grain rice (see p. 175)
2 tablespoons finely chopped parsley
1 medium tomato, in ⅛-inch slices
¼ pound *morcilla* (blood sausage), in
    ¼-inch slices (see glossary)
1 pimiento, homemade or imported,
    cut in strips

Soak the chickpeas overnight in cold water to cover. Drain. The next day heat 6 tablespoons of the oil in a medium skillet. Sprinkle the lamb with salt and brown in the oil. Remove. Add the chopped tomato to the pan and cook 3 minutes.

In a soup pot, place the chickpeas, 6 cups water, the bones, pig's foot, bacon cubes, the lamb, the tomato, and the onion. Bring to a boil, cover, and simmer 1 hour. Add the saffron, cloves, pepper, garlic cloves, and salt and continue cooking until the chickpeas are done, about 1 hour more. Strain the broth and reserve 4 cups. Discard the bones. Bone and finely chop the pig's foot. Reserve along with all the other ingredients from the pot.

In a 12-inch shallow casserole, preferably earthenware, heat the remaining 3 tablespoons of oil. Add the rice and parsley and stir to coat the rice well with the oil. Cook 2 minutes. Pour in the reserved broth, boiling hot, and the other reserved ingredients from the soup pot. Bring to a boil and cook, uncovered and stirring occasionally, 4 or 5 minutes, or until the rice is not soupy but some liquid remains. Decorate the top with the sliced tomato, sliced sausage, and pimiento strips. Bake, uncovered, in a 325° F oven for 20 minutes, or until the liquid is absorbed but the rice not quite done. Let sit 5 minutes, lightly covered with foil, before serving. A tomato salad and a full-bodied red wine like Siglo are fine accompaniments.

ARROZ CON CALABACÍN

(Rice with Zucchini)

I FIND this delicious rice dish most appealing as a side course to complement meat or fish. For those of a vegetarian bent, however, it also makes a nice main course.

Serves 4–6 as a side course

¼ cup olive oil
½ dried sweet red pepper, such as "New Mexico" style (see glossary), stem and seeds removed
1 small tomato, cut in large pieces
1 clove garlic, peeled
1 small onion, chopped

¼ pound zucchini (½ medium zucchini), cut in ½-inch cubes
¼ pound green beans
1 cup short-grain rice (see p. 175)
2 cups chicken broth, preferably homemade
Salt

In a 8–9-inch casserole, preferably earthenware, heat the oil and sauté the dried red pepper until it is softened (careful not to burn). Place in a processor or blender, broken into pieces. In the same oil sauté the tomato and garlic until the garlic turns golden. Place the tomato and garlic in the processor. Add the onion to the casserole and sauté until it is wilted. Stir in the zucchini and green beans and sauté 10 minutes. Add the rice and stir to coat well with the oil.

Blend the processor ingredients until a paste forms. Slowly pour in the broth, heated, and blend until smooth. Add this to the casserole, season with salt, and bring to a boil, then simmer, uncovered and stirring occasionally, 5 minutes, or until the rice is no longer soupy but some liquid remains. Place in a 325° F oven, uncovered, for 15 minutes, or until the liquid is absorbed but the rice is not quite done. Cover lightly with foil and let sit 5 minutes before serving.

PAELLA DE CODORNICES Y SETAS

(Quail and Mushroom Paella)

THIS is one of my favorite *paellas*, in appearance as well as in taste. The mushrooms give the rice a special flavor and the quail are as decorative as they are delicious.

Serves 6–8

A 2½-pound chicken or rabbit
½ pound pork loin, in ½-inch cubes
½ pound pork ribs, divided into in-
    dividual ribs and each split
    in half crosswise
3–4 quail, split in halves
Salt
10 tablespoons olive oil
2 pimientos, homemade or
    imported, chopped
1 tomato, finely chopped

¼ pound green beans, cut in
    halves crosswise
4 cloves garlic, minced
1 medium onion, chopped
1 pound mushrooms, stems trimmed;
    halved or quartered,
    depending on size
3 cups short-grain rice (see p. 175)
6 cups strong chicken broth,
    preferably homemade
Few strands saffron

Cut the chicken into small serving pieces—the whole breast into 4 parts, each thigh into 2 parts, the bony tip of the leg chopped off, the wing tip discarded, and the rest of the wing separated into 2 parts. Sprinkle the chicken, pork cubes, pork ribs, and quail with salt. Heat the oil in a metal *paella* pan with about a 15-inch base. Fry the chicken, pork ribs, and quail until well browned on one side. Turn and add the pork cubes and continue sautéing until everything is well browned. Remove the meats to a warm platter.

Add the pimientos, tomato, green beans, garlic, and onion to the pan. Sauté 5 minutes. Add the mushrooms and sauté 5 minutes more. Stir in the rice and coat well with the oil. Add the reserved pork cubes, then pour in the broth, boiling hot, the saffron, and the salt. Bring to a boil. Cook, uncovered and stirring occasionally, about 10 minutes, or until the rice is no longer soupy but some liquid remains. Bury the chicken pieces and the ribs in the rice. Decorate the top of the *paella* with the quail. Transfer to a 325° F oven and bake, uncovered, 20 minutes, or until the liquid is absorbed but the rice is not quite done. Remove, cover lightly with foil, and let sit 5–10 minutes before serving. A salad and a light red wine like Lan are the only accompaniments necessary.

FIDEUÁ DE MARISCOS

(Noodle and Shellfish Paella)

FIDEUÁ, as the name implies, is a noodle dish (made with *fideos*). What is it doing in a rice chapter? The connection is the *paella* pan and the method of cooking, which give this dish very much the appearance of a *paella* and something of the same taste. Noodles traditionally are of little importance in Spanish cuisine, but Fideuá, which seems to have surfaced only within the last ten years, has become enormously popular. I love Fideuá and find it quite different from any other noodle dish I have ever sampled.

Serves 4

¾ pound halibut steak, or similar
    firm fish, skinned, boned,
    and cut in
    1½-inch cubes
Coarse salt
½ cup olive oil
½ pound small shrimp, shelled
¼ pound large shrimp, in
    their shells

2 cloves garlic, minced
1 teaspoon paprika
⅛ teaspoon cayenne
2 medium tomatoes, skinned
    and chopped
6 cups fish broth (p. 13; make about
    triple the recipe) or
    clam juice
Few strands saffron

¾ pound noodle nests (*fideos*   or Spanish or Italian
    #168)—these noodles are   specialty shops
    about ⅟₁₆ inch thick and   12 very small clams (see p. 11)
    can be found in supermarkets   12 small mussels (see p. 11)

Sprinkle the halibut with salt and let it sit 10 minutes. Heat the oil in a metal *paella* pan with about a 15-inch base, and sauté the small and large, unshelled shrimp briefly, only until they turn pink. Reserve the shrimp. Add the halibut cubes to the pan, sauté lightly for a minute or so, and stir in the garlic, paprika, cayenne, and tomato. Add the fish stock and the saffron and bring to a boil. Add the noodle nests, breaking each nest into 3 parts. Season with salt and cook 3 minutes, uncovered and stirring occasionally, then add the clams and mussels and continue cooking, uncovered, until the noodles are no longer soupy but some liquid remains. Stir in the reserved small shrimp and arrange the large unshelled shrimp on top. Transfer to a 350° F oven and bake 10 minutes. Turn up the heat to 450° F and cook 5 minutes more, or until the liquid is absorbed and the noodles are crusty around the edges.

Chapter 8

MARISCOS
(*Shellfish*)

THE Bar Cervecería Santa Bárbara on a Sunday morning is a sight to behold. This capacious Madrid establishment is packed to the rafters, and negotiating one's way through the door is a feat in itself. Once inside, it is standing room only. The bar reverberates with noise, as customers engage in animated conversations while drinking frothy mugs of beer and eating just one thing: shrimp. Not four or five daintily arranged shrimp, mind you, but mounds of them, which are devoured with alarming speed and just as quickly replaced by the harried waiters who dash to and fro. The surprise is not that this *cervecería*, or beer parlor, is so crowded, for its shellfish is excellent. Rather, it is the mind-boggling price that everyone is paying for his shrimp appetizer— over twenty-five dollars a pound, and unrelentlessly on the rise.

Spaniards take leave of their senses when it comes to shellfish. They will pay five dollars for a single scallop, forty dollars a pound for rare goose barnacles, fifty dollars for a lobster—the price is of little consequence. Although the craving for crustaceans is reaching epidemic proportions, the Spanish love for shellfish is nothing new. Back in the sixteenth century, Emperor Charles V, noted gourmand and gout sufferer, insisted on fresh oysters at his inland retirement retreat at the Yuste Monastery. They were regularly rushed to him by horse relay carriers in record time to preserve their freshness. A similar system exists today to bring shellfish to landlocked Madrid, where the demand is insatiable but quality and freshness, besides, are held in the utmost esteem. Delivery trucks will travel the night from Galicia and the Basque country in the north, as well as from points south in Andalucía and the Levante region in the east, so that fresh-caught *frutas del mar* reach the city by early morning before they have lost the exquisite fresh taste of the sea.

But if you really want to sample Spain's exceptional shellfish at its best, there is nothing quite like sitting at a beachside café, leisurely tackling a tray of unshelled crustaceans, slowly removing their shells, then extracting the delicate morsels of meat from within. I must confess that the Spanish shellfish fever has infected me and my husband, to the extent that no matter where we are in Spain on vacation, we will invariably catch a flight, or drive endless hours, to reach Sanlúcar de Barrameda near Cádiz, where the fresh-caught *langostinos*—aristocrats of the shrimp family—are not to be believed. Oh yes, there are those who will disagree, as must be expected in an individualistic country such as Spain, those who will travel hours on end to the east instead of the south to eat the *langostinos* at Vinaroz in Castellón province. Regional prejudices of this sort abound. The tiny *quisquillas*—shrimp so small that dozens enter into a portion—are popular appetizers in the north but are deemed unfit for serious eating in the south, where they are relegated to broth making and saucy shrimp cocktails. Shrimp from the waters of Málaga are among my favorites, yet proponents of the shrimp from Benicarló are also vociferous in their opinions. The *cigala*, a kind of saltwater crayfish, from the north are the best by some standards, while the southern crayfish receive accolades from others. Lobsters with large claws, called *bogavantes* and equivalent to our northern lobsters, are considered by some to take second place to the spiny lobster, *langosta*, which concentrates its meat in its large tail section. The giant crabs, *centollos*, along with many other crab varieties such as the prized *nécoras* are highly esteemed in the Basque country and Galicia, and every scrap of their delicious meat is utilized, while around Cádiz, fishermen net crabs, tear off one claw, throw back the crab to regenerate the leg, and send these small claws to the city of Cádiz, where they are considered the ultimate delicacy.

Few will disagree that in Galicia and all along the northern coast, some of Spain's finest and rarest shellfish is found. The ugly, fingerlike *percebe* (goose barnacle) is a curious crustacean that fishermen pry loose from storm-battered rocks at the risk of their lives. The *percebe* is considered by many to be the most exquisite (and the costliest) product the sea has to offer. In a category of its own is the *vieira* (scallop), found in Spain only in Galicia. Rather than eating scallops by the dozen, as Spaniards are shocked to find we do, just one precious scallop is served in, and attached to, its own shell. Only scallops fresh from the sea can be kept in their shells, as we keep clams, for the meat deteriorates rapidly. The scallop is, besides, the only shellfish in Spain endowed with religious significance. In Galicia is the city of Santiago de Compostela, one of the three cities in the world designated by the Vatican as "holy," for it was there that the body of Saint James (Santiago in Spanish) was discovered under miraculous circumstances. Since medieval times, pilgrims from all over the world have made their way to Santiago on foot, overcoming incredible hardships, in order to bask in the glory of this magnificent city. In the past, most came seeking cures for their illnesses, and most, unfortunately, were destined to die there. The scallop shell became the symbol of such religiously inspired pilgrimages, and those who did return home pinned scallop shells to their robes, as proof that, indeed, they had reached Santiago, the city of miracles.

I have barely touched the surface of the shellfish Spain has to offer. There are, of course, many varieties of clams, mostly tiny, and mussels are everywhere. Few realize that squid and octopus are also members of the mollusk family, and squid, in particular, is a favorite in Spain and well on its way to popularity in the United States. Octopus and squid are found along the

Spanish coast in many varieties, sizes, and shapes, none more surprising to the
visitor than the delectable *pulpitos* and *calamaritos*, octopus and squid little
more than an inch in size, which hardly make a mouthful.

Recipes for shellfish, as such, are of little importance in Spain. Shellfish is
usually thought of as an appetizer or first course (many more shellfish recipes
appear under Tapas) and is most often simply boiled or grilled. However,
when special preparations do exist, the results are exceptional. Many delicious
regional specialties are included in this chapter: the Catalán lobster with
hazelnuts and chocolate, the Tarragonese shellfish in *romesco* sauce with almonds and dried red peppers, a variety of Galician scallop recipes, Basque
stuffed crab, shellfish in green sauces, squid in ink sauce, and shellfish in
Andalucian sherry sauces. I strongly suggest, besides, that you try any fresh
(not frozen) or, better still, live shellfish in the Spanish style: boiled, cooled to
room temperature, and served in the shell with homemade mayonnaise (p. 104)
or Salpicón Sauce (p. 25) on the side.

GAMBAS
(Shrimp)

FOOD experts seem to agree that deveining shrimp is done exclusively for
aesthetic reasons. In Spain, shrimp are never deveined—in fact, many Spanish
recipes call for cooking and serving shrimp in its shell, in which case deveining
in advance is impossible. It is my opinion that shrimp is much more attractive
whole, rather than with the rough edges and curling caused by deveining.
Consequently, I always leave the shrimp intact. The shrimp in the Tapas
section, similarly, should not be deveined, unless, of course, it is your preference to do so.

GAMBAS EN SALSA VERDE
(Shrimp in Green Sauce)

AN ABUNDANCE of parsley present in green sauces not only gives them their
characteristic color but also provides the principal flavor. Green sauce is
commonly used for other seafoods, such as mussels (p. 17) and hake (p. 225) and
is besides a delicious coating for potatoes (p. 99). Shrimp in Green Sauce is a
lovely dish to serve to guests.

Serves 4

1 pound medium or large shrimp, in
    their shells
Salt
Freshly ground pepper
Flour for dusting
5 tablespoons olive oil

1 cup chopped parsley
¼ teaspoon salt
2 cloves garlic, chopped
¼ cup dry white wine
2 tablespoons finely chopped onion
1½ tablespoons flour

SHRIMP BROTH

1¼ cups water
1 slice lemon
1 slice onion
3 peppercorns

½ bay leaf
¼ teaspoon thyme
1 sprig parsley
Salt

Shell the shrimp, leaving the tail and the shell of the last joint intact. Reserve the shells. To make the broth, place the shrimp shells and the broth ingredients in a saucepan. Bring to a boil, lower the heat, and simmer about 20 minutes. Strain. Reserve ¾ cup.

Sprinkle the shrimp with salt and pepper, then dust with flour. Heat 3 tablespoons of the oil in a large skillet. Fry the shrimp quickly, about 1½–2 minutes. Remove the shrimp to a warm platter. Leave any remaining oil in the pan.

Place the parsley in a blender or food processor with ¼ teaspoon salt and the garlic. Blend until the ingredients are finely minced. With the motor running, pour in the shrimp broth and the wine. Blend until smooth.

Add the remaining 2 tablespoons of oil to the skillet. Sauté the onion until it is wilted. Stir in the 1½ tablespoons of flour and cook a minute. Gradually stir in the sauce from the blender. Cook until the sauce is thickened and smooth. Replace the shrimp in the skillet and cook only until they are heated through. Add salt and pepper to taste. Serve with a reserve white wine, such as Federico Paternina, and Ensalada a la Almoraina (p. 107).

NOTE: The sauce and the shrimp may be made in advance, but without combining them until ready to serve. The sauce, however, may lose some of its bright green color when reheated.

GAMBAS AL JEREZ
(Shrimp in Sherry Sauce)

DRY sherry is the perfect drink with cold boiled shrimp. Logically, sherry should also be an ideal ingredient in a sauce for a shrimp dish, as it is in this recipe.

Serves 4

1 pound medium or large shrimp, shelled, leaving the tail and shell of last joint intact
Butter

¼ cup dry (*fino*) sherry
2 tablespoons finely diced cured ham
1 tablespoon minced parsley

WHITE SAUCE

5 teaspoons butter
4 teaspoons flour
¾ teaspoon Dijon-style mustard
½ cup milk

½ cup fish broth (p. 13) or clam juice
Salt
White pepper

To make the white sauce, melt the butter in a saucepan. Stir in the flour and cook a minute. Add the mustard, then gradually pour in the milk and fish broth. Season with salt and pepper. Cook, stirring constantly, until thickened and smooth.

Place the shrimp in a greased shallow baking pan in 1 layer. Dot with butter. Pour in the sherry and sprinkle on the ham. Broil about 2 minutes, turn the shrimp, and broil about 2 minutes more. Remove the shrimp and the ham to a warm platter. Pour the pan juices into the white sauce. Heat the sauce, then spoon it over the shrimp. Sprinkle with parsley and serve, accompanied by a Green Bean Salad (p. 118). A dry sherry may be served with this dish, or a white wine such as Viña Sol.

LANGOSTINOS GRAN MESÓN
(Prawns in Garlic Sauce)

IN SPAIN shrimp is usually served in its shell, even when in a sauce, for the shells give an added flavor of the sea and keep the shrimp from toughening. You may shell them if you wish, but once you learn to clean shrimp with a knife and fork, it is not at all difficult and becomes part of the pleasure of eating them. In any case, this is a most delicious shrimp preparation.

Serves 4

½ cup olive oil
½ dried red chili pepper,
    seeds removed
6 cloves garlic, lightly crushed
    and peeled
8 bay leaves

2 tablespoons finely minced onion
1 pound large shrimp, in their shells
Salt
1 tablespoon minced parsley
Lemon juice

Heat the oil with the hot pepper, garlic, bay leaves, and onion in a shallow casserole (earthenware is best) until the onion and garlic begin to brown slightly. Add the shrimp, sprinkle with salt, and cook over moderate heat, covered, until the shrimp are done, about 10–15 minutes. Sprinkle with parsley and lemon juice. Serve with an Ensalada de Escalibada (p. 117) and a fine white wine such as Marqués de Riscal.

LANGOSTA CON POLLO

(Lobster with Chicken)

CATALUÑA'S combination of meat and fish has become a world-famous restaurant favorite, although there are those who consider mixing lobster with chicken a heresy and others who believe it is merely a waste of lobster. I find it an interesting combination of tastes that blend easily.

Most restaurants use a standard lobster sauce for this dish, rather than the much more unusual, typically Catalán ingredients used here—a touch of chocolate, almonds, and hazelnuts.

Serves 4

2 whole chicken breasts, split
Salt
Freshly ground pepper
2 live lobsters, about 1½ pounds each
4 tablespoons olive oil
1 medium onion, chopped
2 tablespoons minced parsley
1 bay leaf
½ teaspoon thyme
½ pound fresh or canned tomatoes,
peeled and chopped

1 cup dry white wine
2 tablespoons *aguardiente* or *grappa*,
    found in most liquor stores
Few strands saffron
4 cloves garlic, peeled
16 blanched almonds
10 shelled hazelnuts
1½ teaspoons grated bitter chocolate
⅛ teaspoon sugar

Sprinkle the chicken pieces with salt and pepper. Kill the lobsters (p. 147) and divide them into the tails, large claws, heads, and small claws. Reserve the green liver material (called tomalley).

In a saucepan, place the heads and small claws with water to cover and salt. Bring to a boil, then simmer, covered, for at least 30 minutes. Reserve 1 cup.

Heat the oil in a skillet. Fry the chicken pieces over medium heat until golden on both sides. Remove to a warm platter. Turn up the heat and fry the lobster tails and large claws until they turn pink. Reserve with the chicken. Add the onion to the skillet and sauté until wilted. Add 1 tablespoon of the parsley, the bay leaf, thyme, tomato, wine, *aguardiente*, salt, and pepper. Cover and cook over medium heat for 15 minutes. Add the lobster and chicken to the tomato mixture. Cover and continue cooking about 10 minutes while preparing the processor mixture.

In a processor or blender combine the reserved tomalley, saffron, garlic, almonds, hazelnuts, the remaining tablespoon of parsley, the grated chocolate, and the sugar. Blend until as smooth as possible. Gradually pour in the reserved cup of lobster broth. Pour over the chicken and lobster, stir, cover, and continue to cook 15 minutes more.

To serve, remove the shell from the lobster tails and large claws. Cut the lobster meat into ¼-inch slices. For each serving, give 1 chicken breast piece with lobster slices on top. Pour on the sauce (it may be strained if you prefer). Serve with a salad and a full-bodied white wine such as Marqués de Riscal.

LANGOSTA AL AJO ARRIERO
(Lobster with Red Peppers)

DRIED cod is more commonly found as the main ingredient in this dish, but at Las Pocholas restaurant in Pamplona, lobster is added. (This recipe calls for *only* lobster, which is the way I prefer it.) Las Pocholas is a restaurant made famous in the thirties, when aficionados from all over the world, including Ernest Hemingway, would gather in this city in early July for the "running of the bulls." The restaurant is today owned and managed by the surviving six of nine sisters nicknamed "Las Pocholas"—all unmarried daughters of the restaurant's founder. Two are in charge of the kitchen and the rest take care of the clientele, who dine in the elegant ambience of a seignorial house, wood beamed with soothing green fabric-covered walls and oriental patterned rugs. Although expensive, there is little doubt that this restaurant, which produces many regional specialties, is *the* place to dine in Pamplona.

Serves 2

1¾-pound live lobster
¾ cup olive oil
1 medium onion, finely chopped
5 cloves garlic, minced
2 pimientos, preferably homemade
    (p. 430), finely chopped

1 tablespoon minced parsley
1 tablespoon paprika
Salt
1 tablespoon red wine vinegar

Kill the lobster (p. 147). Leaving on the shell, cut the lobster into small pieces: split the tail lengthwise and cut each half into about 4 pieces. Separate all the small claws. Divide the large claw into the pincer and leg sections. Crush the shells of these large claw pieces lightly for easy removal of the meat.

    Heat the oil in a large, shallow casserole until very hot. Fry the lobster pieces quickly—about a minute, turning once. The lobster will have turned pink. Remove to a warm platter. Pour off ¼ cup of the cooking oil. In the remaining oil, sauté the onion, garlic, pimientos, and parsley very slowly, covered, for about 10 minutes (the onion should not brown). Stir in the paprika, salt, and vinegar. Add the lobster pieces, cover, and cook 10–15 minutes, or until the lobster is just cooked.

    To give this dish a bit more elegance, you may choose to strain or purée the sauce and shell the lobster. I find it much more fun to eat as is, as long as finger bowls are provided. Serve with Salad, Murcia Style (p. 110) and a dry white wine like Viña Sol.

LANGOSTA COSTA BRAVA

(Stuffed Lobster Shells)

Serves 4

4 lobster tails, about 6 ounces each
2 tablespoons olive oil
4 shallots or scallions, minced
¼ pound mushrooms, sliced
    (about 1 cup)
A ¼-pound piece cured ham,
    finely chopped

2 tablespoons minced parsley
½ cup dry white wine
Salt
Freshly ground pepper
Grated Parmesan cheese

WHITE SAUCE

2 tablespoons butter	Salt
2 tablespoons flour	Freshly ground pepper
½ cup milk	Dash nutmeg

Drop the lobster tails into boiling water that has been seasoned according to directions on page 8. Return to a boil and cook about 5 minutes. Cool the lobster, remove the meat, and chop it coarsely. Reserve the shells. Boil down the cooking liquid a bit to give it added strength and reserve ½ cup.

To make the white sauce, melt the butter in a saucepan, add the flour, and cook slowly 1 or 2 minutes. Add the ½ cup of reserved cooking liquid, the milk, salt, pepper, and nutmeg. Stir and cook until thickened and smooth.

Heat the oil in a skillet. Add the shallots, mushrooms, ham, and parsley. Sauté 5 minutes. Add the wine and boil the liquid down to half. Season with salt and pepper if necessary. Add the lobster meat, then mix in the white sauce. Fill the lobster shells. Sprinkle with grated cheese and place in a 450° F oven for 10 minutes. Serve with Ensalada a la Almoraina (p. 107) and a dry Carta de Plata white wine.

SHANGURRO

(Stuffed Crab)

THE Bay of Biscay in Basque country is one of the finest fishing grounds in the world, and giant crabs (*centollos*) are one of the delicacies of Basque cuisine. *Shangurro*, alternately written *changurro* or *txangurro*, is the popular preparation of this crab, made by stuffing the crab shell with the crab meat mixed with a spicy sauce. If you can find crabs with shells large enough for stuffing, use them. Otherwise, scallop shells make an attractive alternative.

Serves 4–6

2 tablespoons olive oil	Salt
1 medium onion, chopped	Freshly ground pepper
2 cloves garlic, minced	Dash cayenne
4 tablespoons finely chopped carrot	¼ teaspoon tarragon
6 tablespoons tomato sauce	1 pound cooked crab meat, preferably
4 tablespoons fish broth (p. 13) or	from Alaskan king crab, cut
clam juice	in ¾-inch pieces (some will
¼ cup brandy, preferably Spanish	also be shredded)
brandy, or Cognac	Bread crumbs
¼ cup white wine	Butter
4 tablespoons minced parsley	

Heat the oil in a skillet and sauté the onion, garlic, and carrot slowly until the carrot is tender. Add the tomato sauce, fish broth, brandy, wine, 2 tablespoons of the parsley, salt, pepper, cayenne, and tarragon. Cover and cook 10 minutes. Add the crab meat and cook 5 minutes more. Place the mixture in crab or scallop shells, sprinkle with the remaining 2 tablespoons of parsley and the bread crumbs, and dot with butter. Bake at 400° F for about 10 minutes, or until the topping is golden. Serve in the shells as a first course or as a main course with a green salad and a dry white wine such as Cepa de Oro.

CANGREJOS AL JEREZ

(Crabs in Sherry)

WHAT a wonderfully attractive and pleasurable meal this makes. If fewer crabs are served per person, this can just as well be a first course for some very special dinner. Note that this is not a saucy dish: the sherry cooks away before serving.

Serves 2

8–12 live hard-shelled crabs, about
    ¼ pound each
Salt
1 stick (¼ pound) sweet butter

3 bay leaves
½ cup dry (*fino*) sherry
1 tablespoon minced parsley
Freshly ground pepper

Place the crabs in a sink and scrub as well as possible under running water. Bring a large pot of salted water to a boil. Add the live crabs and cook 5 minutes. Remove and cool. Scrub more, if necessary.

Melt the butter in a very large skillet. Add the bay leaves and arrange the crabs, shell side up, in the pan. Cook over medium-high heat for 5 minutes, shaking frequently. Turn the crabs and cook 2 minutes more. Turn over again and continue cooking 3 minutes. Add the sherry to the pan and cook until the sherry evaporates. Remove the crabs to a large serving platter. Deglaze the pan with a few tablespoons of water. Add the parsley and pepper. Pour the sauce over the crabs and serve, accompanied by Ensalada de San Isidro (p. 106) and a chilled dry *fino* sherry like Don Zoilo.

VIEIRAS GRATINADAS
(Baked Scallops)

THIS recipe is a typical preparation for scallops, found in many restaurants in Galicia, but most enjoyable to eat at the Hostal de los Reyes Católicos, formerly a sixteenth-century hospital constructed by the "Catholic Kings," Fernando and Isabel, for pilgrims journeying to the city of Santiago de Compostela. Today the hospital is a sumptuous hotel, elegantly decorated with rustic antiques and overlooking the city's splendid cathedral. When the preshelled scallops available to us are prepared in this manner, they take on a flavor similar to their Spanish counterparts.

Serves 4–6

2 tablespoons olive oil	Freshly ground pepper
1 medium onion, chopped	1 tablespoon minced parsley
1 clove garlic, minced	2 tablespoons melted butter
2 thin slices cured ham, chopped	1 pound large (sea) scallops
¼ cup dry white wine	Lemon juice
¾ cup bread crumbs	Butter
Salt	

In a skillet, heat the oil and sauté the onion and garlic until the onion is wilted. Add the ham and sauté briefly. Pour in the wine, cook 2 minutes, then turn off the heat and stir in the bread crumbs, salt, pepper, parsley, and melted butter.

Grease 4 scallop shells and arrange the scallops in the shells. Sprinkle with lemon juice, cover with the bread crumb mixture, and dot with butter. Bake at 400° F for 15 minutes. This may be served as a first course, or as a main course with a green salad and a fine medium-dry white wine such as Viña Esmeralda.

VIEIRAS SANTIAGÜENSES

(Baked Stuffed Scallops)

Serves 4–6

¾ pound sea or bay scallops, finely chopped
1 medium onion, finely chopped
2 cloves garlic, minced
¾ cup bread crumbs
2 tablespoons minced parsley

Salt
Freshly ground pepper
Pinch ground or crushed clove
2 tablespoons olive oil
1 tablespoon white wine
Butter

In a bowl, mix together the scallops, onion, garlic, bread crumbs, parsley, salt, pepper, and clove. Stir in the oil and the wine. Fill scallop shells, dot with butter, and bake at 350° F for about 15–20 minutes. Serve with a salad and a medium-dry white wine like Viña Zaconia. Or serve as a first course.

VIEIRAS DE SANTIAGO

(Scallops, Santiago Style)

THIS wonderful recipe has been immensely popular with guests. It is a welcome change from the ever-present Coquille St. Jacques (St. Jacques is the French name for Santiago, the patron saint of Spain) and replaces the typical white sauce with a spicy tomato and wine sauce.

Serves 4–6

2 tablespoons olive oil
4 tablespoons finely chopped onion
2 cloves garlic, minced
1 pound bay scallops (or sea scallops cut in halves)
2 tablespoons chopped parsley
½ teaspoon thyme
1 dried red chili pepper, seeds removed, crumbled
Salt

Freshly ground pepper
2 cups sliced mushrooms
2 tablespoons brandy, preferably Spanish brandy, or Cognac
¾ cup dry white wine
½ cup tomato sauce, preferably homemade (see p. 218)
Bread crumbs
Butter

Heat the oil in a skillet and sauté the onion and garlic until the onion is wilted. Add the scallops and cook over high heat 2 minutes, stirring. (The scallops should not give off liquid—if they do, remove them and evaporate the liquid.) Lower the heat and sprinkle in the parsley, thyme, chili pepper, salt, and pepper. Add the mushrooms and cook 5 minutes. Pour in the brandy and flame. Then remove the scallops and mushrooms and arrange them in scallop shells or individual casseroles. Add the wine and tomato sauce to the skillet and bring to a boil. Season with salt and pepper if necessary. Simmer 10 minutes, uncovered.

Pour the sauce over the scallops. Sprinkle with bread crumbs and dot with butter. Bake at 450° F for about 10 minutes. Serve with a green salad and a medium-dry white wine such as Sin Rival. These scallops are excellent as a first course for a special dinner.

GRAN ROMESCO
DE PESCADO "SOL-RIC"

(Mixed Seafood in Romesco Sauce)

THE ancient city of Tarragona, where the many monuments of its Roman past are the city's star attraction, is also the home of *romesco*. *Romesco* may refer to a sauce accompanying plainly prepared seafood (see following recipe) or it can be a sauce in which seafood is cooked. The basic ingredients are dried sweet peppers, almonds, and garlic, but the variations, of course, are many. One of our most memorable meals in Spain was at the Sol-Ric restaurant in Tarragona, where we dined on this extraordinary version of Romesco. The sauce was delectable and the seafood the best the Catalán coast has to offer, including tiny octopus no bigger than a thumb joint.

The Sol-Ric restaurant is a country-style house done in the local rustic architecture, whitewashed and wood beamed, with an exceptional collection of Catalán antiques. In the summer the tree-shaded outdoor terrace is a delight. The brothers Tomás, owners of the restaurant, split their duties between the kitchen (brother Simón) and attending to the numerous clients (brother Antonio) who flock from all over Spain and often from far-flung parts of the globe to eat at this restaurant.

Gran Romesco de Pescado is quite an expensive dish—just preparing the cooking broth requires ¾ pound of shrimp, not to mention the lobster and clams that are featured in the main preparation—but I think you will love the results. The sauce, which involves many steps, may be made in advance and the fish added in the final stages of preparation. The dried red pepper is essential to the sauce.

serves 4

4 small fish steaks, about 1¼ pounds
　　and 1 inch thick—the fish
　　must be firm fleshed,
　　like halibut
Coarse salt
1 live lobster, about 1½–2 pounds
12 tablespoons olive oil
¾ pound small shrimp, in their shells
½ medium onion, finely chopped
2 cloves garlic, minced
2 medium tomatoes, finely chopped
3 cups water
Freshly ground pepper
1 dried sweet red pepper such as
　　"New Mexico" style, seeds

and stem removed
　　(see glossary)
12 blanched almonds
6 cloves garlic, peeled
1 slice French-style bread, ¼
　　inch thick
8 jumbo shrimp, in their shells
4 medium squid, cleaned (see p. 216)
　　—reserve the bodies
　　and tentacles
1 dozen small clams (see p. 11)
1 tablespoon minced parsley
　　for garnish

Cut the fish into small serving pieces, removing the skin and bone. Sprinkle the fish steaks well on both sides with coarse salt and let them sit. (This helps to firm the fish so it does not fall apart in cooking and does not give off a lot of liquid.) Kill the lobster (p. 147) and split it lengthwise. Divide each split tail piece into 2 parts crosswise. Separate the small claws from the head and divide the large claws into the leg section and the pincers. Lightly crush the leg and pincer shells. Keep the head and small claws for the broth.

In a large, shallow casserole, heat 3 tablespoons of the oil. Sauté the small shrimp 5 minutes and reserve. In the same oil (add a little more if necessary) sauté the onion and the minced garlic until the onion is wilted. Add the tomato and cook 5 minutes more. Add the reserved small shrimp, the lobster head, and the small lobster legs, the water, salt, and pepper. Bring to a boil, then simmer 40 minutes, uncovered. Strain, pressing with the back of a spoon to extract as much liquid as possible. Reserve 2 cups of the broth. The shrimp will not be used; they may be reserved to mince and mix with mayonnaise for a delicious shrimp salad or to mince and add to the rice of a seafood *paella*— they will be too overcooked to stand on their own.

In a medium skillet, heat 3 more tablespoons of oil. Sauté over medium heat the dried pepper, almonds, the whole garlic cloves, and the slice of bread. Remove the dried pepper when it is softened—do not brown—and the other ingredients as they turn golden. Place all in a processor or blender, breaking the dried pepper into several pieces. Add some salt and beat until the mixture is as fine as possible. Transfer to a mortar and continue to mash to a paste. Reserve.

In a large, shallow casserole, preferably earthenware, place the remaining 6 tablespoons of olive oil. When it is warm, add the paste from the mortar, stirring a few seconds to mix it with the oil. The mixture should sizzle slightly, but not brown. Quickly mix in the 2 cups of reserved shrimp broth, then add the fish steaks, the jumbo shrimp, the lobster pieces. Bring to a boil and simmer, uncovered, for 5 minutes, turning the seafood once. Add the squid and cook 5 minutes more. Do not overcook. Meanwhile, place the clams in a skillet with a little water and bring to a boil. Add the clams to the casserole as they open.

Sprinkle the casserole with parsley, and place in the middle of the table. Serve a little of everything with some sauce. Guests may help themselves to seconds. A fine dry white wine like Federico Paternina Reserva and good crunchy bread for dunking are excellent accompaniments.

MARISCADA A LA PLANCHA
CON SALSA ROMESCU

(Grilled Shellfish with Romesco Sauce)

SHELLFISH grilled, not broiled, with the shells on has a delicious charcoal kind of taste, and the famous *romesco* sauce (more about *romesco*, p. 12) that accompanies it is a perfect *contrapunto*. I have included two versions of this wonderful sauce—the authentic one made with dried sweet red peppers (I thank the Sol-Ric restaurant in Tarragona for the recipe) and another for those who cannot find these peppers. I recommend making the effort to obtain them, however, for they enter into several Spanish recipes in this book, and although substitutions of paprika or pimiento are sometimes possible, the results are not quite the same.

Serves 4

Olive oil
Coarse salt
2 lobsters, about 1–1¼ pounds each,
    split lengthwise, claws
    lightly crushed

1 dozen large shrimp, in their shells
1 dozen clams (see p. 11), at
    room temperature
1 dozen mussels (see p. 11)
Lemon wedges

Make one of the *romesco* sauces, which follow. Coat a stove-top griddle or a large skillet with a teaspoon or so of oil. Heat, then sprinkle with coarse salt. Add the lobster and cook over a high heat about 10 minutes, turning occasionally. Add the shrimp, clams, and mussels and small amounts of oil as necessary to prevent the griddle or pan from scorching. Turn the shellfish occasionally and cook until the lobster and shrimp are done and the clams and mussels have opened (this will only take a few minutes). Serve with lemon wedges and pass the *romesco* sauce. A green salad and a fine dry white wine like Viña Tondonia are appropriate.

ROMESCO SAUCE (1)

1 dried sweet or slightly hot large red
    pepper such as "New Mexico"
    style, seeds and stems removed
    (see glossary)
½ dried red chili pepper,
    seeds removed
1 cup water
½ cup red wine vinegar

¾ cup olive oil
2 slices French-style bread,
    ¼ inch thick
1 large tomato, skinned and chopped
36 blanched almonds (about
    2 ounces), lightly toasted
6 cloves garlic, peeled and chopped
Salt

Place the dried pepper and chili pepper in a saucepan with the water and vinegar. Bring to a boil, then simmer 5 minutes. Drain and cool. In a skillet, heat ¼ cup of the oil. Fry the bread slices until golden on both sides. Remove. In the same oil sauté the tomato for about 3 minutes.

Place in a processor or blender the peppers, fried bread, tomatoes (including the oil in which they were cooked), almonds, garlic, the remaining ½ cup of oil, and the salt. Beat until well blended but with small pieces remaining. Let sit at room temperature until ready to use.

ROMESCO SAUCE (2)

4 tablespoons olive oil
1 medium onion, chopped
3 cloves garlic, chopped
2 fresh tomatoes, skinned
    and chopped
1 pimiento, homemade or
    imported, chopped
2 dried red chili peppers, seeds
    removed, broken into
    small pieces

5 tablespoons fish broth (p. 13) or
    clam juice
2 tablespoons white wine
10 almonds, lightly toasted
1 tablespoon red wine vinegar
Salt
2 cloves garlic, crushed

Heat 2 tablespoons of the oil and sauté the onion and chopped garlic until the onion is wilted. Add the tomato, pimiento, chili pepper, broth, and wine. Cover and cook 30 minutes.

In a processor or blender, grind the almonds. Beat in the vinegar, the remaining 2 tablespoons of oil, the salt, and the crushed garlic. Add the tomato mixture and purée until smooth. Let sit at room temperature until ready to use.

ZARZUELA DE MARISCO
(Shellfish Medley)

THE word *"zarzuela"* has had an interesting, if not tortuous, evolution. *"Zarza,"* from which *"zarzuela"* is derived, originally referred to a bush commonly found in central Spain and led to the naming of a seventeenth-century hunting lodge, frequented by Philip IV, as "La Zarzuela." The king was fond of musical galas, from which Spanish light opera emerged and was christened *"zarzuela."* The word has remained as a musical term referring to satirical and witty Spanish operettas, immensely popular in the nineteenth century, which dealt with simple and folk-oriented themes. Everyday people from the most ordinary walks of life were the celebrated heroes and heroines of these productions and were one reason *zarzuelas* were so pleasing to audiences. Although classified as "light" opera, *zarzuela* is of high musical quality and after a slump of many years is making a strong comeback among music enthusiasts.

The connection between the musical genre and the foods called *zarzuela* is somewhat vague, but it is thought that just as opera is a mixture of song, dance, and theater, so too dishes that form a medley of ingredients and are colorful and inviting receive the same name. Zarzuela de Marisco includes a variety of shellfish in a wonderfully spicy and fragrant sauce. It is a spectacular company dish.

Serves 4

10 tablespoons olive oil
2 live lobsters, killed (p. 147), split
    lengthwise and divided
    into tails and claws
    (discard or keep the head
    and small claws)
12 large shrimp, in their shells
2 tablespoons finely chopped onion
2 cloves garlic, minced
2 tablespoons brandy, preferably
    Spanish brandy, or Cognac
2 medium tomatoes, skinned, seeded,
    and finely chopped

1 teaspoon paprika
1 bay leaf
Freshly ground pepper
Few strands saffron
1 cup dry white wine
1 dozen clams, scrubbed, at room
    temperature (see p. 11)
1 dozen mussels, scrubbed (see p. 11)
Small piece dried red chili pepper
2 tablespoons minced parsley
Lemon wedges

Heat the oil in a very large, shallow casserole (or use 2 if one is not large enough). Sauté the lobster and shrimp until they just turn pink (the lobster may be left a minute more than the shrimp). Remove to a warm platter. In the same oil, sauté the onion and garlic until the onion is wilted. Pour in the brandy and flame. When the flames die, add the tomato, paprika, bay leaf, pepper, and saffron. Cook 3 minutes. Pour in the wine and simmer 5 minutes. Return the lobster and shrimp to the pan. Add the clams and mussels and chili pepper. Cover and cook 10 minutes. (If the clams have not opened, remove the other shellfish and leave the clams a few minutes more.) Serve sprinkled with the parsley and decorated with lemon wedges. A salad and a medium-dry white wine like Brillante are good accompaniments.

TO CLEAN SQUID

HOLDING the body of the squid in one hand and the tentacles in the other, pull out the tentacles. Peel off the ink sac—silvery in color, located beneath the tentacles (this step is necessary only if the ink is to be used in a recipe). Reserve the tentacles if they are to be used, cutting off all waste material but leaving the tentacles in one piece. Remove the skin from the body of the squid and pull off the fins. Turn the squid inside out, remove the cartilage, and wash the body well under running water. Turn the squid to the outside again and dry on paper towels.

CALAMARES EN SU TINTA

(Squid in Ink Sauce)

FOR anyone unfamiliar with ink sauce, the idea of fish cooked in a black liquid may be a bit disconcerting. The ink, however, imparts a subtle flavor that is altogether captivating. This dish is a great favorite in Spain, found in restaurants throughout the country, using either tiny squid, whole and sometimes stuffed, or the larger squid, cut in rings.

Serves 4–6

2 pounds squid, preferably small
　　(about 3 inches total length),
　　with tentacles
4 tablespoons finely chopped cured
　　ham (only if baby squid
　　are being used)
1 pound large squid—only the ink
　　sacs will be used
½ cup dry red wine
2 tablespoons olive oil

1 medium onion, chopped
1 clove garlic, minced
1 medium tomato, peeled, seeded,
　　and chopped
1 tablespoon minced parsley
1 tablespoon flour
1 cup fish broth (p. 13), clam juice,
　　or chicken broth
Salt
Freshly ground pepper

Clean the squid (see preceding instructions). If larger squid are being used, slice them into 1-inch rings. Cut up the tentacles. Small squid will stay whole. For the small squid, chop the tentacles and mix them with the ham. Stuff the body of the squid with this mixture. As the squid cooks, the opening will close and the squid will be reduced to about 1½ inches.

Place the ink sacs, including the extra ones, in a strainer over a small bowl. Press them with a wooden spoon to extract the ink. Pour ¼ cup of the wine through the strainer. Pass the liquid from the bowl through the strainer several times more, until most of the ink color is removed from the remaining pieces. Set aside.

Heat the oil in a large skillet and sauté the onion and the garlic until the onion is wilted. Add the tomato and parsley and cook 5 minutes. Stir in the flour, then add the broth and the remaining ¼ cup wine. Pour in the ink mixture. The sauce should be black. (If it is not, you probably did not have enough ink, but the flavor will still be excellent.) Season with salt and pepper. Add the squid and cook, covered, over a low flame for 2 hours. Serve with, or over, a Rice Ring (p. 191) and accompanied by a full-bodied white wine such as Viña Tondonia.

CALAMARES AL JEREZ

(Squid in Sherry Sauce)

Serves 4

2 pounds squid, cleaned (see p. 216)
　　and cut in rings
2 medium onions, chopped
4 cloves garlic, minced
3 tablespoons olive oil

16 blanched almonds
Few strands saffron
½ cup dry (*fino*) sherry
2 tablespoons minced parsley
Salt

Dry the squid well. In a shallow casserole, sauté the onion and garlic in the oil until the onion is wilted. Place the almonds in a processor with the saffron and grind to a paste. With the motor running, gradually add the sherry. Pour this mixture into the casserole. Add the parsley, salt, and the squid. Cover and cook about 45 minutes, or until the squid is tender, adding some water if the sauce becomes too thick. Serve with rice and a dry white wine like Monopole.

CALAMARES RELLENOS

(Stuffed Squid)

Serves 4

20–24 medium squid, with tentacles
5 tablespoons olive oil
¾ cup chopped onion
4 cloves garlic, minced
¾ pound cured ham, in 2 or 3
    pieces, minced
½ teaspoon paprika

3 tablespoons minced parsley
Salt
Freshly ground pepper
4 teaspoons white wine
5 tablespoons bread crumbs
Flour for dusting

TOMATO SAUCE

About 2 cups

2 tablespoons olive oil
6 tablespoons chopped onion
2 cloves garlic, minced
3 fresh medium tomatoes, skinned
    and chopped, or 6 canned
    plum tomatoes
3 tablespoons tomato paste

3 tablespoons water
2 tablespoons minced parsley
Salt
Freshly ground pepper
Pinch sugar
¾ cup dry white wine

To make the tomato sauce, heat the oil in a shallow casserole and sauté the onion and garlic until the onion is wilted. Add the tomatoes, tomato paste, water, parsley, salt, pepper, sugar, and wine. Cover and simmer 15 minutes. (If this tomato sauce is to be used in other recipes, continue to simmer 1 more hour, then purée and strain.)

Meanwhile, clean the squid well, leaving the bodies in one piece (see cleaning instructions, p. 216). Mince and reserve the tentacles. In a skillet, heat 2 tablespoons of the oil and sauté the onion and garlic until the onion is wilted. Add the minced tentacles to the skillet along with the ham. Cook 2 minutes, turn off the flame and add the paprika, parsley, salt, pepper, wine, and bread crumbs.

Fill the squid bodies with the prepared mixture. Dust with flour and fry in the remaining 3 tablespoons of oil, very briefly, turning once (they should not brown). Transfer to the casserole with the tomato sauce, cover, and cook 1 hour. Serve with a salad and a medium-dry white wine such as Brillante.

PULPO CON PATATINES

(Stewed Octopus with Diced Potatoes)

THE octopus in this dish turns out extremely tender and flavorful—attractive, I am sure, even to those not overly fond of octopus.

Serves 4

6 tablespoons olive oil
1 medium onion, chopped
3 cloves garlic, minced
3½ pounds small octopus, each not
    larger than 1 pound, the
    tentacles cut in 1¼-inch
    lengths, the body cut in
    1¼-inch squares (see p. 23)

1 tablespoon minced parsley
1½ teaspoons paprika
1 bay leaf
Salt
Freshly ground pepper
3 medium potatoes, peeled and diced

Heat 3 tablespoons of the oil in a shallow casserole. Sauté the onion and garlic until the onion is wilted. Add the octopus, parsley, paprika, bay leaf, salt, and pepper. Cover and cook very slowly, 45–60 minutes, until the octopus is tender. During the last 15 minutes of cooking, in a skillet heat the remaining 3 tablespoons of oil to the smoking point. Add the potatoes and cook over medium heat about 15 minutes, turning occasionally, until golden and cooked through. Drain and add them to the octopus. Cover and continue cooking 5 minutes more. Serve with a salad and a dry white wine like Viña Paceta.

Chapter 9

PESCADOS

(Fish)

THE setting is an outdoor café in Cádiz, overlooking the gently lapping Atlantic Ocean and a spectacular bright red summer sunset. We are sipping *fino* sherry and chatting with our friends Pepe and Paqui, lifelong residents of this charming three-thousand-year-old city. A snappily dressed waiter appears with an anguished expression and addresses Pepe:

"I'm so sorry, señor . . . " He hesitates, hardly able to complete his sentence. "The mackerel you requested was fished yesterday. There was none in today's catch."

Pepe eyes the waiter with ill-disguised horror. The offending mackerel is summarily rejected and replaced by an exquisite grilled flounder, fresh that day from the nearby salt marshes. Pepe takes a bite and cannot contain his pride.

"Anyone who wants fish of this quality—no matter how wealthy he may be—has no choice but to come to Cádiz," he boasts.

While there is no doubt that Cádiz has some of the finest fish in the world, it is also true that Spain in general is a fish lover's paradise. Blessed with the longest coastline in Europe and facing the Mediterranean Sea, the fertile Bay of Biscay, and the Atlantic Ocean as well, Spain has an overwhelming variety of fish, from huge open-water species, such as the tuna, to tiny coastal *chanquetes*, no bigger than thumbnails.

In the central plains and mountainous interior areas of Spain, saltwater seafood is less commonly eaten, and dried cod and freshwater fish, especially trout, are more likely to be found. (Central Madrid, of course, is an exception—its people demand, and get, the freshest possible fish, rushed there from all shores of Spain.) When we visit Spain, our trips usually begin in Madrid, continue through the mountains, and gradually wind their way out to the shore. In those weeks our diet changes drastically, from a predominance of pork, lamb, sausage, and potatoes to meals based exclusively on fish and shellfish.

Along the thousands of miles of Spanish coastline, fish reigns supreme and is the focus of all eating. The standard dining dictates that fish should be

followed by meat are thrown to the wind—it is fish or shellfish for *tapas*, fish for first course, and fish as a main course. (My husband has even been known, on occasion, to order fish for dessert!) In Cádiz, the love affair with fish is so intense that eating meat from a four-legged creature comes close to being taboo, and ordering steak, just short of heresy. Indeed, who in his right mind would choose steak when the fish is so fresh and succulent that even traditional meat-and-potato men are transformed overnight into voracious seafood eaters.

Many varieties of fish caught in Spain are the same, or at least in the same family, as those found here—porgy, flounder, bass, cod, and mackerel, for example. There are other local varieties that don't exist in our country, and some others that are not found simply because they are not fished or are thrown back due to lack of demand. Whatever the variety, Spaniards usually prefer their fish small, just as they prefer the meat of small land animals. In the Málaga area, tiny *chanquetes* are netted by the millions, fried, and eaten like potato chips. There are literally hundreds of *chanquetes* in a single order. Fish similar in size to small smelts are the popular size for sardines, red snapper, anchovy, and even flounder. Of special gastronomic interest are the exquisite tiny *angulas*—baby eels—"as tiny as beansprouts," in the words of Ernest Hemingway, which are caught at the mouths of rivers as they complete their three-thousand-mile journey from their place of birth in the Sargasso Sea near Bermuda to their adult living quarters in the fresh waters of Spain's rivers. When the *angulas* are caught by fishermen, they are plunged briefly into hot water to which a piece of cigar has been added for flavor and then distributed to restaurants, where they are almost always prepared "*a la bilbaína*"—in garlic sauce. *Angulas* have a mild taste that is hard to place but pleasing to all and is required eating for every visitor to Spain.

While general categories of fish in Spain are similar to ours, Spaniards make fine distinctions within those categories that leave the average American fish eater, whose main concern is finding fish that is fairly fresh and has not been frozen, shaking his head in amazement. Flounder caught in the salt flats of Cádiz is considered far superior to open-water flounder. *Merluza*—hake—one of Spain's most common fish, is the best in the world when it comes from the Basque country, but better still if hooked rather than netted (the fish fights more, giving more texture to the meat). Baby eels must be eaten only in winter. They have to come from the Basque country, and more specifically from the town of Aguinaga on the Oria River. Sardines are at their best in August, lampreys must come from the Miño River, and salmon has to be from Asturias, and the list goes on.

Although the variety of seafood in Spain is tremendous and, to the casual visitor, quite overwhelming, the real key to the popularity of Spanish fish is freshness. As with shellfish, day-old or frozen (a word that brings instant dismay to the Spanish fish devotee) is not to be tolerated. Boats arrive at ports up and down the coast daily. The fish are bought within minutes of unloading and in many areas, cooked and sold on the spot. In the north, sardines grilled by the women of the port of Santurce are legendary, while in the south, sardines speared and grilled over woodburning beach fires are not to be missed.

So fresh is the fish that in an elegant Cádiz restaurant, El Faro, uncooked and uncleaned whole fish are hand-carried by waiters in crisply starched white jackets to diners for inspection. Only a restaurant that knows that its fish was swimming in the sea just hours before would dare attempt this.

When fish is this fresh, Spaniards like to eat it unaccompanied by irrelevant extra ingredients. It is usually grilled or fried, the preparations best suited to fish of this quality. In Cádiz keeping fish unadorned is carried to extremes. I was once reprimanded for sprinkling lemon juice on freshly fried rounds of whiting. "Lemon on this beautiful fish?" our friend Pepe cried in dismay. "A crime! Lemon is only suitable to mask the taste of less than perfect fish." In the Basque country and Galicia, however, the rough northern climate lends itself to a heartier cuisine, and fish sauces are much more common. The green sauces originated in the north, as did the popular dried salt cod in onion and red pepper sauce called Bacalao a la Vizcaína.

Although in restaurants simple fish preparations are the norm, Spanish regional cooking is most inventive with fish, combining it with locally available ingredients. In Asturias, this means using cider as a cooking liquid; in Galicia, Albariño wine; in the Basque country, Chacolí wine; and in Andalucía, sherry. In the south, almonds and fresh vegetables sometimes enter into fish dishes, and in Galicia the local greens—*grelos*—are mixed with the fish. Recipes for all these wonderful dishes are included here, along with the one recipe without which a Spanish cookbook would not be complete: Fish Fry, Cádiz Style.

PESCADO FRITO A LA GADITANA

(Fish Fry, Cádiz Style)

CÁDIZ, home of Pescado Frito a la Gaditana, is a unique city and by far my favorite destination in Spain. Picture Cádiz: a peninsula three quarters of a mile wide and one mile long and connected to terra firma by nothing more than a narrow isthmus, a city where few buildings are less than two hundred years old and the picturesque streets are hardly wider than alleyways. Cádiz is a city still living in the nineteenth century, and its people, surprise of surprises, are proud of being "old-fashioned" and pleased to be living in a city where life is slow paced and needs are limited. Give the Gaditanos, as the people of Cádiz are called, their magnificent beaches, their abundant supply of fresh seafood, and a few yearly fiestas—in which old and young participate with great gusto—and they would be hard pressed to think of something else they want from life.

In Cádiz the sea is never out of sight and is the lifeblood of the city.

Everyday activity seems to revolve around everything related to seafood. It is the staple of the Cádiz diet, is available in unlimited variety and in many preparations, and is the subject of endless conversation. It is the fried fish, however, that has made Cádiz famous all over Spain. The city has been christened by some as the "Olympus of Fried Fish" because of the excellent quality of its seafood and the knack its chefs seem to have for frying it to just the right point, making it moist, crisp, and greaseless. The owner of the impeccably kept El Faro restaurant in Cádiz, Gonzalo Córdoba Gutiérrez, divulged his secret for perfect fried fish: coat the fish with very coarse flour and fry at exactly 340° F in olive-and-soybean oil. I have followed his instructions and found the results to be outstanding.

Although the fish available in one part of the world is never exactly the same as in another, the variety of fish used in this recipe is close to the selection one would find in Cádiz and is a particularly appealing mixture of seafood flavors.

Serves 4

A 1½-pound whiting, cleaned
4 very small whole baby flounders,
    cleaned, heads removed
12 very small smelts or snappers,
    cleaned, heads on
Milk
Coarse salt
8 small squid, cleaned (see p. 216)
    and cut in ½-inch rings
    (tentacles may also
    be used)

Flour for dusting, preferably a coarse
    flour such as semolina
    (whole-wheat flour may also
    be used)
Olive and salad oils, preferably
    soybean, for frying
1 tablespoon minced parsley
Lemon wedges

Cut the whiting into ¼–½–inch slices, starting at the tail—the bones are soft and a knife will cut through quite easily. The slices from the tail section will be perfect rounds, while as you reach the cleaned stomach area the circles will be opened. Cut off any ragged ends. Soak the flounders and smelts for 30 minutes in milk to cover. Drain and dry. Sprinkle coarse salt on all of the fish, including the whiting and squid. Dust all of the fish with flour.

Heat the oil, at least 1 inch deep, in a skillet until it is very hot (or use an electric fryer heated to 340–70° F). Add the flounders and smelts and fry until they are a deep golden brown. Drain and place on a warm serving platter. Fry the whiting rounds until golden, less than 5 minutes. Drain and add to the platter. Finally, fry the squid until just lightly golden—do not fry more than a minute or two or they will toughen. Drain and arrange on the platter. (At El Faro restaurant the squid rings are sometimes threaded onto long parsley stems, then tied together.)

Sprinkle the fish with parsley and decorate the platter with lemon wedges. Serve with Fried Green Peppers (p. 83) and a full-bodied white Viña Tondonia wine.

MERLUZA A LA VASCA

(Fish Steak in Green Sauce)

Merluza is Spain's most popular and plentiful fish. It is found all over the country and is prepared in endless varieties. Here in the United States, hake is its closest equivalent, although I often use fresh cod instead.

In New York City, Merluza a la Vasca and other hake dishes can be sampled at the Café San Martín, a Spanish restaurant that makes no attempt to look "Spanish," yet serves a wide range of impeccably prepared Spanish specialties. The ebullient and high-spirited ambience, presided over by the restaurant's gracious owner and host, Ramón San Martín, reminds one of the lively café atmosphere of so many restaurants in Spain.

The preparation of Merluza a la Vasca is quite simple and, presented in its own casserole, decorated with clams, mussels, parsley, and chopped egg, it is a dish as pleasing to the eye as it is to the palate.

Serves 4

4 fish steaks, such as hake or fresh cod, about 1 inch thick	2 tablespoons flour
	¾ cup white wine
Salt	¾ cup fish broth (p. 13) or clam juice
Freshly ground pepper	6 tablespoons minced parsley
Flour for dusting	¾ cup peas, fresh or frozen
4 tablespoons olive oil	1 dozen small clams (see p. 11)
1 tablespoon lemon juice	1 dozen small mussels (see p. 11)
4 cloves garlic, minced	1 hard-boiled egg, finely chopped
3 tablespoons minced onion	

Sprinkle the fish with salt and pepper, then dust with flour. Heat 2 tablespoons of the oil in a large skillet. Fry the steaks briefly, about 1 minute a side. Transfer them to 4 individual ovenproof dishes, preferably Spanish earthenware. Sprinkle them with lemon juice.

Wipe out the skillet, then heat the remaining 2 tablespoons of oil and sauté the garlic and onion until the onion is wilted. Stir in the 2 tablespoons of flour and gradually pour in the wine and the broth. Stir until the sauce is thickened and smooth. Add 5 tablespoons of the parsley, the peas, salt, and pepper.

Pour equal amounts of the sauce over each steak. Decorate each dish with 3 clams and 3 mussels. Place the dishes in a 350° F oven and bake about 20 minutes, or until the fish flakes and the shellfish have opened. Sprinkle with the remaining tablespoon of parsley and with the hard-boiled egg. Boiled potatoes may be added if so desired. Note that the clams and mussels are not merely decorative—their juices add flavor to the sauce. Serve with a green salad and a dry white wine like Blanco Seco.

MERLUZA A LA SIDRA

(Fish Steak in Hard Cider Sauce)

HARD cider is the specialty in Asturias in northern Spain and is the region's most popular drink. Serving cider is an art in itself. From a distance of some four feet, the cider is poured from the bottle into wide, unstemmed glasses. Experts accomplish this feat without spilling a drop, but others less experienced usually end up with most of the cider on the floor.

Cider is also a common cooking liquid in these parts, and fish in cider sauce is one of the region's most famous creations. Note that the cider must be hard cider (found in liquor stores), which has a higher alcoholic content and is much drier than common cider.

Serves 4

4 tablespoons olive oil	1 sprig parsley
2 large new potatoes, peeled and thinly sliced	4 fish steaks, such as hake or fresh cod, 1 inch thick
Salt	2 medium onions, finely chopped
1 dozen small clams (see p. 11)	2 cloves garlic, minced
1 bay leaf	2 tablespoons flour
½ teaspoon thyme	1 tablespoon paprika
4 peppercorns	1 cup hard cider
1 slice onion	1 tablespoon minced parsley

Heat 2 tablespoons of the oil in a skillet. Add the potatoes in layers, sprinkle with salt, cover, and cook slowly until the potatoes are tender, turning occasionally, about 15 minutes. The potatoes should not brown. Cover the bottoms of 4 individual ovenproof casseroles, preferably Spanish earthenware, with the potatoes.

Place the clams in a skillet with 1 cup of water. Bring to a boil and remove the clams as they open. Place them around the sides of the casseroles. To the clam liquid, add the bay leaf, thyme, peppercorns, onion slice, and parsley sprig. Add the fish steaks, cover, and simmer about 10 minutes. Drain the fish well and strain the liquid. Reserve 1½ cups (add some water or clam juice if there is not enough liquid). Place the fish steaks over the potatoes in the casseroles.

In a skillet, heat the remaining 2 tablespoons of oil and sauté the onion and garlic until the onion is wilted. Stir in the flour and the paprika and cook over low heat 2 or 3 minutes. Gradually pour in the 1½ cups reserved fish broth and the cider. Sprinkle in the parsley and simmer, uncovered, 10 minutes. Pour the sauce over the fish and bake at 350° F for 15 minutes. Serve in the baking dishes. A green salad and a medium-dry white wine like Marqués de Murrieta is all that is necessary to complete this meal.

MERLUZA A LA MADRILEÑA

(Fish Steaks with Ham and Cheese)

STUFFED with cured ham and cheese, rolled in bread crumbs, and topped with fresh tomato sauce, these cod steaks are among my favorite recipes.

Serves 4

4 fresh cod steaks or hake, about
    1¼ inches thick
4 thin slices cured ham
4 thin slices mild cheese, such as
    Tetilla (p. 432) or Fontina

Flour for dusting
2 eggs, lightly beaten
Bread crumbs
3 tablespoons olive oil

TOMATO GARNISH

1 tablespoon olive oil
1 medium onion, finely chopped
2 ripe tomatoes, finely chopped

1 tablespoon minced parsley
Salt
Freshly ground pepper

Remove the central bone from the cod, thereby dividing each steak into 2 medallions. Remove the skin and cut off the long, thin pieces that hang from each side of the steaks (save them for future use in fish stock). To stuff the fish, with a sharp knife split the steaks in half. Place one slice of ham and one slice of cheese on half of the steaks. Cover with the remaining pieces of fish. Dredge the fish in the flour, coating the sides well. Dip in the egg, then in crumbs. Let sit about 20 minutes to dry before frying.

Meanwhile, prepare the tomato garnish. Heat the 1 tablespoon of oil in a skillet and sauté the onion slowly, covered, until it is wilted. Add the tomato, parsley, salt, and pepper and cook slowly, uncovered, until the tomato is barely tender, about 10–15 minutes. The tomato should have a fresh taste.

In a large skillet, heat the 3 tablespoons of oil until it reaches the smoking point. Add the fish steaks and lower the heat to medium. Brown on each side. Serve with the tomato garnish either over the fish or on the side. Poor Man's Potatoes (p. 97), a green salad, and a full-bodied white wine like Viña Paceta may accompany this dish.

MERLUZA A LA GALLEGA

(Fish Steak, Galician Style)

ANYTHING prepared Galician style is bound to have paprika as an ingredient, as this savory baked fish dish does.

Serves 4

½ cup plus 4 teaspoons olive oil
1 medium onion, chopped
2 cloves garlic, crushed
2 tablespoons minced parsley
2 teaspoons paprika
1½ pounds new potatoes, peeled, cut
    in ⅛-inch slices
1 tablespoon flour

Salt
Freshly ground pepper
Dash ground cloves
1 bay leaf
½ teaspoon thyme
4 fish steaks, such as hake or fresh
    cod, about 1 inch thick

In a shallow casserole, heat ½ cup of the oil and sauté the onion until it is wilted. Stir in the garlic, 1 tablespoon of the parsley, and the paprika. Add the potatoes; shake to coat well with the oil. Sprinkle in the flour, then add water barely to cover. Sprinkle with salt, pepper, cloves, bay leaf, and thyme. Cover and cook 25 minutes, or until the potatoes are just tender.

Divide the potatoes into 4 individual ovenproof casseroles, preferably earthenware. Place a fish steak on top of the potatoes in each dish. Sprinkle with salt and pepper. Dribble the remaining 4 teaspoons of oil over the fish—1 teaspoon to each fish portion. Place in a 350° F oven for 15 minutes, or until the fish flakes.

Sprinkle with the remaining tablespoon of parsley before serving. A green salad and a Marqués de Cáceres dry white wine may accompany this dish.

MERLUZA CON ALCAPARRAS

(Fish Steaks with Capers)

Serves 4

4 fish steaks, preferably hake or fresh
    cod, about 1 inch thick
Salt

Flour for dusting
Oil for frying
2 eggs, lightly beaten

6 tablespoons butter   Lemon wedges
2 tablespoons small capers

Sprinkle the fish with salt, then dust with flour. In a large skillet, heat the oil, at least ½ inch deep. Dip the fish steaks into the beaten egg and place directly in the hot oil. Fry until golden and cooked through.

Meanwhile, in a small saucepan, melt the butter. Add the capers. Pour this sauce over the fish. Serve with lemon wedges and Green Beans and Cured Ham (p. 79). A dry white wine — Campo Viejo, for example — is appropriate.

ROLLO DE MERLUZA

(Fish Roll with Green Sauce)

Serves 4–6

2½ pounds fish steak, such as fresh   3 eggs
    cod, about 1 inch thick   Salt
1 cup bread crumbs   Flour for dusting
½ pound cured ham in 1 or 2   3 tablespoons olive oil
    pieces, diced

GREEN SAUCE

¾ cup minced parsley   2 tablespoons olive oil
3 cloves garlic, chopped   2 teaspoons flour
¼ teaspoon salt

Cook the fish steak as in Pudin de Merluza (p. 59), reserving 2 cups of the cooking liquid (add more water if there is not enough). Shred the fish. Soak the bread crumbs in ½ cup of the reserved liquid. Mix in a bowl the fish, bread crumbs, ham, eggs, and salt, if necessary. Shape the mixture into a roll, about 10 × 3 inches. Coat with flour, then fry in the 3 tablespoons of oil in a deep casserole. Brown on all sides, remove, and wipe out the pot.

To make the green sauce, place the parsley in a processor or blender with the garlic and salt. Blend until as finely chopped as possible. Slowly pour in the remaining 1½ cups of reserved fish broth. In the deep casserole, heat the 2 tablespoons of oil. Stir in the flour, then add the mixture from the processor. Cook until thickened and smooth. Add the fish roll, cover, and cook 20 minutes. To serve, cut the fish roll in thick slices and spoon on some sauce. A refreshing Cucumber, Tomato, and Pepper Salad (p. 106) and a dry white wine like Rinsol are good with this dish.

RAPE CON GRELOS Y ALMEJAS
(Fish Steaks with Greens and Clams)

IN SPANISH cuisine greens are more likely to be combined into soup or meat dishes, but they are also delicious with fish.

Serves 4

½ pound collard greens or Swiss chard, thick stems removed (weight after trimming)
Salt
6 tablespoons olive oil
4 fish steaks, such as monkfish or halibut (about 1 inch thick)
Flour for dusting

Lemon juice
4 tablespoons minced onion
2 cloves garlic, minced
Freshly ground pepper
2 teaspoons vinegar
1 bay leaf
2 tablespoons minced parsley
1 dozen small clams (see p. 11)

Cover the greens with cold water, add salt and 1 tablespoon of the oil, bring to a boil, and cook 5 minutes. Drain and chop coarsely.

Dust the fish with flour. Heat 3 more tablespoons of the oil in a shallow casserole and quickly fry (about 1 minute) the fish until lightly browned on each side. Transfer to a warm platter and sprinkle with lemon juice. Wipe out the pan. Add the remaining 2 tablespoons of oil and sauté the onion and garlic until the onion is wilted. Stir in the greens, salt, pepper, vinegar, bay leaf, and parsley. Return the fish to the pan, arranging the greens around the fish. Cover and cook slowly 15 minutes.

Meanwhile, place the clams in ½ cup water. Bring to a boil and remove the clams as they open. Reserve the broth and chop the clam meat. Add the clams and the reserved broth to the fish and cook 5 minutes more. Serve with a Tomato and Egg Salad (p. 107) and a dry white wine such as Blanco Seco.

LENGUADO CON PIÑONES
"TRES CARABELAS"
(Fillet of Sole with Pine Nuts)

THE Spanish penchant for combining meat and seafood is well known—*paella* is the best example of such a mixture. As unlikely as it may sound, fillet of sole topped with a beef sauce and pine nuts is an extremely pleasant blend of tastes.

Serves 4

4 fillets of sole or flounder (about
    1–1½ pounds)
Flour for dusting
3 tablespoons olive oil
1 tablespoon flour
1 cup beef or veal broth, preferably
    homemade and flavored
    with wine

1 tablespoon lemon juice
Salt
Freshly ground pepper
1 ounce pine (pignoli) nuts (about
    3 tablespoons)

Dust the fillets with flour. Heat the oil in a skillet and fry the fillets until they are golden and cooked through. Transfer them to a warm platter. Add the 1 tablespoon of flour to the remaining oil. Gradually stir in the beef broth and the lemon juice. Cook until the sauce is thickened and smooth. Season with salt and pepper if necessary. Add the pine nuts and pour the sauce over the fish fillets. Serve with Patatas Pobres (p. 97), a green salad, and a Marqués de Riscal dry white wine.

FILETE DE LENGUADO
CON MAYONESA VERDE

(Fillet of Sole with Green Mayonnaise)

Serves 4

4 fillets of sole or flounder
    (1–1½ pounds)
½ cup milk
Salt
Flour for dusting
2 eggs, lightly beaten

Bread crumbs
4 tablespoons olive oil
Rolled anchovies with capers
    for garnish
Lemon slices

GREEN MAYONNAISE

Homemade Mayonnaise (p. 104)
3 tablespoons minced parsley
2 tablespoons capers, finely chopped

½ Pickled Cucumber (p. 105), drained
    and finely chopped

Combine all ingredients for green mayonnaise and chill.

Soak the fish fillets in the milk for 30 minutes, turning occasionally. Drain on paper towels. Sprinkle the fish with salt, dust with flour, coat with beaten egg, then cover with bread crumbs. Let sit for 15 minutes.

Heat the oil in a large skillet. Fry the fillets until golden on both sides and cooked through. Serve decorated with the rolled anchovy and the lemon slices. Pass the mayonnaise separately. Any of the green or red pepper recipes are a nice accompaniment, along with a dry white wine like Viña Tondonia.

LENGUADO AL ALBARIÑO

(Fillet of Sole in Wine and Mushroom Sauce)

ALBARIÑO wine is produced in very limited quantities in Galicia in northwestern Spain and rarely finds its way out of the area. It ideally complements Galicia's seafood, because it is fruity yet dry, making it appropriate also for cooking. I have substituted a medium-dry white wine as its nearest equivalent in this egg-rich sauce.

Serves 4

4 tablespoons olive oil	Freshly ground pepper
4 tablespoons minced onion	2 cups thinly sliced mushrooms
2 cloves garlic, minced	4 fillets of sole or flounder
2 tablespoons flour	(1–1½ pounds)
¾ cup medium-dry white wine	Flour for dusting
¾ cup fish broth (p. 13) or clam juice	4 egg yolks
½ cup milk	2 tablespoons heavy cream
3 tablespoons lemon juice	1 tablespoon minced parsley
Salt	

Heat 2 tablespoons of the oil in a skillet. Add the onion and garlic and sauté until the onion is wilted. Sprinkle in the 2 tablespoons of flour, cook a minute, then gradually stir in the wine, broth, milk, lemon juice, salt, and pepper. Stir until thickened and smooth. Add the mushrooms and simmer the sauce slowly, uncovered, while preparing the fish.

To make the fish, dust the fillets with flour. Heat the remaining 2 tablespoons of oil in a large skillet and sauté the fillets until they are golden and cooked through. Remove to a warm platter.

Mix the egg yolks and heavy cream in a small bowl. Stir in a small amount of the hot white sauce, then return this mixture to the sauce and stir a minute or so. Pour over the fish, sprinkle with parsley, and serve. A salad of Marinated Asparagus (p. 119) and a medium-dry Viña Esmeralda are worthy accompaniments.

FILETES DE LENGUADO CON ALMENDRA

(Flounder Fillets in Almond Sauce)

THIS is a nice all-in-one meal. The dish may be made in advance and placed in the oven when ready to serve.

Serves 4

4 tablespoons olive oil
3 slices day-old French-style bread, ¼ inch thick
2 medium potatoes, in ⅛-inch slices
Salt
Freshly ground pepper
1½ pounds flounder or sole fillets

Flour for dusting
1 onion, chopped
8 blanched almonds
3 cloves garlic, chopped
3 tablespoons minced parsley
1 cup dry white wine
¼ cup water

Heat 2 tablespoons of the oil in a large skillet and fry the bread slices until they are golden on both sides. Remove the bread and reserve. Add the potatoes to the remaining hot oil and sauté them slowly until they are tender but not brown, turning occasionally. Add salt and pepper to taste. Transfer the potatoes to a large, shallow casserole.

Dust the fish with flour and fry in the same oil as the potatoes (add more oil if necessary) until golden. Arrange the fillets over the potatoes in the casserole. Heat the remaining 2 tablespoons of oil in the same skillet and sauté the onion until it is wilted. Meanwhile, place the almonds, garlic, 2 tablespoons of the parsley, and the fried bread in the bowl of a blender or processor and blend until the mixture is finely chopped. With the motor running, add the sautéed onion and gradually pour in the wine and water. Return to the skillet and cook 15 minutes, adding salt and pepper to taste.

Strain the almond sauce over the fish and potatoes, pushing as much of the mixture as possible through the strainer. Bake at 350° F for 15 minutes. Sprinkle with the remaining tablespoon of parsley. Serve with a green salad and a dry white wine such as Marqués de Murrieta.

LENGUADO AL LIMÓN

(Flounder in Lemon Sauce)

A LARGE amount of lemon and a touch of ginger and mustard give this white sauce its excellent flavor and tartness.

Serves 4

4 fillets of flounder or sole
    (1–1½ pounds)
Salt
Flour for dusting
2 tablespoons butter
¾ cup dry white wine

White pepper
½ teaspoon Dijon-style mustard
½ teaspoon powdered ginger
Juice of 1 lemon
¾ cup heavy cream
1 tablespoon minced parsley

Sprinkle the fillets with salt, then dust with flour. Melt 1 tablespoon of the butter in a large skillet and sauté the flounder until golden on both sides and cooked through. Remove to a warm platter. Wipe out the pan. Melt the remaining tablespoon of butter, add the wine, pepper, mustard, salt, ginger, and lemon juice. Bring to a boil and reduce by half. Add the cream, stir, and simmer, uncovered, until the sauce is thickened and smooth. Pour over the fish and serve sprinkled with the parsley. A green vegetable and a dry white wine like Marqués de Murrieta may accompany this dish.

LENGUADO "EL ANTEOJO"

(Fried Flounder with Ham)

THIS dish is done to perfection at the seaside El Anteojo restaurant in Cádiz. (More on Cádiz, p. 223.)

Serves 4

Flour for dusting, preferably a coarse
    flour like semolina
Salt
Freshly ground pepper
4 flounder fillets (1–1½ pounds)
Oil for frying, preferably a mixture
    of olive and soybean oils

A ¼-pound piece cured ham, diced
12 tablespoons butter
2 tablespoons lemon juice
2 tablespoons minced parsley
1 clove garlic, minced

Mix together the flour, salt, and pepper. Coat the fish well. In a large skillet heat the oil, ¼ inch deep, until very hot. Fry the fish quickly until golden on both sides. Transfer to an ovenproof serving platter. Sprinkle with the ham.

Melt the butter in a small skillet and let it brown lightly. Turn off the flame and stir in the lemon juice, parsley, garlic, salt, and pepper. Pour across the middle of the fillets—do not coat the fillets all over with the butter. Place in a 500° F oven for 3 minutes. Serve, spooning on the sauce. Baked Zucchini (p. 86) and a nice dry white wine like Viña Paceta are fitting accompaniments.

BESUGO A LA MADRILEÑA

(Baked Porgy, Madrid Style)

THIS dish is often called Porgy "Mata Mulo"—mule killer—because of the speed with which porgy for the holiday table was rushed by animal carrier from northern fishing ports to Madrid in order to insure freshness. Porgy baked in white wine and tomato sauce is an essential part of the traditional Christmas Eve dinner (see p. 425 for the complete holiday menu).

Serves 4

4 porgies, about ¾ pound each, or 1 large porgy, about 4 pounds, cleaned, heads on	Salt Freshly ground pepper 1 bay leaf
1 lemon, cut in thin wedges	1 cup dry white wine
Juice of 1 lemon	3 cloves garlic, minced
½ cup olive oil	4 tablespoons minced parsley
3 tablespoons chopped onion	6 tablespoons bread crumbs
½ cup tomato sauce, preferably homemade (p. 218)	2 large potatoes, peeled, cubed, and parboiled (optional)

Make 4 incisions on each fish—2 on each side (about 8 incisions—4 to a side if using the large porgy). Insert the lemon wedges so that only the rind is exposed. Sprinkle the fish with lemon juice and let it sit 30 minutes.

Meanwhile, heat 2 tablespoons of the oil in a small skillet. Sauté the onion until it is wilted. Add the tomato sauce, salt, pepper, and bay leaf. Cover and simmer 15 minutes.

Cover the bottom of a roasting pan with 2 more tablespoons of the oil. Place the fish in the pan and sprinkle with salt and pepper. Brush the fish with the remaining oil. Bake at 350° F for 5 minutes. Add ½ cup of the wine and cook 10 minutes.

In a small bowl mix together the garlic, parsley, and bread crumbs. Spoon tomato sauce over each fish, then sprinkle the fish with the garlic mixture.

Pour the remaining ½ cup of wine around the sides of the pan (not over the fish). Bake about 45 minutes more, adding the potatoes, if desired, for the last 20 minutes. Serve with Ensalada de San Isidro (p. 106) and a dry white wine like Viña Tondonia.

URTA A LA ROTEÑA

(Baked Porgy and Peppers with Brandy)

ROTA is a village in southwest Spain with lovely beaches, charming streets, and a magnificent view of the city of Cádiz, shimmering in the sunlight across the bay. Like Cádiz, Rota is known for its seafood, and this porgy dish bears the village's name.

Serves 4

2 porgies, about 2 pounds each, cleaned, heads on	1 bay leaf
6 thin lemon wedges	Salt
8 tablespoons olive oil	Freshly ground pepper
4 medium green peppers, cut in strips	½ teaspoon thyme
4 medium onions, sliced	1 cup dry white wine
5 cloves garlic, minced	½ cup brandy, preferably Spanish
4 medium tomatoes, skinned and chopped	brandy, or Cognac

Make 3 incisions in one side of each porgy. Insert the lemon wedges, leaving the rind exposed. In a large shallow ovenproof casserole, heat 4 tablespoons of the oil, sauté the green pepper, onion, and garlic until the onion is wilted. Add the tomato, bay leaf, salt, and pepper; cover and simmer 10 minutes. Place the fish on top of this mixture. Sprinkle with the remaining 4 tablespoons of oil, the thyme, salt, and pepper. Bake at 350° F for 15 minutes. Pour in the wine and brandy and continue baking about 25 minutes more, or until the fish is done. Serve with a dry white wine such as Marqués de Riscal and a green salad.

BESUGO RELLENO

(Stuffed Porgy)

Serves 4

1 hard-boiled egg, minced
½ cup diced cured ham
1 pimiento, homemade or
    imported, chopped
10 Spanish green olives, with or
    without pimiento, chopped
1 tablespoon minced onion
3–3½-pound porgy, or other mild
    fish, butterflied, head and

tail on, inside bones
    removed, backbone left in
4 tablespoons olive oil
1 clove garlic, minced
1 tablespoon flour
1 tablespoon minced parsley
1½ cups fish broth (p. 13) or
    clam juice

Mix together in a bowl the egg, ham, pimiento, olives, and onion. Stuff the
fish with this mixture, then sew up with a thick needle and thread. In a large,
shallow ovenproof casserole, heat the oil and sauté the garlic lightly (do not
brown). Stir in the flour and parsley, then pour in the broth. Cook until
thickened and smooth. Place the fish in the casserole and bake, uncovered, in a
350° F oven for 30 minutes, basting occasionally. Remove the string before
serving. Accompany by an Ensalada de Escalibada (p. 117) and a Campo Viejo
dry white wine.

BESUGO A LA BILBAÍNA

(Butterflied Porgy, Bilbao Style)

ALTHOUGH this delicious and delicate fish preparation carries the name of the
city of Bilbao, it is all the rage in Madrid, where it appears on the menus of the
most fashionable restaurants. The simple oil and garlic sauce demands the
freshest porgy possible.

Serves 4

4 porgies, about ¾ pound each, heads
    on or off
6 tablespoons olive oil
4 large cloves garlic, sliced
½ dried red chili pepper, cut in
    pieces, seeds removed

Lemon juice
2 tablespoons minced parsley
Lemon wedges

Butterfly the porgies, leaving the backbone joined and removing as much of the rest of the bone as possible. Pat dry. Heat 2 tablespoons of the oil in a large skillet. Open the butterflied porgies and brown them briefly over high heat—a minute or so on each side should be enough. As the porgies fry, remove them to a heated platter, skin side down, and place them in a 300° F oven.

Place the remaining 4 tablespoons of oil, the garlic slices, and the chili pepper in a small skillet. Heat the oil until the garlic begins to sizzle—do not let it brown. Remove from the flame. Take the porgy from the oven and sprinkle it with lemon juice. Spoon on the garlic sauce, sprinkle with parsley, decorate with lemon wedges, and serve. Roast potatoes, Green Bean Salad (p. 118), and a dry white wine like Cepa de Oro are the best accompaniments.

URTA A LA SAL

(Porgy Baked in Salt)

WHEN this fish is brought to the table on a platter, surrounded by salt and accompanied by three sauces, the spectacular presentation is sure to be a conversation piece. The large amount of salt called for in this recipe acts as an insulation and produces an exceptionally tender and juicy fish—it does not make the fish unusually salty. It is a popular preparation in Cádiz, where the same cooking method is also used for boneless loin of pork.

Porgy is delicious prepared "*a la sal,*" but other fish suitable for baking may also be used. The recipe may be increased for any number of portions (the sauce recipes are enough for 4), and larger fish work just as well, although baking time must be appropriately increased (1¼ to 1½ hours for a 3 pound fish). The important things to note are that the fish must be *completely* covered by salt, the salt must be coarse, and the fish scales must *not* be removed.

Serves 1

¾ pound porgy, or other fish, scales and head on
2 cups coarse salt, preferably sea salt
Sprigs parsley
Green Mayonnaise (p. 231), capers omitted and 2 cloves garlic, crushed, added

Salpicón Sauce (p. 25), doubling all ingredients except the oil and vinegar
Romesco Sauce (p. 214)

Grease an oval metal serving platter in which the fish fits fairly snugly. Place the fish on the tray and pour on the salt, covering the fish completely—you may need more or less salt, depending on the pan and fish size. Bake at 350° F for about 40 minutes.

Brush the salt off the top of the fish and decorate the platter with parsley sprigs. Bring to the table for the diners' approval. To serve, brush off all the salt. Remove the skin and discard. Carefully bone the fish and arrange the fillets attractively on individual dishes (the fish will be warm, not hot), garnished, perhaps, with boiled new potatoes and a green vegetable like Green Beans and Cured Ham (p. 79). Pass the sauces. A fine white Reserva wine like Federico Paternina is appropriate.

BESUGO CON PIÑONES

(Porgy in Wine and Pine Nut Sauce)

Serves 4

2 pounds fillet of porgy,
    skin removed
Salt
Flour for dusting
4 tablespoons olive oil
1 large onion, chopped
3 cloves garlic, minced

3 tablespoons pine nuts
2 tablespoons minced parsley
¾ cup medium-dry white wine
¾ cup fish broth (p. 13) or clam juice
1½ tablespoons lemon juice
Freshly ground pepper

Sprinkle the fish with salt and dust with flour. In a large skillet, heat 2 tablespoons of the oil. Fry the fillets over high heat, about a minute to each side. Transfer to a warm platter. Wipe out the pan and add another tablespoon of oil. Sauté the onion, garlic, and pine nuts until the onion is wilted. Transfer this mixture to a processor or blender along with 1 tablespoon of the parsley and the remaining tablespoon of oil. Purée. With the motor running, gradually pour in the wine, ½ cup of the fish broth, the lemon juice, salt, and pepper. Strain into the skillet and stir in the remaining ¼ cup of broth. Add the fillets, spooning some sauce over them. Cover and simmer 15 minutes. Sprinkle with the remaining tablespoon of parsley before serving. This may be accompanied by a green vegetable and a medium-dry white wine such as Brillante.

LUBINA RELLENA

(Striped Bass Stuffed with Mushrooms)

Serves 4

5 tablespoons olive oil
6 tablespoons minced onion
2 cloves garlic, minced
½ pound mushrooms, finely chopped
6 tablespoons bread crumbs
2 tablespoons chopped parsley
Salt

Freshly ground pepper
3 teaspoons lemon juice
2 tablespoons dry (*fino*) sherry
¼ teaspoon paprika
3 pounds striped bass, or similar fish,
    cleaned and boned, head on

Heat 2 tablespoons of the oil in a small skillet. Sauté the onion and garlic until the onion is wilted. Add the mushrooms and cook 5 minutes more. Stir in the bread crumbs, parsley, salt, pepper, 1 teaspoon of the lemon juice, the sherry, and the paprika.

Fill the cavity of the fish with the mushroom mixture. Sew up the fish with a thick needle and a heavy thread. Spread the remaining 3 tablespoons of oil in a roasting pan. Add the fish and turn to coat with the oil. Sprinkle with the remaining 2 teaspoons of lemon juice and some salt. Bake at 350° F for about 45 minutes, or until the fish is done. Remove the thread before serving. A green vegetable and a dry, full-bodied white wine like Viña Paceta are good accompaniments.

LUBINA AL HINOJO

(Fillet of Striped Bass in Fennel Sauce)

THE fennel flavor of this sauce is a perfect complement to striped bass. The fish tastes especially good when eaten on the restaurant terrace of the Parador de Gibralfaro, which from its lofty heights commands a spectacular view of the city of Málaga.

Serves 4

1½ pounds striped bass fillets
Flour for dusting
6 tablespoons butter
2 tablespoons flour

¾ cup fish broth (p. 13) or clam juice
¾ cup dry white wine
½ cup milk
Salt

White pepper   1 tablespoon minced parsley
½ teaspoon crushed fennel seed

Dust the fillets with flour. In a skillet, sauté the fillets in 4 tablespoons of the butter, turning once, until the fish is done. Remove to a warm platter. Wipe out the pan, then melt the remaining 2 tablespoons of butter. Add the 2 tablespoons of flour and cook a minute. Stir in the fish broth, wine, milk, salt, pepper, and fennel. Cook until the sauce is smooth and thickened. Pour over the fish and sprinkle with parsley. Serve with Green Beans and Cured Ham (p. 79) and a dry white wine like Monte Llano.

LUBINA "ALBUFERA"

(Fillet of Striped Bass in Almond Sauce)

THE Albufera is a vast lagoon in the heart of the flat Valencian rice fields, and watching a sunset over its tranquil waters is an experience not to be missed on any visit to Valencia. Food cooked "Albufera Style" found its way into world cuisine by way of the French, who, during the early nineteenth century, occupied much of Spain. The French sauces labeled "Albufera," however, have absolutely no connection with the garlic- and almond-rich sauce referred to as "Albufera" in Spain.

Serves 4

6 cloves garlic   1 tablespoon olive oil
4 tablespoons minced parsley   ¼ teaspoon paprika
¼ teaspoon oregano   1½ cups fish broth (p. 13)
¼ teaspoon mint   2 striped bass, about 1 pound each,
3 tablespoons ground   cut in fillets
     blanched almonds   Strips of pimiento for garnish
2 tablespoons flour

In a food processor or blender, beat the garlic, parsley, oregano, mint, and 1 tablespoon of the ground almonds to a paste. In a skillet, place the flour and remaining 2 tablespoons of ground almonds. Stir in the oil and cook over low heat until the flour and almonds turn golden. Add the paste from the processor and the paprika.

Stirring constantly, mix in the fish broth until the sauce is thickened and smooth. Place the fish fillets on a greased baking dish. Pour on the sauce and cook in a 350° F oven for about 20 minutes. Decorate the fish with strips of pimiento. Serve with Green Bean Salad (p. 118) and a dry white wine such as René Barbier.

CABALLA A LA VINAGRETA

(Mackerel Vinaigrette)

PREPARE SEVERAL HOURS IN ADVANCE.

MACKEREL is a highly prized fish in Spain, and consequently it is often difficult to find. In the seaside city of Cádiz, however, the supply seems to be abundant. Even amateur fishermen catch more than they need and are found on street corners each afternoon selling their day's catch to housewives and restaurateurs alike. In summer the people of Cádiz enjoy mackerel with a cooling vinaigrette.

Serves 4

8 tablespoons olive oil
3 tablespoons red wine vinegar
Salt
Freshly ground pepper
1 teaspoon capers
1 tablespoon minced parsley

2 tablespoons minced onion
2 cloves garlic, crushed
Pinch sugar
4 fillets of mackerel, about ½ pound
    each, skin removed

In a small bowl mix together 6 tablespoons of the oil, the vinegar, salt, pepper, capers, parsley, onion, garlic, and sugar. Grease the broiler. Brush the fish lightly on both sides with the remaining 2 tablespoons of oil. Broil on each side, being careful not to overcook—a few minutes will do. Cool to room temperature. Place in a deep dish, pour on the vinaigrette sauce, and refrigerate, spooning the sauce over the fish occasionally. Serve after several hours with a dry white wine such as Monopole and a green salad with Picadilla Dressing (p. 105).

TRUCHA ESCABECHADA

(Marinated Trout)

PREPARE AT LEAST ONE DAY IN ADVANCE.

SPORTS fishermen from all over the world flock to Spain in early spring to try their luck angling for trout in the country's innumerable and well-stocked mountain streams and rivers. Trucha Escabechada is served cold and is an especially favored preparation during the warm summer months.

Serves 4

4 freshwater trout, about
    ½ pound each
Salt
Freshly ground pepper
Flour for dusting
1 cup olive oil
3 cloves garlic, peeled

2 bay leaves
2 teaspoons thyme
2 tablespoons minced parsley
1 cup fish broth (p. 13) or clam juice
1 cup dry white wine
1 cup red wine vinegar

Clean and dry the trout well, leaving the heads on. Season them inside and out with salt and pepper. Dust with flour. Heat ½ cup of the oil in a large skillet. Fry the trout over medium heat until they are golden brown and cooked through. Remove the trout to a shallow casserole and arrange attractively. Leave the oil in the skillet.

Add the remaining ½ cup of oil to the oil in the skillet and heat. Fry the garlic cloves slowly until they are golden. Cool the oil. Add the bay leaves, thyme, and 1 tablespoon of the parsley. Stir in the broth, wine, vinegar, salt, and pepper. Bring to a boil and continue boiling until the liquid is reduced by half. Pour over the trout. Cool, then refrigerate at least 1 day, spooning the sauce over the fish occasionally. The trout is equally delicious several days later. Serve cold, sprinkled with the remaining tablespoon of parsley. Accompany with an Ensalada de Escalibada (p. 117) and a dry white Preferido wine.

NOTE: After marinating, the trout may also be filleted, cut into small pieces, then served on bread as a *tapa*. The same recipe may be used to make Sardinas Escabechadas (marinated sardines), an equally popular dish in Spain.

TRUCHA A LA NAVARRA

(*Trout with Cured Ham*)

THE mountainous region of Navarra abounds in trout streams and has lent its name to several trout recipes, the most famous one being Trucha a la Navarra. Trout, prized by sportsmen and gourmets alike, is usually prepared as straightforwardly as possible. In this recipe the addition of cured ham to a simply sautéed trout gives interest to the fish without masking or overpowering its delicate flavor.

Serves 4

4 freshwater trout, about ¾ pound
    each, cleaned, heads on
Salt
Freshly ground pepper
Lemon juice
8 thin slices cured ham

Flour for dusting
3 tablespoons olive oil
2 pimientos, homemade or imported,
    cut in strips
Lemon wedges

Sprinkle the trout inside and out with salt, pepper, and lemon juice. Place 1 slice of ham in each trout cavity. Dust the trout with flour. Wrap another piece of ham around the middle of each trout and tie in place with a string. Heat the oil in a large skillet and sauté the fish until well browned on each side and cooked through.

    To serve, remove the string, leaving the ham in place. Decorate with pimiento strips and lemon wedges. Boiled potatoes, a salad, and a dry white wine like Viña Tondonia complete the meal.

SARDINAS A LA MONTAÑESA

(*Sardines, Santander Style*)

THE small sardines in this recipe are wrapped in grape leaves to help them hold together during cooking and to lend a subtle flavor to the fish and to the fresh tomato sauce.

Serves 4

Grape leaves packed in brine, 1 for
    each fish

1 dozen small sardines (about
    1½ pounds)

Salt
Freshly ground pepper
1/4 teaspoon mint
1 medium onion, finely chopped
1 leek or 3 scallions, finely chopped
and well-cleaned

3 medium tomatoes, finely chopped
2 cloves garlic, minced
1/4 cup olive oil
1/2 cup dry white wine
1/2 teaspoon paprika

Separate the grape leaves and drop them into boiling water. Cook 5 minutes and drain well. Season the sardines with salt and pepper. Wrap each in a grape leaf, leaving the heads exposed. Arrange them in crisscrossing layers, seam side down, in a deep pot. Sprinkle each layer lightly with the mint.

In a bowl, mix the onion, leek, tomato, garlic, oil, wine, paprika, salt, and pepper. Pour over the sardines and shake the pot to distribute the sauce. Bring to a boil, cover, and simmer 25 minutes, or until the sardines are done. Turn the contents of the pot out onto a large platter (the sardines may break if you try to serve them directly from the pot). Remove the grape leaves and place 3 sardines on each plate. Spoon the sauce around, not over, them and add a piece of grape leaf as garnish. Serve with a green salad and a dry white wine like Marqués de Cáceres.

BACALAO EN SAMFAINA

(Cod with Eggplant and Peppers)

START PREPARATION AT LEAST ONE DAY IN ADVANCE.

IF THE relatively strong taste of salt cod is not for you, this dish is equally good with fresh fish.

Serves 4

1 pound salt cod, skinned and boned;
fresh tuna, or other fish steaks
Flour for dusting
4 tablespoons olive oil
2 medium onions, chopped
1 pound eggplant, skinned and cubed

2 green peppers, cut in strips
1 pound fresh or canned tomato,
skinned and chopped
1/2 cup dry white wine
Salt
Freshly ground pepper

If using salt cod, soak 36 hours in cold water, changing the water occasionally. Drain and place in a pot of water. Bring to a boil and remove immediately from the flame. Drain and dry the cod.

Cut the cod (or other fish being used) into 1 1/2-inch pieces. Dust with flour. Heat the oil in a large, shallow casserole and fry the fish pieces until golden. Drain. In the remaining oil, sauté the onion, eggplant, and green peppers slowly, about 10 minutes. Add the tomato, wine, salt, and pepper. Cover and cook 20 minutes, or until the vegetables are tender. Add the fish pieces and cook 10 minutes more. A dry, full-bodied white wine such as Marqués de Riscal is appropriate.

BACALAO A LA VIZCAÍNA
(Salt Cod, Basque Style)

START PREPARATION AT LEAST ONE DAY IN ADVANCE.

LOCATED in the northern area of Spain, the Basque country is a lush and mountainous area of rich land, where grassy cliffs abruptly dip down to the Bay of Biscay, one of the finest fishing grounds in the world. Fresh fish is, of course, readily available, but it is dried salt cod, curiously, that is the main ingredient for innumerable well-known Basque specialties. The following is considered one of the supreme dishes of Basque cookery, greatly appreciated by those who have a taste for cod.

Dried sweet peppers (see glossary) are essential for the preparation of an authentic Bacalao a la Vizcaína. The substitution of fresh or canned peppers will produce a good dish, although different in character from the original.

Serves 4

1 pound dried salt cod, boned
    and skinned
4 dried sweet red peppers such as
    "New Mexico" style, seeds
    and stems removed
3 tablespoons olive oil

3 large onions, chopped
2 cloves garlic, lightly crushed
2 sprigs parsley
¼ cup diced slab bacon
½ cup diced cured ham
1 hard-boiled egg yolk

1½ cups hot water	Freshly ground pepper
1 bay leaf	½ dried red chili pepper, seeds
Salt	removed, crumbled

Cover the cod with cold water and soak for 36 hours, changing the water occasionally. Soak the dried sweet peppers for 1 hour in warm water. Drain.

Heat the oil in a skillet and sauté the onion, garlic, and parsley until the onion is wilted. Cover and continue cooking over a very low flame for about 30 minutes. The onions should not brown. Meanwhile, lightly sauté the bacon and ham in a small skillet. Set aside.

Pass the onion mixture to a processor or blender. Add the drained sweet peppers, cut in pieces, and the egg yolk and blend until smooth. With the motor running, gradually add the hot water. Strain and return to the skillet, along with the bay leaf, salt, pepper, ham, bacon, and crumbled chili pepper. Cover and cook slowly 20 minutes more.

Drain the cod and place in a pot with water to cover. Bring to a boil and remove immediately from the flame. Drain. Cut into 1½-inch pieces. In a shallow ovenproof casserole (preferably earthenware), spread a few tablespoons of the onion-and-peppers mixture. Add the cod and cover with the remaining sauce. Place in a 300° F oven, uncovered, and cook until tender, about 1½ hours. Add a little water if the sauce dries out too much. This dish is considered better when reheated the following day. Serve with a full-bodied white wine like Viña Paceta and boiled new potatoes.

ANCAS DE RANA A LA VALENCIANA

(Marinated and Fried Frogs' Legs)

START PREPARATION SEVERAL HOURS IN ADVANCE.

THE swampy rice fields of Valencia are ideal breeding grounds for frogs. Curiously, frogs' legs rarely appear on Valencian restaurant menus, but when they do, they are often marinated and breaded, as in this recipe. Because of the small size of frogs' legs, they make excellent *tapas* for parties—much more interesting than the chicken wings often found on such occasions.

Serves 4

1½ pounds medium frogs' legs	2 eggs, lightly beaten
(approximately 10–12 pairs)	Bread crumbs, preferably homemade
Salt	Oil for frying (a mixture of olive and
Freshly ground pepper	salad oils)
Flour for dusting	

MARINADE

½ cup dry white wine

½ teaspoon thyme

1 tablespoon olive oil

1 tablespoon chopped parsley

1 clove garlic, crushed

Juice of 1 lemon

4 peppercorns

Salt to taste

Mix together all the marinade ingredients. Separate the frogs' legs, if the pairs are joined, and place in a shallow casserole dish. Pour on the marinade. Cover and refrigerate several hours.

Remove the legs from the marinade and drain them on paper towels. Sprinkle on both sides with salt and pepper. Dust with flour, dip in the beaten egg, then roll in the bread crumbs. In a large skillet heat the oil, at least ½ inch deep, and fry the frogs' legs until golden. Drain. They may be kept warm in a 200° F oven for about 30 minutes. Serve with Spicy Lima Beans (p. 80) and a light red wine like Domecq Domain.

Chapter 10

AVES Y CAZA

(Poultry and Game)

I T IS safe to say that game, especially game birds, have wider appeal in Spain than chicken and are easy to find everywhere and at everyday prices. The reason for the abundance of game is twofold. Spain's topography and climate are ideal for the proliferation of game—most of the country is mountainous with sufficient forest lands to harbor large game animals such as deer, bear, wild boar, and wild goat and millions of acres of low mountain brushland, ideal breeding grounds for pheasants, partridge, quail, and rabbits. Besides, there are vast expanses of marshlands in the south and east that ducks and geese call home. In the Basque country, doves are netted as they fly to and from France in the narrow ravines of Echalar in the Pyrenees.

Besides its topography, Spain has abundant game because of its geographic location. It is on the migratory path of millions of European birds that travel to Africa for the winter season. When they return to their homelands in spring, most pass through Spain and many dally there to bear offspring before continuing their journeys. Spring is therefore a delightful time of year to visit Spain, especially the southern areas. Storks with their young can be spotted in every church belfry, and in the Coto Doñana wildlife preserve near Sevilla the sights are endless. An experienced guide can point out hundreds of species that inhabit, or at least spend some time, in the preserve.

Such abundance means that game—especially partridge, quail, and rabbit—are everyday items on restaurant menus, found almost as commonly as chicken. Chicken, by the way, should not be looked down upon—they are often still bred on small farms where they have the run of the grounds and eat whatever their pecking encounters. These conditions produce chickens that have less fat and much more flavor and texture than what we are used to. A simple spit-roasted chicken, bought at a store that specializes in prepared foods, can taste delicious and is especially enjoyable as picnic fare when visiting Spain.

Aves y Caza, poultry and game, will appear on restaurant menus in the limited but delicious preparations one comes to expect from the tourist-oriented Spanish menus that wish to please what is perceived as tourist tastes. Chicken is usually roasted or "*al ajillo*"—garlic fried (my favorite). Quail is roasted and partridge and pheasant stewed in a red or white wine sauce. But visit some of the new regionally oriented restaurants, talk to food-knowledgeable Spaniards, and read some books on Spanish cuisine, and it becomes apparent that in the field of poultry and game, Spanish cuisine shines, putting together unusual and often brilliant combinations of ingredients. Grapes, grape leaves, pears, raisins, figs, olives, eggplant, pine nuts, almonds, *chorizo*, chocolate, shrimp, and lobster all enter into Spanish poultry and game recipes. Most are ideal in taste and presentation for company dinners.

For those unfamiliar with game cookery, there are many exciting ideas included here to expand your culinary repertoire. Some game is less exotic than other. Rabbit and duck, for example, are cooked similarly to chicken and widely available fresh and frozen, often in your local supermarket. Quail is a tiny bird with lots of flavor. Because of its size it lends itself to several elegant presentations—in *escabeche*, in potato nests, enclosed in green peppers, wrapped in grape leaves. It can usually be purchased at specialty butchers (or mail ordered from sporting goods companies) and is well worth the extra effort it may take to find. Pheasant and partridge have more muscular meat and must be cooked with care to avoid toughening. They are generally less accessible but can also be found with a little scouting, usually frozen in specialty shops.

POLLO AL AJILLO

(Chicken in Garlic Sauce)

POLLO AL AJILLO is one of those dishes that has become a part of the Spanish national culinary repertoire and can be found on practically every menu in Spain. Nevertheless, it took me years to find a recipe that was completely satisfactory. I found it finally in the most unlikely place: Osuna, a small southern town in the area referred to as "La Sartén de España"—the frying pan of Spain—not because of the cooking skills of its people, but simply because it is the hottest spot in Spain, and in summer, it is said, eggs that are placed in a pan in the street will fry of their own accord.

The owner-cook at El Mesón del Duque restaurant in Osuna claims that she has a steady clientele of those who make return visits, in spite of the heat, just to eat her Pollo al Ajillo once more.

Serves 4

A 2½–3-pound chicken
4 tablespoons olive oil
1 whole head garlic, peeled
    and minced

Freshly ground pepper
3 tablespoons brandy, preferably
    Spanish brandy, or Cognac
Coarse salt

Cut the chicken into small serving pieces—the whole breast into 4 parts, each thigh into 2 parts, the bony tip of the leg chopped off, the wing tip discarded, and the rest of the wing separated into 2 parts. Dry the pieces well. Heat the oil in a large, shallow casserole. Add the chicken and cook over moderately high heat until the pieces are well browned.

To simplify the arduous chore of chopping garlic, peel the cloves and place them in a food processor; it will mince them very nicely. Add all but 1 tablespoon of the minced garlic to the chicken, along with the pepper and the brandy. Standing well back—the flames may go quite high—ignite the liquid. Stir until the flames subside. Cover and cook slowly about 15 minutes. Sprinkle with the remaining 1 tablespoon of garlic and the salt. Serve, spooning some of the sauce over the chicken. Green Beans and Cured Ham (p. 79) and a light red wine like Marqués de Murrieta are fine accompaniments.

POLLO AL AJILLO "EDELWEISS"

(Garlic Chicken)

THIS is a quick-cooking version of garlic chicken, but nevertheless a most treasured recipe. It comes from the cook at the Edelweiss Restaurant near the Ordesa National Park, an area of spectacular scenery in the Spanish Pyrenees. So taken was my daughter with this chicken that she ordered it on three successive nights. I asked the waiter to ask the cook how he prepared it, and the waiter returned with a scrap of paper on which was neatly printed, each "i" carefully dotted, the following:

GARLIC CHICKEN

Cut up a chicken. Sprinkle it with salt. Place it in a skillet with hot oil. When the chicken is golden, add some crushed garlic cloves. Cook until they are golden, and then enjoy it.

THE COOK

Translated into specifics, the recipe is as follows:

Serves 4

A 2½–3-pound chicken
Coarse salt
6 tablespoons olive oil

10 cloves garlic, unpeeled and
lightly crushed

Divide the chicken into small serving pieces—the whole breast into 4 parts, each thigh into 2 parts, the bony tip of the leg chopped off, the wing tip discarded, and the rest of the wing separated into 2 parts. Dry the pieces well. Sprinkle them with salt.

Heat the oil in a skillet. Fry the chicken until it is golden on all sides and cooked through. Add the garlic cloves and continue cooking until the cloves have browned. Serve, spooning some of the sauce over the chicken and decorating with the garlic. This dish is typically prepared in individual earthenware dishes and served in the cooking dish. Any of the asparagus recipes and a light red wine like Rioja Vega are good accompaniments.

POLLO EN PEPITORIA

(Chicken in Egg, Almond, and Sherry Sauce)

"*Pepitoria*" applies to poultry and game dishes to which egg has been added, either uncooked or hard-boiled, and is a favorite Spanish preparation. Although most often found with chicken, many believe that a hen, slow cooked, produces the tastiest "*pepitoria.*" I have found that a kosher chicken gives the best results. This dish combines all of the ingredients most often associated with Spanish cooking—garlic, saffron, sherry, and almonds—into an unusually savory sauce.

Serves 4

4 tablespoons olive oil
A 3–3½-pound chicken, cut in small
    serving pieces
A ¼-pound piece cured ham, cut in
    julienne strips
1 large onion, chopped
2 cloves garlic, minced
3 tablespoons minced parsley
¼ cup dry (*fino*) sherry

¾ cup chicken broth
Dash nutmeg
¼ teaspoon saffron
1 bay leaf
Salt
Freshly ground pepper
15 blanched almonds
1 hard-boiled egg, finely chopped

In a large casserole, heat the oil and sauté the chicken over a high flame until it is well browned. Pour off all but 1 tablespoon of the oil. Reduce the heat, add the ham, onion, garlic, and 2 tablespoons of the parsley and cook until the onion is wilted. Stir in the sherry, broth, nutmeg, saffron, bay leaf, salt, and pepper. Simmer 10 minutes, uncovered. Remove the chicken, ham, and bay leaf to a heated platter.

In a food processor or blender, chop the almonds until they are finely ground. Gradually add the contents of the casserole and blend until smooth. Return the sauce to the casserole along with the chicken, ham, and bay leaf. Cover and cook in a 350° F oven for 20 minutes, adding more chicken broth if the sauce thickens too much. Sprinkle the hard-boiled egg over the chicken and cook 5 minutes more. Garnish with the remaining tablespoon of the parsley before serving and accompany with a green salad and a light red wine like Cabernet Sauvignon.

POLLO CON HIGOS
(Chicken with Figs)

START PREPARATION SEVERAL HOURS IN ADVANCE.

FIG trees are common all over the Mediterranean coast, but their fruit is usually eaten either fresh or dried and rarely sees the inside of a cooking pot. The Cataláns, however, are particularly predisposed to combine fruits with meats, as in this delicious and unusual preparation of chicken, which I wholeheartedly recommend, even to those of timid tastes.

Serves 4

½ cup medium-sweet white wine
Peel of ½ lemon
A 3–3½-pound chicken, cut in
    serving pieces
Coarse salt

Freshly ground pepper
¼ cup diced slab bacon
1 tablespoon olive oil
3 tablespoons beef broth

FIGS

¾ cup sugar
¾ cup water
½ cup vinegar
1 slice lemon

1 cinnamon stick
1 pound fresh figs or bottled
    figs, drained

To prepare the figs, mix the sugar, water, vinegar, lemon slice, and cinnamon stick in a saucepan. Bring to a boil, then simmer 5 minutes. Add the figs, return to a boil, then simmer 10 minutes more (only 5 minutes for bottled figs). Cover and let sit for several hours. Drain the figs, discarding the lemon and cinnamon.

Place the drained figs in a bowl and add the wine and the lemon peel. Let sit while preparing the chicken. Sprinkle the chicken pieces with salt and pepper. In a large, shallow ovenproof casserole, slowly heat the bacon pieces until they begin to give off their oil and turn golden. Reserve the bacon, leaving its oil in the pan. Add the olive oil, heat, then sauté the chicken until golden on all sides. Turn up the heat and very gradually add the wine in which the figs have been soaking (discard the lemon peel). Boil until the wine is reduced and syrupy. Transfer the casserole to a 350° F oven and cook, uncovered, for 20 minutes, adding water if necessary to prevent burning. Return the casserole to the top of the stove, add the beef broth and figs, cover, and cook 10 minutes more. Serve with a green salad and a light red Reserva wine like Paternina.

PECHUGA DE POLLO VILLEROY

(Béchamel-Coated Fried Chicken)

START PREPARATION SEVERAL HOURS IN ADVANCE.

MANY visitors to Spain return home with a love for Pollo Villeroy, but find it all but impossible to prepare in their own kitchens. The trick lies in chilling the béchamel sauce so that during frying it clings to the chicken. An excellent variation is Gambas Villeroy (p. 10), shrimp prepared in a similar manner.

Serves 4

2 whole chicken breasts, split	½ onion, peeled
Coarse salt	1 sprig parsley
Freshly ground pepper	1 egg, beaten
¼ teaspoon thyme	Bread crumbs
1 bay leaf	Oil for frying

BÉCHAMEL SAUCE

5 tablespoons butter	Salt
6 tablespoons flour	Freshly ground pepper
¾ cup milk	⅛ teaspoon ground nutmeg

Remove the small rib bones from the chicken, leaving the large breast bone intact. Cook the breasts in water to cover with the salt, pepper, thyme, bay leaf, onion, and parsley. (Add also the bones that have been removed.) Cover and cook about 15 minutes—do not overcook. Remove the chicken breasts and continue cooking the broth another 30 minutes. Reserve ¾ cup of the broth for the béchamel sauce. Cool, then chill the chicken.

To make the béchamel sauce, melt the butter in a saucepan, add the flour, and cook a minute or so. Stir in the reserved broth, the milk, salt, pepper, and nutmeg. Cook until the sauce is thickened and smooth. Cool, stirring occasionally.

Dip the cold chicken pieces in the béchamel sauce, coating them completely on all sides. Place the breasts on a plate and refrigerate until the sauce hardens, at least 1 hour. Dip the breasts in the beaten egg, then into bread crumbs to coat. Fry immediately in hot oil, at least 1 inch deep, until the chicken is golden on all sides. Drain. Serve with Spicy Lima Beans (p. 80) and a light red wine like Rioja Clarete.

POLLO CHILINDRÓN

(Chicken with Red Peppers)

THE region of Aragón is the home of a wide variety of *chilindrón* dishes, a word referring to foods cooked with red peppers. Besides chicken, pork (p. 303) and lamb (p. 293) are commonly prepared in this manner. Red peppers seem equally suited to all of these meats, although I am particularly fond of this chicken version.

Serves 4

A 3–3½-pound chicken, cut in
    serving pieces
Coarse salt
2 tablespoons olive oil
1 clove garlic, minced
1 onion, chopped

2 tablespoons diced cured ham
2 pimientos, preferably homemade
    (p. 430), cut in strips
1 tomato, skinned and chopped
Freshly ground pepper

Sprinkle the chicken pieces with salt. Heat the oil in a large, shallow casserole. Brown the chicken well on all sides. Add the garlic and onion and sauté until the onion is wilted. Stir in the ham, then the pimientos, tomato, pepper, and more salt if necessary. Cover and cook 30 minutes. Uncover and continue cooking 20 minutes more—most of the liquid should be evaporated, leaving only a small amount of sauce. A green salad and an Olarra light red wine are appropriate accompaniments.

POLLO EN SAMFAINA
(Chicken and Vegetables)

"*Samfaina*" has the same word root as "symphony" and is probably applied to this dish because of its colorful medley of ingredients, which includes peppers, eggplant, and tomato. This is a light and tasty way to prepare chicken that, if it weren't such an old Catalán specialty, one might be tempted to call "nouvelle."

Serves 4

A 3–3½-pound chicken, cut in
    serving pieces
Coarse salt
2 tablespoons olive oil
A ¼-pound piece cured ham, diced
1 onion, chopped
1 clove garlic, minced
1 eggplant (about ¾ pound), peeled
    or unpeeled and cubed

1 green pepper, cut in strips
1 pound fresh tomato, skinned
    and chopped
1 bay leaf
½ teaspoon thyme
1 tablespoon minced parsley
Freshly ground pepper
½ cup dry white wine

Sprinkle the chicken pieces with salt. In a large, shallow casserole, brown the chicken in hot oil until golden on all sides. Remove to a warm platter. Add the ham and stir fry 1 minute, then add the onion and garlic and sauté until the onion is wilted. Add the eggplant and green pepper. Sauté 5 minutes more. Add the tomato, bay leaf, thyme, parsley, salt, and pepper to taste. Stir in the wine. Return the chicken to the casserole, spooning some sauce over it. Cover and simmer 1 hour. Serve with Watercress and Carrot Salad (p. 108) and a light red wine like Lan.

POLLASTRE AMB GAMBES
(Chicken in Brandy Sauce with Shrimp)

FROM the region that made Langosta con Pollo (Lobster and Chicken, p. 204) famous—Cataluña—comes another chicken and shellfish combination, Pollastre amb Gambes (the name is written in the Catalán language, not Spanish). Here, as in the lobster dish, the tastes of chicken and seafood are surprisingly and deliciously compatible.

Serves 4

A 3–3½-pound chicken, cut in
    serving pieces
Coarse salt
Freshly ground pepper
3 tablespoons olive oil
¼ pound medium-large shrimp, in
    their shells
1 onion, chopped

1 clove garlic, minced
1 carrot, scraped and chopped
¼ cup brandy, preferably Spanish
    brandy, or Cognac
1½ teaspoons flour
½ cup dry white wine
¼ cup beef broth
2 tablespoons minced parsley

Sprinkle the chicken pieces with salt and pepper. Heat the oil in a large, shallow casserole and brown the chicken and the shrimp, removing and reserving the shrimp after 1 minute and continuing to cook the chicken until golden on all sides. Add the onion, garlic, and carrot and sauté until the onion is wilted. Pour in the brandy and, standing well back, flame, stirring until the flames die. Stir in the flour, cook a minute, then add the wine, broth, 1 tablespoon of the parsley, salt, and pepper. Cover and cook 20 minutes. Add the reserved shrimp and continue cooking 10 minutes more. Remove the chicken and shrimp to a warm platter. Strain the sauce and pour it over the chicken and shrimp. Serve, sprinkling with the remaining tablespoon of parsley. A green vegetable, Ensalada de San Isidro (p. 106), and a light red Catalán wine like Cabernet Sauvignon are suitable.

POLLO AL HORNO

(Roast Chicken with Sherry)

THE people of Cádiz like their chicken roasted in this manner. When we visit, we buy it at a takeout store for an exceptional picnic lunch on the beach.

Serves 4

2 tablespoons olive oil
A 3–3½-pound chicken, cut in
    serving pieces
Salt
Freshly ground pepper

1 tablespoon minced parsley
2 cloves garlic, cut in several pieces
¼ cup medium-sweet (*oloroso*) sherry
2 tablespoons lard or butter

Cover the bottom of a roasting pan with the oil. Arrange the chicken pieces in the pan skin side up and sprinkle with salt, pepper, and parsley. Add the pieces of garlic to the pan and pour in the sherry. Dot the chicken with the lard. Place in a 350° F oven and roast about 50 minutes, basting the chicken frequently and adding water as the liquid evaporates. Serve with Greens and Potato Casserole (p. 93) and a light red wine like Imperial.

POLLO AL VINO TINTO

(Chicken in Chorizo and Red Wine Sauce)

A SAUCE as hearty as this one—containing *chorizo*, red wine, and brandy—demands an equally robust red wine, like Sangre de Toro, a good crunchy bread, and a refreshing green salad.

Serves 4

A 3–3½-pound chicken, cut in
   serving pieces
Salt
Freshly ground pepper
Flour for dusting
4 tablespoons olive oil
1 large onion, chopped
1 clove garlic, minced
1 carrot, scraped and finely chopped
1 *chorizo* sausage (2 ounces), chopped

2 tablespoons brandy, preferably
   Spanish brandy, or Cognac
1 pimiento, homemade or
   imported, diced
1 tablespoon minced parsley
1 bay leaf
¼ teaspoon thyme
½ cup chicken broth
1 cup dry red wine

Sprinkle the chicken with salt and pepper. Dust with flour. Heat the oil in a large, shallow casserole and brown the chicken pieces well on all sides. Add the onion, garlic, carrot, and *chorizo* and sauté until the onion is wilted. Add the brandy and carefully flame. Stir in the pimiento, parsley, salt, pepper, bay leaf, thyme, broth, and wine. Cover and simmer about 1½ hours.

POLLO CON PIÑONES

(Chicken with Pine Nuts)

Spanish cooks are fond of combining nuts of many varieties into their sauces. In this case, the delicate flavor of pine nuts is a lovely complement to a chicken simmered in white wine.

Serves 4

A 3–3½-pound chicken, cut in
    serving pieces
Coarse salt
Freshly ground pepper
3 tablespoons olive oil
1 teaspoon flour

2 tablespoons minced shallots
½ teaspoon thyme
2 tablespoons minced parsley
1 bay leaf
½ cup dry white wine
2 ounces pine nuts

Sprinkle the chicken pieces with salt and pepper. Heat the oil in a large, shallow casserole and sauté the chicken until it is golden on all sides. Sprinkle in the flour and stir. Add the shallots, thyme, parsley, bay leaf, wine, and pine nuts. Cover and cook slowly for 30 minutes. Serve with Sautéed Artichokes and Cured Ham (p. 81) and a light red wine like Lan.

POLLO ASADO CON SALSA DE NARANJA

(Roast Chicken with Orange Sauce)

THIS is basically a roast chicken, to which a delicious sweet-sour orange sauce is added when served.

Serves 4

A 3–3½-pound chicken, trussed
Salt
Freshly ground pepper
¾ cup chicken broth,
    preferably homemade

5 teaspoons powdered sugar
3½ teaspoons vinegar
Juice of 2 oranges (about ¾ cup)
2 teaspoons cornstarch

Sprinkle the chicken with salt and pepper. Roast, preferably in an oval earthenware dish, at 350° F for about 1 hour, or until tender and golden, basting occasionally. Remove to a warm platter.

Pour off the fat from the roasting pan, leaving the juices. Add ¼ cup of the chicken broth and deglaze the pan. Reserve this liquid. In a medium skillet, place 4½ teaspoons of the sugar and heat, stirring constantly, until the sugar caramelizes. Remove the pan from the flame and add 3 teaspoons of the vinegar, the orange juice, the remaining ½ cup of broth, and the reserved deglazed pan juices. Add the remaining ½ teaspoon of sugar and the remaining ½ teaspoon of vinegar. Cover and simmer 10 minutes.

Dissolve the cornstarch in water. Add it to the sauce and cook until thickened and smooth, stirring constantly. Cut the chicken into serving pieces and spoon on the sauce. A green vegetable and a light red wine such as Tres Marqueses go well. You might also want to try a Valencian Potato and Orange Salad (p. 113).

POLLO A LA CASTELLANA

(Chicken in Puréed Onion and Wine Sauce)

Serves 4

2 tablespoons olive oil
1 medium onion, chopped
1 clove garlic, peeled
Coarse salt
Freshly ground pepper
A 3–3½-pound chicken, cut in
    serving pieces

3 tablespoons minced parsley
Pinch saffron
½ cup dry white wine
½ cup chicken broth
¼ teaspoon thyme
1 bay leaf

Heat the oil in a shallow casserole. Sauté the onion and garlic until the onion is wilted. Transfer the onion and garlic to a food processor or blender. Salt and pepper the chicken pieces. Brown the chicken in the casserole, adding more oil if necessary.

Meanwhile, add 2 tablespoons of the parsley, the saffron, salt, and pepper to the onion and garlic already in the processor. Blend well. Gradually pour in the wine and chicken broth and beat until smooth. Strain over the chicken pieces. Sprinkle with thyme, add the bay leaf, cover, and cook over a low flame 30 minutes, adding more chicken broth or water if the sauce becomes too thick. Sprinkle with the remaining tablespoon of parsley and serve with Salad, Murcia Style (p. 110) and a light red wine like Diamante.

PECHUGA DE POLLO RELLENA

(Stuffed Chicken Breast)

Serves 4

4 tablespoons chopped green olives,
    with pimiento
4 thin chicken cutlets, cut from
    the breast

Salt
Freshly ground pepper
4 thin slices cured ham
Flour for dusting

4 tablespoons olive oil
6 tablespoons chopped onion
2 cloves garlic, minced
2 tablespoons flour

1 cup chicken broth
1 cup dry white wine
1 tablespoon minced parsley
¼ pound mushrooms, sliced

Place the chopped olives in ¼ cup water and boil 3 minutes. Drain. Season the cutlets with salt and pepper. Cover each with a slice of ham and 1 tablespoon of the chopped olives. Roll. Hold in place with toothpicks.

Dust the cutlets with flour. Heat the oil in a skillet and sauté the cutlets until golden on all sides. Remove them to a shallow ovenproof casserole. Pour off all but 2 tablespoons of the oil from the skillet. Add the onion and garlic and sauté until the onion is wilted. Stir in the 2 tablespoons of flour, then add the broth, wine, parsley, salt, and pepper. Cook, stirring occasionally, for 10 minutes. Stir in the mushrooms. Pour the sauce over the rolled chicken. Cover and bake at 350° F for 25 minutes. Serve with Poor Man's Potatoes (p. 97) and a light red wine like Fino Claret.

POLLO AL AST GLASEADO

(Spit-Roasted Chicken Brushed with Honey and Cumin)

START PREPARATION AT LEAST ONE HOUR IN ADVANCE.

THIS is sweet-sour chicken, Catalán style. Although typically spit roasted, it may also be prepared in the oven.

Serves 4

¼ cup olive oil
1½ tablespoons vinegar
2 teaspoons ground cumin
2 cloves garlic, crushed

2 tablespoons honey
1 teaspoon salt
A 3–3½-pound chicken, trussed

In a small bowl, mix all ingredients except the chicken. Place the chicken in a shallow bowl and pour on the sweet-sour mixture. Marinate for at least 1 hour, turning and brushing the chicken with the marinade frequently.

Roast the chicken on a spit or in an oven pan (preferably an oval earthenware dish) at 350° F for 1 hour. Reserve the marinade and brush the chicken frequently as it roasts. Serve with roast potatoes and a light red wine like Viña Lanciano.

PATO A LA SEVILLANA

(Duck with Olives in Sherry Sauce)

THIS is a most delicious and unusual duck preparation from Sevilla, the most Andalucian of Spanish cities. It utilizes the typical products of southern Spain—the green olives from the groves that cover the parched land as far as the eye can see; sherry wine, made only in Andalucía; and duck from the nearby marshlands of the Guadalquivir River. Pato a la Sevillana makes an elegant meal that is very popular with guests (see Menu Suggestions, p. 424).

Serves 4

1 duck (about 4½ pounds),
    with neck
2 slices onion
2 cloves garlic, peeled
½ cup white wine
½ cup coarsely chopped or sliced
    Spanish green olives,
    without pimiento
2 tablespoons olive oil
1 medium onion, chopped

2 cloves garlic, minced
½ cup dry (*fino*) sherry
½ cup chicken broth
2 carrots, scraped and thinly sliced
1 sprig parsley
¼ teaspoon thyme
1 bay leaf
4 peppercorns
Salt

In the duck cavity, place the onion slices and the whole garlic cloves. Truss. Prick the duck deeply all over with a fork. Place in a roasting pan, along with the neck, if available, and roast at 350° F for 1 hour. Remove the duck to a warm platter and cut in quarters. Drain all fat from the roasting pan and deglaze the pan with ¼ cup of the wine. Reserve these pan juices and discard the neck.

    Place the olives in a small saucepan with the remaining ¼ cup of wine. Boil 5 minutes. Drain. Heat the oil in a shallow ovenproof casserole. Add the chopped onion and minced garlic and sauté until the onion is wilted. Add the sherry, chicken broth, carrots, parsley, thyme, bay leaf, peppercorns, salt, and the deglazed pan juices. Simmer 5 minutes. Add the duck quarters, spooning some sauce over them, cover, and return to the oven for 45 minutes. Remove the duck to a warm serving platter. Strain the sauce into a saucepan, pressing with the back of a spoon to extract as much liquid as possible. Deglaze the oven casserole with a few tablespoons of water or broth and add these juices to the sauce. Stir in the drained olives, heat, and pour over the duck. Serve with Green Bean Salad (p. 118) and a fine light red Reserva wine like Viña Tondonia.

PATO A LA NARANJA

(Duck in Orange Sauce)

THE French will surely dispute such claims, but it seems quite logical that this dish should have originated in Valencia, which supplies oranges to all of Europe and breeds thousands of ducks in its Albufera marshlands.

Serves 4

1 duck (about 4½ pounds), with neck and giblets	3 cloves garlic, peeled
	1 carrot, scraped, in thick slices
Salt	3 oranges
Freshly ground pepper	½ cup semisweet (*oloroso*) sherry
1 onion	Peel of ½ lemon

DUCK BROTH

1 tablespoon olive oil	1½ cups chicken broth
1 onion, coarsely chopped	1 sprig parsley
1 clove garlic, minced	Salt
1 carrot, scraped and sliced	Freshly ground pepper

Prick the duck deeply all over with a fork. Sprinkle inside and out with salt and pepper. Cut 2 slices from the onion and place with 1 clove of the garlic in the duck cavity. Truss. Place the duck in a roasting pan with the remainder of the onion, in 1 piece, the remaining 2 cloves of garlic, and the carrot slices, scattered around the pan. Roast 1 hour at 350° F. Pour off the fat and roast 1 hour more.

While the duck is roasting, prepare the duck broth. Heat the oil in a saucepan and brown the duck neck and giblets well. Add the onion, garlic, and carrot slices and sauté until the onion is wilted. Add the chicken broth, parsley, salt, and pepper. Cover and simmer 1 hour. Strain.

To prepare the oranges, remove the rind—orange part only—from 2 of the oranges and cut the rind into fine julienne strips. Place in a pan with water to cover. Bring to a boil and cook 5 minutes. Run under cold water, drain, and reserve. Remove and discard the white portion of the 2 skinned oranges and separate the oranges into sections. Reserve. Squeeze the remaining orange and reserve the juice.

When the duck is done, remove it to a warm platter. Discard the onion, garlic, and carrot. Skim off as much fat as possible from the pan, then add the sherry. Stir to loosen the particles. Bring to a boil and reduce the liquid by half. Add the lemon peel, orange julienne strips, duck broth, and the reserved orange juice. Cook 2 minutes, then remove the lemon peel and add the reserved orange sections. Cook until they heat through. Cut the duck into serving pieces. Pour on the sauce and serve with a salad and a fine light red Reserva wine like Claret Fino or a rosé wine such as Diamante.

RABBIT

RABBIT is usually bought skinned and often precut into serving pieces. Buy the smallest rabbit available—about 2–3 pounds. If it is not cut, separate the front legs at the shoulder and the hind legs at the hip. Then separate each hind leg section into 2 parts. Cut the rest of the rabbit crosswise into 4–6 pieces, depending on the size of the rabbit.

CONEJO ALIOLI
(Broiled Rabbit with Alioli)

START PREPARATION SEVERAL HOURS IN ADVANCE.

THIS is one of the two most popular ways of eating rabbit in Spain—broiled with seasoned oil, then baked in white wine and dressed with pungent garlic sauce (the more garlic, the better); the other way, Rabbit in Tomato Sauce, appears on page 266.

Serves 4

½ cup olive oil
1 bay leaf, crumbled
½ teaspoon thyme
Alioli Sauce (p. 186), reducing the
    amount of garlic, if desired
A 2½–3-pound rabbit, cut in
    serving pieces

Lemon juice
Salt
Freshly ground pepper
½ cup white wine

Several hours before cooking the rabbit, mix the oil with the bay leaf and thyme to let the flavors blend. Also, prepare the *alioli* sauce and let it sit at room temperature.

Sprinkle the rabbit pieces with lemon juice, then brush them with the oil mixture. Sprinkle with salt and pepper. Grease the broiler tray. Broil the rabbit 10 minutes on each side, basting with the oil mixture. Transfer the rabbit to a roasting pan and place in a 450° F oven. Add the broiler pan juices and the wine and cook 15 minutes more, basting regularly. Pass the *alioli* sauce separately and serve with Sautéed Greens with Croutons (p. 87) and a Gran Condal light red wine.

CONEJO AL PIRINEO

(Rabbit with Almonds and Pine Nuts)

WE OBTAINED this recipe from the congenial young owners of the Posada de Javier in Torrecaballeros, the heart of Castilian baby lamb country, although the recipe had come to them, in turn, from friends in the Catalán area of the Pyrenees. With almonds and pine nuts, it is a wonderful way to serve rabbit.

Serves 4

A 2½–3-pound rabbit, cut in
    serving pieces
Flour for dusting
3 tablespoons olive oil
1 large onion, chopped
1 cup dry white wine
1 tablespoon minced parsley
½ teaspoon thyme

1 bay leaf
Salt
Freshly ground pepper
2 cloves garlic, minced
2 tablespoons pine nuts
¼ cup slivered blanched almonds
    (1½ ounces)

Dust the rabbit with flour. Heat the oil in a casserole and brown the rabbit on all sides. Add the onion and continue cooking until it is wilted. Stir in the wine, parsley, thyme, bay leaf, salt, pepper, garlic, pine nuts, and almonds. Cover and simmer 1½–2 hours, or until the rabbit is very tender. Garlic Green Beans (p. 78) and a light red wine like Cabernet Sauvignon from Cataluña are good accompaniments.

CONEJO CON TOMATE

(Rabbit in Tomato Sauce)

START PREPARATION AT LEAST
ONE HOUR IN ADVANCE.

NEXT to Madrid's Rastro (flea market) is Malacatín, one of the oldest taverns in the city. It displays a fascinating collection of antique bullfighting posters and manages to maintain the ambience of a Madrid long gone. The food there is also traditional *madrileño* fare. The boiled beef dinner, Cocido Madrileño (p. 138), rarely seen these days, and Rabbit in Tomato Sauce, a great favorite that also seems to have disappeared, are both on the menu here. Wines are as traditional as the food—robust Méntrida red wines from the nearby Toledo region.

Serves 4

A 2½–3-pound rabbit, cut in
    serving pieces
1 clove garlic, cut in half
1 cup dry white wine
3 cloves garlic, minced
Coarse salt
Freshly ground pepper
2 tablespoons olive oil
1 large onion, chopped

1 green pepper, chopped
2 cups crushed tomato, fresh
    or canned
¼ teaspoon thyme
2 tablespoons minced parsley
1 bay leaf
½ dried red chili pepper, seeds
    removed, crumbled
3 teaspoons red wine vinegar

Rub the rabbit pieces with the cut clove of garlic, then marinate them in the wine and the minced garlic for at least 1 hour. Drain the rabbit well, reserving the liquid and the garlic.

Sprinkle the rabbit with salt and pepper. Heat the oil in a large, shallow casserole and sauté the rabbit until it is brown on all sides. Remove to a warm platter. Add the onion and green pepper to the pan and sauté until the onion is wilted. Add the tomato, thyme, parsley, bay leaf, hot pepper, vinegar, and the reserved wine and garlic. Cover and cook slowly for 2 hours. Serve with Ensalada de San Isidro (p. 106) and a light red regional wine from Valdepeñas like Molino.

CONEJO A LA CAZADORA
(Rabbit, Hunter Style)

Serves 4

3 tablespoons olive oil
A 2½–3-pound rabbit, cut in
    serving pieces
1 onion, chopped
A ¼-pound piece cured ham, diced
1 clove garlic, minced
2 tablespoons brandy, preferably
    Spanish brandy, or Cognac

1 cup dry white wine
1½ cups chopped tomato or
    tomato sauce
½ teaspoon thyme
1 tablespoon chopped parsley
Salt
Freshly ground pepper
¾ cup sliced mushrooms

Heat the oil in a large, shallow casserole and brown the rabbit on all sides. Add the onion, ham, and garlic and cook until the onion is wilted. Pour in the brandy and carefully ignite. When the flames die down, add the wine, tomato, thyme, parsley, salt, and pepper. Cover and simmer 1½ hours. Stir in the mushrooms and cook 15 minutes longer. Serve with a green salad with Picadilla Dressing (p. 105) and a light red wine like Olarra.

CONEJO CON PISTO
(Rabbit with Red Peppers and Zucchini)

"Pisto" (p. 94) refers to a vegetable medley found in Castilla. When similar vegetables are combined with rabbit, a savory stew results, which needs little more than a salad to make a complete meal.

Serves 4

A 2½–3-pound rabbit, cut in
    serving pieces
Coarse salt
2 tablespoons olive oil
1 onion, sliced
2 cloves garlic, minced
2 pimientos, preferably homemade
    (p. 430), cut in strips

½ pound zucchini (1 medium), in
    ½-inch slices
3 bay leaves
Freshly ground pepper
½ teaspoon thyme
3 tablespoons dry white wine

Sprinkle the rabbit with salt. Heat the oil in a deep casserole and brown the
pieces on all sides. Remove to a warm platter. Sauté the onion, garlic, pimientos,
and zucchini until the onion is wilted. Add the rabbit, bay leaves, salt, pepper,
thyme, and wine. Cover and cook slowly 1–1½ hours, or until the rabbit is
very tender. A light red wine like Spanish Claret is appropriate.

CONEJO EN PEPITORIA

(Rabbit in Egg and Lemon Sauce)

AN EGG and lemon sauce may sound more Greek than Spanish but it is, in fact,
a traditional sauce from the Canary Islands and goes back hundreds of years.
With the additional flavors of artichoke and mushrooms, I think this is perhaps
one of the most interesting ways to prepare rabbit.

Serves 4

2 tablespoons lard or olive oil
A 2½–3-pound rabbit, cut in
    serving pieces
1 medium onion, chopped
¾ cup chicken broth
6 artichoke hearts, halved
Salt

Freshly ground pepper
½ teaspoon thyme
2 tablespoons minced parsley
¼ pound mushrooms, cut in halves
    or quarters
2 egg yolks
2 tablespoons lemon juice

In a deep casserole, heat the lard and brown the rabbit on all sides. Add the
onion and cook until wilted. Stir in the chicken broth, artichokes, salt, pepper,
thyme, and 1 tablespoon of the parsley. Cover and cook slowly 45 minutes. Stir
in the mushrooms and cook 15 minutes more, or until the rabbit is tender.
Remove the rabbit to a serving platter.

    Beat the egg yolks with a fork in a small bowl. Beat in the lemon juice,
then some of the hot sauce from the casserole. Stir the egg mixture into the

casserole and cook over low heat for 1 minute. Pour over the rabbit, sprinkle with the remaining tablespoon of parsley, and serve with a Green Bean Salad (p. 118) and a light red wine like Rioja Clarete.

CONEJO SALMANTINO

(Potted Rabbit)

IN THE mountainous Las Hurdes area in the province of Salamanca, rabbit is prepared in this way—with plenty of vinegar and garlic. The dish is ideally cooked in an earthenware bean pot, which provides even heat and produces a more succulent rabbit.

Serves 4

2 tablespoons olive oil
A 2½–3-pound rabbit, cut in small
    serving pieces
¼ cup vinegar
1 medium onion, finely chopped

Salt
Freshly ground pepper
1 bay leaf
½ head garlic, separated but unpeeled

Heat the oil in a deep casserole, preferably earthenware, and brown the rabbit on all sides. Add the vinegar, onion, salt, pepper, bay leaf, and garlic. Cover tightly and cook slowly about 2 hours. Most of the liquid should be evaporated. If it evaporates too quickly, add a little water. Serve with Peas with Cured Ham (p. 79) and a light red wine such as Olarra.

CODORNICES ESCABECHADAS

(Marinated Quail)

PREPARE SEVERAL DAYS IN ADVANCE.

BEFORE the days of refrigeration, *escabeche* was a common means of preserving meats, especially during game season, when too many partridge, quail, and pheasant were caught for immediate consumption. Fish was also preserved in a similar fashion. Today, *escabeche* remains popular for its piquant and refreshing taste, and dishes such as this elegant quail make ideal summer meals (see Menu Suggestions, p. 425).

Almost any game bird may be prepared in this manner. Cornish hen also works well, but lacks the stronger flavor of game. *Escabeche* dishes will keep under refrigeration for at least two weeks.

Serves 6

12 quail, whole, or 3–6 larger birds, such as partridge* or Cornish hens, split in half
6 tablespoons olive oil
2 medium onions, coarsely chopped
1 head garlic, separated and peeled
2 tablespoons minced shallots
4 carrots, scraped and sliced ⅛ inch thick
1 potato, parboiled, peeled, and cut in quarters (optional)
5 bay leaves
3 sprigs parsley

2 teaspoons thyme
Salt to taste
20 peppercorns
½ celery stalk with leaves
Pinch saffron
¾ cup red wine vinegar (reduce to ½ cup for Cornish hen)
3 cups dry white wine
¾ cup chicken broth, all fat removed
1 lemon, sliced
2 tablespoons chopped parsley
Watercress

*If using partridge, let sit in the refrigerator 2–3 days to help tenderize.

Truss the quail by tucking under the wing tips. For the legs, make a small slit on either side of the bird cavity. Cross the legs and hold them in place by passing the tip of each leg through one of the slits.

The oil will better enhance this dish if it is first prepared in the following manner. Heat it in a small skillet with a piece of lemon peel until the peel turns black. Discard peel. Turn off the flame and add a peeled raw potato to cool the oil. When the oil is at room temperature, discard the potato. Transfer the oil to a large, shallow casserole and sauté the quail slowly until they are well browned on all sides (add a slice of onion to prevent spattering). Transfer the birds to a warm platter.

In the same casserole, sauté the onion, garlic, shallots, carrots, and potato until the onions are wilted. Add the bay leaves, parsley, thyme, salt, peppercorns, celery, and saffron. Stir in the vinegar, wine, and broth. Return the quail to the casserole. Cover and simmer 45 minutes. Remove the birds to a round, shallow serving casserole, preferably earthenware, and arrange them attractively in concentric circles. Reduce the cooking liquid by boiling for 5 minutes, then pour it over the birds. The liquid should cover them, but if it does not, the birds should be turned occasionally when marinating. Cover and refrigerate 3–4 days.

To serve, bring the quail to room temperature and garnish with lemon slices, chopped parsley, and watercress. Accompany by an escarole salad with Picadilla Dressing (p. 105) and a fine light red Reserva wine like Imperial.

CODORNICES ESTOFADAS

(Braised Quail)

Serves 4

2 tablespoons olive oil
Coarse salt
8 quail, trussed (see p. 270)
6 tablespoons finely chopped onion
2 cloves garlic, minced
2 tablespoons brandy, preferably
    Spanish brandy, or Cognac

Freshly ground pepper
1 tablespoon minced parsley
1 bay leaf
½ teaspoon thyme
¾ cup dry white wine

Heat the oil in a large, deep casserole. Salt the quail, then brown them on all sides. Add the onion and garlic and sauté until the onion is wilted. Pour in the brandy and carefully ignite. When the flames die, sprinkle in salt, pepper, parsley, bay leaf, and thyme. Add the wine. Cover tightly and cook about 25 minutes, or until tender. Serve in nests (p. 274) or with Poor Man's Potatoes (p. 97) and a light red wine like Olarra.

CODORNICES CON POCHAS
"SANTO DOMINGO DE LA CALZADA"

(Quail with Beans)

START PREPARATION ONE DAY IN ADVANCE.

SANTO DOMINGO de la Calzada, in the heart of Rioja wine country, is a well-preserved village of noble homes and narrow cobbled streets. Its parador, where I first sampled this wonderful combination of beans and quail, was once a twelfth-century hospital, established by the religious hermit Santo Domingo to care for pilgrims en route to the holy city of Santiago de Compostela (see p. 200). Today this edifice has one of the most dramatic salons of all the paradors, with its sweeping gothic stone arches, black marble floors, wrought iron chandeliers, and antique furnishings.

Besides founding this hospital, Santo Domingo built roads to aid foot-weary travelers—thereby the name by which he is now known and which, in turn, became the name of the village: "Saint Dominic of the Road." This village also boasts an artistically distinguished cathedral that has one curious feature found, I am sure, in no other place of worship in the world. Housed in an ornate cage are a live hen and cock, there to symbolize the miracle that took place when, so the story goes, a roasted chicken set on a dinner table suddenly came to life to declare the innocence of a passing pilgrim accused of theft. To this day pilgrims still stop to pray in this cathedral and to gather a feather or two as a memento of their journey.

Serves 4

1 pound large dried lima beans
5 tablespoons olive oil
Coarse salt
8 quail, trussed (see p. 270)
1 medium onion, finely chopped
2 cloves garlic, finely chopped
1 medium tomato, finely chopped

Freshly ground pepper
1 bay leaf
4 cubes (about 1 inch square)
   slab bacon
2 *chorizo* sausages, 2 ounces each, cut
   in 4 pieces each

Soak the beans overnight in cold water to cover. Drain. Place the beans the following day in 8 cups water. Bring to a boil, cover, and simmer 1½ hours. Meanwhile, heat the oil in a large skillet. Salt the quail and sauté in the oil until they are golden on all sides. Remove to a warm platter. Add the onion and garlic to the pan and sauté until the onion is wilted. Stir in the tomato and cook 3 minutes. Add this to the beans, along with salt, pepper, bay leaf, bacon, *chorizo*, and the quail. Cover and continue cooking 30 minutes more, or until the beans are tender (the quail should not cook longer than 30 minutes).

    Serve the beans and quail in soup bowls with good crusty bread, a mixed salad, and a full-bodied red wine like Viña Bosconia.

CODORNICES ASADAS EN HOJA DE PARRA

(Roast Quail with Grape Leaves)

QUAIL turn out tender and juicy when cooked covered by a grape leaf and wrapped with a strip of bacon. The bacon juices, mingled with a touch of wine, provide an excellent sauce.

Serves 4

8 grape leaves, packed in brine
8 quail, trussed (see p. 270)
12 teaspoons lard
Salt

Thyme
8 thin slices bacon
4 tablespoons chicken broth
4 teaspoons dry white wine

Separate the grape leaves and place them in boiling water for 3 minutes. Drain. Rub the quail well with lard, using about 1 teaspoon of lard per bird. Sprinkle the quail with salt and thyme. Cover each quail with a grape leaf, then wrap a strip of bacon around each breast. Secure with a string. Place in an oven casserole, preferably earthenware. Add the remaining 4 teaspoons of lard, the broth, and the wine. Bake uncovered at 350° F for 30 minutes, adding more broth if necessary, to keep the pan from drying. Remove the string from the quail and pour on the pan juices. Serve with Spicy Potatoes (p. 99) and a full-bodied red Reserva wine like Viña Pomal.

CODORNICES EN ZURRÓN

(Quail in Green Peppers)

THE colorful name of this dish, literally "Quail in a Knapsack," refers to the shoulder bag, or *zurrón*, carried by shepherds in the fields to store their food and belongings. In this recipe the quail are wrapped in cured ham, placed inside green peppers, and baked with tomatoes and pearl onions. The result is a dish as pretty as it is savory.

Serves 4

8 quail, trussed (see p. 270)	8 pearl onions, peeled and parboiled
¼ cup brandy, preferably Spanish brandy, or Cognac	2 carrots, scraped and sliced ¼ inch thick
Coarse salt	2 cloves garlic, minced
Freshly ground pepper	8 large cherry tomatoes
6 tablespoons olive oil	1½ teaspoons flour
8 thin slices cured ham	½ cup chicken broth
8 Italian green peppers, each large enough to hold a quail	¼ cup white wine

Fill the cavity of each quail with about 1½ teaspoons brandy. Sprinkle outside with salt and pepper. Heat the oil in a skillet and sauté the quail until they are brown on all sides. Remove the quail and reserve the oil.

Wrap each quail in a slice of ham. Remove the stem and make a lengthwise slit in each green pepper. Remove the seeds. Place a quail in each pepper. Arrange in a casserole, preferably earthenware, slit side down. Add the onions, carrots, garlic, tomatoes, and the reserved oil. Bake uncovered at 350° F for 30 minutes. Remove from the oven. Sprinkle the flour in the casserole, stir, then add the broth and the wine. Sprinkle in salt and pepper. Continue cooking on top of the stove over low heat for 20 minutes more.

Run briefly under the broiler to brown the peppers. Serve with Ensalada de San Isidro (p. 106) and a full-bodied red Reserva wine such as Gran Coronas Black Label.

CODORNICES AL NIDO

(Quail in a Nest)

WHAT could be prettier than tiny quail placed in nests of crisply fried potatoes? And how wonderful they taste — the sauce in which the birds cook is poured over the quail and seeps into the potatoes, giving them an exquisite flavor. All that is missing is a touch of green watercress to complete the picture.

A potato nest fryer, about 3½ inches in diameter, is needed to make this dish.

Serves 4

Braised Quail (p. 271)	Oil for frying
6 cups shredded peeled potatoes	Watercress

Make the quail according to directions. Meanwhile, soak the shredded potatoes 30 minutes in a bowl of cold water. Drain, then dry as much as possible. Dip the potato nest fryer into oil to coat. Then line it with potatoes, about ¾ cup per nest. Secure the nest with the smaller nest fryer that fits inside.

Dip the nest into hot oil, enough to cover the potatoes, and fry until the potatoes are lightly browned. Drain and keep the nests warm in a 200° F oven until all are fried (you should have 8 nests).

To serve, place 1 quail in each nest, spooning on some sauce. Decorate with watercress and accompany with Ensalada a la Almoraina (p. 107) and a fine light red Reserva wine like Marqués de Cáceres.

OCA CON PERAS

(Baby Goose with Pears)

OCA CON PERAS, the supreme dish of Catalán cookery, combines baby goose with pine nuts, raisins, and pears. After cooking, the pears are coated with crackling caramelized sugar and arranged around the goose — the presentation is magnificent. Goose of the size called for in this recipe is rarely found in this country — use duck instead for delicious results.

Serves 4

A 4-pound baby goose or
 duck, quartered
2 slices onion
3 cloves garlic, peeled
1 bay leaf
7 tablespoons chicken broth
1 tablespoon olive oil
1 medium onion, chopped
1 tablespoon minced parsley

2 tablespoons pine nuts
¼ cup raisins
8 tiny seckel pears or 4 small pears,
 peeled, stems on
2 teaspoons *aguardiente* (see p. 428)
 or *grappa* (available
 in liquor stores)
8 tablespoons sugar
4 tablespoons water

Place the goose pieces in a roasting pan, skin side up, scattering the onion slices, 2 of the garlic cloves, and the bay leaf around the pan. Deeply prick the goose all over with a fork, then roast at 350° F for 1 hour. Remove the goose to a warm platter. Pour off the fat, discard onion, and deglaze the roasting pan with 4 tablespoons of the chicken broth. Reserve these pan juices.

Meanwhile, in a large, shallow casserole, heat the oil and sauté the chopped onion and the remaining clove of garlic, minced, until the onion is wilted. Add the parsley, pine nuts, raisins, and pears and cook 5 minutes, turning the pears. Stir in the remaining 3 tablespoons of chicken broth and the *aguardiente*. Cover and simmer slowly 15 minutes. Add the goose pieces to the casserole and the reserved deglazed pan juices. Cover and continue cooking 45 minutes more. Remove the pears to a warm platter and stand them upright.

In a small skillet, heat the sugar and water and stir constantly until the sugar is lightly caramelized. Quickly pour some sugar syrup over each pear (it will harden right away). To serve, transfer the duck and its sauce to a serving tray. Arrange the pears around the sides. On each plate place 1 pear and a quarter of the goose. Spoon on the sauce. Serve with a light red Reserva wine such as Berberana and a green salad.

NOTE: The caramelized pears will not retain their crunch for very long. Therefore, even if the goose is prepared in advance, caramelize the pears at the last minute.

PERDIZ ESTOFADO "CASA PACO"

(Stewed Partridge)

A PARTRIDGE may be one or two portions, depending on diners' appetites and on the size of the birds. (If the meal has a first course preceding the partridge, half is more than enough.)

This version of stewed partridge comes from Casa Paco, a small tavern in Madrid, and is my husband's favorite recipe for partridge.

Serves 4

2–4 partridge, split in half
4 tablespoons olive oil
1 large onion, chopped
6 cloves garlic, peeled and
    lightly crushed
2 bay leaves

6 peppercorns
1 cup dry white wine
1 carrot, sliced
8 small pearl onions, peeled
Salt

Allow the partridge to sit, uncovered or lightly covered, in the refrigerator for 2–3 days. This helps to tenderize the meat.

Heat the oil in a deep casserole, then brown the birds on all sides. Add the onion, garlic, and bay leaves and cook until the onion is wilted. Add the peppercorns, wine, carrot, pearl onions, and salt. Cover tightly and simmer about 1 hour, or until tender. Parboiled cubed or whole new potatoes may be added for the last 15 minutes of cooking. Serve with a green salad and a light red wine like Marqués de Cáceres.

PERDIZ CON CHOCOLATE

(Partridge in Chocolate-Flavored Sauce)

THE Spaniards quickly acquired a taste for the chocolate they discovered in the New World. Interestingly enough, it was not until much after the conquest that chocolate became the rage in Europe as an ingredient for candies and desserts. Its first use was as a beverage and as a seasoning, lending a unique flavor to meat and game and even to fish (see Langosta con Pollo, p. 204).

Don't be put off by the idea of chocolate in a main-course dish. This sauce will not taste like a Hershey bar; rather, the flavor will be subtle and difficult to place.

Serves 4

2–4 partridge, or other game bird, split in half	1 tablespoon flour
	2 tablespoons vinegar
Coarse salt	½ cup dry white wine
Freshly ground pepper	½ cup chicken broth
3 tablespoons olive oil	2 bay leaves
2 cloves garlic, minced	2 cloves
1 onion, chopped	1 teaspoon grated bitter chocolate

Allow the partridge to sit, uncovered or lightly covered, in the refrigerator for 2–3 days. This helps to tenderize the meat.

Sprinkle the split partridge on both sides with salt and pepper. Heat the oil in a deep casserole and brown the birds well. Add the garlic and onion and continue cooking until the onion is wilted. Stir in the flour. Add the vinegar, wine, broth, salt, pepper, bay leaves, and cloves. Cover and simmer 45 minutes or until tender, skin side down. Remove the birds to a warm platter. Add the chocolate to the sauce and stir until dissolved. Return the birds to the casserole and cook, covered, 10 minutes more.

Serve with roast potatoes or Poor Man's Potatoes (p. 97) and a green Ensalada a la Almoraina (p. 107). A full-bodied wine such as Cerro Añón would complement this dish.

FAISÁN AL MODO DE ALCÁNTARA

(Roast Pheasant with Port)

START PREPARATION TWO OR THREE DAYS IN ADVANCE.

THE story behind the dish known in Spanish as well as in French cookbooks as "Pheasant, Alcántara Style" is almost as interesting as the dish itself. It seems that a monastery of Benedictine monks in Alcántara, in the west-central area of Spain known as Extremadura, was sacked by Napoleon's forces in 1807 as the French swept through Spain on their way to Portugal. The French commander, General Junot, found in the monastery's library a cookbook written by the monks, and he sent this interesting manuscript off to his wife, the Duchess of Abrantes, in France. She included parts of this Spanish cookbook when she later wrote her memoirs, and Escoffier, who incorporated some of the book's recipes into his *Le Guide Culinaire*, declared, "The recipe collection snatched by Junot from the Monastery of Alcántara was the only thing of value obtained by France in that war against Spain."

"Pheasant, Alcántara Style" is perhaps the most famous recipe from that monastery cookbook, and although it is usually thought of as part of elegant French cuisine, Spanish food writers go to great lengths to explain that the recipe is, in fact, Spanish and is proof of the sophistication of early Spanish cuisine. Convincing the world that this dish is Spanish may be a problem, but demonstrating that it is a masterpiece is easy, for the taste is nothing short of extraordinary. Stuffed with liver and truffles, marinated for several days in port wine, then roasted and served with a wine and truffle sauce, "Pheasant, Alcántara Style" is food for the gods.

By our modern standards, a dish containing dozens of truffles is a luxury item not likely to have appeared on the tables of ascetic Benedictine monks. But obviously, almost two hundred years ago truffles were not in demand as they are now and could very well have been a common, if not everyday, recipe ingredient. (Truffles, by the way, grow in Spain as well as in France.) Today, making "Pheasant, Alcántara Style" as the original recipe requires is an expensive operation, for the cost of truffles has skyrocketed. As an alternative, I suggest morels or chanterelles, which give an appropriately "earthy" flavor and aroma to the port wine sauce at a much more accessible price. This pheasant dish is really quite remarkable, truly a jewel of Spanish cookery.

Serves 4

2 dozen small truffles or 3 ounces dried morels or chanterelles; 1 pound if fresh, 6 ounces if canned	Salt
	Freshly ground pepper
	10 duck or chicken livers, gristle removed, cut in 4 pieces each
1 bottle tawny port wine	¼ pound butter
2 pheasants, about 2¼ pounds each, with necks	Lard

Place half of the truffles or morels in a saucepan with ¾ cup of the port wine. Simmer 10 minutes. Drain and slice the truffles or morels. Sprinkle the pheasants inside with salt and pepper. Sprinkle the liver pieces also with salt and pepper. Melt the butter in a medium skillet. Add the livers, cover, and cook slowly about 15 minutes. Purée the livers in a processor or blender, adding a little of the butter if the purée is too thick (it should hold together but not be pasty). Mix the sliced truffles or morels that have been cooked in the port with the liver purée. Fill the bird cavities with this mixture and truss.

Place the pheasants in a deep bowl in which they fit fairly snugly. Cover with the remaining several cups of port, cover the bowl with foil, and marinate 2–3 days in the refrigerator. (If the port doesn't quite cover, either add more port or turn the birds occasionally as they marinate.)

Drain and dry the pheasants, reserving the port marinade. Rub the birds well with lard and season with salt and pepper. Place in a roasting pan (along with the necks if available), preferably earthenware, and roast at 350° F, turning occasionally and basting regularly, for about 24 minutes to the pound. (Time per pound for each bird.) Do not overcook.

While the pheasant is roasting, place the port marinade and the remaining truffles or morels, whole, in a saucepan and simmer until the liquid is reduced by half. During the last 10 minutes of roasting, add the reduced port with the truffles or morels to the roasting pan and cover the pheasant breasts with foil. Finish roasting, split the birds in half, and serve half for each portion. (It is not as much as it looks to be, for the legs and wings of this game bird are usually tough and not eaten.) Serve with roasted new potatoes and a full-bodied, elegant Reserva red wine like Viña Bosconia.

Chapter 11

CARNES

(Meats)

HOW does one begin to describe the tenderness, the succulence, the golden crunchy exterior of a baby lamb or pig that is little more than two weeks old? Such delicacies await the traveler to Spain—especially central Spain, where these meats have reached cult status. Friends in Madrid think nothing of traveling hundreds of miles on a Sunday afternoon just for the pleasure of eating baby lamb from Sepúlveda near Segovia. Others swear by the meats of Cándido in Segovia, the Posada de Javier in Torrecaballeros, Mesón Terete in Haro, and Casa Florencio in Aranda del Duero. Not that the love for beautifully roasted meat is anything new—rather, it is the most primitive form of cooking known to man, taken in the twentieth century to the heights of gourmet cooking.

Those who love Spanish roasts are very specific in their requirements for the best: the lamb or pig must be less than a month old. It must never have run in the fields and must have had nothing but mother's milk for nourishment (therefore the name "*lechal*" lamb—from *leche*, milk). When eating lamb, it must be the forequarter; some go so far as to insist that the left forequarter is superior to the right because the young lamb invariably lies down on his right side, toughening the meat a smidgen on that side. Baby lamb and pig must be prepared in an earthenware dish in a woodburning oven; some specify that the wood has to be thyme or rosemary or oak, for each gives a different fragrance to the meat. Better still is to roast the meat in a baker's oven; the tradition still exists in some villages for townsfolk to carry their meats to the local bakery for roasting. The ultimate test comes in cutting: if the roast is top quality, it can be cut with the edge of a plate—no knife necessary.

Surprisingly, it is still apparently economically feasible in Spain to market such tiny animals, and the production seems to keep pace with the demand. Prices are high, but not unreasonable. Part of the reason lies in the mountainous Spanish terrain, where grazing on a large scale for large animals is just not possible. This means that beef also is eaten quite young—veal is much more common than mature beef—and the limited grazing land is left to the dairy cows.

Because of the gastronomic love for young animals and the roasting tradition, Spaniards prefer their meats simply prepared—roasted, grilled, or quick fried. It is the best way to prepare meats of this caliber, which could hardly be improved by the addition of sauces and garnishes. Of course, such young animals are almost impossible to find in the United States. I can only hope that my readers will have the pleasure of eating these delicacies in Spain. In this chapter I have concentrated, therefore, on recipes that translate well and do not depend upon these exquisite meats for success. Two versions of roast lamb appear—the sauces are very tasty, more seasoned than those of a baby roast would be, and prepared in the Spanish manner. There is veal and pork also in the tradition of the roasts and grills.

Although simply prepared meats are the most common in Spain, each region does have its specialties, which are either stews, meats in combination with peppers, or sausage and chopped meat dishes. *Fricandó*, veal made with ground almonds, and Estofado a la Catalana, beef with bitter chocolate, both come from Cataluña. Extremadura has a stew rich in paprika and garlic and another piquant with lemon juice, called *cochifrito*. The Rioja region cooks pork with local red peppers, and in Asturias pork is baked in Asturian apple cider. Specialty meats, particularly tripe and kidneys, are popular all over and appear in many regional variations, such as kidneys in sherry sauce, from Andalucía, and tripe with *chorizo*, typical of Madrid.

No matter what the preparation, the general accompaniment to meats is fried potatoes. Rice rarely appears as a side course, except when it is served with kidneys in sherry sauce or with squid in ink sauce. Since there is no rice to blend with the sauce, meats with sauces usually are served in their own individual casserole dishes with no accompaniment. A Spaniard relies on his first course to provide him with vegetables and uses bread to absorb the sauces.

CHULETA DE TERNERA
AL AJO CABAÑIL

(Veal Chops, Shepherd Style)

"*Ajo Cabañil*" refers to any sautéed meat prepared with garlic, vinegar, and paprika—a winning mixture of ingredients and typical of the region of Murcia.

Serves 4

2 tablespoons olive oil
4 rib veal chops, about ¾ inch thick
2 cloves garlic, minced
Salt

Freshly ground pepper
½ teaspoon paprika
1 tablespoon vinegar
1 tablespoon chicken broth or water

Heat the oil in a large skillet and fry the chops over a high flame until they are well browned. Lower the heat, add the garlic, salt, pepper, paprika, vinegar, and broth. Cover and cook slowly about 15 minutes, or until the meat is done as desired. Serve with roast potatoes, Peas with Cured Ham (p. 79), and a light red wine like Imperial.

CHULETA DE TERNERA HORTELANA

(Veal Chops with Ham,
Mushrooms, and Pimiento)

THE colorful, finely chopped vegetables that cover these chops make them extremely attractive and perfect for company dinners. They are especially good when served with Poor Man's Potatoes (p. 97) and an elegant Watercress and Carrot Salad in Anchovy Dressing (p. 108). Use only the best veal available.

Serves 4

3 tablespoons olive oil
½ cup minced onion
1 clove garlic, minced
2 tablespoons minced cured ham
1 cup finely chopped mushrooms
2 pimientos, homemade (p. 430) or
    imported, finely chopped

Coarse salt
Freshly ground pepper
¼ teaspoon thyme
4 rib veal chops, about 1 inch thick
¼ cup dry white wine
1 bay leaf
1 tablespoon minced parsley

Heat 2 tablespoons of the oil in a medium skillet and sauté the onion and garlic until the onion is wilted. Add the ham, mushrooms, pimiento, salt, pepper, and thyme. Cook 5 minutes more.

Meanwhile, sprinkle the chops with salt and pepper. Heat the remaining 1 tablespoon of oil in a large skillet and sauté the chops slowly until they are cooked—they should be slightly pink within (about 15 minutes). Remove them to a warm platter. Deglaze the pan juices with the wine. Season with salt and pepper and add the bay leaf. Cook slowly 2 or 3 minutes, adding some water or chicken broth if necessary. Arrange the vegetable mixture on top of the chops. Pour on the sauce and sprinkle with parsley. This lovely dish requires a fine reserve wine such as the light red Viña Tondonia.

NOTE: To prepare the chops in advance, cook them over high heat until brown but not cooked through. Deglaze the pan, prepare the vegetables, and arrange them over the chops. To serve, cover the pan and heat until the chops are done, about 15 minutes.

CHULETA DE TERNERA CON HABAS

(Veal Chops and Beans)

START PREPARATION ONE DAY IN ADVANCE.

GALICIA is known for its superior veal, which is an integral part of this wonderful dish from Duna-2 in La Coruña, an excellent restaurant with a rich and varied menu of Galician specialties. Note that this is not a stew—the veal and beans remain separate but complementary, and the veal must therefore be top quality.

Serves 4

½ pound dried beans, such as white kidney or small limas	3 tablespoons tomato sauce
1 veal bone	½ dried red chili pepper, seeds removed, crumbled
2-ounce piece of slab bacon	1 bay leaf
1 small leek	Coarse salt
2 tablespoons olive oil	Freshly ground pepper
⅓ cup chopped onion	4 loin veal chops, about 1 inch thick
2 cloves garlic, minced	1 tablespoon minced parsley

Soak the beans overnight. The next day, drain them, then place in a pot with water to cover. Add the veal bone, bacon, and leek. Bring to a boil, cover, and simmer slowly 1 hour.

In a medium skillet, heat 1 tablespoon of the oil, sauté the onion and garlic until the onion is wilted. Add this to the beans, then stir in the tomato sauce, chili pepper, bay leaf, salt, and pepper. Cover and continue cooking until the beans are tender, about 1–1½ hours more. Remove from the flame and let sit while preparing the chops.

To make the chops, heat the remaining tablespoon of oil in a large skillet. Salt the chops and brown over high heat. Reduce the heat and continue cooking until the chops are done—they should still be slightly pink (about 15 minutes). Serve, with the beans next to, not over, the chops. Sprinkle with parsley. Fresh Beet Salad (p. 116) and a nice light red reserve wine like Claret Fino complete the meal.

TERNERA A LA EXTREMEÑA

(Veal with Chorizo and Green Peppers)

FOR some reason, this veal dish seems to appear on the menu of every Spanish restaurant in New York City and is very popular among the public.

Serves 4

1½ pounds veal cutlets, sliced thin
Coarse salt
1 tablespoon olive oil
1 medium onion, chopped
1 clove garlic, minced
1 green pepper, finely chopped
1 *chorizo* sausage (2 ounces),
    thinly sliced

6 tablespoons dry (*fino*) sherry
6 tablespoons chicken broth
2 tablespoons tomato sauce
½ teaspoon thyme
1 bay leaf
Freshly ground pepper

Sprinkle the cutlets on both sides with salt. Heat the oil in a large, shallow casserole. Brown the cutlets over high heat and remove them to a warm platter. Reduce the heat and sauté the onion, garlic, and green pepper for 5 minutes. Add the *chorizo* and cook 2 minutes more. Stir in the sherry, chicken broth, tomato sauce, thyme, bay leaf, salt, and pepper. Return the cutlets, spoon some sauce over them. Cover and cook slowly 15 minutes.

Serve with a green salad and a full-bodied red wine like Viña Real.

FILETES DE TERNERA EMPANADOS
(Breaded Veal Cutlets, Spanish Style)

SIMPLE breaded veal cutlets are a pleasant standby at almost any restaurant in Spain. But the ones I prepared in my home never had the "taste" of Spain until I realized that there are slight subtleties in making these cutlets that can make all the difference. With a touch of parsley, a squirt of lemon juice, and, most importantly, a few tablespoons of olive oil for frying, I no longer have to wait for a trip to Spain to eat my favorite "Spanish" veal cutlets.

Serves 4

1 egg	1 pound veal cutlets, sliced very thin
1 teaspoon lemon juice	Salt
Bread crumbs	Freshly ground pepper
1 tablespoon minced parsley	3 tablespoons olive oil

Beat together the egg and lemon juice. Combine the bread crumbs with the parsley. Sprinkle the cutlets on both sides with salt and pepper. Dip the cutlets in the egg mixture, then coat with the bread crumbs, pressing so that they adhere well. Let the cutlets dry for 20 minutes.

Heat the oil to the smoking point. Lower the heat and fry the cutlets until golden. Serve with Sautéed Green Peppers and Pimientos (p. 84). A light red wine—Diamante, for example—is a good choice.

ESCALOPINES MADRILEÑOS
(Veal Medallions with Fresh Tomato Sauce)

THIS dish is served at the elegant restaurant of the spectacular Hostal de San Marcos in León, surely one of the most beautiful hotels in the world.

Serves 4

1 tablespoon minced parsley	4 tablespoons olive oil
1 clove garlic, crushed	2 eggs, lightly beaten
1/4 cup flour	
1½ pounds veal medallions, in very thin slices	

TOMATO SAUCE

1 tablespoon olive oil	1 tablespoon minced parsley
1 medium onion, finely chopped	Salt
2 fresh tomatoes, finely chopped	Freshly ground pepper

To make the tomato sauce, heat the 1 tablespoon of oil in a skillet and sauté the onion until it is wilted. Add the tomato, parsley, salt, and pepper and cook slowly, uncovered, until the tomato is barely tender, about 10–15 minutes. The sauce should have a fresh taste.

To prepare the veal, combine the parsley, garlic, and flour. Coat the veal with this mixture, pressing with the palm of your hand so that it adheres well. In a skillet heat the 4 tablespoons of oil to the smoking point. Dip the floured veal in the beaten egg and then place the veal directly in the hot oil. Fry quickly. As the pieces brown lightly, remove them to a warm platter and continue frying the rest of the pieces. Serve with the tomato sauce on the side. Baked Stuffed Potatoes with Cured Ham (p. 100) are an excellent accompaniment, and perhaps a light red reserve wine such as Marqués de Cáceres.

TERNERA ASADA

(Roast Veal)

Serves 6

2 tablespoons olive oil	¼ teaspoon thyme
A 3-pound boneless veal roast, cut from the leg or loin	Salt
	Freshly ground pepper
1 onion, peeled and quartered	About 1 cup dry white wine

Heat the oil in a large, heavy casserole and brown the meat on all sides. Add the quartered onion and cook 5 minutes more. Transfer the meat to a roasting pan. Season with thyme, salt, and pepper. Deglaze the casserole juices with ¼ cup of the wine and add to the roasting pan. Add another ¼ cup of the wine and roast in a 350° F oven about 1¼ hours, or about 25 minutes to the pound. As the liquid evaporates, add more of the wine. Slice and serve the roast with its juices. Green Beans and Potatoes, Galician Style (p. 95) would be a good accompaniment, along with a light red wine like Rioja Vega.

CALDERETA DE TERNERA
(Potted Veal Roast)

Serves 6

2 tablespoons olive oil
A 3-pound boneless veal roast, cut
    from the leg or loin
2 large onions, coarsely chopped
2 cloves garlic, lightly crushed
½ cup dry (*fino*) sherry

½ cup chicken broth or water
2 cloves
Salt
Freshly ground pepper
¼ pound quartered mushrooms

Heat the oil in a deep casserole. Brown the veal on all sides. Add the onion and garlic and sauté until the onion is wilted. Add the sherry, broth, cloves, salt, and pepper. Cover and cook over a low flame, about 1½ hours. Add the mushrooms and continue cooking 15 minutes more.

Slice the veal and serve with the sauce and with boiled potatoes (2 tablespoons of the sauce added to the potato cooking liquid give added flavor). A light red wine—Lan, for example—will go well with the veal.

FRICANDÓ DE TERNERA
A LA CATALANA
(Veal Stew, Catalán Style)

THIS dish produces an extremely tender veal in a subtly flavored sauce, which has the typically Catalán addition of a paste of almonds, garlic, saffron, and parsley.

Serves 4

1½ pounds boneless veal, such
    as shoulder, cut in
    1½-inch cubes
Salt
Flour for dusting
4 tablespoons olive oil
1 medium onion, chopped
2 tomatoes, skinned and chopped

1 cup dry white wine
1 cup veal or chicken broth
1 bay leaf
1 sprig parsley
¼ teaspoon thyme
Salt
Freshly ground pepper
6 medium mushrooms, quartered

6 blanched almonds	Few strands saffron
2 cloves garlic, chopped	1 tablespoon minced parsley

Sprinkle the veal pieces with salt, then dust with flour. Heat 2 tablespoons of the oil in a deep casserole. Add the veal and sauté until brown on all sides. Remove the meat to a warm platter.

Add the onion to the casserole and sauté until wilted, adding more oil if necessary. Add the tomato and wine, bring to a boil, and reduce the liquid by half. Return the veal to the pot, then add the broth, bay leaf, parsley sprig, thyme, salt, pepper, and mushrooms. Cover and simmer 1 hour.

In a processor, grind the almonds until a paste forms. Beat in the garlic, saffron, minced parsley, and the remaining 2 tablespoons of oil. Add this mixture to the veal and cook 30 minutes more. A Green Bean Salad (p. 118) and a light red wine such as Diamante would make fine additions to the meal.

ROAST LAMB

To approximate the roast lamb served in Spain, buy the youngest and smallest lamb available. Roast, if possible, in a shallow earthenware casserole, which distributes the heat more evenly and helps produce a superior roast. In Spain, by the way, they like to eat their lamb well done.

CORDERO ASADO, ESTILO CASTELLANO
(Roast Lamb, Castilian Style)

Casa Botín is a landmark in Old Madrid, famed for its roast suckling pig and roast baby lamb. Two hundred fifty years ago Casa Botín was a *posada*, or inn, in the heart of Madrid's old commercial center, where weary journeymen could rest their horses and rent a room. Because of the traveler's need for nourishment, *posadas* often became restaurants as well. Roast meats were served then and are still the specialty now at Casa Botín, where little has changed since the days of the *posada* and where the very same woodburning oven, decorated with brightly colored tiles, still roasts the meats to perfection.

Serves 6

3–4-pound leg of baby lamb, or a
    3–4-pound piece of leg,
    preferably the shank portion
2 tablespoons lard
Salt
Freshly ground pepper
¼ teaspoon paprika
1 clove garlic, crushed
2 cups water

2 cloves garlic, peeled
3 slices onion
1 bay leaf
2 sprigs parsley
2 tablespoons vinegar
¼ teaspoon rosemary
¼ teaspoon oregano
¼ teaspoon ground cumin
Juice of 1 lemon

Preheat the oven to 450° F. Rub the lamb with the lard, then sprinkle with salt, pepper, and paprika. Rub in the crushed garlic. Roast the lamb 15 minutes.

Meanwhile, bring the remaining ingredients to a boil in a saucepan.

Reduce the oven to 350° F. Pour about ½ cup of the liquid over the meat and continue roasting, 12–20 minutes to the pound, depending on the desired doneness. Baste every 10 minutes with more liquid, replenishing the liquid in the saucepan with more water if necessary, and keeping it simmering all the while the lamb is roasting. Slice and serve with the sauce, roast potatoes, Sautéed Greens with Croutons (p. 87), and a full-bodied red reserve wine such as Viña Turzaballa.

CORDERO ASADO A LA SEPULVEDANA

(Roast Lamb, Sepúlveda Style)

ANOTHER tasty version of roast lamb, from the village of Sepúlveda in the province of Segovia, the area in Spain most famous for lamb.

Serves 6

3–4-pound leg of baby lamb, or a
    3–4-pound shank portion
    of a leg of lamb

Salt
Freshly ground pepper
½ teaspoon thyme

4 cloves garlic, crushed	3 tablespoons semisweet
3 tablespoons lard	(*oloroso*) sherry

Rub the lamb with salt, pepper, thyme, garlic, and the lard. Place in a roasting pan in a 350° F oven. After 30 minutes, add the sherry to the pan. Check every 10 minutes, basting the meat and adding water if necessary to prevent the juices from burning, until the meat is the desired doneness (a total of 12–20 minutes per pound, which ranges from medium-rare to well done). Serve with fried potatoes and Sautéed Lima Beans and Ham (p. 81). A full-bodied Rioja wine such as Viña Real is appropriate.

CHULETA DE CORDERO EMPANADA

(Béchamel-Coated Breaded Lamb Chops)

START PREPARATION TWO HOURS IN ADVANCE.

THERE is extra work involved in preparing these chops—they must be marinated, fried, dipped in white sauce, then browned again—but I think the juicy and crunchy chops that result are delicious.

Serves 4

½ cup olive oil	12 small, rib lamb chops, about ½
3 cloves garlic, crushed	inch thick
1 tablespoon minced parsley	2 eggs
Salt	Bread crumbs
Freshly ground pepper	Oil for frying

WHITE SAUCE

7½ tablespoons butter	1¼ cups milk
9 tablespoons flour	Salt
1 cup chicken broth	Freshly ground pepper

In a shallow dish combine the ½ cup olive oil with the crushed garlic, parsley, salt, and pepper. Add the chops, turn to coat, and let them marinate 2 hours or more at room temperature. Drain. Lightly grease a large skillet and heat until very hot. Fry the chops until done to taste. Drain on paper towels, patting both sides to absorb the grease.

To make the white sauce, melt the butter in a saucepan. Add the flour and cook a minute or so. Gradually add the broth, milk, salt, and pepper. Cook, stirring constantly, until very thick and smooth. Cool and spread the sauce out in a flat dish. Coat the chops lightly with the white sauce, on both sides and along the rib bone. Place the chops on a greased platter and refrigerate 30 minutes, until the sauce solidifies.

Beat the eggs with a fork in a shallow dish. Dip the chops in the egg, then in the bread crumbs. Heat the oil, ⅛ inch deep, in a large skillet. Brown the chops quickly on each side and drain. Serve with Pisto Manchego (p. 94) and a full-bodied red wine, perhaps Campo Viejo.

CORDERO ESTOFADO
(Smothered Lamb)

VINEGAR and a whole head of garlic give this stew its excellent flavor.

Serves 6

3 tablespoons olive oil	1 bay leaf
3 pounds boneless lamb, cut in	1 teaspoon paprika
2-inch cubes	½ cup red wine vinegar
1 large onion, chopped	Salt
1 whole head garlic, separated	Freshly ground pepper
but unpeeled	

Heat the oil in a deep casserole. Add the meat cubes and brown well on all sides. Add the onion and sauté until wilted. Stir in the garlic cloves, bay leaf, paprika, vinegar, salt, and pepper. Cover and cook over a low flame about 2 hours, or until the meat is tender. Add some water during cooking if necessary. Serve with Green Beans and Cured Ham (p. 79) and a full-bodied wine from Penedés — Gran Coronas, for example.

CALDERETA EXTREMEÑA
(Lamb Stew, Extremadura Style)

Serves 4

1 tablespoon olive oil	1¾ pounds boneless lamb, cut in
1 tablespoon lard	2-inch cubes (or use lamb
6 cloves garlic, peeled	pieces with some bone)

1 small onion, chopped
1 bay leaf
½ teaspoon thyme
2 teaspoons paprika
½ dried red chili pepper,
    seeds removed

Salt
Freshly ground pepper
¾ cup dry red wine
¼ cup water
1 pimiento, homemade or imported
1 tablespoon vinegar

Heat the oil and lard in a deep casserole. Slowly fry the cloves of garlic until they are lightly browned. Remove them and reserve. Add the lamb pieces to the oil and brown over high heat. Lower the flame, add the onion, and sauté until it is wilted. Stir in the bay leaf, thyme, paprika, chili pepper, salt, and pepper. Pour in the wine and boil a minute to reduce slightly. Add the water, cover, and cook 30 minutes.

Meanwhile, place the reserved garlic in a processor or blender with the pimiento and mix until finely chopped. With the motor running, pour in the vinegar and enough liquid from the meat (a few tablespoons) to form a smooth, thick sauce. Add this to the lamb, stir, and continue cooking until the meat is tender, at least 1 hour more, adding more water if the sauce thickens too much. Serve with boiled new potatoes, a green salad, and a full-bodied red wine such as Sangre de Toro.

CORDERO AL CHILINDRÓN

(Lamb and Red Pepper Stew)

Chilindrón style is the typical way to prepare lamb in Navarra, and nowhere is this dish better prepared than at Las Pocholas restaurant in Pamplona (see p. 205).

Serves 4

2 tablespoons olive oil
2–2½ pounds lamb (the amount
    depends on whether you
    prefer your stew with or
    without bones), cut in
    2-inch pieces
Salt
Freshly ground pepper

1 medium onion, chopped
1 clove garlic, minced
3 pimientos, homemade (p. 430),
    cut in strips
1 pound fresh or canned
    tomatoes, chopped
1 tablespoon minced parsley
1 bay leaf

Heat the oil in a deep casserole and sauté the meat until it is well browned. Sprinkle with salt and pepper. Add the onion and garlic and continue cooking until the onion is wilted. Add the pimientos, tomato, parsley, salt and pepper (if necessary), and the bay leaf. Cover and simmer 1½–2 hours, or until the meat is tender. Serve with boiled or roast potatoes and a green salad like Salad, Murcia Style (p. 110). Solar de Samaniego, a full-bodied red wine, is appropriate.

COCHIFRITO

(Potted Lamb with Lemon)

A FAMILY favorite, especially good with Poor Man's Potatoes (p. 97).

Serves 4

1 tablespoon olive oil
1 tablespoon butter
2 pounds lamb, cut in 2-inch cubes
    (or use lamb pieces with bone
    and increase the weight)
Salt

Freshly ground pepper
2 cloves garlic, minced
¼ cup lemon juice
¼ cup chicken broth or water
1 teaspoon dry (*fino*) sherry

Heat the oil and butter in a deep casserole until the butter begins to brown. Add the lamb and cook over a moderately high flame until the pieces are well browned. Lower the heat, season with salt and pepper, and add the garlic. Cook 5 minutes more. Stir in the lemon juice, broth, and sherry. Cover and cook over a very low flame, 1½–2 hours, or until the meat is very tender. Add some water during cooking if necessary, but remember that this dish should not have a large amount of sauce. You might serve a full-bodied Siglo wine with it.

ALBÓNDIGAS "SANT CLIMENT"

(Lamb Meatballs in Brandy Sauce)

TAHULL lies in a valley of the Pyrenees and is best known for its beautifully preserved church, San Clemente (Sant Climent in the Catalán language), one of the most outstanding works of Romanesque architecture in all of Spain. The village, however, was all but abandoned until well-heeled city dwellers succumbed to its charms and bought all the homes, leaving the exteriors intact while constructing luxurious living quarters within. The village now prospers, and its only eating establishment, Restaurante Sant Climent, is bustling at lunchtime. On a recent visit the *"plato del día"* was meatballs, and although they didn't sound terribly appealing, I gave them a try. They turned out to be the best meatballs I had ever eaten. Besides preparing them for dinner, I often serve them as party appetizers.

Makes 6 dinner portions or about 60
appetizer-size meatballs

2 pounds ground lamb (see *Note*)
2 eggs
4 cloves garlic, crushed
4 tablespoons chopped parsley
Salt
2 tablespoons coarsely ground pepper
1 cup bread crumbs

4 tablespoons dry red wine
2 tablespoons olive oil
1 onion, chopped
¼ cup brandy, preferably Spanish
    brandy, or Cognac
3 tablespoons tomato sauce
1 cup beef or lamb broth (see *Note*)

Combine the ground lamb, eggs, garlic, parsley, salt, and pepper. In a separate bowl, soften the bread crumbs in the wine, then add the crumbs to the meat mixture. Mix well. Form about 25 meatballs (or make them bite-size if they are to be used as appetizers). Heat the oil in a large casserole and brown the meatballs on all sides. Add the onion and continue cooking until it is wilted. Pour in the brandy. Staying well away from the pan—the flames may go quite high—ignite the liquid. Stir until the flames subside. Add the tomato sauce and the broth. Salt to taste. Cover and cook slowly 45 minutes. Parboiled potatoes may be added for the last few minutes of cooking. Serve with a full-bodied wine—try Viña Pomal.

NOTE: If you buy lamb (with some bone) and grind it in a processor, you will be assured a low fat content. And, the bones and scraps may be used to make the broth needed in the sauce.

FILETE EMPANADO
(Breaded Beefsteak)

THIS is quite simple, but one of the best-liked meat dishes in my household.

Serves 4

1 clove garlic, chopped
2 tablespoons chopped parsley
½ teaspoon salt
1–1¼ pounds beef, such as round,
    sliced very thin

2 eggs, lightly beaten
Bread crumbs
5 tablespoons olive oil

Mash the garlic, parsley, and salt in a mortar, or use a blender or processor if you wish. Spread this mixture on the meat with a rubber spatula (it need not be evenly distributed), hitting with the heel of your hand so that it adheres. Dip the meat in the egg, then coat with the crumbs. It is best to let the meat sit at least 20 minutes before frying so that the coating dries.

Heat the oil in a large skillet. Over high heat, cook the meat, only until the coating browns. Keep the cooked pieces on a heated platter or in a 200° F oven while frying the remaining pieces. This is excellent with Sautéed Pimientos (p. 83) and a full-bodied red wine like Cerro Añón.

CARNE A LA CASTELLANA
(Castilian-Style Sliced Beef)

Serves 4

5 tablespoons olive oil
2 onions, sliced
2 cloves garlic, minced
4 long, thin slices cured ham, each
    cut in 4 pieces

1½ pounds beef, such as sirloin, cut
    in ¼-inch-thick slices
2 tablespoons flour
1½ cups beef broth
½ cup dry red wine

In a skillet heat 2 tablespoons of the oil. Sauté the onion and garlic slowly, covered, until the onion is tender. Stir in the ham pieces and remove from the flame.

In a separate skillet, heat another tablespoon of the oil to the smoking point. Fry the beef slices very quickly, just to brown. Remove to a warm platter. Add the remaining 2 tablespoons of oil to the skillet and stir in the flour. Cook for a minute, then add the broth and wine. Stir until smooth and thickened. Add the onion mixture and cook 5 minutes. Return the meat to the pan and cook for a minute, just until the meat is heated. Serve with an Ensalada a la Almoraina (p. 107). Viña Real, a full-bodied red Rioja, would be an appropriate wine selection.

ENTRECOTE AL QUESO CABRALES

(Steak with Blue Cheese Sauce)

THIS dish is found in Asturias, where *Queso Cabrales*, a delicious strong blue cheese aged in caves and wrapped in leaves, is produced. The cheese is shipped to most parts of Spain and can be found in food specialty shops. When visiting Spain, be sure to try it. In the United States, a Roquefort cheese may be substituted.

Serves 4

¼ pound Cabrales (p. 431) or
    other blue cheese
4 teaspoons white wine
1 teaspoon lemon juice
1 tablespoon minced parsley
1 clove garlic, crushed

Dash paprika
Dash pepper
1 tablespoon butter
4 steaks, such as rib or club,
    1 inch thick
Salt

Mix together in the top of a double boiler the cheese, wine, lemon juice, parsley, garlic, paprika, and pepper. Cook, stirring occasionally, until smooth. Keep the sauce warm while the steak is cooking.

    Heat the butter in a skillet until it starts to brown. Sauté the steaks until cooked to taste. Remove to a warm platter. Deglaze the pan with water or broth and season with salt. Add 2 tablespoons of these juices to the cheese sauce. Pour the sauce over the steaks and serve immediately. A full-bodied reserve wine such as Viña Bosconia is a fitting accompaniment, as is a green salad with El Aliño Dressing (p. 104).

SOLOMILLO ALL-I-PEBRE
(Beef Roast in Garlic Sauce)

"All-i-pebre" is a Catalán expression referring to anything in a garlic and pepper or paprika sauce. This beef is a cross between a roast beef and a pot roast—the meat turns out medium rare (or to taste) but with the bonus of a very tasty stewing sauce. Beef tenderloin—the Chateaubriand section—gives the best results, although other cuts usually associated with beef roasts can also be used.

Serves 4

1½–1¾ pounds beef tenderloin, or
    a roast beef cut, such as
    sirloin tip or round
Coarse salt
Flour for dusting
2 tablespoons lard or olive oil
8 small pearl onions, peeled and cut
    in half lengthwise

1½ tablespoons red wine vinegar
3 cloves garlic, crushed
1 tablespoon minced parsley
¼ teaspoon freshly ground pepper
½ cup beef broth

Sprinkle the meat with salt, then dust with flour. Melt the lard in a deep casserole and brown the meat on all sides. Add the onions and vinegar. Cook slowly, covered, turning occasionally, about 15 minutes. Meanwhile, in a blender or processor, mix together the garlic, parsley, and pepper. Gradually add the broth. Pour this mixture over the beef and continue cooking, covered, about 10–15 minutes more, or until done to taste. Slice the meat and serve with the sauce and onions, accompanied by roast potatoes and an Ensalada de San Isidro (p. 106). This dish deserves a full-bodied Reserva wine such as Viña Real.

ESTOFADO A LA CATALANA
(Catalán-Style Beef Stew)

"Catalán Style" in cooking usually refers to the use of chocolate, nuts, or sausage in a dish. This stew has the chocolate—just a small amount to lend a lovely tartness to the sauce—and *butifarra*, the typical sausage of the region.

Serves 4

1 tablespoon olive oil
¼ pound slab bacon, cut in 3 or
    4 pieces
2 pounds beef chuck, cut in
    1½-inch cubes
1 large onion, chopped
4 cloves garlic, peeled
1 tablespoon flour
1 cup dry white wine
1 sprig parsley
1 bay leaf

⅛ teaspoon oregano
¼ teaspoon thyme
½ cup beef broth or water
Salt
Freshly ground pepper
½ teaspoon grated bitter chocolate
2 large potatoes, peeled, cubed, and
    parboiled
16-inch *butifarra* sausage (p. 55), or
    4 sweet Italian-style sausages

Place the oil and bacon in a deep casserole. Cook slowly until the bacon gives off its oil. Add the meat, turn up the flame, and brown well. Add the onion and garlic and cook until the onion is wilted. Sprinkle in the flour, then add the wine, parsley, bay leaf, oregano, thyme, and broth. Season with salt and pepper. Cover and cook about 2 hours, or until the meat is tender. Stir in the chocolate, add the parboiled potatoes, and continue cooking until the potatoes are tender, about 10 minutes.

In a separate pan, sauté the sausage. Serve the stew with the sausage, sliced, arranged around the dish, and a Green Bean Salad (p. 118). A full-bodied wine, such as the Catalán Red Penedés of René Barbier, stands up well to this robust stew.

ESTOFADO DE VACA

(Garlic Beef Stew)

GARLIC, when cooked for so long a time, loses its pungency. It lends a pleasant flavor to this stew without being at all overpowering.

Serves 4

2 tablespoons olive oil
2 pounds beef for stew, such as chuck,
    in 1½-inch cubes
1 onion, chopped
1 whole head garlic, separated
    and peeled
1 teaspoon flour

1 cup dry white wine
2 cloves
Salt
Freshly ground pepper
1 tablespoon minced parsley
1 bay leaf
¼ teaspoon thyme

Heat the oil in a deep casserole. Brown the meat well on all sides. Add the onion and garlic and continue cooking until the onion is wilted. Stir in the flour, then add the wine, cloves, salt, pepper, parsley, bay leaf, and thyme. Cover and simmer 1½–2 hours. Serve with boiled or roast potatoes and a full-bodied wine such as Coronas.

RABO DE TORO A LA ANDALUZA

(Oxtail Stew)

As MIGHT be expected, Rabo de Toro is native to Andalucía, a land of bulls and bullfighters. More specifically, this dish is said to be from Córdoba, a delightful city that conserves its rich Jewish past in the narrow streets of its old quarter and where the city's magnificent Arab mosque is a constant reminder that Córdoba was once the Moorish capital of Spain and the cultural capital of the Western world. Córdoba is a city that bursts with flowers, nowhere more beautifully or more proudly displayed than in the many communal patios, typical of the city. Any visit to Córdoba is not complete without seeing the lovely patios that have won top prizes in the city's annual patio competition.

Nor would a visit to Córdoba be complete without a visit to its most charming and highly regarded El Caballo Rojo restaurant, where Rabo de Toro is served. It is a dish that utilizes the tasty and very tender tail of the bull or ox to produce a rich, fork-tender stew with a wonderfully winy sauce.

Serves 4

3½–4 pounds oxtail, cut in 2-inch-thick rounds	Salt
1 medium onion, in thick slices	Freshly ground pepper
2 carrots, scraped and cut in thick slices	2 tablespoons olive oil
2 sprigs parsley	3 cloves garlic, minced
2 bay leaves	3 tablespoons chopped cured ham
½ teaspoon thyme	1 medium onion, chopped
½ stalk celery	½ teaspoon paprika
	2 tablespoons flour
	1 cup dry white wine

Trim some of the fat from the oxtails. Place them in a deep casserole and barely cover with water. Add the onion slices, carrot slices, parsley, 1 of the bay leaves, thyme, celery, salt, and pepper. Bring to a boil, skim off the foam, cover, and simmer 3 hours. Remove the oxtails to a warm platter and reserve 1 cup of the cooking liquid, skimming off the fat. Keep the rest for future use as stock or soup. Wipe out the casserole.

Heat the oil in the casserole and slowly sauté the garlic, ham, chopped onion, the other bay leaf, and the paprika until the onion is wilted. Stir in the flour, then the wine and the reserved 1 cup of cooking liquid. Cook until smooth and thickened. Return the oxtails to the casserole, taste for salt and pepper, then cover and cook 1 hour more. Serve with a green vegetable and a full-bodied Rioja wine such as Viña Pomal.

COCHINILLO ASADO

(Roast Suckling Pig)

IF YOU can find pigs that are small enough, this Castilian specialty is one of the most exquisite dishes imaginable. Cochinillo should be roasted in a woodburning baker's oven, using woods such as pine, thyme, or ash to give added fragrance to the roast. It may also be done in a home oven.

Serves 4

5 tablespoons lard
3 cloves garlic, lightly crushed
  and peeled
A 7-pound baby pig, head on

Salt
1 tablespoon dry white wine
Thyme

In a small saucepan, melt the lard with 2 of the crushed garlic cloves. Keep warm. Butterfly the pig by splitting the underside and leaving the backbone and the head intact. Pound to flatten slightly. Sprinkle on both sides with salt.

Put the pig in an shallow earthenware roasting pan, with a tablespoon of water and the wine, skin side down. Place in a 450° F oven, roast 10 minutes, then reduce the heat to 350° F and continue roasting until the side facing down begins to brown (be careful not to let it stick to the pan). Turn the pig, skin side up, and pierce the skin with a fork. Cover the ears with foil to prevent burning. Continue roasting, basting frequently with the lard, until the skin is deeply golden and crunchy. Figure cooking time at somewhere around 3 hours. Remove from the oven and brush once more with the lard. Sprinkle with salt. To the pan juices add a sprinkling of thyme and the remaining clove of garlic, well crushed. A little more wine may also be added. Remove the foil from the ears and present the Cochinillo at the table. Then quarter, remove the head, and serve with its juices. Poor Man's Potatoes (p. 97) and a light red wine, perhaps a Reserva like Claret Fino, are excellent accompaniments.

CHULETAS DE CERDO A LA ASTURIANA

(Pork Chops with Apples in Cider Sauce)

HARD cider, produced in Asturias, enters into many recipes of the region. Accompanied by apples, it is particularly complementary to this pork dish. Another well-known Asturian dish, Merluza a la Sidra (p. 226), also uses cider in its preparation.

Serves 4

4 loin pork chops, about
    ¾–1 inch thick
Salt
Flour for dusting
1 tablespoon olive oil
2 tablespoons butter

½ pound apples, peeled, cored, and
    sliced about ½ inch thick
½ cup chicken broth
½ cup hard cider, available in liquor
    stores (see glossary)
Freshly ground pepper

Season the chops with salt, then dust with flour. Heat the oil and butter in a large skillet. Lightly brown the chops on both sides. Remove to a warm platter. Add the apple slices to the pan and sauté in the remaining oil, turning once, for 1 minute.

In an ovenproof casserole, arrange half of the apple slices, the chops on top, then the remaining apples. To the skillet add the broth, cider, salt, and pepper. Boil 3 minutes, then pour the liquid over the chops in the casserole. Cover tightly and bake at 350° F for 35 minutes, or until the chops are cooked and tender. Serve with boiled new potatoes, a green salad, and a hard, very dry cider, if available. Otherwise, a light red wine such as Lan is appropriate.

CHULETAS DE CERDO AL JEREZ DULCE

(Pork Chops with Sweet Sherry)

A NICE contrast of tastes, *oloroso* sherry lending a pleasant sweetness to the chops. Do not substitute cream sherry—it is too sweet.

Serves 6

3 tablespoons olive oil
6 loin pork chops, 1 inch thick
3 ounces slivered blanched almonds

½ cup medium-sweet (*oloroso*) sherry
Salt

Heat the oil in a large skillet. Sauté the chops over high heat until they are brown on both sides. Lower the flame and continue cooking until the chops are cooked through. Transfer them to a warm platter.

Add the almonds to the remaining oil in the skillet. Sauté until the almonds are lightly golden. Deglaze the pan with the sherry. Salt to taste. Simmer 5 minutes, then pour over the chops. Serve with Poor Man's Potatoes (p. 97), eliminating the garlic. Viña Lanciano, a light red wine, would complement this dish.

CHULETAS DE CERDO A LA RIOJANA

(Pork Chops, Rioja Style)

ALSO called "*chilindrón,*" this pork chop and red pepper combination is a favorite all over Spain. In general, any dish designated "*a la riojana*" means that the delicious red peppers from the Rioja region of Spain were used in its preparation.

Serves 4

2 tablespoons olive oil
4 loin pork chops, about
 ¾–1 inch thick
1 medium onion, chopped
1 clove garlic, minced

3 pimientos, homemade (p. 430), cut
 in strips
2 fresh or canned tomatoes, chopped
Salt
Freshly ground pepper

Heat the oil in a large, shallow casserole and brown the chops quickly. Add the onion and garlic and cook until the onion is wilted. Add the pimientos, tomato, salt, and pepper to the chops. Cover and simmer until the chops are cooked through, about 20 minutes. Roast potatoes and a light red wine like Marqués de Cáceres are fine accompaniments.

CHULETAS DE CERDO CON
PIMIENTOS Y JAMÓN

(Pork Chops, Peppers, and Ham)

THIS is a variation of the preceding recipe, which eliminates the tomato and adds cured ham and green pepper. It is difficult to decide which is better.

Serves 4

4 tablespoons olive oil
2 medium onions, sliced
1 green pepper, cut in strips
1 pimiento, homemade (p. 430),
      cut in strips
1 clove garlic, minced

4 loin pork chops, about
      ¾–1 inch thick
A ¼-pound piece cured ham, diced
Salt
Freshly ground pepper

Heat 2 tablespoons of the oil in a large skillet and sauté the onion, green pepper, pimiento, and garlic for 5 minutes. Cover and continue cooking over low heat until the peppers are tender.

Meanwhile, heat the remaining 2 tablespoons of oil in a large, shallow casserole. Brown the chops quickly over high heat. Add the ham and sauté briefly. Spread the onion-and-pepper mixture over the chops. Sprinkle with salt and pepper. Cover and cook slowly 20 minutes, or until the chops are done. Serve the chops with the pepper mixture on the side. Marqués de Murrieta, a light red wine, is a good choice, as is an Ensalada a la Almoraina (p. 107).

CHULETAS DE CERDO CON CIRUELA PASA

(Pork Chops with Prunes)

START PREPARATION SEVERAL HOURS IN ADVANCE.

MOST dishes that combine meat with fruits are of Catalán origin. This delicious dish of pork chops in a sweet prune sauce is a fine example.

Serves 4

½ pound pitted prunes
Salt
Freshly ground pepper
4 loin pork chops, about ¾ inch–
      1 inch thick
½ cup red wine

½ cup water
1 cinnamon stick
2½ teaspoons sugar
2 tablespoons olive oil
½ teaspoon cornstarch
½ teaspoon water

Soak the prunes several hours in warm water to cover. Salt and pepper the chops. Let them sit while finishing the preparation of the prunes. Drain the prunes and place them in a saucepan with the wine, water, cinnamon, and sugar. Simmer slowly, covered, about 20 minutes. Remove the prunes, leaving the liquid in the saucepan.

Heat the oil in a large skillet. Sauté the chops until brown on both sides and cooked through. Meanwhile, heat the reserved prune liquid. In a small cup dissolve the cornstarch in the ½ teaspoon of water and add to the prune liquid. Stir until thickened, clear, and smooth. Return the prunes to the liquid. Spoon the prunes and the sauce over the chops. A light red wine such as Lan is appropriate, and boiled new potatoes may be served.

CHULETAS DE CERDO A LA MADRILEÑA

(Seasoned Broiled Pork Chops)

A TOPPING of garlic, parsley, onion, and paprika makes these simply broiled chops special.

Serves 4

Salt	2 tablespoons minced parsley
Freshly ground pepper	3 tablespoons minced onion
4 loin pork chops, 1 inch thick	1½ teaspoons paprika
2 cloves garlic, minced	3 tablespoons olive oil

Salt and pepper the chops. In a small bowl mix the garlic, parsley, onion, paprika, and olive oil.

Heat the broiler, grease the broiler pan, and arrange the chops. Spread half of the garlic mixture over the chops and place the pan 4–5 inches from the flame. Broil the chops about 5 minutes. Turn, spread with the remaining mixture, and broil 5 minutes more, or until the chops are cooked through but still juicy. Serve with mashed potatoes and Molino, a wine from the central region of Spain.

LOMO DE CERDO ADOBADO

(Seasoned Pork Loin)

START PREPARATION AT LEAST ONE DAY IN ADVANCE.

WHILE living in Madrid, whenever I was stumped for a dinner menu or temporarily out of ingredients, I would go down to the local *ultramarino* store, a kind of delicatessen (so called because its products once came from "beyond the sea"), and order several slices of Lomo Adobado. When sautéed and served with mashed potatoes and either Garlic Green Beans (p. 78) or Peas with Cured Ham (p. 79), it was always one of my favorite "quick" meals. Lomo Adobado is also a common *tapa* in bars throughout Spain, where it is served on slices of bread.

Serves 4

1 tablespoon paprika
2 cloves garlic, crushed
3 tablespoons olive oil
¼ teaspoon thyme

1 bay leaf, crushed
Salt
1½ pounds boned pork loin roast
Oil or butter for frying

In a small bowl, mix the paprika, garlic, olive oil, thyme, bay leaf, and salt. Coat the meat on all sides with this mixture. Place in a shallow bowl and cover with foil. Refrigerate at least overnight, although the meat will be more flavorful after several days. It will keep more than a week.

To serve, slice the meat to the desired thickness (it is usually sliced thin) and sauté in oil or butter. Deglaze the pan juices and pour over the meat slices. A light red wine from Rioja—Berberana, for example—goes well, as do mashed potatoes.

LOMO DE CERDO CON LECHE

(Pork Roast Simmered in Milk)

WHEN pork is cooked in milk, the result is an exceptionally tender and subtly flavorful meat. It has long been a favorite of mine.

Serves 4–5

1 tablespoon lard or olive oil
2 pounds boned pork loin
1 medium onion, coarsely chopped
1 carrot, scraped and
        coarsely chopped

2 cups warm milk
2 cloves garlic, unpeeled
3 peppercorns
Salt
1 tablespoon minced parsley

Heat the lard in a deep casserole. Brown the meat on all sides. Add the onion and carrot and cook until the onion is wilted. Stir in the warm milk, garlic, peppercorns, and salt. Bring to a boil. Lower the heat and simmer, covered, about 2 hours. (Don't worry—the sauce will look curdled.)

Remove the meat to a warm platter. Purée the sauce in a processor or blender, strain it, and return to the casserole. Add the meat and heat briefly. Slice the meat, add the sauce, and sprinkle with the parsley. Serve with a light red wine such as Rioja Vega, roast potatoes, and Sautéed Asparagus (p. 88).

LOMO DE CERDO CON ESCALIBADA

(Pork Roast with Peppers and Eggplant)

Escalibada, a Catalán mixture of eggplant and peppers, makes a delicious salad (p. 117), as well as an excellent accompaniment to roast pork. I particularly like this dish with spicy Salsa Picante—cucumber and caper sauce. To make the sauce, you will need Pickled Cucumbers (p. 105), which, if you don't happen to have them on hand, will take a few hours to marinate.

Serves 4

2-pound boneless pork loin roast
1 clove garlic, crushed
Thyme
Salt
Freshly ground pepper

2 red peppers
1 green pepper
A ½-pound eggplant
1 tablespoon olive oil
1 tablespoon minced parsley

SALSA PICANTE

4 tablespoons finely chopped onion
1 tablespoon tarragon vinegar
1½ teaspoons white wine
1 Pickled Cucumber (p. 105), minced
¼ teaspoon small capers or large
     capers, chopped

1 tablespoon tomato sauce
Salt
1 tablespoon butter
2 teaspoons minced parsley

To make the Salsa Picante, in a small saucepan place the onion, vinegar, and wine. Bring to a boil, then simmer slowly about 5 minutes, until the liquid is absorbed. Add the cucumber and capers. Mix in the tomato sauce and salt and cook slowly, uncovered, 10 minutes more. Stir in the butter and parsley. Keep warm on the back of the stove.

Rub the roast with the crushed garlic. Sprinkle with thyme, salt, and pepper. Place in a 450° F oven, reduce the heat to 350° F, and roast for 15 minutes. Add the whole red and green peppers and the eggplant to the roasting pan. Continue cooking for 30 minutes, turning the vegetables occasionally. Remove the vegetables. Skin the eggplant and the peppers and remove the seeds from the peppers. Slice these vegetables in strips. Combine the peppers and eggplant on a platter (the vegetable strips should be kept in rows, not tossed together) and sprinkle with salt and pepper. Drizzle with the olive oil and garnish with the parsley. Keep warm (this should not be hot) and continue to roast the meat until it is done, a total of 30–35 minutes to a pound.

Deglaze the pan juices with a few tablespoons of broth or water. Slice the meat and pour on some of the juices. Serve with the vegetables on the side and pass the Salsa Picante. A light red wine such as Viña Tondonia is appropriate.

FILETES DE CERDO "CANTAMAÑANAS"

(Pimiento- and Cheese-Filled Pork Cutlets)

"Cantamañanas" is not a word you will find on a menu; it's just an expression used by some Spanish children we know to refer to these pork cutlets, which they invariably request when visiting their grandmother.

Serves 4

1 pound pork cutlets, thinly sliced	Flour for dusting
4 slices mild cheese, such as Tetilla	2 eggs, lightly beaten
(p. 432) or Fontina	Bread crumbs
2 pimientos, homemade or imported,	3 tablespoons olive oil
cut in strips	

Match up the cutlets by size and shape so that 2 will fit together. Place a slice of cheese and several strips of pimiento over half of the cutlets. Top with the other halves. Pound the edges lightly to seal. Dust with flour, dip in the beaten egg, then coat with crumbs. Let sit about 20 minutes.

Heat the oil in a large skillet and fry the cutlets. Keep them warm in a 200° F oven as the others cook. Serve with Potatoes in Green Sauce (p. 99) and a full-bodied red wine such as Sin Rival.

MANOS DE CERDO RELLENAS

(Stuffed Pig's Feet)

START PREPARATION SEVERAL HOURS IN ADVANCE.

You must like the gelatinous consistency of pig's feet to appreciate this dish, and if you do, this version, stuffed with mushrooms, is outstanding. In the region of La Mancha, pig's feet are customarily served with mashed potatoes.

Serves 2

2 pig's feet, split in halves	½ carrot, scraped and cut in
2 cubes slab bacon, about 1 inch each	thick slices

1 small onion, peeled and studded
    with 4 cloves
1 sprig parsley
¼ teaspoon thyme
1 bay leaf
1 cup dry red wine

3 cups chicken broth
4 peppercorns
Salt
Olive oil
Bread crumbs

STUFFING

5 tablespoons butter
¼ cup minced onion
2 cloves garlic, minced
1⅓ cups finely chopped mushrooms
    (about ½ pound)

1½ tablespoons minced parsley
3 tablespoons bread crumbs
4 teaspoons dry white wine
Salt
Freshly ground pepper

Tie the halved pig's feet at 1-inch intervals so they do not fall apart in cooking. Place them in a deep pot and add the bacon, carrot, peeled onion, sprig parsley, thyme, bay leaf, red wine, broth, peppercorns, and salt. Bring to a boil, then cover and simmer most of the day (at least 7 or 8 hours). The pig's feet must be extremely tender. Remove from the pot very carefully, cool, and take off the string. Gently remove the bones, being careful again to keep the feet whole.

To make the stuffing, melt the butter in a medium skillet. Sauté the minced onion until it is wilted. Add the garlic, mushrooms, and minced parsley and cook 5 minutes. Turn off the flame and stir in the 3 tablespoons of bread crumbs, white wine, salt, and pepper. Stuff the pig's feet with this mixture.

Spread a few tablespoons of olive oil in a flat dish. Coat the feet with oil, then carefully roll them in the bread crumbs. Place in a baking dish, skin side up, and broil 4–5 inches from the flame for 3–4 minutes, or until golden. Serve with a hearty red wine like Coronas.

PICADILLO

(Marinated Pork and Potatoes)

START PREPARATION ONE DAY IN ADVANCE.

A TASTY Spanish-style hash from Rioja.

Serves 4

⅓ cup olive oil
1 bay leaf, crumbled
Salt
Freshly ground pepper
1 tablespoon chopped onion
1 clove garlic, crushed

1 tablespoon chopped parsley
2 teaspoons paprika
1¼ pounds pork loin, in
   ½-inch cubes
3 large potatoes, boiled and cubed

In a large bowl mix the oil, bay leaf, salt, pepper, onion, garlic, parsley, and paprika. Add the meat pieces and stir to coat well. Cover and marinate several hours or, preferably, overnight (refrigerated).

Heat 1 tablespoon of the marinade in a large skillet until the oil is very hot. Add the meat pieces and stir fry until they begin to brown. Add the potatoes and continue stir frying until the meat is completely cooked and the potatoes are brown. Serve with a green vegetable and a light red wine like Lan.

CAZUELA DE LOMO Y BUTIFARRA

(Pork and Sausage Casserole)

THIS is a Catalán specialty, as is any recipe that includes *butifarra* sausage. The chops turn out tender and tasty, with the added spice provided by the sausages.

Serves 4

1 tablespoon olive oil
4 boneless pork loin chops,
   ¾ inch thick
½ pound *butifarra* (p. 55),
   sweet Italian, or
   breakfast-style sausage

1 medium onion, chopped
2 cloves garlic, minced
½ cup dry white wine
4 fresh or canned plum
   tomatoes, chopped
1 bay leaf

Salt   1 tablespoon chopped parsley
Freshly ground pepper

Heat the oil in a shallow ovenproof casserole. Brown the chops and the
sausage. Add the onion and garlic and sauté until the onion is wilted. Stir in
the wine, tomato, bay leaf, salt, pepper, and parsley. Cover and bake at 350° F
for 30 minutes. Slice the sausage and serve with the chops and the sauce,
accompanied by a green salad and a full-bodied wine of the region such as
Red Penedés of René Barbier.

LOMO RELLENO DE SALCHICHA

(Sausage Rolled in Pork Fillet)

Serves 4

1 pound uncooked sausage links,   1 onion, chopped
    homemade (p. 57) or   1 clove garlic, minced
    breakfast style   1 carrot, scraped and finely diced
8 very thin slices (½–¾ pound)   1 tablespoon minced parsley
    pork loin   ¾ cup dry red wine
Flour for dusting   Salt
2 tablespoons olive oil   Freshly ground pepper

Wrap each sausage in a slice of pork loin. Secure with a toothpick. Dust with
flour. Heat the oil in a large, shallow casserole and sauté the sausage rolls until
brown on all sides. Sprinkle in the onion, garlic, and carrot and continue to
cook until the onion is wilted. Add the parsley, wine, salt, and pepper. Cover
and cook slowly 30 minutes. Serve with boiled or roast potatoes, Fresh Beet
Salad (p. 116), and a full-bodied red wine such as Carta de Oro.

SALCHICHAS CON HIGOS AGRI-DULCES

(Sausages with Sweet-Sour Figs)

PREPARE THE FIGS ONE DAY IN ADVANCE.

IN THE sixteenth century, sweet-sour sauces were quite common, perhaps as a
means to disguise poor-quality foods. Over the years such sauces disappeared

from Spanish cuisine, and this dish—discovered in Extremadura, where some of the most "primitive" Spanish cooking still exists—is a rare example of this type of sauce. The combination of sausages with sweet-sour figs is quite striking, however unlikely it may sound, and I highly recommend it. When the sausages and figs are cut in smaller sizes, this dish makes an exciting *tapa*.

Serves 4

1½ pounds sausages, preferably homemade (p. 57), otherwise sweet Italian or breakfast-style sausage may be used
1 tablespoon olive oil

4 tablespoons white wine
2 teaspoons tomato sauce
Salt
Freshly ground pepper

SWEET–SOUR FIGS

1 cup sugar
1 cup red wine vinegar
1 cinnamon stick
4 cloves

1 slice lemon
1 pound fresh small green figs, or 1 pound bottled figs in syrup, drained

To make the figs, combine the sugar, vinegar, cinnamon, cloves, and lemon slice in a saucepan. Bring to a boil, then simmer 5 minutes. Add the figs, cover, and simmer 20 minutes (for bottled figs, simmer 5 minutes only). Cool the figs in the syrup and let them sit, covered, at room temperature overnight.

Cook the sausages in the oil and 2 tablespoons of the wine until the wine evaporates and the sausages are cooked and brown. Remove the sausages to a warm platter. Pour most of the fat from the pan. Deglaze the pan with 4 tablespoons of water and the remaining 2 tablespoons of wine. Add the tomato sauce, salt, and pepper and simmer 2 minutes, uncovered.

Drain the figs (the syrup will not be used). Add them to the pan, along with the sausages. Cover and cook briefly until the figs are heated. This dish may be accompanied by a full-bodied red wine such as Viña Vial and a green salad.

NOTE: To serve as an appetizer, cut each sausage into 3 or 4 slices. Cut the figs in halves or quarters, depending on size. Spear pieces of sausage and fig on toothpicks. Serve with the sauce.

BUTIFARRA CON SETAS
(Baked Sausage and Mushrooms)

IN CATALUÑA, a mushroom is not a mushroom—it may be a *pinetell, rovellón, múrgola, cuireny, rossinyol, cama-sec, ou de reig, peu de rata,* or *oronja,* and the list goes on. Nowhere else in Spain is there such a passion for mushrooms and such discrimination between one variety and another. Changing the type of mushroom used in a recipe, Catalán mushroom lovers will agree, can change the entire character of a dish. Butifarra con Setas, one of the area's most famous dishes, is made with the local white sausage in combination with wild mushrooms. We, unfortunately, will have to settle for whatever mushrooms are available, but the results are still excellent—either as a first-course serving or a quick meal in itself.

Makes 4 main-course portions

1 tablespoon olive oil
1½ pounds *butifarra* sausage
    (p. 55), sweet Italian, or
    breakfast-style sausage
¼ cup dry white wine
1 pound mushrooms, whole, or cut
    in halves or quarters if large

1 clove garlic, minced
1 tablespoon minced parsley
Salt
Freshly ground pepper

Heat the oil in a large ovenproof casserole, preferably Spanish earthenware. Brown the sausage and pour off any excess fat. Add the wine to the pan to deglaze. Mix in the mushrooms, sprinkle with garlic, parsley, salt, and pepper, and place in a 400° F oven, uncovered, for about 20 minutes. This may also be made in individual casserole dishes. An Ensalada de Escalibada (p. 117) and a full-bodied Coronas wine, both native to Cataluña, are perfect accompaniments.

CANELONES
(Meat-Filled Pasta)

CANELONES came to Spain by way of the port of Barcelona when, in the sixteenth century, Italy was ruled by the Spanish crown and communication between the two countries was close. Although other types of pasta are still uncommon in Spain, Canelones are found everywhere. The dish is now considered quite Spanish and should properly be a part of any Spanish cookbook.

A recipe for pasta is included, although in Spain every grocery store sells squares of fresh pasta, exclusively for the preparation of Canelones. You may use instead your own recipe, purchase fresh pasta in sheets, or buy packaged manicotti shells.

Serves 4–5

2 tablespoons olive oil
1 medium onion, finely chopped
1 clove garlic, minced
1½ pounds mixture of ground beef, veal, and pork
1 chicken liver, chopped
4 tablespoons minced cured ham
1¼ cups tomato sauce, preferably homemade (p. 218)

1 tablespoon dry (*fino*) sherry
2 tablespoons minced parsley
1 egg, lightly beaten
2 tablespoons bread crumbs
6 tablespoons grated Parmesan cheese
Salt
Freshly ground pepper
Butter

DOUGH

1 egg
2 tablespoons melted butter

½ cup water
1½ cups flour

WHITE SAUCE

5 tablespoons butter
5 tablespoons flour
2 cups milk
3 tablespoons grated Parmesan cheese

Salt
Freshly ground pepper
Dash of nutmeg

To make the dough, beat the egg in a bowl and mix in the butter and water. Stir in the flour. Knead lightly until smooth and elastic. Cover and let sit 1½ hours.

Meanwhile, make the filling. Heat the oil in a skillet and sauté the onion and garlic until the onion is wilted. Add the meat mixture and the chicken liver and brown. Stir in the ham, cook a minute, then add ¾ cup of the tomato sauce, the sherry, and the parsley. Cook 10 minutes, uncovered. Add the egg, bread crumbs, 3 tablespoons of the cheese, salt, and pepper.

Roll the dough as thin as possible. Cut into 4-inch squares and let them dry 10 minutes. Place in boiling salted water to which 1 tablespoon of oil has been added. Do not crowd. Cook 15 minutes, or until just tender. Drain and run under cold water. Dry on paper towels.

Pour the remaining ½ cup of tomato sauce into a baking pan in which the Canelones will fit snugly. Place about 2 tablespoons of the meat filling on each pasta square. Roll and arrange seam side down in the baking pan.

To make the white sauce, melt the butter in a saucepan. Add the flour and cook a minute or so. Gradually stir in the milk, cheese, salt, pepper, and nutmeg. Cook until thickened and smooth.

Pour the white sauce over the Canelones. Sprinkle with the remaining 3 tablespoons of cheese, dot with butter, and bake at 450° F for about 10 minutes, or until bubbly and lightly browned on top. Serve with Cucumber, Tomato, and Pepper Salad (p. 106) and Viña Lanciano, a light red wine.

LOMBARDA RELLENA

(Stuffed Red Cabbage)

THE sweetness of the red cabbage blends beautifully with the sausage-and-apple filling of this yuletide dish.

Serves 4

1 medium head red cabbage
2 tablespoons olive oil
1 medium onion, finely chopped
1 pound breakfast-style sausage meat
    (homemade, p. 57)
1 clove garlic, minced
1 tablespoon minced parsley
¼ cup dry red wine

½ apple, peeled, cored, and diced
½ cup cooked rice
Salt
Freshly ground pepper
2 eggs, lightly beaten
½ cup beef broth
1 tablespoon melted butter
2 tablespoons grated cheese

Select and separate 8 of the large outer leaves of the cabbage (if the leaves are hard to separate, boil the cabbage head briefly). Chop the rest of the cabbage to make about 2 cups. Place the whole leaves in boiling water until they are tender enough to fold for stuffing—do not overcook, or the leaves will lose their color. Drain.

Heat the oil in a skillet and sauté the onion until it is wilted. Add the sausage meat and separate it with a fork as it browns. Pour off the excess fat, then add the garlic, parsley, chopped cabbage, wine, and apple. Cook, uncovered, 15 minutes. Remove from the flame and stir in the cooked rice, salt, and pepper. Mix in the eggs.

Fill each cabbage leaf with several tablespoons of the filling. Fold up 2 sides of the cabbage leaves, then roll to enclose the filling. Cover the bottom of a roasting pan with the broth and the melted butter. Arrange the stuffed cabbage in the pan seam side down and sprinkle with grated cheese. Bake in a 350° F oven for about 30 minutes, adding more broth as necessary. Serve with a light red wine such as Marqués de Cáceres and a green salad.

PIMIENTOS Y CALABACINES RELLENOS
(Stuffed Green Peppers and Zucchini)

Serves 6

2 tablespoons olive oil
2 large onions
3 cloves garlic
2 pounds chopped beef, or a mixture
    of beef, veal, and pork
Salt
Freshly ground pepper
2 tablespoons minced parsley
2 tablespoons dry red wine

2 tablespoons minced cured ham
2 fresh tomatoes, skinned
    and chopped
3 medium zucchini
½ cup uncooked short- or
    long-grain rice
6 green peppers
¾ cup tomato sauce, preferably
    homemade (p. 190)

Heat the oil in a skillet and sauté the onion and garlic until the onion is wilted. Add the chopped meat and continue cooking, stirring frequently, until the meat is lightly browned. Season with salt and pepper. Add the parsley, wine, ham, and chopped tomato. Cut the zucchini in half crosswise and hollow them out, adding the flesh to the meat mixture and reserving the shells. Continue cooking this mixture 5 minutes. Stir in the rice and cook 5 minutes more, uncovered. Cut off the caps of the green peppers (reserve them) and scoop out the seeds and the membrane.

Dilute the tomato sauce with ¾ cup water. Season with salt and pepper. Pour into a baking dish. Stuff the zucchini and peppers about ¾ full with the meat mixture. Close the peppers with the reserved caps. Arrange in the baking dish and bake at 350° F for about 1 hour, basting occasionally and adding more water as the sauce thickens. Serve with a light red wine such as Spanish Claret.

HOJAS DE PARRA RELLENAS
(Stuffed Grape Leaves)

I SHALL never forget my surprise when one day, while living in Madrid, I decided to treat friends to an authentic Greek meal. I imported a jar of Greek vine leaves and proceeded to make *dolmades*. My friends found them most interesting and unusual, but their maid, a recent arrival from a small Spanish village in La Mancha, informed us that stuffed grape leaves were eaten all the time in her hometown! The Spanish preparation is a bit different from the Greek, but the idea is the same.

Serves 4

16–20 grape leaves, packed in brine
½ pound veal, with some fat on it
1 cup chopped cured ham
1 chicken breast, boned and skinned
2 tablespoons minced parsley
2 large cloves garlic, minced

Salt
Freshly ground pepper
10 tablespoons beef broth
2 slices bread, crusts removed, soaked
   and squeezed dry
2 tablespoons tomato sauce

Separate the grape leaves and drop them into boiling water. Remove after 5 minutes. Drain and dry on paper towels.

Grind together in a processor the veal, ham, and chicken. Mix in the parsley, garlic, salt, pepper, 4 tablespoons of the broth, and the bread. Place about 2½ tablespoons of the filling in the center of each grape leaf. Fold up 2 sides of the grape leaves, then roll to enclose the filling.

In a large pot, mix the remaining 6 tablespoons of broth and the tomato sauce. Arrange the stuffed leaves in layers, seam side down. Cover with an inverted plate that will press down on the leaves. Cover the pot with a lid and slowly simmer 30 minutes. Serve with the juices poured over and with a Cucumber, Tomato, and Pepper Salad (p. 106). These are also very good cold. A light red wine like Viña Lanciano would be an appropriate accompaniment.

CEBOLLAS RELLENAS

(Stuffed Onions)

THIS dish is native to the Balearic island of Mallorca.

Serves 4

8 large onions
1 tablespoon olive oil
1 clove garlic
1¼ pounds ground beef
Salt
Freshly ground pepper
Dash nutmeg
Dash cinnamon

1 tablespoon minced parsley
2 tablespoons dry white wine
2 tablespoons heavy cream
2 tablespoons bread crumbs
2 tablespoons grated cheese
Butter
1 cup beef broth

Peel the onions and trim the ends. Place them in boiling salted water for 15 minutes. Drain. Slice about ½ inch off the tops, then scoop out the centers, leaving a ¼-inch shell. Reserve the scooped-out pieces and chop them (1 cup will be used — save the rest for future use).

In a skillet, heat the oil, then sauté the 1 cup reserved chopped onion with the garlic until the onion is wilted. Add the ground beef and cook until brown. Sprinkle with salt, pepper, nutmeg, cinnamon, and parsley. Stir in the wine, cream, bread crumbs, and 1 tablespoon of the cheese. Fill the onions with this mixture, sprinkling on the remaining cheese. Dot with butter and place in a roasting pan. Pour in the beef broth and bake at 350° F for about 40 minutes, adding some water if the broth evaporates. Serve with some liquid spooned over the onions and with a green vegetable and a light red wine such as Marqués de Murrieta.

FRICADELAS

(Beef Patties)

AN INTERESTING variation on a hamburger from Cartagena in Murcia.

Makes 4–6 meat patties

2 slices bacon, chopped
1 pound ground beef
1 cup finely chopped escarole
Salt
Freshly ground pepper

1 tablespoon dry (*fino*) sherry
4 tablespoons olive oil
4–6 slices French-style bread, ¼ inch thick

In a small skillet, lightly sauté the bacon. Mix together the beef, bacon, escarole, salt, pepper, and sherry. Divide into 4–6 meat patties. Heat 1 tablespoon of the oil in a large skillet and cook the patties over a medium-high flame until the meat is cooked to taste.

Meanwhile, heat the remaining 3 tablespoons of oil in a skillet. Lightly fry the bread slices. Serve the patties on the fried bread, pouring on the pan juices. A green vegetable and Potato and Beet Salad (p. 116) could accompany these patties, along with a full-bodied red wine like Viña Vial.

HÍGADO CON PIMIENTOS

(Calves' Liver and Green Peppers)

THIS is a wonderful way to serve liver—smothered in peppers and onions.

Serves 4

3 tablespoons olive oil
2 medium onions, sliced
3 green peppers, cut in strips
Coarse salt

1 pound calves' liver, in thin slices
¼ cup dry white wine
Freshly ground pepper

Heat the oil in a skillet. Sauté the onion until it is tender. Reserve. In the same oil (add more if necessary), sauté the green peppers for 2 minutes, stirring, then cover and cook slowly until they are tender, about 10–15 minutes more. Reserve with the onions.

Salt, then fry the liver in the same pan (again adding oil if necessary) over high heat until the liver is cooked to taste. Remove to a warm platter. Deglaze the pan with the wine, then pour these juices over the liver. Return the onions and peppers to the skillet, season with salt and pepper, and cook until the vegetables are heated through. Serve over the liver. Spicy Potatoes (p. 99) and Ensalada a la Almoraina (p. 107) are good accompaniments, along with a full-bodied wine such as Campo Viejo.

HÍGADO EN AJO CABAÑIL

(Calves' Liver with Garlic and Vinegar)

THIS piquant vinegar-and-paprika combination is the perfect foil for the strong taste of sautéed liver.

Serves 2

2 tablespoons olive oil
½–¾ pound calves' liver, in thin slices
2 cloves garlic, minced
2 tablespoons red wine vinegar

½ teaspoon paprika
Salt
Freshly ground pepper

Heat the oil in a skillet and fry the liver very quickly over high heat until brown on both sides, but not yet cooked. Add 6 tablespoons water to deglaze the pan, then add the garlic, vinegar, paprika, salt, and pepper. Continue cooking to the desired doneness, adding more water if too much of the liquid evaporates. Serve with a green vegetable and a full-bodied red wine—Viña Real, for example.

FÍGADO CON RUIBARBO

(Liver in Sorrel Sauce)

THIS delicious and most unusual dish is found in the historic city of Segovia at the Mesón de Cándido, one of the oldest and most charming inns in Spain. Housed in a delightful centuries-old building at the foot of the city's two-thousand-year-old Roman aqueduct (still in use today), this cozy and rustic restaurant has a huge display of memorabilia, from the many gastronomic awards received by its longtime owner, Cándido, to photographs and signatures of illustrious guests, with a special display cabinet reserved for royal signatures only. Many regional Castilian specialties appear on the menu at Mesón de Cándido. The baby lamb and suckling pig, roasted in woodburning ovens, are by now legendary and attract diners from all over the globe. One of Cándido's lesser-known dishes is Fígado con Ruibarbo—liver cooked in a sauce of lettuce, sorrel, vinegar, and wine—a preparation that unquestionably gives liver a wonderful new taste.

In Spain, Fígado con Ruibarbo, as the name indicates, is prepared with rhubarb leaves, but these leaves are not eaten in this country and, indeed, are considered poisonous. To avoid confusion, I have substituted sorrel leaves, which come from the same plant family.

Serves 4

3 tablespoons olive oil
1 medium onion, slivered
1¼ pounds calves' liver, in 1 piece,
    then cut in 1¼-inch cubes
1½ teaspoons flour
1 teaspoon paprika
⅛ teaspoon cayenne
1 heart of romaine lettuce (about 2
    ounces), chopped
¼ pound sorrel leaves, stems trimmed
    (if unavailable, use 2

teaspoons sorrel purée,
    available in specialty shops)
¼ cup red wine vinegar
¾ cup dry red wine
2 cloves garlic, chopped
½ teaspoon thyme
1 bay leaf
Salt
Freshly ground pepper
1 tablespoon minced parsley

Have all ingredients assembled in advance and all cutting and chopping completed before beginning; otherwise the liver will overcook. Heat the oil in a skillet and quickly brown the onion and liver over a high flame. Lower the heat and stir in the flour, paprika, and cayenne. Add the chopped lettuce and the whole sorrel leaves. Sauté briefly, just until the leaves are wilted. Stir in the vinegar, wine, garlic, thyme, bay leaf, salt, and pepper. Simmer just a minute or so, or until the liver is done—it should be lightly pink within. Sprinkle with parsley and serve with a salad and a full-bodied red wine like Cerro Añón.

RIÑONES AL JEREZ

(Kidneys in Sherry Sauce)

IN SPAIN one rarely finds kidneys prepared any other way except "al jerez"—in sherry sauce. And, indeed, the taste of sherry is the perfect complement to kidneys, making them thoroughly appealing even to someone like me who is not ordinarily a fan of kidneys.

Kidneys quickly acquire an off taste when not completely fresh—be sure to buy from a first-class butcher.

Serves 4

4 very fresh veal kidneys (about 3 pounds)	2 onions, chopped
Juice of 3 lemons	2 cloves garlic, minced
Coarse salt	2 tablespoons minced parsley
Freshly ground pepper	3 tablespoons flour
2 tablespoons olive oil	1½ cups dry (*fino*) sherry
	1½ cups dark beef broth

Let the whole kidneys sit in the lemon juice for 10 minutes. Cut the kidneys into ¾-inch cubes, removing all fat and membrane. Run them under hot water to rinse and drain on paper towels. Sprinkle with salt and pepper.

Heat the oil in a skillet and sauté the kidneys over high heat for 1 minute. Remove them to a warm platter. Add the onion, garlic, and parsley to the pan and sauté until the onion is wilted, adding more oil if necessary. Stir in the flour and cook a minute. Add the sherry and the beef broth, stirring until thickened and smooth. Cover and simmer 10 minutes. Strain, discarding the onion, then return the sauce to the pan. Add the kidneys and simmer 5–10 minutes, or until the kidneys are just faintly pink within. It is very important not to overcook, for the kidneys become tough. Serve with a Rice Ring (p. 191) and a light red reserve wine like Imperial. If you try the kidneys as a *tapa* or first course, a chilled dry sherry such as La Ina is appropriate.

BROCHETA DE RIÑONES

(Kidney Brochette)

Serves 4

2 very fresh veal kidneys, about
    ¾ pound each
Juice of 3 lemons
16 mushroom caps
¼ pound slab bacon, in 1-inch cubes
A ¼-pound piece cured ham, cut in
    ¾-inch cubes

Eight 1-inch bread cubes (with crust)
2 eggs, beaten
Bread crumbs
Oil for frying

Soak the whole kidneys in the lemon juice for 10 minutes. Cut into 1-inch cubes, discarding fat and gristle. Rinse in hot water and dry on paper towels. On each of eight 8-inch skewers, place 1 piece of kidney, a mushroom cap, bacon, kidney, mushroom, kidney, ham, and kidney, ending with a cube of bread. Dip the skewers in the egg, coating on all sides, then roll in the bread crumbs. Heat the oil, at least ½ inch deep, in a large skillet, large enough so that the skewers will lie flat. Fry the brochettes over medium-high heat until well browned on both sides (turn them with tongs). Do not overcook or the kidneys will toughen—they should be slightly pink within. Serve with Limas with Artichoke and Cumin (p. 95), a green salad, and a light red wine like Cabernet Sauvignon.

NOTE: These brochettes may instead be broiled, eliminating the bread crumbs and egg, again being careful not to overcook them.

CALLOS A LA MADRILEÑA

(Tripe, Madrid Style)

SPANIARDS, my husband in particular, are great lovers of tripe. This spicy version from Madrid is especially popular, and I am convinced that even those who think they dislike tripe will enjoy it prepared in this manner. At least they will love the sauce. Cooking time varies greatly for tripe, but the important thing is for it to be very tender before eating. Sometimes it is necessary to leave the pot on the stove most of the day. Tripe is best when prepared the day before and then reheated. It will keep for many days in the refrigerator and is equally appropriate as a first course or as a hearty meal.

1 pound beef tripe
½ cup dry white wine
1 fresh or canned small
    tomato, chopped
1 pig's foot, split in half
2 sprigs parsley
10 peppercorns, lightly crushed
2 cloves, crushed
Dash of nutmeg
2 bay leaves
½ teaspoon thyme

Salt
1 small onion, coarsely chopped
6 cloves garlic, peeled
2 tablespoons olive oil
1 small onion, finely chopped
¼ pound *chorizo*, in ¼-inch slices
¼ cup diced cured ham
1 tablespoon flour
1 tablespoon paprika
½ dried red chili pepper, seeds
    removed, crumbled

Rinse the tripe well. Place in a pot and cover with water. Bring to a boil, then drain immediately. Cut the tripe into 1½-inch squares and return it to the empty pot. Add 3 cups water, wine, tomato, pig's foot, parsley, peppercorns, cloves, nutmeg, bay leaves, thyme, salt, the coarsely chopped onion, and the garlic. Cover and cook over a very low flame for 4–5 hours, or until almost tender.

In a medium skillet, heat the oil and sauté the finely chopped onion until it is wilted. Add the *chorizo* and ham and cook 5 minutes. Stir in the flour and paprika and cook a minute. Add ½ cup of cooking liquid from the pot and stir until the mixture thickens. Add this and the chili pepper to the tripe and cook 1–2 hours more, covered. Uncover and cook another 1–2 hours, or until extremely tender.

Remove the bone from the pig's foot and discard. Cut the meat into pieces and stir into the tripe. Serve in soup bowls or shallow individual casserole dishes, preferably earthenware, accompanied by a green salad and plenty of good crusty bread for dunking. A hearty red wine from the region—Balada, for example—is needed for this dish.

Chapter 12

PANES, BOLLOS Y MASAS

(Breads, Rolls, and Pastry Doughs)

A N OLD retired Spanish baker bemoaned the bygone days when bread was *really* bread—no commercial leavening agents, no air-filled loaves. In spite of his pessimism, there is not as yet a great need for home bread baking in Spain, for the bakery product coming from neighborhood stores is still a solid loaf with excellent flavor and a superb crust. Its quality is high no matter where one travels, since government law controls the purity of ingredients and the bread's density.

There are, of course, regional variations. Castilla in central Spain, known as *"Tierra de Pan"* (Land of Bread), has ideal conditions for growing superior wheat, and its bread is generally considered the finest in Spain. Northern Spain produces large quantities of corn and rye, and these ingredients, quite naturally, are used in bread baking. Breads found in small villages are generally less refined than those found in large cities. *Candeal*-style breads, large round country loaves, are heavy and coarse textured and very satisfying with country foods and excellent for dunking in hearty sauces. Bread found in Madrid is equally delicious, but is baked in long loaves of fine crumbs and crackling crusts. In villages off the beaten track, the bread is still sometimes baked in woodburning ovens. Such is the case in the charming village of Capileira, one of a succession of lovely untouched villages in the Alpujarra mountain range, where two elderly black-clad ladies take charge of bread baking for the entire village from their primitive home oven of stone and brick.

Sampling breads in cities and villages all over Spain is one of my favorite pastimes. However, reproducing them in my kitchen is another matter because of the difference in flours and ovens. When I lived in Spain, I was unable to bake a light American-type cake because the flour available there was not made for such delicate products. On the other hand, that flour produced a wonderful loaf of bread that the flour available to home bakers in America cannot reproduce. In Spain, when my daughter was desperate for a multilayered birthday cake, I would resort to imported cake mixes. In the United States, I have experimented and created several delicious breads that come as close as possible to the Spanish loaves of which I am so fond.

Just as a Spanish lunch or dinner table would never be complete without its loaf of bread, so too a Spanish breakfast or tea would be unthinkable without a variety of sweet breads, which are sometimes used with sandwich fillings for snacks. The quality of the sweeter breads is not regulated and depends wholly on the caliber of the bakery. In Madrid, for example, you will be assured of top quality by visiting two longtime bakeries, Mallorca and Lhardy. Many of the sweet breads to be found in those establishments—the *suizos, ensaimadas,* and *medias-noches,* to name a few—are included in this chapter.

When buying breads in Spain, remember that table breads and sweet breads are usually sold in different types of bakeries. A *panadería* (from the word *pan*—bread) sells only that, while a *pastelería* (from the word *pastel*—pastry) provides sweet breads, pastries, cookies, and candies.

Eating bread in Spain is a treat, and for a Spaniard an essential part of every lunch and dinner meal. Baking bread at home is an exciting and rewarding experience and the only way to sample authentic Spanish breads outside of Spain.

PAN DE PUEBLO

(Basic Long Loaf)

THESE are loaves that everyone seems to love. They are relatively foolproof to prepare, and I always keep a supply on hand in my freezer.

Makes 2 long loaves

1¼ cups warm water
1 package dry yeast
3¼ cups bread flour or unbleached,
    all-purpose flour

3 teaspoons coarse salt
Cornmeal or bread crumbs
    for sprinkling
1 egg white for brushing

In a small cup mix ¼ cup of the warm water with the yeast. While this mixture sits, mix the flour and salt in a large bowl. Add the softened yeast and the remaining cup of warm water. Mix with a wooden spoon, then turn out onto a working surface (the dough will not yet hold together) and knead 10 minutes, adding more flour if necessary. Place the dough in a bowl greased with oil, turn to coat with the oil, cover with a towel, and place in a warm, draft-free spot (an unlit oven with a pilot light is good) for about 3 hours, or until double in size.

Punch down the dough and knead 5 minutes. Divide into 2 equal parts. Roll each piece into an oblong about 5 × 20 inches. Starting with a long side, roll up tightly, jelly-roll fashion. Pinch to seal the seam and the ends. Place the loaves, seam side down, on a cookie sheet that has been sprinkled with cornmeal or bread crumbs. Slit the tops in several places, diagonally, with a sharp knife. Place in a warm spot again for 1 hour, or until double in size.

Preheat the oven to 450° F and place a pan of water on the oven floor. Bake the bread on the middle-upper rack 5 minutes. Remove the pan of water and continue baking the bread 5 minutes more. Mix the egg white in a small bowl with 1 teaspoon water. Brush it on the bread and continue baking until brown and crusty, about 5–10 minutes more.

PAN CANDEAL

(Country-Style Bread)

START PREPARATION TWO DAYS IN ADVANCE.

A DESCRIPTION of bread baking in earlier times, given to me by a Spanish baker, inspired me to combine his primitive techniques with modern methods, resulting in a bread just slightly sour from its two days of aging without yeast, but in the end containing yeast to insure proper rising. I am very pleased with this hearty loaf that emerged from my experimentation, and I have used the same technique in preparing my rye bread and corn bread recipes.

Makes 1 round loaf

3½ cups bread flour or unbleached, all-purpose flour	3 teaspoons coarse salt
1¼ cups warm water	Cornmeal or bread crumbs for sprinkling
1 package dry yeast	1 egg white for brushing

Mix 3 cups of the flour with 1 cup of the warm water. Turn onto a working surface and knead 5 minutes, adding more flour if necessary—the dough should be very firm. Let the dough rest 5 minutes, then knead again 5 minutes more. Dust the dough with flour and place in a bowl, cover with foil, and leave in a draft-free spot, such as a cupboard, for 2 days. At the end of that time the dough should have expanded slightly and will have a faint aroma of vinegar.

Soften the yeast in the remaining ¼ cup of warm water. Add the remaining ½ cup of flour and mix this dough with the dough already prepared. Knead, incorporating in the process the salt and as much flour as necessary to form a smooth elastic dough. The kneading should take about 5 minutes. Place the dough in a bowl greased with oil, turn to coat with the oil, and cover with a towel. Let rise in a warm spot 2½–3 hours, or until about double in bulk.

Punch down the dough and knead 5 minutes, adding more flour if necessary. Shape into a firm round loaf by folding the sides of the dough toward the center several times, then pinching the bottom to seal. Place, pinched side down, in an 8 × 8-inch square cake pan that has been sprinkled with cornmeal or bread crumbs. Slash diagonally twice. Let rise 1 hour more, or until doubled in bulk, in a warm spot.

Preheat the oven to 425° F. Place a pan of water on the oven floor. Bake the bread 5 minutes on the middle-upper shelf of the oven. Remove the pan of water. Bake 10 minutes more, then brush with the egg white, which has been mixed with 1 teaspoon water. Remove the loaf from the cake pan and place directly on the oven rack. Bake about 2 minutes more, or until the bread sounds hollow when tapped on the bottom.

PAN GALLEGO DE CENTENO
(Galician Rye Bread)

START PREPARATION THREE DAYS IN ADVANCE.

GALICIAN breads and cheeses, especially the cheese known as *tetilla* (see Spanish Cheese, pp. 431–432), are characteristically round and culminate in a twist that makes them look like huge chocolate kisses.

Makes 1 large round loaf

4½ cups bread flour	2 tablespoons coarse salt
2½ cups dark rye flour	2 tablespoons lard or vegetable
½ cup cornmeal	shortening, softened
2½ cups warm water	2 teaspoons caraway seeds
2 packages dry yeast	Cornmeal or bread crumbs
4 teaspoons sugar	for sprinkling

In a large bowl, mix 3½ cups of the bread flour, the rye flour, cornmeal, and 2 cups of the warm water. Turn onto a work surface and knead 5 minutes, adding more bread flour if necessary—the dough should be very firm. Let the dough rest 5 minutes. Knead again 5 minutes more until smooth. Dust with flour and place in a bowl. Cover with foil and leave in a warm draft-free cupboard for about 36 hours. The dough should have expanded a bit and have a slight aroma of vinegar.

Soften the yeast and sugar in the remaining ½ cup of warm water. Add the remaining 1 cup of bread flour and incorporate this mixture into the dough that has been resting, along with the salt, softened lard, and caraway seeds. Turn out onto a work surface and knead 5 minutes, adding more flour as necessary. Place in a large bowl greased with oil, turning the dough to coat, cover, and let rise in a warm place about 2–2½ hours, or until doubled in bulk.

Punch the dough down, knead 5 minutes more, adding flour if necessary, and shape into a ball. Twist the center of the dough to make the typical Galician "cap." Place on a cookie sheet sprinkled with cornmeal or bread crumbs and let rise 1 hour, or until double in size.

Heat the oven to 425° F. Place a pan of water on the oven floor. Bake the bread on the middle-upper rack for 5 minutes. Remove the pan of water and bake 5 minutes more. Lower the heat to 350° F and continue baking 20 minutes more. Remove the bread from the cookie sheet and place directly on the oven rack. Bake about 2 minutes more, or until the bread is well browned and sounds hollow when tapped on the bottom.

PAN DE CEBADA

(Corn and Barley Bread)

START PREPARATION ONE DAY IN ADVANCE.

A HEAVY and strongly flavored bread found only in Galicia, where it is eaten with sardines. It is a great accompaniment for pâté, especially the Partridge and Liver Pâté (see p. 62), or for cold fish, such as Marinated Trout (see p. 242).

If you wish to use the bread to make appetizer rounds, divide the dough into four long loaves. When barley flour is unavailable, whole barley may be finely ground in a coffee grinder.

Makes 1 large round loaf

2 cups cornmeal	2 packages dry yeast
3½ cups water	4 tablespoons warm water
1 cup barley flour	5 teaspoons salt
4½ cups plus 4 tablespoons whole-wheat flour	Cornmeal or bread crumbs for sprinkling

Mix the cornmeal and the 3½ cups water in a saucepan. Bring to a boil, stirring constantly, then continue cooking a few minutes until quite thick. Cool.

In a large bowl, mix the barley flour, 4½ cups of the whole-wheat flour, and the softened cornmeal. Turn out onto a work surface and knead 5 minutes (it will take a little work before it begins to hold together). Let the dough rest 5 minutes, then knead 5 minutes more, adding more whole-wheat flour if necessary. Form into a ball, dust with flour, and place in a foil-covered bowl in a warm spot, such as a kitchen cabinet, for 24 hours.

At the end of the 24 hours, dissolve the yeast in the 4 tablespoons of warm water. Mix in the remaining 4 tablespoons of whole-wheat flour. Add this yeast mixture to the dough, along with the salt. Knead 2 minutes, adding more whole-wheat flour if necessary. Let rest 2 minutes, then knead 3 minutes more. Place in an oiled bowl, turn to coat with the oil, cover with a towel, and let rise in a warm place for about 3 hours. It will not quite double in bulk.

Punch the dough down and knead 5 minutes more. Shape into a ball. Place on a cookie sheet that has been sprinkled with cornmeal or bread crumbs. Slash the top twice and let rise 1 hour more. Again, it will not quite double.

Place the bread in a 425° F oven on the middle-upper rack. Place a pan of water on the oven floor. Bake 5 minutes, then remove the pan of water. Bake 5 minutes more, then reduce the heat to 350° F. Continue baking about 20 minutes more. Remove the bread from the cookie sheet and place directly on the oven rack. Bake about 5 minutes more, until it is well browned and sounds hollow when tapped on the bottom.

HORNAZO

(Sausage-Stuffed Country Bread)

THIS typically Castilian bread, almost a meal in itself, is prepared at Easter time. It incorporates large pieces of *chorizo* and blood sausage and whole eggs, so that each piece of bread produces a surprise slice of something. This filling is traditional, although variations are, of course, possible—different types of sausage may be used, or cured ham may replace the bacon.

Makes 1 large loaf

Pan de Pueblo (p. 325)
3 tablespoons olive oil
¼ pound slab bacon, diced
¼ pound *morcilla* (blood sausage), in
    2 pieces (see glossary)

¼ pound *chorizo* (2 sausages), each
    sausage cut in half crosswise
2 hard-boiled eggs, shelled
Cornmeal or bread crumbs,
    for sprinkling

Let the bread dough rise for the 3-hour period as indicated, or until doubled in bulk. Heat the oil in a skillet and lightly sauté the bacon, blood sausage, and *chorizo*.

Punch down the dough and knead in 3 tablespoons of the oil in which the sausage has cooked and the diced bacon, adding more flour as necessary. Shape into a ball. With a knife, make slits in the dough and push in the pieces of blood sausage, *chorizo*, and the whole eggs. Close the dough over the pieces, pinching well to seal. Place the dough, pinched side down, on a cookie tray lightly sprinkled with cornmeal. Flatten the dough slightly. Let rise in a warm spot for 1 hour, or until doubled in bulk.

Place the bread in a 450° F oven, middle-upper shelf. Put a pan of water on the oven floor. Bake 5 minutes, then remove the pan of water. Continue baking about 15 minutes more, or until well browned.

MEDIAS-NOCHES

(Miniature Egg Buns)

MEDIAS-NOCHES (the word means "midnight") are very pretty, small sweet buns glazed with egg. They are popular as tea sandwiches when spread with butter and filled with thin slices of ham—cured or boiled—or cheese.

Makes 18–20 buns

1 package dry yeast
¼ cup warm water
1¾ cups bread flour or unbleached,
    all-purpose flour
½ teaspoon salt
5 teaspoons sugar

3 tablespoons milk
2 eggs, lightly beaten
2 tablespoons butter, melted
    and cooled
1 egg yolk, beaten, for brushing

Dissolve the yeast in the warm water. Place the flour in a bowl, mix in the salt and sugar, then add the milk, softened yeast, the 2 eggs, and the cooled butter. Turn out onto a floured work surface and knead, adding more flour as necessary and throwing the dough forcefully to the counter several times until it is smooth and elastic—the dough will be soft, but should not be sticky.

Divide the dough into 1½-inch balls. Shape between the palms into ovals and place on an ungreased cookie sheet. Flatten slightly. Let the dough rise in a warm spot for about 30 minutes, or until double in size. Brush the rolls with the egg yolk mixed with a teaspoon of water and bake at 350° F until very well browned, about 15 minutes. Serve the rolls soon after baking.

ROSCÓN DE REYES

(Holiday Bread)

NO HOLIDAY is more eagerly awaited in Spain than El Día de los Reyes Magos—the Day of the Three Kings (Epiphany)—on January 6. On this date every year, so the legend goes, the Three Wise Men journey to Spain on camels, bearing gifts for all Spanish children. They use ladders to gain access to city apartments and leave presents in the children's shoes, which have been carefully laid out the night before, along with fodder for the hungry camels. Kids who have not been good during the year fear the worst: that the kings will fill their shoes with black coals instead of toys.

Roscón de Reyes is baked and eaten only at this time of year. It is a delicious sweetened bread, coated with sugar and candied fruits, and it always contains a surprise—either a coin or a small ceramic figurine, which is to bring luck for the year to the fortunate person who finds it in his piece of bread.

Makes 1 large bread ring

1 package dry yeast	½ teaspoon salt
¾ cup warm water	2 eggs
1 tablespoon orange flower water (often found in Italian food shops. If unavailable, substitute strong tea)	1 tablespoon brandy, preferably Spanish brandy, or Cognac
	½ cup milk, scalded and cooled
	5 cups unbleached, all-purpose flour
½ teaspoon grated lemon rind	Candied fruit slices (orange, lemon, etc.)
6 cloves	
¼ pound butter	1 egg, lightly beaten
1 tablespoon lard or vegetable shortening	1½ tablespoons sugar, preferably coarse, for sprinkling
½ cup sugar	

Dissolve the yeast in ¼ cup of the warm water. Simmer the remaining ½ cup of warm water with the orange flower water, lemon rind, and cloves for 10 minutes, covered. Cool. Discard the cloves.

Cream the butter, lard, the sugar, and the salt. Beat in the 2 eggs, then add the brandy, milk, the water-and-lemon mixture, and the softened yeast. Gradually mix in the flour with a wooden spoon until a soft and slightly sticky dough is obtained. Knead on a floured working surface, adding more flour as needed, about 5 minutes, until smooth and elastic. Place the dough in a large oiled bowl, turn to coat with the oil, cover with a towel, and place in a warm spot, such as an unlit oven, to double in size, about 2 hours. Punch down and knead again 5 minutes. Insert a good luck coin—perhaps a silver dollar or half-dollar —or some other appropriate object, such as a cute miniature ceramic animal.

Shape the dough into a large ring, pinching the ends to seal. Place on a lightly greased cookie sheet. Decorate with the fruit slices, pushing them slightly into the dough. Let the ring rise in a warm spot about 1 hour, or until double in size. Brush with the egg, which has been mixed with a teaspoon of water, sprinkle with sugar, and bake in a 350° F oven 35–40 minutes, or until a deep golden brown.

PAN QUEMADO

(Valencian Sweet Bread)

A SPECIALTY of Valencia, these pretty and delicious miniloaves are commonly served for breakfast or as afternoon snacks. The name "Burnt Bread" refers to the rich golden color of the bread and its meringue topping.

Makes 4 small loaves

1 package plus 1 teaspoon dry yeast	¾ cup salad oil
¼ cup warm water	Pinch salt
3 eggs, at room temperature	4 cups unbleached all-purpose flour
⅔ cup sugar	1 egg white
1 tablespoon butter, softened	2 teaspoons sugar for sprinkling

Soften the yeast in the warm water. Beat together the 3 eggs and the ⅔ cup of sugar with an electric beater until light colored and fluffy. Beat in the softened butter, softened yeast, oil, and salt. Stir in the flour a little at a time. Turn the dough out onto a floured work surface and knead 5 minutes. Place in an oiled bowl, turn to coat with the oil, cover with a towel, and let sit in a warm spot for 3 hours (the dough will not rise very much).

Shape the dough into 4 smooth round loaves. Place them on a greased cookie sheet and let them rise 4 hours more (again, they will not expand dramatically). Beat the egg white until stiff but not dry. Cover each loaf with a smooth cap of the egg white, being careful not to disturb the dough so that it does not deflate. Sprinkle each loaf with ½ teaspoon of the sugar. Bake 35 minutes at 300° F, or until the loaves are a deep golden color. Pan Quemado is delicious spread with butter.

TORTELES

(Sweet Filled Bread Rings)

A SPECIALTY of Cataluña and Mallorca, Torteles, or *"Tortells"* as they are called in the Catalán language, are a common offering in cafeterias all over Spain with midmorning coffee.

Makes three 5-inch rings

½ package (1½ teaspoons) dry yeast
½ cup warm water
2 cups unbleached, all-purpose flour
¼ teaspoon salt
1 egg

¼ cup granulated sugar
1½ tablespoons salad oil
Melted butter
1 egg, beaten
Powdered sugar for dusting

FILLING

2 ounces blanched almonds
¼ cup sugar
3 ounces boiled potato (about ¼ of
    a medium potato), peeled

¼ teaspoon grated lemon rind

To make the dough, in a small bowl dissolve the yeast in ¼ cup of the warm water. Add ½ cup of the flour, turn out onto a board, and knead lightly, adding flour if necessary, until a ball forms and the dough is smooth. Slit the top, wrap in a towel, and let sit in a warm place while preparing the rest of the dough.

In a bowl mix the remaining ¼ cup of warm water with the salt, the egg, and 2 tablespoons of the granulated sugar. Add the remaining 1½ cups of flour and turn out onto a working surface, kneading until all the flour is incorporated. Knead together the 2 balls of dough, gradually incorporating the remaining 2 tablespoons of granulated sugar and the oil, adding a little more flour if necessary. Knead until smooth and elastic. Wrap in a towel and let sit in a warm spot about 10 minutes while preparing the filling.

To make the filling, grind the almonds in a processor or blender until as fine as possible. With the motor running, gradually add the ¼ cup of sugar, then beat in the potato and lemon rind.

Divide the dough into 3 equal pieces. Grease a working surface and a rolling pin and roll 1 piece of the dough into a rectangle about 24 × 5 inches and about the thinness of a coin. Brush the dough with some melted butter. Place ⅓ of the filling in a thin cord along one long side of the dough, close to the edge. Roll up, jelly-roll fashion. Pinch to seal, then shape into a circle, sealing the ends together. Repeat for the other 2 pieces of dough.

Place the rings on a cookie sheet, seam side down, and place in a warm, draft-free spot for about 3 hours, or until double in size. Gently brush with the beaten egg, which has been mixed with a teaspoon of water, and dust with the powdered sugar. Bake at 400° F, on the middle-upper rack of the oven, about 10 minutes, or until lightly browned. Serve fresh from the oven or reheated.

SUIZOS

(Sugar-Topped Sweet Rolls)

SUIZOS are the most popular of all sweet rolls and are sure to be a part of any "continental" breakfast selection at a Spanish hotel.

Makes 12 rolls

½ package (1½ teaspoons) dry yeast
½ cup warm water
2 cups unbleached, all-purpose flour
¼ teaspoon salt
1 egg

¼ cup sugar
1½ tablespoons oil
12 teaspoons sugar for topping
1 egg, beaten, for brushing

Follow the instructions to make Torteles (preceding recipe), through the kneading process.

Divide the dough into 12 balls. Shape each into an oval and make a slash lengthwise down the center. Place on a cookie sheet and let rise in a warm spot for 3 hours, or until double in size. Fill the slash opening of each roll with 1 teaspoon of the sugar. Brush the roll tops (not the sugared part) with the beaten egg, which has been mixed with a teaspoon of water. Bake at 350° F 10–15 minutes, or until well browned. Serve fresh from the oven or reheated.

ENSAIMADAS

(Sweet Snail-Shaped Rolls)

ANOTHER typical breakfast and afternoon tea bread.

Makes 18 rolls

½ package (1½ teaspoons) dry yeast
½ cup warm water
2 cups unbleached, all-purpose flour
¼ teaspoon salt
1 egg

¼ cup granulated sugar
1½ tablespoons oil
Melted butter
Powdered sugar for dusting

Follow the instructions for Torteles (p. 333), through the kneading process.

Divide the dough into 9 equal pieces. Take 1 piece and roll between the palms to form a ½-inch-thick rope. Place on an unfloured counter. Roll to 30 inches long and about 2 inches wide. Brush with melted butter—but not quite to the edges. Roll tightly, jelly-roll fashion. Pinch to seal. Cut the roll into 2 equal pieces. Curl each piece loosely into a spiral or "snail" shape. Pinch to close the spiral. Repeat for the remaining 8 pieces. Place the snails on a cookie sheet, seam side down, with the ends of the spirals near the edges of the pan to prevent uncurling. Place in a warm spot for 3 hours, or until doubled in bulk.

Brush the rolls with water, then dust with powdered sugar. Bake in a 350° F oven until lightly browned, about 10 minutes. Cool slightly, then dust again with powdered sugar. Serve fresh from the oven or reheated.

TORTA DE CHICHARRONES

(Sweet Crackling Bread)

Makes 1 round loaf

½ recipe for Pan de Pueblo (p. 325)
1 cup finely diced salt pork or fatback
1 egg, lightly beaten

¼ cup sugar
¼ teaspoon lemon rind
1½ tablespoons sugar for sprinkling

Prepare the bread dough according to instructions, and let it rise 3 hours, or until doubled in bulk, as indicated. Slowly fry the fat pieces until golden and crunchy. Drain. Reserve 1 tablespoon of the fat.

After the bread dough has doubled, punch down and knead in the egg, fried pork, the ¼ cup of sugar, lemon rind, and the tablespoon of rendered fat, adding some flour until the dough is no longer sticky.

Sprinkle a cookie tray with flour. Place the ball of dough in the center and flatten with hands to a circle less than ½ inch thick. Sprinkle with the 1½ tablespoons sugar. Let rise 1 hour, or until about doubled in bulk. Bake at 350° F about 20 minutes, or until well browned.

HOJALDRE

(Puff Pastry)

PUFF pastry is extremely popular in Spanish cooking and is commonly used for desserts as well as with meat or fish fillings for main courses or appetizers. Its use in Spain goes back centuries, and Spanish food writers claim that it is a Spanish invention. I will remain apart from this controversy, except to note that I adore puff pastry no matter what the filling or country of origin.

Until I recently discovered Julia Child's new, easy, and foolproof method of making puff pastry, I had long ago concluded that I did not have the patience to prepare this delicate dough on a regular basis. Now I make it all the time and keep it on hand in the refrigerator or freezer. I suggest you do the same, for not only is it used in many recipes in this book, it has endless possibilities for other recipes you may find elsewhere or create yourself. This recipe is adapted from Julia Child's *Julia Child & Company*. The quantity is more than enough for any recipe in this book.

Makes 2 ¾ pounds

3 cups unbleached all-purpose flour	6½ sticks chilled unsalted butter
1 cup cake flour	1 cup iced water
1½ teaspoons salt	

Mix together the all-purpose and cake flours. Stir in the salt. Cut the sticks of butter in half lengthwise, then in half again, lengthwise. Now cut into ½-inch cubes and add to the flour. Rub the cubes of butter between your fingers to flatten them into flakes, combining them at the same time with the flour. Refrigerate the mixture 10 minutes (the butter must be kept firm throughout the process). Add the cold water and stir until the dough roughly holds together.

Turn the dough onto a lightly floured work surface. Pat into a rectangle about 18 inches long and 8 inches wide. Sprinkle the top of the dough with flour. With the aid of a knife, fold one side over the top, then fold over the other side, business-letter fashion. Lift the dough, flour the work surface again, flour the top of the dough, then roll out with a rolling pin to the previous size, making the folded sides the width and the open ends the length. (Remember, all this must be done rapidly — if the butter softens, refrigerate briefly.) Fold up a second time in the same manner, roll out again, then repeat 2 more times, flouring surfaces as necessary and ending with the dough folded. Wrap in plastic wrap. Refrigerate 40 minutes. Roll and fold twice more, and the dough is ready to use or to store for future use in the refrigerator or freezer.

MASA DE EMPANADILLA

(Dough for Meat or Fish Turnovers)

Dough for 40 turnovers

1 cup water
¼ teaspoon salt
3 tablespoons butter
3 tablespoons salad oil

2½ cups unbleached,
   all-purpose flour
1 egg

In a saucepan, heat the water, salt, butter, and oil over a medium flame until the butter is melted. Remove from the heat. Add the flour all at once and stir until completely incorporated. Beat in the egg with a wooden spoon until the dough is smooth. Turn the dough onto a floured work surface and knead briefly, adding flour if necessary, until the dough is smooth and elastic and no longer sticky. Cover and let sit 30 minutes. Roll the dough very thin and cut into 3-inch circles.

MASA DE EMPANADA (1)

(Dough for Meat or Fish Pie)

*Dough for 11-inch round pie
or 10 × 15-inch rectangular pie*

1 package dry yeast
¼ cup warm water
3 tablespoons lard or
    vegetable shortening
3½ cups unbleached,
    all-purpose flour

1½ teaspoons salt
2 eggs, lightly beaten
½ cup warm milk

Soften the yeast in the warm water. Melt the lard and cool slightly. In a large bowl, combine the flour and the salt. Add the eggs, melted lard, the yeast mixture, and the warm milk. Turn the dough out onto a floured work surface and knead briefly, 2 or 3 minutes, adding flour as necessary, until the dough is smooth and elastic. Place the dough in a large oiled bowl, turning to coat with the oil. Cover the bowl with a towel and place in a warm spot for 1½ hours. Knead the dough another 2 or 3 minutes, then return to the bowl, cover, and let rise 1 hour more. Continue as directed in the Empanada recipes.

MASA DE EMPANADA (2)

(Dough for Meat or Fish Pie)

Dough for 10 × 15-inch pie

2 medium onions, thinly sliced
2 slices bacon, cut in 1-inch pieces
3 cloves garlic, minced
1 cup salad oil
5⅓ cups unbleached,
    all-purpose flour

2 teaspoons dry yeast
1½ teaspoons salt
1½ cups warm water

Slowly sauté the onion, bacon, and garlic in the oil until the onion is wilted. Strain the oil, reserving the oil and, separately, the onion, bacon, and garlic.

In a large bowl, mix the flour and the dry yeast. Dissolve the salt in the warm water and add the water to the flour. Turn the dough onto a floured surface. Gradually incorporate ½ cup of the reserved oil, kneading in about 2 tablespoons at a time and adding more flour as necessary. Save the remaining reserved oil to use in the preparation of the filling.

Place the dough in a large oiled bowl, turning to coat. Cover and let sit in a warm spot (inside a kitchen cabinet is good) for 12 hours, or overnight. Continue as directed in the Empanada recipes.

MASA DE EMPANADA (3)

(Dough for Sardine Pie)

Dough for 8-inch pie

⅔ cup cornmeal
1⅓ cups unbleached,
    all-purpose flour
1 teaspoon salt
7 tablespoons lard or
    vegetable shortening

1 small egg (about 3 tablespoons),
    lightly beaten
5 tablespoons water

Mix the cornmeal, flour, and salt together in a bowl. Cut in the lard by rubbing it between your fingers into the flour. When it is well distributed, stir in the egg and water and form into a ball. Knead until smooth. Let the dough rest, covered, several hours before using.

Chapter 13

POSTRES

(Desserts)

NOWHERE in Spanish cuisine is the Moorish influence more pronounced than in dessert making; almonds, egg yolks, and honey have been the mainstays of most Spanish confections since the Arabs left their culinary and cultural marks on Spain many centuries ago. After the Moors were expelled in 1492, the dessert tradition was carried on by nuns confined to convents, who developed their own recipes and sold their sweets at holiday time to help support their religious institutions. To this day these convent recipes are jealously guarded secrets, and the nuns' creations may still be purchased at certain convents in Spain. Many famous Spanish sweets, especially *yemas*—egg yolk candies—still bear the names of their religious orders. *Yemas de Santa Teresa* come from the Carmelite nuns of Ávila; *Yemas de San Leandro*, from the San Leandro order in Sevilla; *Yemas de San Pablo*, from Cáceres in Extremadura; and *Yemas de Segovia*, from the nuns of the city of Segovia.

The discovery of the New World brought a completely new taste to the art of dessert making and proved a sensation in Europe: chocolate. One oft-told story is that the wife of Louis XIV of France, the Spanish Infanta María Teresa, had a dreadful complexion and black teeth pocked with cavities due to her excessive fondness for chocolate, which was still relatively unknown in seventeenth-century France, but soon to become the favorite of the Western world. In Spain, however, chocolate never reached its full potential in dessert making and was used, and continues to be used today, mainly in drinks and in candies, but rarely in cakes or pastries.

In spite of María Teresa's excesses, Spaniards never developed a passion for sweets. It is therefore understandable that restaurants tend to have very simple dessert menus. Fruit and cheese are always offered, as well as flan and often ice cream; more elaborate desserts only occasionally make an appearance. Excellent pastries do, of course, exist, and in great variety—the selection at a fine *pastelería* is truly overwhelming—but are reserved for other occasions, such as between-meal snacks, as a part of afternoon teas, or as Sunday treats. Children are often found after school munching on hero bread containing chunks of chocolate, and pastry shops are packed on Sundays with customers dressed in their holiday finest, purchasing delectable miniature pastries to go calling on weekends.

Not only are certain desserts marked for special times of day or for particular days of the week, but many, besides, are associated with specific religious holidays. On All Saints Day, Huesos de Santo, "Bones of the Saint," and Buñuelos de Viento, light and airy fritters, make their appearance; at Christmas, almond-rich *turrón* and marzipan candies are presented at the end of the holiday meal. Three Kings Day (Epiphany), on January 6, brings Roscón de Reyes, a holiday bread ring. Buñuelos de Cuaresma, similar to Buñuelos de Viento, announce the Lenten season. Torrijas, sugar-coated fried bread, and Tarta Pasiega, a kind of cheesecake, are commonly found at Easter. The May 16 festival for Madrid's patron saint, San Isidro, brings out the Buñuelos de San Isidro, cream-filled puffs, and on August 12, Rosquillas de Santa Clara, iced doughnuts, suddenly fill the pastry shops for Saint Clara's Day. Such sweets vanish as rapidly as they appear and will rarely be found again, until the following year.

When considering Spanish desserts, certain characteristics come to mind. Ground almonds are used in abundance and often replace flour in cake baking. Baking powder is rarely used; beaten egg whites are invariably the leavening agent in cakes. Milk desserts are often spiced with cinnamon and lemon peel rather than vanilla, and anisette liqueur is frequently added. Anise seeds are used to flavor fried pastries, which are commonly coated with honey, the sweetener preferred to sugar. Fried desserts are perhaps the most popular sweets in Spain, and although they consist of little more than flour and water, they are as irresistible as pretzels or potato chips.

More than any other factor, the heavy use of egg yolks characterizes Spanish dessert making, especially in the preparation of custards and candies. Since Spaniards are not a wasteful people, the question always arises: what happens to all those leftover egg whites? There are only a handful of desserts that depend upon egg whites—meringues and the iced dessert Leche Merengada, for example—so they can hardly account for the dozens of egg whites left over after preparing such rich desserts as *yemas* or Tocino del Cielo. The explanation that makes most sense to me is that egg whites have traditionally been in demand for wine making. Although the practice is dying, there are still many wine companies in Rioja and Jerez de la Frontera that use the time-honored process of clarifying wines by beating in egg whites (in the same way that they are beaten into consommé) to carry away with them any particles that can make the wine (or the soup) cloudy. Think of the thousands of egg whites needed in wine making—at R. López de Heredia wineries we were informed that eight egg whites go into each barrel of Reserva wine. This must have led years ago to some creativity in the kitchen and the invention of countless recipes to utilize the egg yolk.

Until now your only familiarity with Spanish desserts may have been flan, and although enjoying this world-famous custard is a delightful and refreshing way to end a meal, this chapter, I trust, will provide many other exciting and unusual alternatives.

FRIED DESSERTS AND PUFF PASTRY

CHURROS

(Breakfast Fritters)

AT EVERY Spanish festival or carnival, one is sure to find a huge cauldron of bubbling oil where Churros are quickly fried, shaped into loops, and threaded onto reeds that are then knotted for easy carrying. They are meant to be purchased immediately after frying, usually by the dozens, and are munched by visitors as they wander about taking in the sights.

Churros are nothing more than a fried batter of flour and water, but they are essential to a Spanish breakfast, dipped either in sugar or in a cup of coffee or thick hot chocolate (p. 397). If one is out on an all-night binge—a *juerga*, as it is called—it is the custom to end the evening by eating Churros and hot chocolate at a *churrería*, or *churro* store, which opens by dawn.

While recognizing the nutritional limitations of Churros, I adore them and would not think of eating anything else for breakfast in Spain. Although by custom they are available only in the morning hours and at teatime, there is really no reason they can't be eaten for dessert as well. Just remember that Churros do not keep and must be eaten immediately.

Makes 30 fritters

2 cups water
1 tablespoon salad oil
¼ teaspoon salt

2 cups flour
Oil for frying
Granulated sugar for dipping

Place the water, oil, and salt in a saucepan and bring to a boil. Add the flour all at once, reduce the heat, and stir vigorously with a wooden spoon until a ball forms. Cool slightly. Using a Churro maker (available in some Spanish specialty shops) or otherwise a pastry bag or cake decorator fitted with a ⅜-inch fluted tube (#105 is good), press the dough out into strips 4 inches long (the strips may also be shaped into loops). The fluted shape is essential. Otherwise the pastries will turn out hard and doughy. Heat the frying oil, at least ½ inch deep, in a skillet until it is very hot. Reduce the heat to medium and fry the Churros, turning once, until they barely begin to color. Do not fry more than 3 or 4 at a time so that you can keep a watchful eye to prevent overcooking. Drain. Serve warm and dip in sugar.

PESTIÑOS AL ANÍS

(Anise-Flavored Fried Pastries)

PREPARE SEVERAL HOURS IN ADVANCE.

"Pestiño" originally referred to a room where bread or pastries were baked. Today the word applies to these delicious anise-flavored pastries, which puff when fried and are then dipped in honey and dusted with powdered sugar. Although the yield of seventy may seem excessive, it is impossible to eat only one, and I guarantee that they will disappear in the blink of an eye.

Makes 70–80 pastries

½ cup salad oil
Peel of ½ lemon
2 tablespoons anise seeds
½ cup dry white wine

2 cups flour
Oil for frying
1 cup honey (12-ounce jar)
Powdered sugar for dusting

Place the oil in a small frying pan with the lemon peel and heat over a high flame until the peel turns black. Remove the pan from the flame and discard the peel. Cool slightly, then add the anise seeds. Cool the oil completely.

Strain the oil into a bowl, discarding the anise seeds. Mix in the wine and flour. Knead lightly into a smooth ball. Wrap the dough and let it sit for 30 minutes.

Roll out the dough on a lightly floured board to the thinness of a coin. Cut into 2 × 1-inch rectangular pieces. Let the pieces sit 30 minutes.

In a saucepan, mix the honey with 4 tablespoons water. Bring to a boil, then simmer 15 minutes while frying the pastries. Heat the oil, at least ½ inch deep, in a skillet to the smoking point. Reduce the heat to medium. Add as many dough pieces as will comfortably fit and fry until they are lightly browned, turning once. (They will puff.) Drain on paper towels.

Dip the Pestiños into the honey and place them on a wire cooling rack so that the excess honey may drip off. Arrange them attractively in an overlapping "starburst" design on a round serving tray and dust with powdered sugar. Pestiños stay crisp for many days and in my opinion are better the following day. They should be prepared, in any case, several hours before serving so that the honey has a chance to penetrate the crisp pastry.

BORRACHUELOS

(Fried Pastries with Anise and Sesame Seeds)

THESE pastries are similar to Pestiños, but larger, more moist, and seasoned with sesame seeds.

Makes 60 pastries

⅔ cup salad oil
Peel of ¼ orange
2 teaspoons sesame seeds
1 teaspoon anise seeds
⅓ cup sweet white wine
⅓ cup dry white wine

3 tablespoons orange juice
2¾ cups flour
Oil for frying
1 cup honey (12-ounce jar)
4 tablespoons water
Powdered sugar for dusting

Heat the ⅔ cup of oil with the orange peel until the peel turns black. Remove from the flame, discard the peel, and cool the oil. Pour the oil into a bowl and add the sesame seeds, anise seeds, sweet and dry wines, and the orange juice.

Gradually add the flour. Turn the dough out onto a working surface. Knead lightly, adding flour if necessary. Wrap and let rest 30 minutes.

Take ¾-inch balls of dough and roll out into ovals about 4 × 2 inches. Heat the frying oil, at least ½ inch deep, until it is very hot. Reduce the heat to medium and fry the pastries until lightly browned. Drain.

Heat the honey and water in a saucepan. Simmer 5 minutes. Dip the pastries in the honey and let drain on wire cooling racks. Roll in powdered sugar and arrange on a platter. They will keep for several days.

TORRIJAS

(Sugar-Coated Fried Bread)

START PREPARATION TWO HOURS IN ADVANCE.

WHO but the Spanish could take a simple slice of bread and transform it into the country's most beloved dessert? Spaniards wax ecstatic over Torrijas, in this their simplest form or in their more elaborate guise: the Tostadas of the following recipe.

Serves 4

8 slices day-old long loaf bread, ¾ inch thick. The bread should not be airy (Pan de Pueblo, p. 325, is ideal)
1 cup milk
3 tablespoons sugar

1 cinnamon stick
Peel of ½ lemon
Oil for frying
2 eggs, lightly beaten
Granulated sugar for dusting
Cinnamon for dusting

Place the bread in a single layer in a deep dish. In a saucepan, bring to a boil the milk, sugar, cinnamon stick, and lemon peel. Simmer 10 minutes. Discard the cinnamon and lemon peel and pour the milk evenly over the bread slices. Let sit 2 minutes, then transfer the bread slices to a dry dish. Let them sit at least 2 hours to dry.

Heat the oil, at least ½ inch deep, in a skillet. Dip the bread slices in the beaten egg and fry in the oil, turning once, until golden. Drain well. Roll in sugar, sprinkle with cinnamon, and serve immediately.

TOSTADAS

(Fried Bread and Honey)

A DELICIOUS variation of the preceding Torrijas.

Serves 4

½ cup milk
⅓ cup honey
8 slices day-old long loaf bread, ¾
    inch thick (Pan de Pueblo,
    p. 325, works very well)

Oil for frying
1 egg, beaten

SYRUP

½ cup sugar
½ cup water

¼ cup white wine
Peel of ½ lemon

Heat the milk to lukewarm. Stir in the honey, pour into a deep dish, then dip the bread slices in this mixture, turning several times to coat well. Place the bread on a platter and let it sit 1 hour.

To make the syrup, combine all syrup ingredients in a saucepan, bring to a boil, then simmer 10 minutes. Keep warm until ready to use.

In a skillet, heat the oil, at least ½ inch deep, until it is very hot. Reduce to medium. Dip the bread slices in the beaten egg, then fry until golden on both sides. Drain. Place on a deep dish and pour on the syrup. Eat while still warm.

Tostadas are still good 1 or 2 days later. To reheat, place the bread and its syrup in a 350° F oven until heated and crisp.

BUÑUELOS DE VIENTO

(Fritters)

"PUFFS OF WIND"—a perfect name for these tiny, light-as-air doughnuts. They are typically eaten on All Saints Day, November 1, a date of great importance on the Spanish calendar (see p. 389).

Makes about 50 puffs

1 cup water
6 tablespoons butter, cut in pieces

¼ teaspoon salt
2 teaspoons granulated sugar

1 cup flour
¼ teaspoon lemon rind (optional)
4 eggs

Oil for frying
Powdered sugar for dusting

Heat the water, butter, salt, and granulated sugar slowly in a saucepan until the butter has melted and the water comes to a boil. Add the flour all at once. Lower the heat, add the optional lemon rind, and stir with a wooden spoon until a ball forms. Cook, flattening and turning the dough with a wooden spoon for 2 minutes. Remove from the flame and cool a minute or so. Beat in the eggs 1 at a time. After each addition the dough will become slippery but will gradually smooth out. (This is much more easily done in a processor — before adding the eggs, transfer the dough to the bowl of a processor. Mix 15 seconds. Add the eggs all at once and process 30 seconds more.)

Drop the dough by the teaspoon into hot oil at least 1 inch deep. Fry fairly slowly, turning the doughnuts occasionally until they are completely puffed and hollow within (they will be about twice their original size). Drain. Cool, then dust with powdered sugar. Eat the same day.

BUÑUELOS DE SAN ISIDRO

(Cream-Filled Fritters)

SAN ISIDRO is the patron saint of Madrid, and the May holiday is greeted by a full week of bullfight activity. These cream-filled puffs are also traditional during that week and can commonly be found in all the local bakeries.

To make Buñuelos de San Isidro, prepare Buñuelos de Viento (preceding recipe). Before sprinkling with powdered sugar, cut open a flap in the top of each puff. Fill with custard (p. 366). Close the flap, then sprinkle with powdered sugar. The custard may also be injected if you have a device for that purpose known as a Bismarck filler.

ROSQUILLAS RIOJANAS

(Miniature Anise-Flavored Doughnuts)

START PREPARATION TWO HOURS IN ADVANCE.

BEFORE the days of measuring cups and spoons (which are still not widely used in Spain), any recipe calling for eggs used the egg half shells to measure other ingredients in the dish, as in this old family recipe provided by my mother-in-law. I discovered that a half egg shell of a medium–large egg is almost exactly 2 tablespoons, but it is far more fun to use the egg-shell system than to use measuring spoons.

Makes 40 small doughnuts

6 half egg shells of salad oil (¾ cup)
1½ teaspoons anise seeds
1 egg
4 tablespoons granulated sugar
6 half egg shells of dry white wine
    (¾ cup)

2½ cups flour
Oil for frying
Powdered sugar for dusting

Heat the oil with the anise seeds in a small skillet until the seeds are brown. Cool the oil, then strain, discarding the anise. In a bowl, beat the egg until light and frothy. Gradually add the sugar, then the cooled oil and the wine. Stir in the flour gradually to make a dough that can be worked with the hands but is slightly sticky. Cover the bowl with foil and let the dough rest for 2 hours.

With floured hands, roll the dough into ½ × 4-inch ropes. Shape into rings, pressing the ends together so they are firmly joined. Heat the frying oil, at least 1 inch deep, to the smoking point in a skillet. Lower the heat to medium-high and fry the doughnuts, turning 2 or 3 times during frying. The doughnuts should brown slowly and be removed when golden. Drain and cool the doughnuts, then roll in sifted powdered sugar. Arrange on a serving dish and sift additional powdered sugar over them (some cinnamon may also be dusted on).

BREVAS DE SORIA

(Custard-Filled Small Doughnuts)

IT IS sound policy in Spain to follow the crowds and eat where everyone seems to be. This theory led us for breakfast in Soria, the beloved city of the famous poet Antonio Machado, to a small corner cafeteria, where all Soria seemed to be eating these delicious doughnuts with a cup of coffee.

Makes about 30 small doughnuts

1 package dry yeast
¼ cup warm water
3½ cups flour
½ teaspoon salt

½ cup sugar
1 egg, lightly beaten
1 cup warm milk
2 tablespoons butter, melted

½ recipe for Custard Filling   Oil for frying
   (following recipe)   Granulated sugar for dusting

Dissolve the yeast in the warm water. Mix together in a bowl the flour, salt, and the ½ cup of sugar. Add the egg, then stir in the milk, butter, and the yeast mixture. Turn onto a working surface and knead a minute or so, just until the dough is smooth and no longer sticky, adding more flour as necessary. Place in a greased bowl, cover with a towel, and leave in a warm spot until doubled in bulk, about 1½ hours.

Meanwhile, prepare the custard according to instructions, omitting the lemon peel and adding ¼ teaspoon of vanilla after the custard has cooked. Cool, stirring occasionally.

Punch down the dough, divide and shape into 2 × 1-inch ovals. Let the pieces sit 1 hour more on a cookie tray in a warm spot. In a skillet, heat the oil, at least ½ inch deep, until it is very hot. Lower the heat to medium and fry several doughnuts at a time, turning frequently, until golden and well puffed. Drain and cool. Roll in sugar. Slit the doughnuts lengthwise with a sharp knife, as for a baked potato, and fill each doughnut with about 1 teaspoon of custard. These doughnuts are best when eaten soon after cooking.

BARTOLILLOS

(Custard-Filled Fried Pastries)

BARTOLILLOS are a specialty of Madrid.

Makes 15–20 pastries

½ cup salad oil   Pinch salt
Peel of ½ lemon   Oil for frying
½ cup white wine   Powdered sugar for dusting
2 cups flour   Cinnamon for dusting

CUSTARD FILLING

2 cups milk   ½ cup sugar
Peel of ½ lemon   ½ cup flour
5 egg yolks   1 tablespoon butter

To make the dough, place the ½ cup of oil in a small frying pan with the lemon peel and heat over a high flame until the peel turns black. Discard the peel and cool the oil. Transfer the oil to a bowl and add the wine, flour, and salt. Work into a ball with your hands, kneading lightly. Wrap up the dough and let it sit 30 minutes.

Meanwhile, prepare the custard. Heat the milk with the lemon peel to the boiling point. Reduce the heat and simmer 10 minutes. Discard the lemon peel. Place the egg yolks in a saucepan and gradually stir in the sugar. Beat with a wire whisk until the yolks are pale yellow. Beat in the flour and gradually add the hot milk. Cook over moderate heat, stirring constantly, until thickened and smooth and no flour taste remains. Remove from the heat and stir in the butter. Cool, stirring occasionally.

While the custard is cooling, roll out the dough on a floured working surface to the thinness of a nickel. Cut into triangles 2 × 3 × 3 inches. Let the pieces sit another 30 minutes.

Place about 1 teaspoon of custard down the middle of half of the triangles. Cover with the remaining triangles and seal the edges well with a fork. Heat the oil, at least ½ inch deep, and fry the triangles over moderate heat until golden. Drain and dust with powdered sugar and cinnamon.

BANDA DE ALMENDRA

(Almond and Marmalade Puff Pastry Strips)

IF YOU have puff pastry on hand, this is an extremely quick and very elegant dessert.

Makes 12 small pastries

½ pound puff pastry, homemade (p. 336) or frozen
¾ cup Quince Marmalade (p. 380), Candied Squash (p. 381) or

other fruit preserves, such as apricot
⅓ cup sliced almonds
Powdered sugar for dusting

Prepare the puff pastry and marmalade according to instructions. Roll the dough out to ⅛ inch. Cut into 4 × 1½-inch strips. Bake on a cookie tray in a 425° F oven on the upper rack, removing after 7 minutes. Spread about 1 tablespoon of preserves on each strip. Return to the oven for about 5 minutes more, until the pastries are golden. Remove and cool slightly. Arrange the almonds in overlapping rows along the length of the pastry. When cool, dust with powdered sugar.

CANUTILLOS

(Custard Horns)

CUSTARD HORNS are specialties of Navarra, where they are often served warm sprinkled with cinnamon and powdered sugar.

Makes about 15 pastries

10 ounces puff pastry, homemade
    (p. 336) or frozen
Custard Filling (p. 366), at
    room temperature

Egg yolk for sealing
Powdered sugar for dusting
Cinnamon for dusting

Prepare the puff pastry and custard according to instructions. Roll the puff pastry dough to the thinness of a dime. Cut into ½-inch-wide strips and wrap, in slightly overlapping circles, around 4-inch-long baking horns. If more than 1 strip is needed for each horn, be sure to seal the seams well with egg yolk. Place on a cookie tray, seam side down. Bake at 425° F on the upper rack until the horns are golden, about 5 minutes. Cool slightly. Remove the forms.

    Fill the horns with the custard, then return them to a 350° F oven for about 5 minutes, or until the custard has heated. Dust with powdered sugar and cinnamon and serve warm.

CASADIELLES

(Walnut-Filled Turnovers)

A POPULAR sweet in northern Asturias.

Makes 20 turnovers

Puff pastry, frozen or preferably
    homemade (p. 336)
1 cup coarsely ground walnuts
½ cup sugar
¼ teaspoon cinnamon

1 tablespoon anisette liqueur
1 tablespoon butter, melted
    and cooled
1 egg, lightly beaten, for sealing
Granulated sugar for dusting

Prepare the puff pastry according to instructions. Mix together the nuts, sugar, and cinnamon. Stir in the anisette and butter.

Roll the puff pastry to ⅛ inch. Cut into 4-inch circles. Fill each circle with 3 teaspoons of the walnut mixture. Brush the edges with the beaten egg, fold the circles in half, and press with a fork to seal well. Bake in a 450° F oven on the upper rack for about 10 minutes, or until the turnovers are golden. Dust with sugar. Serve warm or at room temperature.

PASTELES DE HIGO

(Fig and Candied Squash Pastries)

DRIED figs and candied squash form the unusual pastry filling for this delightful invention of Simón Tomás, of the Sol-Ric restaurant in Tarragona (more on Sol-Ric and Tarragona on pp. 211).

Makes 12 pastries

Puff Pastry (p. 336)
12 tablespoons Candied
    Squash (p. 381)
12 dried figs, hard stems removed,
    lightly mashed

Egg yolk for sealing
Powdered sugar for dusting
Cinnamon for dusting

Prepare the puff pastry and candied squash according to instructions. Roll out the puff pastry to ⅛-inch thickness and cut into 4 × 4 × 6-inch triangles. On half of the triangles place a tablespoon of the candied squash. Place a mashed fig in the center. Cover with the remaining triangles, sealing the edges with a little egg yolk and crimping with a fork. Bake at 425° F on the upper rack of the oven for 10–15 minutes, or until golden. Cool slightly, dust with powdered sugar and cinnamon, and serve warm.

TECLA DE YEMA

(Candied Egg Yolk Pastries)

Makes 9–10 pastries

¾ pound puff pastry, homemade
    (p. 336) or frozen

Candied Egg Yolks (p. 386)

Prepare the puff pastry and candied egg yolks according to instructions. Roll the puff pastry to ⅛-inch thickness and cut into 3½ × 1½-inch rectangles.

Spread on a heaping teaspoon of filling, not reaching to the edges. Cover with a second rectangle and seal the edges by crimping with a fork. Bake on the upper rack of the oven at 450° F for 10–15 minutes, or until golden.

MILK AND CUSTARD
AND OTHER EGG DESSERTS

ARROZ CON LECHE A LA ASTURIANA

(Rice Pudding, Asturian Style)

ASTURIAS claims to be the home of rice pudding, and while the assertion is doubtful, there is no question that the best rice pudding in Spain is made here. Its secret lies in the enormous quantity of milk used, which boils down over a three-hour period to form a rich and creamy pudding. Brandy and anisette give extra flavor, and the burnt sugar topping adds a special crunch. I thank Mr. Gil Lus of the Casa Fermín restaurant in Oviedo for this excellent recipe.

Serves 6

12 cups milk
2 cinnamon sticks
Peel of ½ lemon
Pinch salt
⅔ cup short-grain rice (do not
    substitute long-grain)
    (see p. 175)

1¼ cups sugar
1 tablespoon anisette liqueur
1 tablespoon brandy, preferably
        Spanish brandy, or Cognac
2 tablespoons butter

TOPPING

Cinnamon

6 tablespoons sugar

Bring the milk to a boil with the cinnamon sticks, lemon peel, and salt. Lower the heat, add the rice, and simmer *very* slowly, uncovered, stirring frequently and vigorously with a wooden spoon during the first few minutes to prevent the rice grains from sticking together. It will take about 3 hours for the rice to cook and the milk to reduce. During that time the pudding should be stirred every 10 minutes or so. Add the sugar, anisette, and brandy and cook, stirring,

10 minutes more. The pudding should be about the consistency of soft custard. If it has not thickened sufficiently, boil over high heat briefly, stirring constantly, until it reaches that point. Add the butter and stir until melted. Cool to room temperature, stirring occasionally.

Divide the pudding into 6 wide and shallow (about 5 inches across) dessert dishes (earthenware is traditionally used). Leave at room temperature. Right before serving, sprinkle each with first the cinnamon, then 1 tablespoon of the sugar. To caramelize the sugar, either heat a salamander used for that purpose and apply it to the surface of the custard or, if such a tool is unavailable, heat a saucepan (the width of the dessert dish) containing 2 tablespoons of oil (to prevent scorching) until the pan is very hot. Rest the bottom of the pan over the custard for a second until the sugar caramelizes. Wipe the bottom of the pan and reheat between applications. Serve immediately (the sugar will stay hard only for a short time) at room temperature. The pudding is best when eaten the same day. Refrigerate if kept overnight.

PUDIN DE MANZANA CON NATILLAS

(Apple Pudding with Custard Sauce)

THIS delicious dessert is a specialty at Casa Cámara in Pasajes de San Juan, a quaint seaside village right outside the bustling port area of San Sebastián. The restaurant is housed in a centuries-old structure that has been a restaurant for 125 years and was founded by the present owner's great-grandfather, whose portrait hangs in the attractive dining room that overlooks the sea. The house has been lovingly and painstakingly restored, as we witnessed when taken on a tour by the proud owner.

Save this dessert for a day when you have other chores in the kitchen—the apples cook for three hours and must be stirred occasionally.

Serves 6

2½ pounds apples, peeled and cored   ¼ teaspoon lemon rind
5 tablespoons sugar   ¼ teaspoon cinnamon
4 tablespoons sweet butter   Pinch salt
1 teaspoon lemon juice   2 eggs, lightly beaten

CARAMELIZED SUGAR

8 tablespoons sugar   4 teaspoons water

CUSTARD

2 eggs, slightly beaten   2 cups hot milk
¼ cup sugar   ½ teaspoon vanilla
⅛ teaspoon salt

Coarsely grate the apples and place them in a heavy saucepan with the sugar, butter, lemon juice, lemon rind, cinnamon, and salt. Cook very slowly, covered, about 3 hours, stirring occasionally. Uncover and turn up the flame for 2 or 3 minutes to evaporate any remaining liquid, stirring constantly. Cool slightly, then mix in the eggs.

Grease 6 custard cups. To caramelize the sugar, in a small, heavy skillet, combine the sugar and water and cook over a medium-high flame, stirring constantly, until the sugar is lightly caramelized. Pour into the custard cups. Add the apple mixture to the custard cups and place the cups in a pan of hot water. Bake at 350° F for 1½ hours. Remove the cups from the water and cool to room temperature.

To make the custard, combine with a wire whisk the eggs, sugar, and salt in a heavy saucepan. Gradually stir in the hot milk. Cook the mixture, stirring constantly, over hot but not boiling water until the custard coats a spoon. Add the vanilla and cool, stirring occasionally.

To serve, loosen the sides of the pudding with a knife and turn out onto dessert dishes. Spoon on the custard. This dessert is best when served at room temperature.

LECHE FRITA

(Fried Custard Squares)

"FRIED MILK," a custard that is crunchy on the outside and creamy within, is a typical Spanish dessert found all over the country but said to be from the

Basque country. With one teaspoon of anisette liqueur poured over each square and ignited, Leche Frita al Anís is created.

Makes sixteen 2-inch squares

2 cups milk	1 egg, beaten
Peel of ½ lemon	Bread crumbs
1 cinnamon stick	Oil for frying
3 egg yolks	Powdered sugar for dusting
3 tablespoons granulated sugar	Cinnamon for dusting
5 tablespoons cornstarch	

Bring the milk with the lemon peel and the cinnamon stick to a boil. Lower the heat and simmer 10 minutes.

In a saucepan, beat the egg yolks with a wire whisk until they are lemon colored. Beat in the granulated sugar, then the cornstarch. Stir in a few tablespoons of the hot milk, then gradually stir in the rest. Cook over moderate heat, stirring constantly, until thickened and smooth. Remove at the first sign of a boil. Discard the lemon peel and cinnamon stick. Give the custard a vigorous stir to release steam, then pour into a greased 8-inch square pan. Let cool, undisturbed, then refrigerate until the custard becomes hard.

Cut the custard into 2-inch squares, dip them in the beaten egg, then coat with bread crumbs. Fry in very hot oil, at least ½ inch deep. Drain, dust with a mixture of powdered sugar and cinnamon, and serve immediately. Leche Frita can be kept warm if necessary for about 30 minutes in a 200° F oven.

CREMA CATALANA

(Catalán Custard)

CREMA CATALANA, a custard with a candied sugar coating, is often available in restaurants, especially in the region around Barcelona. It is a great favorite of mine.

Serves 4

2 cups milk	7 tablespoons sugar
Peel of ½ lemon	1½ tablespoons cornstarch
1 cinnamon stick	Ground nutmeg (optional)
4 egg yolks	

Bring the milk to a boil with the lemon peel and cinnamon stick. Simmer 10 minutes, then discard the lemon peel and cinnamon. With a wire whisk, beat the egg yolks and 3 tablespoons of the sugar until lemon colored. Beat in the cornstarch. Stir in a few tablespoons of the hot milk, then add the egg yolk mixture to the rest of the milk. Cook over moderate heat, stirring constantly, for about 5 minutes, or until thickened and smooth and no cornstarch taste remains. Remove at the first sign of a boil. Give a vigorous stir to release steam, and pour the custard into 4 dessert dishes, which should be wide and shallow (about 5 inches across). Typically, they are earthenware. Cool undisturbed, then refrigerate.

Before serving, sprinkle 1 tablespoon of sugar (and a dash of nutmeg, optional) evenly over each custard. To caramelize the sugar, use a hot metal "branding iron" (a salamander), about the width of the dessert dish. If this is unavailable, I have gotten good results by heating a saucepan (place a few tablespoons of oil inside to prevent scorching), the width of the custard dishes, until very hot. Place the bottom of the pan on the custard and hold it there briefly until the sugar is brown and crunchy. Wipe off the bottom of the pan, reheat, and repeat for the other dishes. Serve immediately — the sugar will stay hard for only about 30 minutes.

NATILLAS CON NUECES

(Soft Custard with Walnuts)

A SIMPLE but very satisfying dessert.

Serves 4

2 cups milk	3 tablespoons sugar
Peel of ½ lemon	⅛ teaspoon salt
4 egg yolks	2 ounces walnut pieces

Bring the milk with the lemon peel to a boil. Reduce the heat and simmer 10 minutes. Discard the lemon peel. Beat the egg yolks in the top of a double boiler with the sugar and salt until the yolks turn pale yellow. Gradually stir in the milk. Cook in the double boiler until the custard is thickened, stirring constantly. Divide into 4 dessert dishes, preferably wide, shallow earthenware dishes. Cool, then chill. Before serving, sprinkle with walnut pieces.

FLAN DEL GRAN FLANERO

(Caramel Custard)

Iberia, James A. Michener's exceptionally perceptive study of Spain and its people, describes a man known in Madrid circles as "El Gran Flanero" – the Great Flan Maker. The story goes that each morning he cooks up a prodigious amount of flan, then sits back to await the arrival of a procession of Madrid society notables—from bullfighters to businessmen—who would not dream of making any crucial decisions without first eating one of the maestro's "good luck" flans. This recipe, which is adapted from the Gran Flanero, produces an exceptionally rich and smooth custard.

Serves 6

3 whole eggs
3 egg yolks
¼ teaspoon grated lemon rind

6 tablespoons sugar
2½ cups milk

CARAMELIZED SUGAR

10 tablespoons sugar

5 teaspoons water

To make the caramelized sugar, heat the sugar and water in a small skillet over a medium-high flame, stirring constantly, until the sugar has turned a golden color. Remove from the heat immediately and pour into 6 ovenproof custard cups.

To make the custard, beat together lightly with a wire whisk the whole eggs and the yolks. Add the lemon rind, sugar, and milk. Pour into the caramelized cups and place the cups in a pan of hot water. Cook on top of the stove over a medium flame for 1 hour. Transfer to a 350° F oven and continue cooking 25 minutes, or until a knife inserted in the custard comes out clean. Remove the cups from the water and cool, then refrigerate. To serve, loosen the sides of the custard with a knife and invert onto dessert dishes.

TOCINO DEL CIELO

(Rich Caramel Custard)

TOCINO DEL CIELO may taste a bit like flan, but it is missing one of flan's main ingredients—milk. It is very rich, but is served in small portions, and, in spite of the abundance of egg yolk, is a very refreshing and seemingly light dessert. Its name poetically flows from the tongue in Spanish, but does not fare so well in translation: "Fat from Heaven" certainly does a disservice to this lovely custard.

It is said that Tocino del Cielo was invented by convent nuns in southern Spain, who used in its preparation the egg yolks given to them by the local wineries. The egg whites had been used for wine clarification, and as an act of charity, these wine producers donated the leftover yolks to the nuns so that they could sell their sweets at a good profit.

Makes sixteen 2-inch squares

2¼ cups cold water	10 egg yolks
1½ cups sugar	2 whole eggs
Peel of 1 lemon	1 teaspoon almond liqueur (optional)

CARAMELIZED SUGAR

¼ cup sugar	1 teaspoon lemon juice
2 teaspoons hot water	

To caramelize the sugar, mix the sugar, water, and lemon juice in an 8-inch square baking pan. Place the pan over a high flame, stirring the dissolved sugar constantly, until it turns a light caramel color. This will take less than a minute; watch carefully. Remove immediately from the flame and tilt the pan so that the sugar coats the entire bottom. Cool.

To make the custard, in a saucepan mix 1½ cups of the cold water with the sugar and lemon peel. Bring to a boil over a medium flame. Add the remaining ¾ cup of water and cook to the string stage (about 20 minutes). Remove from the flame and cool slightly. Discard the lemon peel.

In a bowl, beat the egg yolks and the whole eggs with a wire whisk until smooth but not foamy. Pour in the sugar syrup very slowly, beating constantly. Pour the mixture into the caramelized pan. Cover tightly with foil and place the pan in a larger pan of hot water. The water should reach halfway up the sides of the custard pan. Place on top of the stove, bring the water to a boil, and cook over medium heat for 12 minutes.

Heat the oven to 350° F. Place the custard pan (in the pan of water) in the oven and bake 13 minutes. Remove from the oven and let the custard sit in the water until the water cools. Loosen the edges of the custard with a knife and turn onto a dish. Cut into 2-inch squares. Transfer the squares to a dry serving dish and refrigerate until ready to serve.

Strain the caramelized sugar that has remained and mix with the almond liqueur. When ready to serve, pour this syrup over the custard squares. The custard looks very attractive when placed in shallow paper muffin cups.

FLAN DE NARANJA

(Orange Custard)

Serves 6

6 eggs
5 tablespoons sugar

Juice of 4 oranges (about 1⅓ cups)
1 teaspoon grated orange rind

CARAMELIZED SUGAR

8 tablespoons sugar

4 teaspoons water

To caramelize the sugar, place the sugar and water in a small skillet. Heat over a medium flame, stirring constantly until the sugar has a golden color. Pour immediately into 6 custard cups.

To make the custard, lightly beat the eggs with a wire whisk until light colored. Beat in the sugar, then gradually add the orange juice and the orange rind. Pour into the custard cups, place them in a pan of hot water, and bake at 350° F for 45 minutes, or until a knife inserted in the custard comes out clean. Remove from the pan of water and cool.

To serve, unmold and spoon on the caramelized sugar.

FLAN DE COCO

(Coconut Custard)

START PREPARATION TWO HOURS IN ADVANCE.

Serves 5

⅜ cup grated fresh coconut
1⅞ cups milk
½ cup plus 2 tablespoons condensed
    milk (sweetened)

3 eggs
1½ tablespoons sugar

CARAMELIZED SUGAR

5 tablespoons sugar

2½ teaspoons water

Soak the coconut in ½ cup of the milk for 2 hours. To make the caramelized sugar, heat the sugar and the water in a small skillet and cook, stirring constantly, until the sugar turns a light golden color. Divide into 5 ovenproof custard cups.

In a saucepan, heat the remaining 1⅜ cups milk and the condensed milk over a medium flame, stirring, until it reaches a boil. Remove from the flame.

In a bowl, lightly beat the eggs with a wire whisk, then beat in the sugar. Drain the coconut and discard the milk in which it has soaked. Stir the coconut into the eggs, then gradually add the hot milk.

Pour the custard into the caramelized cups. Place the cups in a pan of hot water and bake at 350° F for about 45 minutes, or until a knife inserted in the custard comes out clean. To serve, unmold onto dessert dishes.

FLAN DE MANZANA

(Apple Custard)

Serves 4–5

APPLES

¼ cup light brown sugar, packed
½ cup water
¼ teaspoon cinnamon

1 apple, peeled, cored, and cut in ⅛-inch slices

CARAMELIZED SUGAR

5 tablespoons sugar

2½ teaspoons water

CUSTARD

4 tablespoons sugar
2 cups milk
⅛ teaspoon salt

1-inch piece vanilla bean
2 whole eggs
2 egg yolks

To make the apples, heat the brown sugar, water, and cinnamon in a saucepan until the sugar is completely dissolved. Add the apple pieces and simmer until they are tender. Drain the apples and arrange them in the bottom of 4 or 5 greased custard cups.

To caramelize the sugar, in a small skillet heat the sugar and water over a medium flame, stirring constantly, until the sugar is lightly caramelized. Pour it immediately into the custard cups over the apple slices.

To make the custard, mix the sugar, milk, salt, and vanilla bean in a saucepan. Bring to a boil, then simmer 10 minutes. Discard the vanilla bean.

Lightly beat the whole eggs and egg yolks in a bowl with a wire whisk. Gradually pour in the hot milk and mix well. Divide the custard into the prepared custard cups, place them in a pan of hot water, and bake at 350° F for 45–60 minutes, or until a knife inserted in the custard comes out clean. Cool, then chill. To serve, unmold the custard onto dessert dishes.

MERENGUES DE FRESA

(Strawberry Meringues)

NOTHING is more likely to light up the eyes of a Spanish youngster than a bakery display of *merengues*. These are not the slow-baked, cookielike meringues we commonly find here, but meringues that are slightly crunchy on the outside, soft and custardy within, and meant to be eaten with a spoon. My favorites are the flavored meringues, particularly the ones made with fruit syrups and topped with fresh fruit.

Makes 20 small meringues

¼ pound strawberries (about
    8 medium-size), hulled, or
    any other berry
½ cup hot water
1 cup granulated sugar
4 egg whites

14 drops lemon juice
2 tablespoons powdered sugar
Powdered sugar for dusting
Strawberries, or other berries,
    for garnish

In a processor or blender, purée the strawberries and beat in the hot water. Strain into a saucepan and stir in the granulated sugar. Bring to a boil, then simmer over a very low flame until the syrup reaches the soft-crack stage (when a small amount is dropped into ice water, hard threads will form that can be bent but not broken). This will take about 25–30 minutes.

When the syrup is almost ready, beat the egg whites with the lemon juice. When the egg starts to stiffen, add the 2 tablespoons of powdered sugar and continue beating until stiff but not dry. Very gradually pour the hot syrup into the egg whites, beating all the while with an electric beater. Continue beating for 10 minutes.

Drop the meringue by 3 tablespoonsful into miniature paper baking cups (the meringues may be made larger or smaller). Dust heavily with powdered sugar. Place the cups on a cookie sheet and bake at 500° F for 1 minute. Take the meringue cups off the pan and cool. Decorate with wedges of strawberry — about 1 strawberry for each meringue.

VARIATIONS: The meringues may be made plain, omitting the fruit and cooking instead the peel of ½ lemon with the sugar syrup.

To make coffee meringues, substitute ½ cup weak coffee for the ½ cup water.

CREMA DE JEREZ
(Chocolate Sherry Chiffon Pudding)

Serves 6

1½ packages gelatin
1 cup sweet (cream) sherry
1 cup milk
3 ounces unsweetened chocolate, cut
    in pieces
¼ cup finely ground hazelnuts

2 eggs, separated
1 cup plus 2 tablespoons sugar
1 teaspoon vanilla
½ cup heavy cream
Whipped cream for garnish (optional)

Dissolve the gelatin in ¼ cup of the sherry. Place the milk, chocolate, and the softened gelatin in a saucepan and cook over medium heat until the chocolate is completely melted and the gelatin dissolved. Add the hazelnuts and cool, stirring occasionally.

Beat the egg yolks with ¾ cup of the sugar and the vanilla. Add the remaining ¾ cup of sherry. Stir this mixture into the cooled chocolate mixture.

Beat the egg whites with the remaining 6 tablespoons of sugar until stiff and glossy. In another bowl, beat the heavy cream until stiff. Stir the chocolate mixture into the whipped cream. Gradually fold this into the egg whites, mixing gently but thoroughly so that there are no lumps. Pour into individual dessert dishes and refrigerate until set. Serve, if desired, with whipped cream.

CUAJADA CON MIEL
(Rennet Pudding with Honey)

FRESHLY made, all-natural rennet pudding is a far cry from the heavily sweetened and artificially flavored packaged junket usually available here. In Spain, it is most often prepared unsweetened with honey poured over it. Recently, rennet pudding has become a very popular dessert among Spaniards and is found in many restaurants.

Serves 4

3 cups milk
1 cinnamon stick
3 rennet tablets, crushed (available in
     some specialty food shops)

Honey
Chopped walnuts (optional)

Heat the milk with the cinnamon stick until it is very warm but not hot. Add
the crushed rennet and stir gently until the tablets are completely dissolved but
the milk has not yet begun to set. Discard the cinnamon. Pour into dessert
dishes (in Spain narrow earthenware mugs without handles are used) and let sit
1 hour, undisturbed. Refrigerate. Serve with honey. You may also sprinkle on
some chopped walnuts.

If you prefer to have the custard sweetened, omit the honey and add 4½
tablespoons sugar to the milk before heating.

NOTE: I once ate a delicious version of Cuajada in the lovely mountain village
of Morella. Before the pudding completely set, a square of cake soaked in a
sherry syrup was added, then sprinkled with cinnamon. To make such a cake,
follow the recipe for Bizcocho Borracho a la Crema (p. 365), adding 2 ounces
(about ½ cup) ground almonds to the cake batter. Make the syrup from the
following ingredients: ¾ cup sugar, ¾ cup water, 1 cinnamon stick, and ¾
cup sweet (*oloroso* or cream) sherry. Omit the custard filling.

FILLOAS A LA CREMA

(Custard-Filled Dessert Pancakes)

START PREPARATION SEVERAL HOURS IN ADVANCE.

A TYPICAL Galician dessert that, when flamed with anisette, makes a nice
ending to a dinner party.

Serves 6

PANCAKES

1 egg
½ cup milk
½ cup water
1 cup flour
1 teaspoon sugar

Pinch salt
3 tablespoons butter
Granulated sugar for dusting
1 tablespoon anisette liqueur

FILLING

9 egg yolks   ¾ cup milk
9 tablespoons sugar

To make the pancakes, combine the egg, milk, water, flour, sugar, and salt in a processor or blender. Mix until smooth. Let the batter rest several hours before using.

To make the filling, beat the egg yolks in the top of a double boiler with a wire whisk, then add the sugar and continue beating until the mixture is smooth and lemon colored. Heat the milk in a saucepan. Gradually stir the milk into the yolk mixture. Place over hot water and cook, stirring constantly, until the mixture is thickened. If any lumps appear, strain. Cool.

To cook the pancakes, grease a small skillet or crêpe pan and heat. Swirl in just enough batter to coat the pan, about 1 tablespoon. When the pancake has set, turn and cook the other side. Do not brown. The pancakes may be cooked in advance and kept between pieces of wax paper until ready to use.

To serve, spread 1 tablespoon of the filling on each pancake. Fold in quarters. Melt the 3 tablespoons of butter in a large skillet or chafing dish. Gently heat the folded pancakes. Turn, dust with sugar, pour in the anisette, and ignite.

If anisette is not desired, fill the pancakes as directed. Fold, then heat in the oven in a buttered pan, turning once. To serve, dust with powdered sugar and cinnamon.

CAKES AND TARTS

BIZCOCHO BORRACHO A LA CREMA
(Custard-Filled, Liqueur-Flavored Cake)

IT IS traditional in Spain to cut cakes in squares rather than wedges. So it is with this delicious "drunken" cake, so-called because it is soaked in liquor—in this case, rum and orange liqueur. For added elegance, I like to cut the cake into very small squares, petit four–style, lightly caramelize the sugar topping, and serve in miniature paper cups. This is a great "finger" dessert for large parties.

Makes 36 small cake squares

4 eggs
½ cup sugar
1 cup flour

2 tablespoons butter, melted
        and cooled
Powdered sugar for dusting

SYRUP

6 tablespoons sugar
6 tablespoons water
1 cinnamon stick

5 tablespoons rum
4 tablespoons orange liqueur, such as
        Gran Torres or Grand Marnier

CUSTARD FILLING

1 cup milk
Peel of ½ lemon
3 egg yolks

¼ cup sugar
¼ cup flour
2 teaspoons butter

To make the cake, beat the eggs and sugar with an electric beater until the mixture is light and fluffy, about 3 minutes. Gradually mix in the flour, then the melted butter. Pour the batter into a greased and floured 8-inch square baking pan. Bake at 350° F for about 25 minutes, or until the cake springs back when pressed in the center. Cool slightly.

While the cake is baking, prepare the syrup. In a saucepan mix together the sugar, water, and cinnamon stick. Bring to a boil, then simmer 5 minutes. Remove from the heat and discard the cinnamon. Mix in the rum and the orange liqueur. While the cake is still in the pan and still warm, pour half of the syrup evenly over the cake. It will take only a moment for the syrup to soak in. Then carefully turn the cake out onto a dish and pour the remaining syrup over the other side.

To make the custard, heat the milk with the lemon peel to the boiling point. Reduce the heat and simmer 10 minutes. Discard the lemon peel. Place the egg yolks in a saucepan and gradually stir in the sugar. Beat with a wire whisk until the yolks are pale yellow. Beat in the flour and gradually add the hot milk. Cook over moderate heat, stirring constantly, until thickened and smooth and no flour taste remains. Remove from the heat and stir in the butter. Cool, stirring occasionally.

Split the cake and fill it with the custard. Cut the filled cake into 36 squares. Dust each one heavily with powdered sugar. Heat a thin metal object, such as a skewer (protect your hand with a potholder). When it is very hot, press it on the tops of the cakes, making a gridiron design by caramelizing the sugar. Reheat and wipe off the skewer as necessary. Serve the cakes in miniature paper baking cups.

TARTA DE SANTIAGO

(Almond Cake)

ALMOND cakes are associated with Galicia, even though the almonds must be brought from the south, where almond trees grow. This version (there is another that is flat and candy-like) is a lovely moist cake made without flour. It is best after it has had a chance to sit for several hours, so that the cream moistens the cake.

Makes one 2-layer cake

1 cup sugar
¼ teaspoon grated lemon rind
7 eggs, separated
½ pound almonds, with skins,
    finely ground

¼ teaspoon cinnamon
Chopped or ground almonds
    for garnish

TOPPING

½ pint heavy cream
¼ teaspoon sugar

1 teaspoon very strong
    coffee (optional)

Cream the sugar, lemon rind, and egg yolks until the mixture is light and fluffy. Stir in the almonds and cinnamon. Beat the egg whites until they are stiff but not dry. Stir a few tablespoons of the egg white into the almond mixture, then fold in the rest of the egg whites. Pour into 2 greased 8-inch layer pans and bake at 350° F for 45 minutes, or until the cakes are well browned. Cool briefly, then remove the cakes from the pans.

To make the topping, whip the cream with the sugar and coffee until stiff. Spread between the cake layers, then coat the top and sides of the cake. Garnish with chopped or ground almonds.

BRAZO DE GITANO

(Custard-Filled Cake Roll)

"Brazo de Gitano" literally means "Arm of a Gypsy," which I suppose refers to the elongated shape of this typically Spanish rolled cake. Why it is the arm of the gypsy in particular is a mystery to me.

Makes 1 rolled cake
(at least 8 servings)

¼ pound sweet butter	1 cup sifted flour
3 eggs	⅛ teaspoon salt
½ cup sugar	Powdered sugar for dusting
½ teaspoon grated lemon rind	Cinnamon for dusting

FILLING

2¾ cups milk	¾ cup flour
1 cinnamon stick	3 tablespoons sweet
Peel of ½ lemon	(cream) sherry
8 egg yolks	1 tablespoon butter
¾ cup sugar	2 ounces pine nuts

To make the cake, melt the butter and cool. Beat the eggs with an electric beater until foamy. Gradually add the sugar and the lemon rind. Beat until very light and fluffy, about 4 minutes. Stir in the flour, which has been mixed with the salt. Lightly fold in the cooled butter. Heat the oven to 375° F and grease well a 10 × 15-inch cookie pan (the type that has a small rim). Pour in the batter, distributing evenly. Bake on the middle-upper rack for 9–10 minutes, or until the cake is done, but only lightly golden on the bottom (otherwise the cake will be difficult to roll).

Dust heavily with powdered sugar a piece of thin cloth, at least the length of the cake and a few inches wider. Invert the cake while still warm onto the cloth. Trim any brown edges. Roll the cake in the cloth, being sure the ends are well covered. Cool and leave wrapped until ready to fill.

To make the filling, bring the milk to a boil with the cinnamon and lemon peel. Simmer 15 minutes. Discard the cinnamon stick and the lemon peel. With a wire whisk, beat the egg yolks in a heavy saucepan. Beat in the sugar and continue mixing until the eggs have a pale yellow color. Stir in the flour. Gradually add the hot milk and 2 tablespoons of the sherry. Cook over a medium flame, stirring constantly, until the custard is thickened and smooth and begins to bubble. (The custard may seem lumpy for a while, but will smooth out when done.) Remove from the heat and stir in the butter and remaining tablespoon of sherry. Cool, stirring occasionally.

When the custard is at room temperature, unroll the cake, leaving it on the cloth. Spread with the custard and sprinkle on the pine nuts. Reroll, using the cloth to aid in rolling. Transfer to a serving dish. Sift powdered sugar over the cake and dust with cinnamon. Serve, preferably, at room temperature. A glass of sweet dessert sherry such as Hartley and Gibson Cream is a lovely accompaniment.

TARTA "HUERTO DE CURA"
(Orange Ice Cream Cake)

PREPARE ONE DAY IN ADVANCE

ENRICHED with frozen orange custard and flavored with orange liqueur, Tarta "Huerto de Cura" from the city of Elche (see p. 169) is an elegant variation of ice cream cake. Two recipes from this chapter are needed for its preparation, but fortunately, all work is completed the day before.

Serves 8

½ recipe Frozen Orange Custard (p. 383), using 2 teaspoons orange rind and omitting the blackberry topping
Bizcocho Borracho (p. 365), omitting the syrup and filling
1 pint vanilla ice cream, softened

8-ounce jar English orange marmalade, heated to soften slightly
½ cup orange liqueur, such as Gran Torres or Grand Marnier
½ pint heavy cream, whipped
Powdered coffee for dusting

Prepare the Frozen Orange Custard according to instructions. Using an 8-inch round baking pan, make the Bizcocho. When the custard is frozen and the cake cool, quickly assemble the ice cream cake. Slice the cake into 3 layers. Spread the first layer with the softened vanilla ice cream. Cover with the second layer of cake, top this with the custard, and cover with the remaining cake layer. Spread the top with the softened orange marmalade. Place in the freezer overnight to harden, lightly covered with foil.

To serve, soften the cake slightly. Cut into wedges, and place them on their sides on individual dishes. Pour about 1 tablespoon of orange liqueur on each portion so that it penetrates the cake. Top with whipped cream and a light dusting of coffee.

MANTECADAS DE ASTORGA
(Spanish-Style Cupcakes)

MANTECADAS, light-as-air cupcakes that are nice for teas, are found all over Spain with many variations. They are sometimes more like cookies than cake, and most often are made with lard. These from Astorga, a town in the butter-producing province of León, are particularly well known.

In Spain, Mantecadas are traditionally baked in square or rectangular paper molds. You may achieve this effect by mitering the corners of foil cupcake liners or by making your own from parchment paper. If you make the Mantecadas round, of course, they will taste just as good.

Makes 20 cupcakes

¼ pound sweet butter
3 eggs
½ cup sugar
1 cup sifted flour

⅛ teaspoon salt
¼ teaspoon cinnamon
Powdered sugar for dusting

Melt the butter and cool. Beat the eggs with an electric beater until they are foamy. Gradually add the sugar and beat until very light and fluffy, about 4 minutes. Stir in the flour that has been mixed with the salt and cinnamon. Lightly fold in the cooled butter. Fill the cupcake liners ⅔ full. Bake at 350° F for 15 minutes, or until just lightly golden. These are best when eaten soon after baking. They may be dusted with powdered sugar.

PAN DE MUNICIÓN

(Chocolate Custard Cake)

THIS recipe, which dates back to the last century, produces a dense, bitter chocolate taste in a cake that borders on a custard. When chocolate was brought from the New World, it was used essentially as a seasoning and as a drink. It was not until the nineteenth century that it became immensely popular in Europe as a dessert ingredient.

Makes 1 loaf

1⅓ cups cocoa
½ cup orange flower water (available
    in Italian specialty shops)
½ cup water
4 tablespoons butter, softened
¾ cup plus 1 tablespoon sugar

4 eggs
½ cup ground almonds
½ teaspoon grated orange rind
2 egg whites
¼ cup chopped almonds

CHOCOLATE SAUCE

1⅓ cups milk
3 squares unsweetened chocolate
Pinch salt
⅓ cup sugar

2 teaspoons cornstarch
1 teaspoon vanilla
⅓ cup heavy cream

In a bowl, mix the cocoa with the orange flower water and the water until smooth. In another bowl, cream the butter and sugar until light and fluffy. Beat in the whole eggs, then stir in ¼ cup of the ground almonds, the cocoa mixture, and the orange rind.

Beat the egg whites until stiff but not dry. Fold them into the chocolate mixture along with the chopped almonds. Pour the batter into a greased 9¼ × 5¼-inch loaf pan. Bake at 350° F for 40 minutes. Cool, then turn out of the pan onto a serving dish.

To make the chocolate sauce, heat the milk, chocolate, and salt in a double boiler, stirring occasionally. When the chocolate is melted, add the sugar and cook until it is dissolved. Mix the cornstarch with enough cold water to form a paste. Add it to the chocolate and stir until smooth, thickened, and no cornstarch taste remains. Cool, then add the vanilla. Thin with the heavy cream (the sauce should be the consistency of heavy cream).

To serve, cut the cake in slices and pour on some of the chocolate sauce. Sprinkle with the remaining ¼ cup ground almonds.

TARTA DE NARANJA

(Orange Almond Cake)

Makes one 8-inch cake

4 eggs, separated
½ cup sugar
Grated rind of 2 oranges

¼ pound blanched almonds,
finely ground

SYRUP

Juice of 2 oranges
⅓ cup sugar

1 cinnamon stick
1 teaspoon orange liqueur

Beat the egg yolks, sugar, and orange rind until fluffy and lemon colored. Gradually beat in the almonds. In another bowl, beat the egg whites until stiff but not dry. Fold into the yolk mixture. Turn into a greased and floured 8-inch square or round layer pan. Bake at 350° F for about 45 minutes, or until the cake is well browned. Cool slightly, then remove the cake from the pan onto a serving dish.

To make the syrup, mix together in a saucepan the orange juice, sugar, and cinnamon stick. Bring to a boil, then simmer 5 minutes. Remove from the flame and add the orange liqueur. Cool, then pour evenly over the cake.

TARTA DE MANZANA

(Apple Tart)

THIS is quite rich—serve small portions.

Makes one 9-inch tart

DOUGH

¼ pound sweet butter
½ cup sugar
1 egg yolk

1½ cups sifted flour
Pinch salt
⅛ teaspoon baking powder

CUSTARD

1 cup milk
Peel of ½ lemon
3 egg yolks

¼ cup sugar
¼ cup flour
1½ teaspoons butter

FILLING

¼ cup sugar
1 teaspoon lemon juice
½ teaspoon cinnamon

4 apples, peeled, cored, and cut into
¼-inch slices

TOPPING

½ cup apple jelly

To make the dough, cream the butter and gradually beat in the sugar, then the egg yolk. Combine the flour with the salt and baking powder and stir into the butter mixture. Work with hands to form a ball. Press the dough with your fingers into and up the sides of a loose-bottom quiche pan. Refrigerate while preparing the custard.

To make the custard, heat the milk with the lemon peel to the boiling point. Reduce the heat and simmer 10 minutes. Discard the lemon peel. Place the egg yolks in a saucepan and gradually stir in the sugar. Beat with a wire whisk until the yolks are pale yellow. Beat in the flour and gradually add the hot milk. Cook over moderate heat, stirring constantly, until thickened and smooth and no flour taste remains. Remove from the heat and stir in the butter. Cool, stirring occasionally.

While the custard is cooling, combine in a small bowl the sugar, lemon juice, and cinnamon for the filling. Mix with the sliced apples.

Spread the custard over the dough and arrange the apples on top in overlapping circles. Bake at 350° F for about 1 hour, or until the crust is well browned. Cool.

In a small saucepan, melt the apple jelly. Spoon over the apples to glaze the tart. Remove the sides of the quiche pan, leaving the tart on the bottom circle. Serve at room temperature or chilled.

FLAÓN

(Sixteenth-Century Cheesecake)

THIS is an unusually flavored flat cheesecake, which is a specialty of Ibiza and is described in Ruperto de Nola's 1525 cookbook (see p. xiii). A similar dessert, Tarta Pasiega, is found in pastry shops during the Easter season.

Makes one 8-inch tart

2 eggs
½ pound cottage cheese
½ cup sugar
⅛ teaspoon mint
⅛ teaspoon anisette liqueur

3 tablespoons honey
1 teaspoon rose water (available in pharmacies)
Cinnamon for dusting

DOUGH

1 cup flour
¼ teaspoon salt

2½ tablespoons water
3 tablespoons salad oil

To make the dough, mix the flour and salt and stir in the water and oil. Roll out, fold in 3 parts, business-letter fashion. Roll again and fold and roll 2 more times. Fit into an 8-inch, loose-bottom quiche pan, covering the bottom and the sides with the dough.

In a bowl, beat the eggs with the cheese, sugar, mint, and anisette. Spread onto the dough and bake 40 minutes at 350° F, or until the filling is set.

Mix together the honey and rose water. Dribble this mixture over the pie, then dust with cinnamon. Serve warm.

TARTA DEL CONVENTO

(Puff Pastry Tart)

"*El Convento*" of the recipe title refers to the lovely *parador*, or government inn, Vía de la Plata at Mérida, a building that was once an ancient convent. The grounds are thought to be the site of an earlier religious structure, the Temple of Concord of Augustus, dating back to Roman times. The city of Mérida was once a Roman capital and to this day boasts one of the best-preserved Roman theaters in the world, along with the remains of its graceful aqueduct.

The restaurant of the *parador* has received several gastronomic awards for its fine regional cooking. One of its most exciting dishes is Sausages with Sweet-Sour Figs (p. 311), and its dessert menu features this puff pastry tart.

Makes one 7 × 12-inch tart (serves 6–8)

Puff pastry, preferably homemade
  (p. 336) or frozen

FILLING

½ cup water
⅓ cup granulated sugar
3 egg whites
Few drops lemon juice

1 teaspoon powdered sugar
¼ teaspoon vanilla
1 cup heavy cream

CHOCOLATE GLAZE

3 ounces unsweetened chocolate
10 tablespoons sugar

6 tablespoons water

Divide the puff pastry dough into 3 parts; roll 1 part on a floured working surface into a 10 × 15-inch rectangle (refrigerate the other 2 parts). Transfer the dough to a lightly greased cookie sheet of the same size and refrigerate. Prepare the other 2 pieces of dough in the same manner (if 3 cookie sheets are not available, you will have to bake the dough in 2 or more stages). Heat the oven to 450° F. Prick the dough all over with a fork. It is best to bake 1 sheet at a time, or as many as will fit on the upper rack of the oven. Bake 10 minutes, opening the oven every 2 minutes or so to prick the dough some more so that it does not puff too much. The dough should be well browned all over (don't worry if the edges overcook). Cool, then trim the edges to make rectangles 7 × 12 inches.

To make the filling, place the water and granulated sugar in a saucepan. Bring to a boil, then simmer until the syrup reaches the soft-ball stage, about 15–20 minutes. Meanwhile, beat the egg whites with the lemon juice until foamy. Add the powdered sugar and vanilla and continue beating until the eggs are stiff but not dry. Slowly beat in the hot syrup and continue beating for 10 minutes. Refrigerate until cold. Whip the cream, then fold it into the egg white mixture.

Place 1 sheet of pastry on a serving dish. Spread ½ of the filling on the sheet, cover with a second sheet, and spread the remaining filling on top. Cover with the third piece.

To make the chocolate glaze, melt the chocolate, either in a double boiler or by leaving it in a pan on top of a warm stove. In a saucepan, mix the sugar and water. Bring to a boil, then simmer until it reaches the string stage. Slowly pour the syrup into the chocolate, stirring vigorously. Keep warm until ready to use, so that it does not harden. Spread the chocolate over the top layer of the tart. To serve, cut into rectangular or square serving pieces.

COOKIES

POLVORONES SEVILLANOS

(Powdered Sugar Cookies)

THESE typical Spanish holiday cookies are of Arab origin, but just about every country in the Western world has some version of a sugar cookie. Sevilla is famous for its cookies, but they are also found throughout Spain. Although often made with lard, butter produces a finer cookie. My version is, I believe, the last word in sugar cookies and my most solicited recipe.

The Spanish sometimes serve these cookies in the afternoon to guests, accompanied by a glass of anisette liqueur, such as Anís del Mono.

Makes about 20 cookies

½ pound sweet butter, at
    room temperature
1 egg yolk
1 tablespoon powdered sugar
1 tablespoon brandy, preferably
    Spanish brandy, or Cognac

2 cups flour
½ teaspoon cinnamon
About 2 cups powdered sugar, sifted,
    for dusting

Cream the butter with an electric beater until light colored and fluffy. In a small cup, mix together the egg yolk and the tablespoon of powdered sugar. Stir in the brandy. Beat this mixture into the creamed butter.

Sift the flour with the cinnamon. Gradually incorporate the flour with a spatula or a wooden spoon into the butter mixture. The dough should be slightly sticky. With floured hands shape the dough into ovals, about 2 inches long and ½ inch high. Place on an ungreased cookie sheet. Bake at 300° F for about 30 minutes. The cookies should not brown. Cool slightly 2–3 minutes.

Sift the powdered sugar onto a sheet of wax paper. Roll the warm cookies carefully in the sugar, coating them lightly on all sides. Cool the cookies completely, then dust heavily with more powdered sugar. To serve, you may place the cookies in miniature paper cupcake liners.

GRANADINAS

(Almond Cookies)

WHAT could be more beautiful than Granada in spring, its valleys awash with white almond blossoms, the snowcapped peaks of the Sierra Nevada glittering in the sunlight. It is little wonder that Boabdil, the last Moorish ruler of this lovely city, burst into tears when he looked back on his beloved city from the mountains that would become his place of exile. ("You weep like a woman over that which you could not defend as a man," his mother reprimanded.) Under Arab rule Granada had been transformed into a veritable garden, where almond, lemon, and orange trees grew in profusion, filling the air with the fragrance of their blossoms.

Granadinas, native to Granada, are rich in almonds, and I have been known to eat them by the dozen.

Makes 20 cookies

1 cup flour
¾ cup finely ground
    blanched almonds

½ cup sugar
Pinch salt
¼ teaspoon cinnamon

¼ pound (½ cup) lard or   1 egg, lightly beaten
     vegetable shortening   Powdered sugar for dusting

Place the flour in a heavy skillet over low heat and cook about 7 minutes, stirring occasionally with a wooden spoon. Do not let the flour brown. This process gives the flour a "nutty" flavor. Cool, then transfer the flour to a bowl and mix in the almonds, sugar, salt, and cinnamon. Work in the lard and egg with your hands until a dough forms. Shape the dough into 1-inch balls and place them on an ungreased cookie sheet. Flatten the centers of the cookies with your index finger. Bake them in a 300° F oven for about 30 minutes, or until they are golden. Cool. Dust with powdered sugar.

These cookies will stay crisp several weeks in a metal tin. In Spain, however, they are eaten soft. To soften, wrap the cookies lightly in wax paper and leave them for about 6 days.

LENGUAS DE GATO

("Cat's Tongue" Cookies)

THESE wafer-thin, crisp cookies are found in pastry shops all over Madrid and are ideal accompaniments to ice cream or custard desserts.

Makes 70 cookies

¼ pound sweet butter   2 egg whites, unbeaten
¾ cup powdered sugar   ¾ cup flour
¼ teaspoon vanilla   Pinch salt
⅛ teaspoon lemon rind (optional)

Cream the butter until light colored and fluffy. Add the sugar, vanilla, and lemon rind and continue beating another minute. Add the egg whites and beat until the mixture is smooth and very light textured. Gradually stir in the flour and add the salt.

Put the dough in a pastry bag or cake decorator fitted with a ¼-inch round opening (#11 or #12). Press the dough onto a greased cookie sheet in 2½-inch lengths, well spaced (the dough will spread when baked). Bake at 350° F for 5 minutes, or until the cookies are very lightly browned around the edges. Remove them immediately from the pan with a flexible pancake turner and cool. Be sure to watch the cookies carefully as they bake—they burn in a flash.

FRUIT DESSERTS

MANZANAS ASADAS

(Almond- and Raisin-Filled Baked Apples)

TRY serving these delicious apples with a dessert sherry such as Hartley and Gibson Cream.

Serves 4

2 tablespoons light rum
1 tablespoon water
2 tablespoons raisins
4 large apples, suitable for baking
Lemon juice
2 egg yolks

6 tablespoons sugar
2 ounces blanched almonds, lightly
    toasted and ground
3 tablespoons butter, melted
    and cooled

Mix the rum, water, and raisins in a small saucepan. Heat until warm. Remove from the flame and let sit.

Peel the apples and core them, leaving a base of ½ inch at the bottom and a hollowed cylinder of about 1½ inches in diameter. Rub the apples with lemon juice to prevent discoloration. In a small bowl, mix the egg yolks, 5 tablespoons of the sugar, the almonds, and the butter. Drain the raisins, reserving the liquid. Add the raisins to the egg mixture.

Fill each apple with about 2 tablespoons of the filling. Place the apples in a shallow ovenproof pan and pour in the reserved liquid from the raisins plus another ½ cup of water and the remaining 1 tablespoon of sugar. Bake at 350° F for 30 minutes, basting occasionally and adding more water if the liquid evaporates. Cover and continue baking another 15–20 minutes, or until the apples are tender. Serve warm.

PLÁTANOS CON MIEL Y PIÑONES

(Bananas with Honey and Pine Nuts)

A DESSERT using bananas is bound to be from the Canary Islands. These delicious bananas take only 4 minutes to prepare. They may be made in a chafing dish at the table.

Serves 4

4 tablespoons sweet butter
4 bananas, peeled and cut in half
    lengthwise and crosswise
½ cup honey
3 tablespoons warm water

1 teaspoon lemon juice
3 tablespoons anisette liqueur
4 tablespoons pine nuts

Melt the butter in a skillet or chafing dish, add the bananas, and sáuté, turning once, for 1 minute. In a small bowl, mix together the honey, water, and lemon juice. Add to the bananas and cook slowly 1 minute. Add the anisette and cook 2 minutes more. Sprinkle with the pine nuts and serve hot. This is also very good over vanilla ice cream.

ZURRACAPOTE

(Stewed Prunes and Apricots)

PREPARE SEVERAL HOURS IN ADVANCE.

FROM the Basque country, a traditional Christmas Eve dessert with a wonderfully spicy flavor.

Serves 4–6

1 cup full-bodied red wine
1 cup water
1 cup firmly packed brown sugar
1 cinnamon stick

Peel of ½ lemon
½ pound dried prunes
½ pound dried apricots

In a saucepan place the wine, water, brown sugar, cinnamon, and lemon peel. Bring to a boil, then simmer 5 minutes. Add the prunes and apricots, cover, and simmer 15 minutes more. Turn off the heat and let the fruit sit at least a few hours in the syrup. Serve warm. This will keep for weeks in a jar, refrigerated or at room temperature.

PERAS CON VINO

(Pears in Wine Sauce)

PREPARE ONE DAY IN ADVANCE.

Serves 4

2 cups water
½ cup sugar
2 slices lemon
2 cinnamon sticks

4 pears, peeled but not cored,
    stems on
¾ cup red wine

In a saucepan bring the water and sugar to a boil. Add the lemon slices, cinnamon sticks, and pears. Simmer, covered, for 10 minutes. Add the wine and simmer 10 minutes more, or until the pears are tender. Remove the pears and boil down the sauce until it is slightly thickened and syrupy. Return the pears to the syrup and let them sit at room temperature overnight. To serve, core the pears, cut in slices, and arrange in overlapping rows on dessert dishes, decorating each dish with a cinnamon stick or a slice of the lemon. Spoon on some of the syrup.

DULCE DE MEMBRILLO

(Quince Marmalade)

QUINCE, a relative of the apple, has been used by man since ancient times. It is fairly easy to find preserved in bottles or tins, especially in Spanish and Greek specialty shops. Sometimes it is available fresh, in which case it is quite simple to make your own jam. It may be used as is, to spread on bread or toast, or it can be used for the puff pastries, Banda de Almendra (p. 350).

Makes 1 cup marmalade

2 quince, about 1½ pounds, peeled,
    cored, and cut in ½-inch rings

10 tablespoons sugar

Place the quince in a saucepan with water to cover. Bring to a boil, then cover and simmer about 15 minutes, or until the quince is tender. Drain. Transfer the quince to a processor or blender and purée. Gradually beat in the sugar. Return this mixture to the saucepan and cook very slowly for 20 minutes, stirring frequently. Cool. Place in a crock or bottle.

CABELLO DE ÁNGEL

(Candied Squash)

CANDIED squash, called Cabello de Ángel (angel's hair) because of its golden color, is commonly used in Spanish pastry making as a filling or topping. It is used in two recipes in this chapter—as a topping for Banda de Almendra (p. 350) and mixed with figs in Pasteles de Higo (p. 352).

Makes 1 cup

1-pound wedge spaghetti squash	5 tablespoons water
	Peel of ½ lemon
¾ cup sugar	1 cinnamon stick

Place the squash in a saucepan with water to cover. Bring to a boil, cover, and simmer until tender, about 15–20 minutes. Cool. Scrape off the pulp with a fork and discard the shell.

In a saucepan, place the sugar, water, lemon peel, and cinnamon stick. Heat until the sugar is dissolved. Add the squash, bring to a boil, and cook, uncovered, for 35 minutes, stirring frequently. The mixture will have the consistency of a thick jam. Store in a covered jar, refrigerated.

FROZEN DESSERTS

LECHE MERENGADA
(Cinnamon-Flavored Ice Milk)

SUMMER in Spain is always heralded by the addition of Leche Merengada to café menus. Although ice cream is popular all year round, for some reason Leche Merengada can be found only from the middle of June to the beginning of September. Café Gijón, a lively turn-of-the-century coffeehouse frequented by writers and artists, is the preferred place for Leche Merengada in Madrid. There is nothing to equal it for summer refreshment. When served in glasses over chilled black coffee, Leche Merengada becomes a delicious drink called Blanco y Negro (p. 393).

Serves 6

3 cups milk
1 cup heavy cream
¾ cup plus 2 tablespoons sugar
Peel of 1 lemon

2 cinnamon sticks
4 egg whites
Few drops lemon juice
Cinnamon for dusting

Bring to a boil the milk, cream, ¾ cup of the sugar, the lemon peel, and the cinnamon sticks. Reduce the heat and simmer 30 minutes, stirring occasionally. Cool, then refrigerate until cold. Remove the lemon peel and cinnamon sticks.

Beat the egg whites with the lemon juice until they form soft peaks. Gradually add the remaining 2 tablespoons of sugar and continue beating until stiff but not dry. Slowly beat in the cold milk mixture.

Freeze in ice cube trays, or preferably in an ice cream machine, following manufacturer's instructions. To serve, scoop into parfait glasses and dust with cinnamon.

BABARRÚA DE NARANJA CON SALSA DE MORA

(Frozen Orange Custard with Blackberry Sauce)

ACTUALLY a custard, this sherbetlike dessert is an exceptionally refreshing end to a meal.

Serves 6

1½ teaspoons gelatin
¼ cup cold water
¼ cup heavy cream
1¾ cups orange juice
1 cup plus ½ teaspoon sugar

4 eggs, separated
½ teaspoon orange rind
3 teaspoons orange liqueur, such
    as Gran Torres or
    Grand Marnier

TOPPING

1 cup blackberry preserves

3 teaspoons orange liqueur

Soften the gelatin in the cold water. In a saucepan, mix the cream and ¼ cup of the orange juice. Add the gelatin and heat to dissolve. Cool.

Beat together 1 cup of the sugar, the egg yolks, and the orange rind, then gradually add the gelatin mixture, the remaining 1½ cups of orange juice, and the orange liqueur. Beat the egg whites with the remaining ½ teaspoon of sugar until stiff but not dry. Fold the egg yolk mixture into the egg whites. Soft freeze in an ice cream machine or freezer tray, then freeze completely in a covered container in the freezer.

To make the topping, mix together the preserves and the orange liqueur. To serve, thaw the frozen custard slightly and scoop into dessert bowls. Spoon on the blackberry sauce.

HELADO DE CIRUELA PASA "IRENE"

(Prune Ice Cream in Orange Liqueur Sauce)

GUESTS rave about this ice cream dessert but are never able to pinpoint the taste as prune. (Read about Irene on p. 126.)

Serves 6

¼ pound dried prunes
2 pints vanilla ice cream

½ cup orange liqueur, such as Gran
Torres or Grand Marnier

Cook the prunes according to package directions. Reserve the liquid. Chop the prunes and return the pits to the reserved liquid to give it added flavor.

Soften the ice cream in a large bowl. Fold in the prunes with a rubber spatula and return the ice cream to the freezer to harden. Strain the prune juice. (There should be about ½ cup—if there is more, you may wish to boil it down for added strength.) Mix with the orange liqueur. To serve, scoop the ice cream into individual dessert dishes and spoon on a few tablespoons of the sauce.

SORBETE DE TURRÓN

(Turrón Ice Milk)

Turrón (see p. 430), a candy of almonds and honey, lends itself beautifully to ice cream, either as a topping (following recipe) or incorporated into the ice cream. *Turrón* ice cream is a favorite in Spain and available in most ice cream parlors. This version is most simple to prepare and needs no ice cream machine.

Serves 4–6

5 ounces (½ package) Jijona (soft)
  turrón, crumbled
1½ cups powdered milk
½ cup sugar
½ cup heavy cream

½ cup water
12 ice cubes, crushed
5 ounces (½ package) Alicante (hard)
  turrón, broken into pieces

Place in a saucepan the crumbled Jijona *turrón*, powdered milk, sugar, cream, and water. Heat until the sugar dissolves. Cool. Transfer to a processor or blender and beat until smooth.

Add the crushed ice and blend with an on/off motion until no large pieces remain. Add the Alicante *turrón* and blend also with the on/off motion until no large pieces remain. Refrigerate until hardened. This is excellent served with a chocolate syrup.

HELADO CON TURRÓN
"LOS CARACOLES"
(Ice Cream with Turrón)

As ONE approaches the Caracoles restaurant in the old quarter of Barcelona, the tantalizing aroma of roasting chickens fills the air. Dozens of chickens sizzling and turning on spits outside the restaurant provide an inviting first view of a charming establishment that has been around almost 150 years and has been visited by most of the world's notables, as autographed photographs lining the walls clearly demonstrate. Los Caracoles has a varied menu that includes its namesake—snails; the Catalán specialty, Butifarra con Setas (Baked Sausage and Mushrooms, p. 313), an excellent roast suckling pig; and this extremely simple ice cream dessert that has a topping of *turrón* candy (see p. 430).

Serves 6–8

5 ounces (½ package) Jijona (soft) *turrón*

2 pints vanilla ice cream

Very simply, crumble the *turrón* over the ice cream and serve. A most delicious combination of tastes.

SORBETE DE CHAMPÁN "IRENE"
(Champagne Sherbet)

ANOTHER delight from that talented cook in the Pyrenees, Irene (see p. 126).

Serves 4–6

½ cup sugar
¾ cup water
Peel of 1 orange
Peel of 1 lemon
1¼ cups orange juice

¼ cup lemon juice
¾ cup champagne (for Spanish sparkling wines, see wine chart)

Bring to a boil the sugar, water, and fruit peels. Simmer 30 minutes and remove fruit peels. Add the orange juice, lemon juice, and champagne and transfer to a freezer tray or ice cream machine. Serve slightly softened.

CANDIES

YEMAS DE SANTA TERESA

(Candied Egg Yolks)

PREPARE ONE DAY IN ADVANCE.

SPANISH candies originated centuries ago in convents, where the nuns prepared such goodies for holiday treats. Santa Teresa, of course, is well known for her sixteenth-century writings on mysticism and was the energetic founder of the Descalza reform movement of Carmelite nuns. Her convent was known for these candies, and they were therefore christened with Santa Teresa's name.

Yemas are still made by nuns today but are also found in pastry shops. They are made from egg yolks, which after cooking and sweetening are shaped into small circles that look just like the original yolks.

Makes 12 candies

½ cup sugar
¼ cup water
1 cinnamon stick
5 egg yolks

⅛ teaspoon lemon juice
Grated rind of ½ lemon
Granulated sugar for dusting

Place in a saucepan the ½ cup of sugar, the water, and the cinnamon stick. Bring to a boil and simmer until the syrup reaches the soft-ball stage. Remove from the heat and discard the cinnamon stick.

With a wire whisk, beat the egg yolks, lemon juice, and lemon rind until the yolks become pale yellow. Add this mixture to the hot syrup in a slow stream, beating constantly. Continue cooking over moderate heat about 4 minutes, beating all the time, until it thickens. Remove from the heat and continue beating until the candy stiffens, then place the saucepan in a bowl of ice and beat with a wooden spoon until it becomes very stiff.

Cover a cookie sheet with wax paper and butter it lightly. Transfer the candy to the wax paper and, with a buttered rubber spatula, shape into a long, thin roll, 12 inches long by 1 inch thick. Chill until the candy is stiff enough to handle.

Slice the roll into 1-inch lengths. Using buttered hands, shape each piece into a circle, or "yolk." Roll in sugar. Arrange the candies in a dish and cover with foil. Let them sit overnight to become slightly crusty on the outside. Place in foil or paper candy cups.

YEMAS DE COCO
(Coconut Candies)

START PREPARATION TWO DAYS IN ADVANCE.

Makes about 10 candies

3 ounces (about ¾ cup) grated
    fresh coconut
¾ cup milk
6 tablespoons sugar

1 teaspoon brandy, preferably Spanish
    brandy, or Cognac
Granulated sugar for dusting

Soak the grated coconut in the milk overnight, refrigerated. Drain well. Place the coconut and the 6 tablespoons of sugar in a small saucepan. Dissolve the sugar over low heat, then continue cooking 5 minutes more over a medium flame, stirring constantly. The mixture should be quite stiff—if there is too much liquid, turn up the flame to evaporate it. Stir in the brandy and remove from the flame. Cool. When still slightly warm, shape the candy into ¾-inch balls. Roll in granulated sugar and place in paper or foil candy cups. Let sit, covered with foil, overnight to dry the candy.

BOCADILLOS DE MONJA
(Almond and Egg Yolk Candies)

PREPARE TWO DAYS IN ADVANCE.

BOCADILLOS DE MONJA, like Yemas de Santa Teresa, originated in the convents of Spain and are still known by their religious name, "Nun's Morsels."

Makes 12–15 candies

5 ounces (about 1 cup)
    blanched almonds
¼ teaspoon grated lemon rind
1 cup water

2 egg yolks
¾ cup granulated sugar
Powdered sugar for dusting

Grind the almonds as fine as possible in a food processor or blender. Mix in the lemon rind and place the nuts in a saucepan with the water. Bring to a boil and continue boiling 5 minutes. Strain the almonds over a bowl, reserving the liquid (there will be a few tablespoons). Cool. Transfer the almonds to another bowl. Add the egg yolks and mix well.

Boil the almond liquid in a saucepan with the granulated sugar until it reaches the thread stage. Pour the syrup gradually over the nut mixture, mixing constantly. Return to the saucepan and cook 5 minutes more, stirring constantly, until thickened. Cool by placing the saucepan over a bowl of ice and mixing until the candy stiffens. Refrigerate until hard enough to handle.

Dust your hands with powdered sugar. Form the candy into 1-inch balls and roll them in powdered sugar. If the sugar is absorbed, roll the candies again in the sugar. Place on a dish and let the candies dry, uncovered, for 2 days. To serve, place the candies in tiny paper or foil cups.

MELINDRES DE YEPES
(Marzipan Candies)

START PREPARATION ONE DAY IN ADVANCE.

MARZIPAN came to Spain centuries ago by way of the Arabs and has remained a popular sweet ever since.

Makes about 50 candies

½ pound blanched almonds	4 tablespoons water
1 cup sugar	Powdered sugar for dusting

GLAZE

½ cup powdered sugar	1 teaspoon lemon juice
1 egg white	

In a processor or blender, grind the nuts to a paste. Add the sugar and continue beating. With the motor running, add the water to form a malleable dough.

Dust a working surface with powdered sugar. Shape the dough into doughnuts the thickness of a pencil and about 1½ inches in diameter. Place them on a cookie sheet. Leave uncovered overnight to dry.

To make the glaze, beat the powdered sugar and egg white until white, creamy, and thickened. Add the lemon juice and beat 5 minutes more. Dip the top of each candy in the glaze. Put the candies back on the cookie sheet and let them sit until the glaze hardens.

HUESOS DE SANTO

(Candied Egg Yolk in Almond Roll)

START PREPARATION ONE DAY IN ADVANCE.

THIS candy is eaten on All Saints Day, November 1, a holiday related to our Halloween, but celebrated in quite a different fashion. It is the day when the living pay their respects to the souls of the dead by spending the day at family burial grounds.

In their typically irreverent manner, the Spanish have named this candy "Bones of the Saint," an apt description indeed, for these hollowed white candy rolls filled with candied egg yolk do look amusingly like bones.

Makes 10 candies

2 ounces potato (about ¼ of a large potato)
½ cup sugar
¼ cup water

⅛ teaspoon lemon rind
3½ ounces (about ⅞ cup) finely ground almonds

FILLING

6 egg yolks
6 tablespoons sugar

4 tablespoons water

COATING

1 cup sugar
½ cup water

2 teaspoons lemon juice

Boil the potato in its skin. When it is tender, skin, then pass through a strainer. Combine the sugar, water, and lemon rind in a saucepan. Bring to a boil and cook to the hard-ball stage—the sugar will have thickened and darkened slightly. Add the ground almonds and stir with a wooden spoon. Mix in the potato and continue cooking and stirring until the mixture leaves the sides of the pan. Remove from the flame and cool until the candy is stiff enough to handle. Turn out onto a floured working surface and flatten to about ½ inch. Let dry 1–2 hours, turning occasionally with the aid of a knife.

Roll out the candy on a floured surface to ¼–⅜-inch thickness. Cut into 2 × 3-inch rectangles and roll them lengthwise around a ½-inch cylindrical object to form a "bone"—the handle of a wooden spoon works very well. Remove the cylinder and place the candies, seam side down, on a cookie sheet. Let dry and harden, uncovered, overnight.

To make the filling, in a small bowl beat the egg yolks with a wire whisk until light colored. Combine in a saucepan the sugar and water and boil until it reaches the hard-ball stage. Gradually add the egg yolks in a thin stream, beating constantly with the wire whisk. Continue cooking and stirring with a wooden spoon until the mixture stiffens. Cool. With the aid of a pastry tube (or a small spoon if a tube is not available), fill the "bones" with the yolk mixture.

To make the coating, boil the sugar and water to the hard-ball stage. Remove from the flame and add the lemon juice. Beat with a wire whisk until the sugar syrup turns white, thickens, and forms a ball. Remove from the pot and cool. Place the sugar ball in the top of a double boiler with 1 teaspoon hot water and heat until the sugar is completely liquefied. Dip the candies in the liquid, then let them dry at least 1 hour.

ALMENDRAS GARRAPIÑADAS

(Candied Almonds)

THE pushcart vendor is still a common sight in Spain, especially in southern cities. Stroll the lushly shaded Alameda in Málaga, for example, and you will find a vendor every few feet of the way. Along with the usual plastic nonsense, you can buy such delights as slices of fresh coconut, a variety of roasted nuts, sunflower seeds, roasted chickpeas, and *chufas*, or tiger nuts, from which the wonderfully refreshing drink, *horchata* (see p. 391), is made. One of the vendor's most popular items is Almendras Garrapiñadas, which he often prepares himself. They are a pleasure to munch on a lazy summer afternoon.

¼ pound almonds with skins	2 tablespoons honey
½ cup sugar	2 teaspoons water

Place the almonds on a cookie tray and toast them lightly in a 300° F oven for about 8 minutes, shaking occasionally.

In a heavy skillet, mix together the sugar, honey, and water. Cook over a medium flame, stirring constantly, until the sugar is melted and well caramelized. Add the almonds and stir with a wooden spoon until they are completely coated with the sugar.

Turn the candy out onto a greased marble slab or counter. While the sugar is hardening, continuously move the nuts with a wooden spoon, so that the sugar adheres to them. When cool enough to handle but not yet completely hard, separate the nuts, each one with its sugar coating, and let them harden completely.

Chapter 14

BEBIDAS

(Drinks)

SPANIARDS like their drinks simple, and except for summertime gin and tonics, mixed drinks have never become popular. The general rule is that wines, liquors, and liqueurs, as well as nonalcoholic beverages, should be pure and unadulterated.

The most outstanding exception to this rule is *sangría*, a wonderfully refreshing summer drink that became immensely popular through advertising, then fell into disrepute because of bottling. It is as distasteful to bottle *sangría* as it is to can *paella* and *gazpacho*, although these atrocities are also committed. One Spanish food commentator writes, " . . . canned *paella* . . . My God, what a travesty! Like trying to can the sun . . . or poetry." The same may be said for *sangría*. It must be mixed with sweet succulent fruits shortly before drinking to preserve its lovely fresh flavor.

One of the most unusual and refreshing Spanish drinks is *horchata*, a creamy beverage of Arab origin that tastes vaguely like coconut milk, but is made from tiger nuts, which, to my knowledge, are not available in the United States. In Spain the plant grows around Valencia, where the best *horchata* is still found. Because of its popularity, *horchata* was eventually bottled, but just as in the case of *sangría*, it is a far cry from the freshly made product. Fortunately, a national chain of ice cream stores, called La Jijoneca, came to the rescue and now brings fresh *horchata* to all of Spain. It is a drink that when chilled to the point of soft-freeze is not to be missed on a hot summer afternoon or evening.

In the mornings, Spanish children wake up to huge cups of thick hot chocolate. Everyone else drinks very strong and syrupy espresso coffee. At breakfast time, coffee is served in large cups with lots of hot milk to cut its strength. In the afternoon and evening, however, it is consumed black (Spaniards who visit the United States are always horrified by the watery liquid we call coffee), and with outrageous quantities of sugar. Espresso coffee is often accompanied by a glass of Spanish brandy or a dry Spanish anisette.

There are several hot alcoholic drinks that are regional specialties and make excellent, but powerful, after-dinner drinks. By all means try the flaming Galician drink, *queimada*, and the Catalán *cremat* coffee. For cold evenings at home alone, snuggle up to the hot milk, almond, and brandy drink called *ponche.*

Spain's pride, of course, are its table wines and sherries, which should come first on any list of Spanish drinks to try (see Chapter 15, "The Wines of Spain").

SANGRÍA

START PREPARATION SEVERAL HOURS IN ADVANCE.

NOTHING is more satisfying in summer than an icy cold *sangría*. When I think of Spain, some of my most pleasant thoughts are of beach-side restaurants, where one goes in bathing suit straight from a dip in the Mediterranean to eat *paella* and sip *sangría.*

Sangría slides down easily, so prepare plenty, increasing this recipe by any amount desired.

Makes about 4 cups

1 bottle (24 ounces) dry, full-bodied red wine, preferably of Spanish import from Valencia or Valdepeñas (see wine chart)
2 tablespoons orange juice
2 tablespoons orange liqueur (optional), such as Gran Torres or Grand Marnier

1 tablespoon sugar
Orange and lemon slices
Apple and/or peach wedges
1 cup club soda or sparkling water

Mix together in a large pitcher all ingredients except the club soda. Cover and refrigerate several hours or overnight. Add the club soda and ice cubes. Serve very cold in balloon-shaped wineglasses or in Spanish earthenware mugs (without handles).

SANGRÍA BLANCA

(White Wine Sangría)

START PREPARATION ONE DAY IN ADVANCE.

WHITE *sangría*, to my knowledge, is not found in Spain, but due to the great popularity of white wines in the United States, it has caught on here.

Makes 4 cups

1 bottle (24 ounces) dry white wine
6 teaspoons sugar, or to taste
2 tablespoons orange liqueur, such as
  Gran Torres or Grand Marnier

Orange and lemon slices
Apple and/or peach wedges
1 cup club soda or sparkling water

Mix all ingredients except the club soda in a large pitcher. Cover and refrigerate overnight. To serve, add the club soda and ice cubes.

BLANCO Y NEGRO

(Cinnamon-Flavored Ice Milk with Coffee)

JUST like an ice cream soda, Blanco y Negro ("White and Black") is eaten with a long spoon and sipped through a straw. Its glacial iciness can make one forget the heat of summer.

Blanco y Negro is dessert and coffee all in one.

Serves 6

Leche Merengada (p. 382)
1½ cups strong black coffee, preferably espresso, chilled

Make the Leche Merengada according to instructions. Pour ¼ cup chilled coffee into each of 6 parfait glasses, then add scoops of Leche Merengada. Serve immediately.

MAZAGRÁN

(Lemon-Flavored Iced Coffee)

MY HUSBAND'S favorite summer refresher.

Serves 1

3 teaspoons sugar, or to taste
¾ cup strong cold coffee
1 teaspoon lemon juice

Crushed ice
½ cup water or club soda
1 slice lemon

Mix the sugar, coffee, and lemon juice in a tall glass. When the sugar is dissolved, add the crushed ice, water or soda, and the slice of lemon. This drink may also be made with the addition of a small amount of brandy.

LIMONADA MADRILEÑA

(Lemonade, Madrid Style)

PREPARE SEVERAL HOURS IN ADVANCE.

A CROSS between a lemonade and a *sangría*, this drink is most refreshing.

Makes 4 cups

1 cup freshly squeezed lemon juice
1 cup water
2 cups dry red wine

1 peach, cut in thin wedges
3 tablespoons sugar
4 lemon slices

Combine all ingredients. Refrigerate several hours. Serve in tall glasses with lots of ice.

CREMAT

(Catalán Coffee)

A BRACING drink for a cold winter's eve. You might want to top the Cremat with heavy cream, plain or whipped, for an elegant finale to a special dinner.

1 cup brandy, preferably Spanish   ½ cup anisette liqueur
   brandy, or Cognac (no   ¼ cup sugar
   need to use your very   2 cinnamon sticks
   best V.S.O.P.)   Peel of ½ lemon
1 cup light rum   3 cups strong hot coffee

Mix in a pot (a shallow Spanish earthenware casserole is typically used) the
brandy, rum, anisette, sugar, cinnamon sticks, and lemon peel. Heat slowly,
then ignite, standing well back and being sure that nothing flammable is
nearby. Burn 10–15 minutes, or until the liquid is reduced from 2½ cups to
1½ cups. (You may put the flame out occasionally, by putting on a lid, to see
how much liquid remains.) Put out the flames. Add the hot coffee, then pour
into Irish coffee glasses, mugs, or large balloon-shaped wineglasses.

QUEIMADA

(Flaming Liqueur with Apples)

QUEIMADA is an awesomely potent brew of ancient origin. A longtime resident of Galicia and close friend, Chalo Peláez, describes the rituals that
accompany the drinking of this hot liqueur: "Galicia is the land of legend,
where, on typically foggy nights, when the mist hangs low over forest and sea,
witches gather, it is said, under a magical oak tree to brew the Queimada. We
prepare it today much as they supposedly did—by combining in an earthenware pot over an outdoor fire large quantities of a local liquor called 'orujo,'
some sugar and slices of apple. The liquid is ignited, lighting up the heavy
night air, and the pot is slowly stirred to the accompaniment of ancient Celtic
chants, which echo through the forests. So important is the tradition of the
Queimada in Galicia that contests are held each year to choose the 'Gran
Maestro of the Queimada,' a title of almost mystical significance, which brings
great respect to the holder."

   Ideally this drink should be prepared out-of-doors, but our friend Chalo
prepared it for us in our living room. With the lights dimmed, everyone seated
on the floor, and Celtic chants in progress, the effect was terrific, but the
flames leaped too high for my comfort. I suggest using instead the more
prosaic surroundings of the kitchen stove.

Serves 6

5 tablespoons sugar   Italian equivalent, *grappa*,
2 cups *orujo*, also known as   is found in liquor stores)
   aguardiente, p. 428. (Its   ½ apple, cored, in 8 wedges

Sprinkle 3 tablespoons of the sugar in a chafing dish or large, shallow casserole, preferably earthenware, about 12 inches in diameter. Stir in the *orujo* and apple slices.

Place another tablespoon of sugar in a large serving spoon. (The spoon should, ideally, be earthenware too, so that it doesn't conduct heat—otherwise, protect your hand with a potholder.) Fill the rest of the bowl of the spoon with liquor from the casserole. Ignite the spoon, holding it over—not in—the casserole. (At this point the lights should be lowered and the Celtic chanting begun!) Flame the spoon until the sugar starts to bubble and caramelize. Lower the spoon into the casserole and carefully ignite the pot, stirring. While this burns, add another tablespoon of sugar to the spoon, fill it with the liquor, and caramelize again. Stir into the casserole. Continue burning a few more minutes—the longer you burn, the lower the alcohol content will be. With a soup ladle, spoon the liquid and apple slices into small earthenware mugs, small punch cups, or demitasse cups (no saucers).

NOTE: Queimada can also be made into an excellent dessert (serves 4). Increase the apples to 3, each cut in 16 wedges. Reduce the liquor to 1 cup and leave the sugar the same. Follow the above instructions, cooking until the flames die. Continue cooking until the apples are tender and the liquid is reduced and syrupy. The apples may then be served and are delicious over vanilla ice cream.

PONCHE DE COÑAC

(Hot Milk, Almond, and Brandy Punch)

A SOOTHING nightcap, especially indicated when one is not feeling up to par. In spite of its brandy content, it is commonly served to children in Spain when they have come down with *"la gripe"*—flu. It is, however, equally enjoyable when one is in perfect health.

Serves 4–5

16 blanched almonds, chopped
2½ tablespoons sugar
2 cups milk
4 egg yolks

4 tablespoons brandy, preferably Spanish brandy, or Cognac
½ teaspoon vanilla

Grind the almonds in a blender or processor. Gradually pour in the sugar and milk. Transfer to a saucepan and heat to the boiling point. Meanwhile, in a small bowl beat the egg yolks until smooth and light colored. Gradually add the brandy and vanilla. Stir the yolk mixture into the hot milk. Strain into glasses and serve immediately.

CHOCOLATE

(Spanish-Style Hot Chocolate)

HOT chocolate is typically served at breakfast or teatime with Churros (p. 342) or fried bread pieces (*picatostes*), which are dunked in this thick and rich chocolate drink.

Makes 1 cup

1 cup milk
1 ounce unsweetened chocolate, cut
    in small pieces

8 teaspoons sugar, or to taste

Mix together the milk, chocolate, and sugar. Heat over a low flame, stirring with a wire whisk, until the chocolate is completely dissolved. Turn up the heat and bring to a boil. Allow the mixture to bubble up to the top of the saucepan. Remove immediately from the heat and beat with the wire whisk. Repeat boiling and beating 3 more times, then tilt the pan and beat the hot chocolate well with the wire whisk until it is very frothy. Serve immediately.

Chapter 15

THE WINES OF SPAIN

Wine brings feelings of happiness and optimism. The wines of
Cariñena, Priorato, Alella, Rioja, Jerez, Córdoba and Málaga have
the sun of Spain concentrated within them, and are the joy of its
people.

Diccionario de Vinos Españoles

THE wines of Spain, quintessentially Spanish in their taste, are the ideal
accompaniment to the foods of Spain. Nothing quite complements Cocido
Madrileño, Paella a la Valenciana, Fabada Asturiana, Perdiz Estofado, or
Tortilla Española, to take a few examples, like a wine whose roots are in the
very same soil that produced the ingredients for these most typically Spanish
dishes. Yet since the wines of Spain are in the tradition of Bordeaux and
Burgundy wines, they are also good with a wide variety of other cuisines.
Couple this with the comparatively low prices of these fine wines, and the
reasons for becoming a fan of *vinos españoles* are compelling indeed.

Spanish wines are being discovered all over the world and are winning
prizes and much praise. These are exciting times for the wines of Spain, and
the quality and selection in the United States are increasing by leaps and
bounds. America is fast becoming one of Spain's biggest markets. The "oaky"
taste of the Rioja region's wines, a result of long and painstaking aging, and
the blending of different grape varieties (a process common to all Spanish
wines) contribute to the special characteristics of the wines of Spain and make
them stand out from other wines of the world.

But the age-old snob appeal of French wines lingers on and in some ways is
a blessing for those of us who love Spanish wines—it keeps the prices down
and keeps availability up. The Spanish reserve wines of 1970; for example—
one of the best years for Spanish wines in the past two decades—may still be
purchased at relatively moderate prices.

My husband and I have done our best to take advantage of this situation to
build up a wine cellar based on the finest Spain has to offer. It has been a

haphazard process consisting of chance finds in small and otherwise unremarkable wine shops and at other times persistent searches (with the aid of cooperative wine merchants) for particular bottles known to exist in this country in small quantities. Such a search yielded in one instance a case of Vega Sicilia 1953, the crème de la crème of Spanish wines that commands top prices here and abroad and is in a class by itself. We have also supplemented our cellar with purchases in Spain of wines not imported or long gone from the American market, wines all the more pleasurable to drink because of the memorable miles of travel they covered with us across Spain.

When speaking of Spanish wines, the region most frequently referred to is Rioja. (Sherry from Jerez is, of course, even better known but will be discussed separately [p. 413].) Rioja is an area in north-central Spain and is one of the largest producers of quality wines in Spain today. Another area that makes top-notch wines is Penedés, near Barcelona. Almost all regions of Spain, however, have vines under cultivation, more vines, in fact, than any other country in the world. In some areas—Valdepeñas and Valencia, for example— production is enormous, but the wines are young and meant for everyday consumption. These wines usually reach us in three-liter jugs and are ideal for casual drinking or as the base for a fine *sangría*. In other areas, production is extremely small, filling only local needs. These are the wines that never reach American shores, but you will want to sample them on a visit to Spain and know about them in the event that they are one day imported.

If you travel to Galicia in northwest Spain, for example, be sure to sample the fascinating Albariño white wine, fruity yet dry; and the red and white Ribeiro wines, the whites light and fruity, the reds very dry, syrupy, and raspberry colored. The whites are exceptionally good with Galicia's extraordinary scallops. In the Barcelona area, try the Alella district's smooth red wines and their famous dry whites. Tarragona's powerful Priorato wines, amber-colored whites and deep-toned reds, also hail from Cataluña. When in the Basque country, the only thing to drink is their Txakoli, an acidic, low-grade "green" wine, which is the ideal accompaniment to the area's excellent and varied seafood, as well as being an ingredient in many a seafood recipe. The wines of Cariñena, in the province of Aragón, are tough, powerful wines— the strongest unfortified wines in the world, reaching up to 18 per cent alcohol, as compared to 11–12 per cent for most table wines—which nicely complement the equally robust cuisine of the region. The hearty wines of Chinchón and Méntrida from central Spain near Toledo and the mountain wines of Morella and Albarracín are all highly suited to the stew and bean dishes indigenous to these areas. Every region in Spain has its characteristic wines, and when traveling in Spain, it is best to pass up the Rioja and Penedés wines, which are widely available here, and try instead the local varieties, which almost invariably will be the house wines listed on area menus.

The making of wine in Spain goes back over two thousand years, but the production of quality wines is a more recent development, dating back to the last century. It was Spain's good fortune—and France's great misfortune—that a tragic plague was to hit France's vineyards in the mid-nineteenth century, cutting short that nation's progress in the area of wine making. The Phylloxera disease, caused by an insect that attacked the roots of the plants, spread rapidly throughout France, bringing complete devastation to the vines and spelling financial disaster for wine producers. Enterprising Frenchmen then turned to Spain to renew their wine production. They searched for areas with climatic and soil conditions similar to those they had left behind in France, looking at the same time for areas fairly close to their homeland where some wine production was already in progress. They found two places that met all their requirements: Rioja and Penedés, where they hastened to establish themselves, setting up the refined systems of wine production that had been developed in France. The French prospered, while the Spanish learned new wine-making techniques.

As the plague subsided, the French returned home, replanting their vineyards and reactivating their wine industry. But the methods they left behind in Spain endured and are partly responsible for the outstanding quality of Rioja and Penedés wines today. It should be noted, however, that wine in Spain never was and never will be a copy of French wine. The climate is different, the vines produce different grape varieties that must be handled in their own special ways, and, of course, over the years Spanish wine growers have developed their own ideas and methods of utilizing their native products to the fullest.

RIOJA WINES

I RECENTLY visited the Rioja region to find out what makes Rioja wines different from other wines of the world. My husband and I were there in April, when the twisted bodies of bare vine stumps contrasted sharply with the geometrically perfect rows of plantings—a far cry from the lushly laden plants that would appear in September. Even with the absence of grapes, there was no doubt that we were in wine country. Along with the acres of tilled land, which produces outstanding vegetable crops as well as grape vines, the main road to Haro, wine capital of the region, is lined with *bodegas,* as the wine companies are called, many of them well over a century old. Although most of these *bodegas* trace their origins to the arrival of the French in the nineteenth century, vineyards were cultivated in Rioja long before this event. By 1560, in fact, Rioja wines were already prospering, leading growers to form a control board to regulate Rioja wine production and prevent fraud. One of the world's first trademarks was that of the Rioja producers, who combined their initials into a logo that was used as a stamp of quality. Today the Designation of Origin label, which appears on the back of all Rioja bottles, is a guarantee of quality and proof of origin.

It was not by chance that Rioja was from early times a prospering wine-growing region, for the area unites all the ideal conditions to produce fine wines. Located along the Oja River (Río Oja, from which Rioja is contracted), a tributary of the majestic Ebro River, the Rioja region is at a point in Spanish geography where the cold and wet Atlantic climate of the north meets the hot and arid Mediterranean climate of the south. Some experts attribute the special characteristics of Rioja wines to this unique location.

Rioja is subdivided into three parts, the Rioja Alta (Upper Rioja), Rioja Alavesa (northern Rioja, comprising part of the province of Álava), and the Rioja Baja (Lower Rioja). Rioja Alta and Alavesa are the northernmost areas, more influenced by the Atlantic climate, with long, although not extreme, winters and much rainfall. Rioja Baja, on the other hand, is farther south and has warmer and drier conditions, which are less ideal for wine production. Consequently, 65 per cent of all Rioja production and most of its top-quality wines come from the two northern regions. There are, of course, exceptions to the rule—in my mind, one of the finest wines of Rioja belongs to the Bodegas Muerza located in San Adrián in Lower Rioja.

Rioja wines are a highly personalized blend of four grapes, each *bodega* having its own formula for mixing them. The *tempranillo* grape, a variety native to the region, accounts for 50–75 per cent of all grapes used and gives the Rioja wines a special taste—it is said to add "spice" to the wine, to give it a fruity flavor and a magnificent deep ruby color. Of the three other grape types used in making Rioja wines, two others also are native strains—the *graciano*, very perfumed, which gives a wonderful bouquet and freshness to the wine, and the *mazuelo*, high in tannin, giving the wine its acidity and contributing to its lovely color. The *garnacha* grape is found elsewhere in Europe and provides a high degree of alcohol while not adding significantly to the wine's color or aroma. White wine accounts for only 10 per cent of Rioja production but is of exceptionally high quality and extremely pleasing to the palate. The "oaky" taste of these whites, some of them aged up to six years in barrel before bottling, is an indication of their body and character.

Climate and grape variety are two of the components that make Rioja wines unique. The third is the laborious process of barrel aging, which gives Rioja wines their wonderful "woody" and earthy flavor. Simple Riojas spend from one to three years in American oak, a type of wood that has proved over the years to be the most appropriate. However, those Riojas destined to be great wines, the Reservas, are aged anywhere from eight to ten years in barrels. Although it was the French who brought this technique to Rioja, it is interesting that in France today such lengthy aging is extremely rare. Rioja wines, however, maintain the tradition and stand up well to such prolonged aging; it is not unusual to find Rioja wines from the turn of the century that are still in exquisite condition.

Rioja wines not only are subjected to careful aging in the barrels, but also spend many years in bottles in the *bodegas* to continue the aging process before being released for sale. It is the practice in other countries to sell wines immediately and depend on the buyer to age the wines. Rioja *bodegas* take no such chances, keeping enormous stocks of bottled wine in storage until the wine meets their rigorous requirements. The exceptional Reserva wines are kept the longest, often remaining ten to fifteen years or more in *bodega* before being sold. Such a system assures the buyer that any Rioja wine he purchases is ripe to drink. Of course, wines continue to develop in the bottles for many more years, and keeping a Rioja wine longer, in proper conditions, can only bring further improvement.

RIOJA RESERVA WINES

THE Riojas that I find most exciting are the Reservas, for they are old wines that have been lovingly cared for. When a Rioja bottle reads "Reserva" or "Gran Reserva" and "Reserva Especial" (finer still than Reservas), you know an excellent wine is in your possession, for only exceptional harvests—perhaps one or two in a decade—will become Reservas. In recent times the years 1964 and 1970 have produced outstanding wines (see vintage chart, pp. 405–406). Although prices are climbing, Reserva wines are still quite modestly priced. The wine chart lists the Reservas generally available in the United States (pp. 407–408).

Obviously the long years of aging Rioja wines can create a financial burden for the *bodegas* by tying up capital for prolonged periods of time. One wonders how long this can continue without a change in methods of production or a lowering of quality. The *bodegas* I visited in Rioja provided clues to how they are dealing with these problems now and how they will in the future. At Federico Paternina, for example, one of the largest wineries in the world and the largest Rioja exporter, the answer is modernization and appeal to a mass market. Many critics contend that such methods can only lead to lower quality. The answer remains to be seen, for Paternina still has large reserves of quality wines from years past.

For R. López de Heredia, on the other hand, where oak barrels are handmade on the premises and reserve wines still clarified with egg whites and the bottles filled by hand, the answer lies in maintaining high standards and a good reputation (eliminating the need for extensive publicity) and in keeping the business in the family. But change is inevitable—already the aging period has been reduced by many companies to save on costs, as well as to cater to a market looking for "lighter" wines. These concessions may eventually alter the taste and quality of Riojas. All the more reason to stock up now!

PENEDÉS WINES

THE wines of the Penedés region of Cataluña, stretching south of Barcelona along the Mediterranean coast and into the mountainous interior, are fast becoming hot items on the wine market, especially those wines produced by the family-operated Miguel Torres company. Their light whites, called Viña Sol, are exceedingly popular with the American public; their reds, Coronas in particular, are winning international acclaim for their outstanding quality.

Be advised that the "reserva" label on Penedés wines has a different meaning from similar Rioja labeling. "Reserva" in Rioja means outstanding vintage coupled with extended aging. In Penedés, "reserva" refers only to the selection of superior grapes; the aging period is short, no different from the aging of ordinary wines (a maximum of two years). Penedés wines are, in general, much younger wines than Rioja, and producers are riding on the crest of the worldwide taste today for lighter wines. Penedés producers are also much more open to innovation and to French influences and are therefore less tradition-bound than most Rioja *bodegas*. There is much experimentation with French grape varieties (in particular the Cabernet Sauvignon), great interest in the mechanical harvesting of grapes, and much less emphasis on barrel aging. Their wines, therefore, are a much more international-style product, without the very "Spanish" traits of the Riojas.

RIBERA DEL DUERO WINES

THE most exciting wine region in Spain today is the Ribera del Duero, which spans principally the provinces of Burgos and Valladolid. These top quality wines, crisp and fruity, are receiving rave reviews from American wine connoisseurs, and I expect that more and more wineries of the region will bring their product to the United States in the future.

For years the wines of the Vega Sicilia winery were the only ones mentioned from the Ribera del Duero, and they remain in a class by themselves. This small establishment produces a unique wine highly prized in Spain and little known elsewhere in the world because of its tiny production. We are geared to think of Spanish wines as bargains—again Vega Sicilia stands out from the crowd, for it is the most expensive Spanish wine on the market today. Vega Sicilia produces two wines, both red: the Valbuena and the Reserva Único. They are more acidic than Rioja wines and have an exceptional bouquet and flavor. Both are imported to the United States, but the supply is extremely limited.

The wines of Spain are as exciting and unique as Spain's cuisine, and, ideally, one should not be sampled without the other. I have included wine suggestions with many recipes and hope this will enable those who are relatively unfamiliar with Spanish food and wine to make wine selections that will pleasantly complement the foods. I am confident that a familiarity with

Spanish wines can only lead to greater appreciation and admiration for these fine wines.

Vintages

Vintage information on Penedés and most Ribera del Duero wines is not available prior to the 1970's. However, since Penedés wines are usually consumed when quite young, it would be highly unusual to find a bottle more than ten years old. And although Ribera del Duero wines age well, most of the region's quality wines are of recent production.

	RIOJA	PENEDÉS	RIBERA DEL DUERO
1928	Very Good	—	—
1934	Very Good	—	—
1943	Very Good	—	—
1947	Very Good	—	—
1952	Excellent	—	—
1954	Good—Very Good	—	—
1955	Very Good	—	—
1956	Good	—	—
1959	Very Good	—	—
1960	Good	—	—
1961	Good	—	—
1962	Very Good	—	—
1963	Average–Good	—	—
1964	Excellent	—	—
1965	Poor	—	—
1966	Average	—	—
1967	Average	—	—
1968	Very Good	—	—
1969	Average	Average	—
1970	Excellent	Very Good	—
1971	Average	Good	Average
1972	Poor	Excellent	Average
1973	Good	Very Good	Very Good
1974	Average	Poor	Good
1975	Good	Very Good	Good
1976	Good	Excellent	Very Good
1977	Poor	Good	Poor

	RIOJA	PENEDÉS	RIBERA DEL DUERO
1978	Good—Very Good	Excellent	Average
1979	Good	Average	Good
1980	Good	Very Good	Good
1981	Excellent	Very Good	Excellent
1982	Very Good	Very Good	Very Good
1983	Very Good	Good	Very Good
1984	Average	Very Good	Average
1985	Very Good	Very Good	Very Good
1986	Very Good	Good	Very Good
1987	Good	Average	Good
1988	—	Very Good	—

All the wines listed in this section are imported to the United States. However, finding a liquor store with a large selection of Spanish wines is somewhat of an adventure. Within a small neighborhood you may find one liquor store with two or three brands, while a few blocks away another will have a completely different stock. So it is useful to shop around. Remember too that Spanish wines, except the Reservas, are usually blended, and therefore the quality is quite uniformly high, with less variation according to vintage than might otherwise be expected.

The wines are divided into several categories: *Reservas* are the oldest wines, selected from the best vintages. *Light Reds* (*claretes*) are Bordeaux-style wines that generally go well with "light" meats such as veal or chicken and with many egg and rice dishes. *Full-bodied Reds* are similar to Burgundy wines and are usually associated with beef, game, sausage, and bean dishes. *Dry and Medium-Dry Whites* most often accompany fish and shellfish. *Dry and Medium-Dry Rosés* are sometimes recommended for duck or chicken dishes and occasionally for fish. Such classifications are extremely elastic and vary according to personal preferences. The ingredients used in the preparation of a dish can also affect the type of wine used.

Many recipes in this book recommend specific brands and types of wines for certain dishes. If the brand suggested is not available, substitute another wine in the same category—or, of course, you may choose to select a different type of wine entirely.

Starred wines are personal favorites found to be exceptionally good.

Table Wines

DRY LIGHT RED RESERVES

Wines	Producers	Area	Price Range
*Berberana 1952, 1970 1973, 1975, 1978	Bodegas Berberana	Rioja	$$-$$$
*Claret Fino 1966	Bodegas Bilbaínas	Rioja	$$$
*Conde de los Andes 1952, 1959	Federico Paternina	Rioja	$$$$
*Gran Zaco 1962	Bodegas Bilbaínas	Rioja	$$$
Imperial 1966, 1968, 1975	Compañía Vinícola del Norte de España	Rioja	$$-$$$
*Marqués de Cáceres 1970, 1973, 1975	Marqués de Cáceres	Rioja	$$-$$$
*Marqués de Murrieta 1952, 1973, 1975	Marqués de Murrieta	Rioja	$-$$$
Marqués de Riscal 1964, 1965, 1966, 1970	Marqués de Riscal	Rioja	$$$$
*Marqués de Villamagna 1973	Campo Viejo	Rioja	$$
*Olarra 1970, 1973, 1975	Bodegas Olarra	Rioja	$$
Paternina 1967	Federico Paternina	Rioja	$$
René Barbier 1978	René Barbier	Penedés	$
*Reserva 890, 1973	La Rioja Alta	Rioja	$$$
*Reserva 904, 1973	La Rioja Alta	Rioja	$$
Reserva Especial 1973	Martínez Lacuesta	Rioja	$$
Royal Rioja 1975	Bodegas Franco-Españolas	Rioja	$
*Único 1960, 1965, 1972	Vega Sicilia	Valladolid	$$$$
*Viña Lanciano 1970	Bodegas Lan	Rioja	$$
Viña Monty 1975, 1976	Bodegas Montecillos	Rioja	$$
*Viña Tondonia 1964, 1968, 1970, 1973	R. López de Heredia	Rioja	$$

*Personal Preference

$ = inexpensive; $$ = moderate; $$$ = expensive; $$$$ = very expensive

DRY FULL-BODIED RED RESERVES

Wines	Producers	Area	Price Range
*Carlomagno 1970	Carlos Serres	Rioja	$$
Carlos Serres 1970	Carlos Serres	Rioja	$$
Carta de Oro, 1973, 1975	Bodegas Berberanas	Rioja	$$
Carta de Plata 1973, 1975	Bodegas Berberanas	Rioja	$$
*Cerro Añón 1973, 1975	Bodegas Olarra	Rioja	$$
Gran Coronas 1979	Miguel Torres	Penedés	$$
*Gran Coronas Black Label 1973, 1975, 1977	Miguel Torres	Penedés	$$$
*Gran Sangre de Toro 1975, 1979, 1986	Miguel Torres	Penedés	$$
Lagunilla, 1973, 1975	Bodegas Lagunilla	Rioja	$$
*Solar de Samaniego 1968, 1970, 1973	Bodegas Alavesas	Rioja	$$-$$$
*Viña Bosconia 1964, 1968, 1970, 1973	R. López de Heredia	Rioja	$$-$$$
*Viña Pomal 1966, 1970, 1973	Bodegas Bilbaínas	Rioja	$$-$$$
*Viña Real 1966, 1973, 1975	Compañía Vinícola del Norte de España	Rioja	$$-$$$
*Viña Turzaballa 1966	Ramón Bilbao	Rioja	$$

DRY WHITE RESERVES

Wines	Producers	Area	Price Range
*Federico Paternina 1970, 1976, 1977, 1979	Federico Paternina	Rioja	$$
Gran Viña Sol 1976, 1977, 1983	Miguel Torres	Penedés	$$
*Gran Vina Sol Reserva Especial 1976, 1977	Miguel Torres	Penedés	$$
Reserva Limousin 1980, 1981	Marqués de Riscal	Valladolid	$$
*Viña Tondonia	R. López de Heredia	Rioja	$$

*Personal Preference

$ = inexpensive; $$ = moderate; $$$ = expensive; $$$$ = very expensive

DRY LIGHT RED

Wines	Producers	Area	Price Range
*Cabernet Sauvignon	Jean León	Penedés	$$
Clarete Fino	Martínez Lacuesta	Rioja	$
Diamante	Bodegas Franco-Españolas	Rioja	$
*Gran Condal	Bodegas Rioja Santiago	Rioja	$$
*Imperial	Compañía Vinícola del Norte de España	Rioja	$$
*Lan	Bodegas Lan	Rioja	$
Lar de Barros	Inviosa	Extremadura	$$
Los Molinos	Bodegas Félix Solis	Valdepeñas	$
*Marqués de Arienzo	Pedro Domecq	Rioja	$$
*Marqués de Cáceres	Marqués de Cáceres	Rioja	$$
*Marqués de Murrieta	Marqués de Murrieta	Rioja	$$
Marqués de Riscal	Marqués de Riscal	Rioja	$$
Mauro	Bodegas Mauro	Ribera del Duero	$$
Monte Llano	Ramón Bilbao	Rioja	$
*Muga	Bodegas Muga	Rioja	$
*Olarra	Bodegas Olarra	Rioja	$
*Pesquera	Bodegas Alejandro Fernandez	Ribera del Duero	$$$
Protos	Bodegas Ribera Duero	Ribera del Duero	$$
*Remelluri	Remelluri	Rioja	$
René Barbier	René Barbier	Penedés	$
Rioja Bordón	Bodegas Franco-Españolas	Rioja	$
Rioja Clarete	Compañía Vinícola del Norte de España	Rioja	$
*Rioja Vega	Bodegas Muerza	Rioja	$
*Valbuena	Vega Sicilia	Valladolid	$$$
*Viña Alberdi	La Rioja Alta	Rioja	$$
Viña Albina	Bodegas Riojanas	Rioja	$
Viña Ardanza	La Rioja Alta	Rioja	$$
*Viña Cumbrero	Bodegas Montecillo	Rioja	$
Viña Berceo	Bodegas Gurpequi	Rioja	$$

*Personal Preference

$ = inexpensive; $$ = moderate; $$$ = expensive; $$$$ = very expensive

DRY LIGHT RED (cont'd)

*Viña Lanciano	Bodegas Lan	Rioja	$
Viña Monty	Bodegas Montecillo	Rioja	$
*Viña Tondonia	R. López de Heredia	Rioja	$$
*Viña Zaco	Bodegas Bilbaínas	Rioja	$$
*Yllera	Bodegas Yllera	Ribera del Duero	$$

DRY FULL-BODIED RED

Wines	Producers	Area	Price Range
Burgella	Juan Hernández	Valencia	$
Campeador	Martínez Lacuesta	Rioja	$
*Campo Viejo	Campo Viejo	Rioja	$
*Carlomagno	Carlos Serres	Rioja	$
Carta de Oro	Bodegas Berberanas	Rioja	$
Carta de Plata	Bodegas Berberanas	Rioja	$
*Cerro Añón	Bodegas Olarra	Rioja	$$
Coronas	Miguel Torres	Penedés	$
Faustino	Bodegas Faustino Martínez	Rioja	$
Iberia	Iberia	Valdepeñas	$
José García	José García	Tarragona	$
Masía Bach	Masía Bach	Penedés	$
Monte Real	Bodegas Riojanas	Rioja	$
Monte Seco	Ramón Bilbao	Rioja	$
Prado Enea	Bodegas Muga	Rioja	$
Sangre de Toro	Miguel Torres	Penedés	$
Siglo	Age	Rioja	$
*Solar de Samaniego	Bodegas Alavesa	Rioja	$
Tres Ríos	Bodegas Gallegas	Orense	$
*Viña Ardanza	La Rioja Alta	Rioja	$$
*Viña Bosconia	R. López de Heredia	Rioja	$
*Viña Pomal	Bodegas Bilbaínas	Rioja	$
*Viña Real	Compañía Vinícola del Norte de España	Rioja	$$
Viña Santa Digna	Miguel Torres	Penedés	$$
*Viña Vial	Federico Paternina	Rioja	$$
Zapardiel	Zapardiel	Valdepeñas	$

*Personal Preference

$ = inexpensive; $$ = moderate; $$$ = expensive; $$$$ = very expensive

DRY WHITE

Wines	Producers	Area	Price Range
Blanco Seco	Bodegas Olarra	Rioja	$
Campo Viejo	Campo Viejo	Rioja	$
Canchales	Bodegas Riojanas	Rioja	$
*Cepa de Oro	Bodegas Bilbaínas	Rioja	$
Cerro Añón	Bodegas Olarra	Rioja	$
Chalais	Juan Hernández	Valencia	$
Chardonnay	Jean León	Penedés	$$
*Ermita D'Espiells	Juvé y Camps	Penedés	$
Faustino	Bodegas Faustino Martínez	Rioja	$
Gran Condal	Bodegas Rioja Santiago	Rioja	$
Iberia	Iberia	Valdepeñas	$
José García	José García	Tarragona	$
Los Molinos	Bodegas Félix Solís	Valdepeñas	$
*Marqués de Cáceres	Marqués de Caceres	Rioja	$
*Marqués de Murrieta	Marqués de Murrieta	Rioja	$$
*Marqués de Riscal	Marqués de Riscal	Valladolid	$
*Martin Codax Albariño	Martin Codex	Galicia	$$
*Masía Bach	Masía Bach	Penedés	$
Monopole	Compañía Vinícola del Norte de España	Rioja	$$
Monte Blanco	Ramón Bilbao	Rioja	$
Monte Llano	Ramón Bilbao	Rioja	$
Muga	Bodegas Muga	Rioja	$
Oro Ribeiro	Bodegas Arnoya	Galicia	$
Parxet	Marqués de Alella	Alella	$$
Privilegio	Pedro Domecq	Rioja	$
Puerta Vieja	Bodegas Riojanas	Rioja	$
Reciente	Bodegas Olarra	Rioja	$
René Barbier	René Barbier	Penedés	$
Rioja Blanco	Compañía Vinícola del Norte de España	Rioja	$
Siglo	Age	Rioja	$
Solar de Samaniego	Bodegas Alavesas	Rioja	$
*Viñadrián	Bodegas Gurpegui	Rioja	$
Viña Cumbrero	Bodegas Montecillo	Rioja	$

*Personal Preference

$ = inexpensive; $$ = moderate; $$$ = expensive; $$$$ = very expensive

DRY WHITE (cont'd)

Viña Gravonia	R. López de Heredia	Rioja	$
*Viña Paceta	Bodegas Bilbaínas	Rioja	$
Viña Sol	Miguel Torres	Penedés	$
Viña Soledad	Bodegas Franco-Españolas	Rioja	$
Viña Tondonia	R. López de Heredia	Rioja	$$

MEDIUM-DRY WHITE

Wines	*Producers*	*Area*	*Price Range*
Brillante	Bodegas Bilbaínas	Rioja	$
Lan Blanco	Bodegas Lan	Rioja	$
Monte Haro	Federico Paternina	Rioja	$
Monte Real	Bodegas Riojanas	Rioja	$
*Viña Esmeralda	Miguel Torres	Penedés	$$
*Viña Zaconia	R. López de Heredia	Rioja	$

DRY ROSÉ

Wines	*Producers*	*Area*	*Price Range*
De Casta Rosado	Miguel Torres	Penedés	$
Don Miguel	Don Miguel	Penedés	$
*Las Campanas	Vinicola Navarra	Navarra	$$
Marqués de Cáceres	Marqués de Cáceres	Rioja	$
Rosado Fino	Martínez Lacuesta	Rioja	$

MEDIUM-DRY ROSÉ

Wines	*Producers*	*Area*	*Price Range*
Brillante	Bodegas Bilbainas	Rioja	$
Siglo	Age	Rioja	$

*Personal Preference

$ = inexpensive; $$ = moderate; $$$ = expensive; $$$$ = very expensive

SHERRY: THE NOBLE WINE

SHERRY—Jerez—one of the world's oldest wines, savored and praised over the centuries for its fine quality and unique taste, is, at the same time, one of the most misunderstood and maligned of all wines. Surely the time has come to erase the image of sherry as a drink sipped by little old ladies in staid English parlors and let it take its rightful place among the great wines of the world.

Although sherry complements many cuisines, it is absolutely indispensable if one wants to eat in Spanish style. Nothing quite compares to the crisp taste of a cold glass of dry sherry with *tapas*, and, indeed, once one has relaxed along the banks of the Guadalquivir River in southern Spain, eating exquisite fresh prawns and savoring a fine sherry, it is difficult to imagine a drink more sublime. Sherry takes many forms, from bone dry to syrupy sweet and all ranges in between. It is so versatile that besides being ideal with appetizers, in its sweeter forms it is perfect with desserts. It is also indispensable in Spanish cookery, entering into fish and meat sauces as well as adding exciting flavor to desserts. The frequency with which the expression "*al jerez*" is used to describe Spanish recipes attests to the exceptional esteem in which sherry is held in Spanish cuisine.

Sherry, like Champagne or Cognac, takes its name from its place of origin, Jerez (Heh-reth') in southwest Spain. (The British, age-old sherry drinkers, mispronounced the name as "sherry," which today is its name worldwide.) Jerez is an area of vast estates, more tradition-bound than any other region of Spain. Many of the great names of Spanish nobility call Jerez their home and follow a life-style of elegance and gentility that has all but disappeared from modern Spain. In sherry country, time seems to stand still, and one is taken back to a more gracious era of living. Sherry is a part of that way of life and insures, to some extent, its survival, for making sherry demands loving care and devotion, as no other wine-making process does. Its quality depends upon those for whom tradition is a way of life.

The history of Jerez and its sherry goes back thousands of years, when Phoenician settlers introduced grape vines to the area. In more recent centuries, sherry accompanied many famous Spanish expeditions of discovery. Magellan's ship left for its world-encompassing journey from Sanlúcar de Barrameda, in the heart of sherry country, carrying 417 jugs and 253 casks of sherry. Columbus, who set sail from southern ports, carried sherry on all three of his voyages, for sherry, due to its fortification, was not subject to spoilage. Other items of sherry lore: the *Mayflower* was once a sherry ship running between the Spanish port of Cádiz and Plymouth, England. And warfare between Spain and England in the eighteenth century was the setting for another curious sherry story. In the famous battle of Trafalgar near Cádiz, in which Lord Nelson lost his life, it is said that Nelson's body was "pickled" for the long journey home to England in a keg of sherry!

Sherry is made elsewhere in the world, most notably in California and in

Italy, where it goes by the name "Marsala." But only Jerez unites all the optimum conditions for sherry production. The complex interplay of air, sun, soil, aging, and tradition exists nowhere else in the world.

Climate is one of the keys to successful sherry production. The very predictable weather conditions of Jerez, where the sun shines most of the year, mean that grape crops are of uniformly high quality. The chalky *albariza* soil, found only in Jerez, is just as important for the proper development of the vines, for it crusts and locks in the limited moisture supply below the ground. Nature more or less controls these early stages of sherry production, but from the time of the September harvest, or *vendimia*—a time of great festivity in Jerez—man's role in sherry making becomes important. After fermentation has begun, the *capataz*, the official wine taster for each sherry company, makes a preliminary and tentative classification of the newly formed wine into three categories: *fino* (dry), *oloroso* (medium-sweet), and undetermined—wine that will be distilled into a neutral brandy and used for sherry fortification. The great mystery of sherry is that grapes from the same harvest and vineyard will develop differently, some tending toward sweetness, others to dryness. Man has no control over this—he can only taste, then classify that which has already been determined by nature, which is why the taster plays such an important role in sherry production. At the prestigious Pedro Domecq company, the chief taster is none other than the dapper José Ignacio Domecq, a direct descendant of the company's early founders. He has been the taster at Domecq for forty years and is fondly referred to around the world as "The Nose" because of his enormous olfactory abilities and also because of the generous size of his nose. It is he alone who will determine the ultimate quality and taste of Domecq sherries.

Next comes the aging process in which sherry, contrary to table wines, will be exposed to light and air in vast sun-filled naves. As befits the wine from the liveliest and sunniest region of Spain, there are no dank, dark, and somber cellars involved in sherry making. Light and air, which would spell disaster for table wines, contribute to sherry's unique taste. Wines stay in these naves for two years, during which time the drier ones will develop *flor*, a yeast that seems to exist only in Jerez and is one reason dry sherries are not found elsewhere. The master taster then further subdivides the sherries and sends them along to the final *solera*, or blending stage. Sherry kegs are placed in rows, then in tiers, usually five kegs high. The oldest wines are at the bottom in kegs more than a century old that may still contain traces of sherry from the nineteenth century (blending makes it impossible to determine the exact contents of barrels). The youngest wines are at the top, and as they age they are transferred to the next level, while the upper kegs are refilled with younger wines. This is the first step of a laborious process that will eventually end many years later when these wines reach the lowest level and are drawn off for bottling. Such blending eliminates vintages and is another factor in the consistently high quality of sherry wines. Don't be misled by a sherry bottle that reads, to take an example, "Solera 1895." This does not refer to a vintage, but rather to the year when a *solera* system of blending was begun, which has been in use ever since.

Three more steps must be taken before bottling: the sherry is clarified by beating in egg whites to carry away any sediment, the sweetness is varied, again according to the dictates of the taster, and the wine is fortified to its full 16–20 per cent alcohol content. Fortification limits the use of sherry to before and after meals: for most tastes, it is too strong to accompany a main course.

There are basically four kinds of sherry. *Fino* is the most common dry sherry, the favored aperitif all over Andalucía. It is very pale in color and so dry that those accustomed to thinking of sherry as a sweet drink sometimes have difficulty getting used to it. But sherry devotees consider it the aristocrat of the sherry family and regard the sweeter varieties as inferior wines (it is true that the best grapes do go into making *finos*). If you are trying this wonderful wine for the first time, be sure to have cold shrimp or salted almonds on hand to fully appreciate what an exquisite accompaniment this wine can be. *Manzanilla* is a variety of *fino*, is extremely dry and produced only in the town of Sanlúcar de Barrameda. *Manzanilla* has a unique salty tang, attributed to the vineyards' proximity to the Atlantic Ocean. Although production is limited, one or two brands of this sherry are available in the United States. *Amontillado* is a pale almond color, less dry than a *fino* but equally appropriate before a meal. *Oloroso,* meaning "fragrant," is a deep amber color and definitely in the dessert category, although Dry Sack, widely advertised as an aperitif, falls into this grouping. Cream sherry, slightly thick and syrupy and deeper in tone than the *oloroso*, is perhaps the most popular sherry in America, sipped with desserts, over coffee, or simply as a soothing late evening drink on a cold night. (The damp British climate is probably one reason these sweet sherries are so very popular in that country.)
country.)

The best way to learn about sherries is by comparison tastings. Line up four sherries in order of sweetness and, starting with the driest, sample each one. It is more fun still to organize a sherry tasting with friends and accompany the drinks with an interesting array of *tapas* for the dry sherries and desserts for the sweeter sherries. (See the Menu Suggestions section for party ideas, p. 425.) In this way you can help spread the word that sherry, in all its forms, is a wonderful wine, well worth adding to your wine repertoire.

NOTE TO SHERRY CHART

Sherries are blended and fortified wines, and therefore the variations are endless. The following chart groups sherries into very general categories, and within each classification there will be sherries slightly drier or sweeter than others.

Fino and *manzanilla* are the driest sherries and are always served chilled. They go with any kind of appetizer, but are most delicious with nuts and shellfish. *Amontillado* is a bit sweeter, but is also served chilled and as an accompaniment to appetizers. *Oloroso* and cream sherries are drinks to serve at room temperature with desserts, *oloroso* with light desserts and cream sherry with rich desserts. Those who like sweet aperitifs enjoy *oloroso* as a cocktail, chilled, and there are many who love cream sherry as a nightcap. There are about sixty sherry companies in Spain, and each usually offers a full range of sherries from dry to sweet, many of which are available in the United States.

Fine wines are always enhanced by beautiful clear crystal glasses, and sherry is no exception. It is appalling to see how some establishments serve sherry, sometimes in metal stemware and filled to the brim. Sherry glasses must be clear in order to fully appreciate the beautiful color and clarity of the wine; stemmed for elegance, as well as for keeping hands off the glass so that they don't warm a chilled sherry; tulip shaped, tapering slightly at the top to hold the bouquet and to allow the nose to savor the wine. They must be large enough, comfortably holding two ounces with a breathing space of about one inch to the rim for the release of the wine's bouquet. In Spain a glass called a *copita* is traditionally used, but it is sometimes difficult to find in America. As an alternative, a large whiskey-sour glass may be used, or any cordial glass; you should always look for glasses that curve inward at the mouth.

The following chart should prove invaluable to the wine customer and merchant alike, for although every liquor store stocks dozens of sherries, rarely will you be able to ascertain what type of sherry is in each bottle. Often the labels simply don't say, or sometimes they provide misleading information. To clear up the confusion, I have devised this chart, which is, to my knowledge, the only complete guide to sherries that is available in the United States.

Sherries

DRY SHERRIES

(*Fino* and *Manzanilla*)

Names	Producers	Price Range
*Barbadillo Manzanilla	Antonio Barbadillo	$$
Don Fino	Sandeman	$$
*Don Zoilo	Don Zoilo	$$
El Palacio	González Byass	$
Fino Apitiv	Sandeman	$$
Fino Feria	Duff Gordon	$$
*Fino Quinta	Osborne	$$
Gran Barquero (Montilla wine)	Perez Barquero	$$
*Hartley & Gibson Fino	A.R. Valdespino	$
*Hartley & Gibson Manzanilla	A.R. Valdespino	$
*Jarana	Emilio Lustau	$$
*La Ina	Pedro Domecq	$$
*Manzanilla La Gitana	Vinícola Hidalgo	$
Palomino Dry	Palomino & Vergara	$
Pando	Williams & Humbert	$$
Pinta	Duff Gordon	$$
Savory & James Fino	Savory & James	$
Savory & James Fino Manzanilla	Savory & James	$
*Tío Pepe	González Byass	$$
*Tres Palmas	M. Ant. de la Riva	$
Wisdom & Warter Pale Fino	Wisdom & Warter	$

*Personal Preference
$ = inexpensive; $$ = moderate; $$$ = expensive; $$$$ = very expensive

MEDIUM–DRY SHERRIES

(*Amontillado*)

Names	Producers	Price Range
Bristol Dry	Harvey	$$
Carlito	Williams & Humbert	$$
Club Dry	Duff Gordon	$$
Don Zoilo Medium	Don Zoilo	$$
*Dos Cortados (rare)	Williams & Humbert	$$$
Dry Don	Sandeman	$$
El Cid	Duff Gordon	$$
El Palacio	González Byass	$
*Hartley & Gibson Amontillado	A.R. Valdespino	$
Osborne Amontillado	Osborne	$
Palomino Amontillado	Palomino & Vergara	$
*Peninsula Palo Cortado	Emilio Lustau	$$
Primero Amontillado	Pedro Domecq	$$
Royal Amontillado	M. Ant. de la Riva	$
*Royal Ambrosante (rare)	Sandeman	$$$
*Royal Esmeralda (rare)	Sandeman	$$
Savory & James Amontillado	Savory & James	$
*Sibarita Rare	Pedro Domecq	$$$$
Wisdom & Warter Extra Amontillado	Wisdom & Warter	$

MEDIUM–SWEET SHERRIES

(*Oloroso*)

Names	Producers	Price Range
Almancenista	Emilio Lustau	$$
Armada Cream	Sandeman	$$
Don Nuño	Emilio Lustau	$$
*Dry Sack	Williams & Humbert	$$
Duff Gordon #28	Duff Gordon	$$
*Imperial Corregidor (rare)	Sandeman	$$$

*Personal Preference
$ = inexpensive; $$ = moderate; $$$ = expensive; $$$$ = very expensive

MEDIUM-SWEET SHERRIES (cont'd)
(*Oloroso*)

*Imperial Oloroso (rare)	Pedro Domecq	$$$$
Niña	Duff Gordon	$$
*Rio Viejo	Pedro Domecq	$$
*Royal Corregidor (rare)	Sandeman	$$$
Shooting Sherry	Harvey	$$

SWEET SHERRIES
(*Cream*)

Names	Producers	Price Range
Alvear Fino Cream (Montilla wine)	Alvear	$
Alvear Pedro Ximénez (Montilla wine)	Alvear	$
Argueso Pedro Ximénez (very sweet)	A.R. Valdespino	$$
*Bristol Cream	Harvey	$$
Bristol Milk	Harvey	$$
*Celebration Cream	Pedro Domecq	$$
Canasta Cream	Williams & Humbert	$$
Character	Sandeman	$$
Delicate Cream	Wisdom & Warter	$
Double Century Cream	Pedro Domecq	$
El Palacio Cream	González Byass	$
Gran Barquero (Montilla wine)	Pérez Barquero	$
*Hartley & Gibson Cream	A.R. Valdespino	$
Osborne Cream	Osborne	$
Palomino Cream	Palomino & Vergara	$
Royal Cream	M. Ant. de la Riva	$
Sandeman Fine Rich Cream	Sandeman	$$
Santa María	Duff Gordon	$$
Savory & James Cream	Savory & James	$

*Personal Preference

$ = inexpensive; $$ = moderate; $$$ = expensive; $$$$ = very expensive

SWEET SHERRIES (cont'd)
(*Cream*)

Names	Producers	Price Range
*Venerable Rare-Ximénez (very sweet)	Pedro Domecq	$$$$
Vina #25 (very sweet)	Pedro Domecq	$$

NOTE TO DESSERT WINES, SPARKLING WINES, BRANDIES, AND LIQUEURS

Many Spanish brandies are made by the French Cognac process and are of exceptionally fine quality. Most come from Jerez and are distilled from sherry, although the Torres company in Cataluña has also begun to produce and export some excellent brandies. In the higher price ranges, the carefully aged Spanish brandies are every bit the equal of their French counterparts, but, as with Spanish wines, the brandies have a "Spanish" quality all their own.

Sparkling Spanish wines are also made by French methods, developed in Champagne. The Penedés region near Barcelona (and more specifically, the town of San Sadurní de Noya,) is one of the largest sparkling wine producers in the world, and its wines have gained wide acceptance in domestic and foreign markets, competing remarkably well with French Champagne. In the United States the selection of *cavas*, as they are called in Spain, has increased dramatically. They are fresh and fruity, low priced and top quality, and I highly recommend them.

There are few Spanish liqueurs available in the United States market. They are very pleasant, often herbally scented, and sometimes quite sweet.

Dessert Wines, Sparkling Wines,
Brandies, and Liqueurs

DESSERT WINES

Names	Producers	Area	Characteristics	Price Range
*Extrísimo	Masía Bach	Penedés	Oaky, sweet white	$
Gran Vino Sansón	Luis Barceló	Málaga	Very sweet syrupy, taste of raisins	$$

SPARKLING WINES
Champagne Method
(Cavas)

Names	Producers	Area	Characteristics	Price Range
Conde de Haro	Bodegas Muga	Rioja	Very dry	$$
Brut Zero	Castellblanch	Penedés	Very dry	$$
Extra	Castellblanch	Penedés	Dry	$$
Cristal	Castellblanch	Penedés	Medium-dry	$$
*Gran Codorníu	Codorníu	Penedés	Very dry	$$$
Blanc de Blanc	Codorníu	Penedés	Very dry	$$
*Brut Clásico	Codorníu	Penedés	Very dry	$$
Brut Natural	Codorníu	Penedés	Very dry	$$
Brut de Noir (Rosé)	Codorníu	Penedés	Very dry	$$
Blanc de Blanc	Conde de Caralt	Penedés	Very dry	$

*Personal Preference
$ = inexpensive; $$ = moderate; $$$ = expensive; $$$$ = very expensive

SPARKLING WINES (cont'd)

Brut Barroco	Freixenet	Penedés	Very dry	$$
Blanc de Blanc	Freixenet	Penedés	Very dry	$$
Brut Nature	Freixenet	Penedés	Very dry	$$
Carta Nevada Brut	Freixenet	Penedés	Very dry	$$
Cordón Negro	Freixenet	Penedés	Very dry	$$
Carolina Brut	Joseph Masachs	Penedés	Very dry	$$
*Reserva de la Familia	Juvé y Camps	Penedés	Very dry	$$
*Gran Cru	Juvé y Camps	Penedés	Very dry	$$$
Gran Tradición	Marques de Monistrol	Penedés	Very dry	$$
*Blanc de Blanc	Marqués de Monistrol	Penedés	Very dry	$
Blanc de Blanc	Paul Cheneau	Penedés	Very dry	$$
*Lembey	Pedro Domecq	Penedés	Very dry	$$
Brut Reserva	Segura Viudas	Penedés	Very dry	$$

AGED BRANDIES

Names	Producers	Area	Characteristics	Price Range
*Cardenal Mendoza	Sánchez Romate	Jerez	Full-bodied, very smooth and aromatic	$$$$
*Carlos I	Pedro Domecq	Jerez	Good bouquet, extremely smooth	$$$
*Conde de Osborne	Osborne	Jerez	Old, mellow, Dalí bottle	$$$$
*Gran Duque de Alba	Zoilo Ruiz Mateos	Jerez	Full-bodied, smooth, excellent bouquet	$$$$
Imperial	Miguel Torres	Penedés	Smooth and aromatic	$$$
*Lepanto	González Byass	Jerez	Very old, very dry and smooth	$$$$
*Marqués de Domecq	Pedro Domecq	Jerez	Extraordinarily old brandy of very limited production	$$$$

*Personal Preference

$ = inexpensive; $$ = moderate; $$$ = expensive; $$$$ = very expensive

OTHER BRANDIES

Names	Producers	Area	Characteristics	Price Range
Fundador	Pedro Domecq	Jerez	Average everyday brandy	$$
Felipe II	Agustín Blázquez	Jerez	Average everyday brandy	$$
*Magno	Osborne	Jerez	Good everyday brandy	$$
Soberano	González Byass	Jerez	Good everyday brandy	$$
Terry Centenario	Terry	Jerez	Average everyday brandy	$$
Three Vines	Pedro Domecq	Jerez	Average everyday brandy	$$
Tres Torres	Miguel Torres	Penedés	Average everyday brandy	$$
Veterano	Osborne	Jerez	Average everyday brandy	$$

LIQUEURS

Names	Producers	Area	Characteristics	Price Range
Aguardiente Chinchón	La Chinchonera	Chinchón	Dry, anise flavor	$$
Anís Chinchón	La Chinchonera	Chinchón	Sweet, anise flavor	$$
*Anís del Mono Dulce	Vicente Bosch	Badalona (Barcelona)	Sweet, anise flavor	$$
*Anís del Mono Seco	Vicente Bosch	Badalona (Barcelona)	Dry, anise flavor	$$
*Licor 43 Mirabilis	Diego Zamora	Cartagena (Murcia)	Sweet, vanilla taste	$$
*Miguel Torres Orange Liqueur	Miguel Torres	Penedés	Brandy-based orange herbal liqueur	$$
Pacharán	Distillerías Vianas	Navarra	Sweet, made from bilberries	$$

Menu Suggestions

THESE menus are designed, in general, as three-course meals. If you wish appetizers besides, make selections from the Tapas chapter.

DINNER MENUS

Menu 1

Shellfish Vinaigrette

Seafood-Flavored Rice, Alicante Style

Eggplant, Artichoke, Pepper, and Tomato Salad

Dry white Rioja wine

Fruits and Cheeses

Espresso coffee and Carlos I brandy

Menu 2

Cold Fish Timbale with Mayonnaise Dressing

Dry white Rioja wine (optional)

Veal Chops with Ham, Mushrooms, and Pimiento

Poor Man's Potatoes

Light red Rioja wine

Frozen Orange Custard with Blackberry Sauce

Espresso coffee and Lepanto brandy

Menu 3

Shrimp Cocktail, Spanish Style

Dry white Rioja wine (optional)

Duck with Olives in Sherry Sauce

Roast Potatoes

Salad, Murcia Style

Light red Reserva wine

Prune Ice Cream in Orange Liqueur Sauce

"Cat's Tongue" Cookies

Menu 4

Gazpacho (Cold Tomato Soup)

Paella (Chicken and Seafood Rice)

Escarole Salad with Tomato and Cumin Dressing

Sangría

Flan del Gran Flanero (Caramel Custard)

Espresso coffee and Licor 43 liqueur

Menu 5

Garlic Soup, "Casa Irene"

Dry (*fino*) sherry (optional)

Mixed Seafood in *Romesco* Sauce

Cucumber, Tomato, and Pepper Salad

Dry white Penedés wine

Catalán Custard

Coffee and Duque de Alba brandy

HEARTY WINTER MENUS

Menu 6

Asturian Bean Stew
Mixed Salad, San Isidro Style
Valdepeñas full-bodied red wine
Rice Pudding, Asturian Style

Menu 7

Soup of *Cocido*
Boiled Beef and Chickpea
   Dinner (*Cocido*)
Valdepeñas full-bodied red wine
Cream-Filled Fritters

COLD SUMMER MENU
(Prepare entirely one day in advance)

Menu 8

White *Gazpacho* with Grapes,
   Málaga Style
Medium-dry white Rioja
   wine (optional)
Marinated Quail
Green Bean Salad
Light red Rioja wine
Cinnamon-Flavored Ice Milk
Powdered Sugar Cookies

SEAFOOD DINNER

Menu 9

Mussels in Green Sauce
Bonito and Tomato Soup,
   Basque Style

Fish Steaks with Ham and Cheese
Garlic Green Beans
Dry white Rioja wine
Fruits and Cheeses

SPECIAL OCCASION MENUS

Traditional Christmas Eve Dinner
Menu 10

Onion and Almond Soup
Baked Porgy, Madrid Style
Dry white Rioja wine
Roast Turkey
Baked Red Cabbage and Apples
Light red Reserva wine
Fruits and Cheeses
Turfon candy
Marzipan Candies
Espresso coffee and Marqués de
   Domecq brandy

Medieval Supper
Menu 11

Garlic Soup, Castilian Style
Marinated Trout
Dry white Penedés wine
Roast Lamb, Castilian Style
Eggplant with Cheese
Full-bodied red Rioja wine
Custard-Filled Dessert Pancakes
Flaming Liqueur with Apples

Tapas and Sherry-Tasting Party
Menu 12

Stuffed Mussels
Anchovy and Pimiento Spread
Marinated and Fried Frogs' Legs

Menu 12 (cont'd.)
Chicken and Ham Croquettes
Cod Puffs
Tuna Turnovers
Veal Turnovers
Chorizo with Wine and Pimientos
Potato Omelet
Ensaladilla Rusa
Marinated Mussels
Shrimp Pancakes
Sausages with Sweet-Sour Figs
Lamb Meatballs in Brandy Sauce
Manzanilla sherry
Fino sherry
Amontillado sherry
Small Desserts (no forks necessary)
Anise-Flavored Fried Pastries
Bizcocho Borracho a la Crema
Almond and Egg Yolk Candies
Miniature Anise-Flavored Doughnuts
Custard Horns
Oloroso sherry
Cream sherry

LUNCHEON MENUS

Menu 13

Eggplant with Shrimp and Ham
Watercress and Carrot Salad in
    Anchovy Dressing
White Penedés wine
Orange Ice Cream Cake

Menu 14

Tomato and Green Pepper Pie
Soft-Set Eggs with Shrimp
    and Spinach

Dry white Rioja wine
Fig and Candied Squash Pastries

BRUNCH MENUS

Menu 15

Lemonade, Madrid Style
Potato Omelet
Asturian-Style Sausage or
    Catalán Sausage
Basic Long Loaf Bread
Almond and Quince Puff
    Pastry Strips

Menu 16

Sausage Buns
Baked Mushrooms and Eggs
Stewed Prunes and Apricots
Almond Cookies

REGIONAL MENUS

Galacian Dinner
Menu 17

Beef, Beans, and Greens Soup,
    Galician Style
Pork Pie
Galician red wine
Almond Cake

Asturian Dinner
Menu 18

Onion, Tuna, and Tomato Omelet
Pork Chops with Apples in
    Cider Sauce

Asturian Cider
Walnut-Filled Turnovers

Basque Dinner
Menu 19

Stuffed Crab
Butterflied Porgy, Bilbao Style
Green Beans and Cured Ham
Dry white Rioja wine
Fried Custard Squares

Castilian Dinner
Menu 20

Tripe, Madrid Style
Stewed Partridge
Peas with Cured Ham
Full-bodied red Rioja wine
Sugar-Coated Fried Bread

Catalán Dinner
Menu 21

Baked Sausage and Mushrooms
Shellfish Medley (*Zarzuela*)
Green Salad with Creamy
   Almond Dressing
Catalán Custard

Andalucian Dinner
Menu 22

Baked Eggs with Ham, Sausage,
   and Asparagus
Porgy Baked in Salt
Dry white Rioja wine
Custard-Filled Cake Roll
Oloroso sherry

Valencian Dinner
Menu 23

Marinated and Fried Frogs Legs
Traditional Valencian *Paella*
Potato and Orange Salad
White Penedés wine
Orange Almond Cake

Rioja Dinner
Menu 24

Mixed Vegetables, Rioja Style
Chicken with Red Peppers
Spicy Potatoes
Light red Rioja wine
Pears in Wine Sauce

A Glossary of Spanish Foods and Cooking Equipment

Aguardiente, also called *orujo*, is a powerful Spanish liqueur popular as a drink in Galicia and used very sparingly in cooking. Its Italian equivalent, *grappa*, is widely available here, and although it has a lower alcohol content than the Spanish liqueur, it is an adequate substitute.

Bacon, slab, is simply bacon in a block rather than in thin slices. It is often used in Spanish cooking, diced or cut in chunks. Although thin sliced bacon will give the desired flavor, it burns too easily and cannot take the heat that cubes of bacon can. It also does not provide texture. Slab bacon is often found in supermarkets.

Butifarra sausage is a white sausage that comes from Cataluña. It is spiced with cinnamon, nutmeg, and cloves and used extensively in Catalán cooking. A recipe for *butifarra* can be found on page 55. Otherwise, Italian sweet sausage is a passable substitute.

Chorizo is the most typical Spanish sausage, heavily scented with paprika and garlic. It is eaten cold and sliced or fried as an appetizer and also enters into many cooked dishes. You may make your own *chorizo* (p. 54) or buy it in any Spanish specialty food store, as well as in some supermarkets. Spanish-style, as opposed to South American–style, *chorizo* is mild. *Chorizo* that is less cured is most often used in cooking while the harder and drier *chorizos* are eaten as cold cuts.

Cider (sidra) is a hard, very dry cider that is the typical drink of Asturias in northern Spain, often replacing wine as a lunch or dinner accompaniment. It is also used to make sauces for meat and fish. Use only hard cider available in liquor stores. It is a bit sweeter than the Asturian cider (and therefore not as appropriate as a dinner drink) but works very well in cooking. A sparkling cider imported from Spain is often found in Spanish markets. This product is quite sweet and meant to be used like champagne, not as a cooking liquid.

Codfish, dried salted (bacalao), is a favorite in Spain in interior areas with no access to the sea, as well as in the north, where fresh fish is plentiful. Its strong flavor is not to everyone's liking, but when well prepared in an interesting sauce, it can be outstanding. Look for cod that is well dried and white—avoid pieces that have a yellow cast to them. Cod that has been boned and skinned before drying is much easier to handle and to eat. Each cod recipe gives instructions for the preparation of cod suitable for that recipe, but all call for a soaking period of 24 to 36 hours to remove the salt.

Earthenware dishes (cazuelas), glazed on the inside and rough and unfinished without, are the most common pieces of Spanish cooking equipment. Spanish cooks prefer earthenware because it heats evenly and it retains heat long after the dish has been removed from the stove. These dishes, usually wide and shallow, come in individual as well as casserole sizes and are often for sale in Spanish markets, imported from Spain. Other earthenware dishes are now sometimes found in department stores and kitchen specialty shops but do not usually have the proper size or shape to be used as *cazuelas*. If earthenware dishes are to be used on top of the stove, as they frequently are in Spain, they should first be treated to prevent cracking. (I also like to place a metallic mesh burner cover over the flame to better distribute the heat.) There are two methods recommended. The old-fashioned Spanish way, suggested by Señor Moneo at the Casa Moneo Spanish market in New York City, works very well: rub the unglazed outer sides and bottom of the casserole with a cut clove of garlic, then rub with oil so that the oil penetrates the clay. Place about ¼ inch of oil inside the dish, then place in a 300° F oven for about 20 minutes. The dish is then ready to use. A simpler method calls for filling the *cazuela* half full of water and adding ½ cup of vinegar. Slowly bring to a boil on top of the stove and boil until the liquid has evaporated. Even after treatment, never pour very cold liquid into a hot dish or vice versa.

Ham, cured (jamón serrano), is used in a surprising variety of Spanish recipes. Italian prosciutto is the closest cured ham available here. Try to find prosciutto that is not too salty or dry (Daniele and Citterio are two very good brands). Never substitute smoked cured ham—it will give an entirely different flavor that is not appropriate to Spanish cooking.

Many recipes call for cured ham diced or in cubes. Buy the ham, therefore, in slices at least ¼ inch thick. When larger pieces are required—for example, in soups—it is best to buy the narrow end of the ham in a piece at least 1 inch thick.

Lard, or solidified rendered pork fat, is used in baking as well as in frying, sautéing, and basting meats and fowl. Although used sparingly in this book, when it is called for, it lends a special flavor to foods, and I recommend its use. However, for main courses, olive oil may be substituted; in baking, vegetable shortening may be used. When buying lard, look for packages labeled "100% pure lard" (such as the Tobin brand) and skip those that contain chemical preservatives. Better still, render your own lard from "leaf lard," available in butcher shops.

Morcilla is a Spanish blood sausage often used in stews and sliced and fried as an accompaniment to eggs or as an appetizer. When it is of excellent quality, it is one of my favorite sausages—otherwise I prefer not to eat it. The *morcilla* found vacuum packed is usually not very good. Look for the unpackaged kinds found in Spanish markets. The type called "Argentinian" is quite good, but I most enjoy the *morcilla* that contains rice, sometimes called "Colombian style." If top-quality *morcilla* cannot be found, it can usually be omitted from recipes without drastically changing the character of the dish.

Olive oil is the oil used almost exclusively in Spanish cooking—except in dessert making, when salad oil is more commonly used. An unsaturated fat, olive oil is excellent for those watching cholesterol. Olive oil may be highest quality extra virgin (unrefined, less than 1% acidity), virgin (less than 1.5% acidity) or pure (chemically refined). Virgin oils are generally more fruity and complex and used when a more assertive flavor is desired (in salads, for example). Use pure oils for general cooking and frying.

Paprika, ground sweet red pepper, can be made from many different varieties of red pepper. For authentic flavor, use paprika *(pimentón)* imported from Spain.

Peppers, dried hot red, are a common ingredient in many Spanish dishes, used to give a slight hotness to a sauce. They are often added in a single piece, or broken into large pieces, and are not meant to be eaten. The seeds are not used. You may substitute crushed red pepper, available in all supermarkets, but this will contain the pepper seeds, which will give added spiciness. Using crushed pepper also means that the pepper pieces will be distributed throughout a sauce, which is not always desirable.

Peppers, dried sweet red (ñoras, pimientos romescos, or *pimientos choriceros),* lend a wonderfully earthy taste to foods, are used in several rice dishes, and are essential in two of the most outstanding dishes of Spanish cuisine, Bacalao a la Vizcaína and Gran Romesco de Pescado. Although hot red peppers of numerous varieties can be found here in Mexican and South American markets, the dried sweet peppers are hard to get. The closest I have found to the sweet red pepper used in Spain is an elongated dried pepper called "New Mexico," which has just a slight piquantness that it loses in cooking. It is well worth the effort to find dried sweet peppers for the special character they give to several dishes in this book. I have tried a combination of paprika and pimientos as a substitute (about 3 teaspoons paprika and 1 pimiento to each dried red pepper), but I really do not find this mixture an adequate substitute.

Pimiento is nothing more than the Spanish word for peppers, but in English it has come to mean red peppers that are preprepared by cooking, skinning, and seeding. Pimientos are used extensively in Spanish cooking. If using canned pimientos, purchase only those imported from Spain—domestic pimientos are mushy and fall apart in cooking. It is, of course, preferable to make your own, especially since red peppers seem to be available now all year round. Simply place the red peppers in a roasting pan and bake at 375° F for 35 minutes, turning once. Peel off the skin and remove the seeds. They may be kept refrigereated for several days, wrapped in foil or in a covered container.

Saffron (azafrán), an Arab word for "yellow," consists of the stigmas of a purple crocus flower. Saffron adds color and a distinct flavor, somewhat akin to tea, to Spanish rice dishes as well as to other main-course meals. Most of the world's saffron comes from Spain, and because of the arduous process of collection, it is the most expensive spice in the world. Its strong flavor means that it is always used in small quantities. Substitutes, such as tumeric and Mexican marigold petals, will lack the flavor and aroma of saffron and should not be used in Spanish cooking.

Salt, coarse, sometimes called kosher salt, is recommended for use in *all* recipes calling for salt, although in some it is more important than others. Meats and poultry that are sprinkled with salt before sautéing fry better when coarse salt is used. It is also much better for sprinkling on foods already cooked, for it does not penetrate the foods as fine salt does. Coarse salt is essential for the fish dish Urta a la Sal. If, however, the salt is going to dissolve in cooking, fine salt will do just as well. I have indicated coarse salt in recipes when that type of salt is most important.

Turrón is a Spanish almond and honey candy of Arab origin that comes in a crackling hard bar (Alicante style) and in a soft marzipanlike form (Jijona style). Both are available, especially during the Christmas season, in Spanish markets, imported from Spain. *Turrón* is excellent eaten as a candy and is used besides in several dessert recipes in this book. Despite a visit to a *turrón* factory in Jijona, Spain, and innumerable attempts to produce a recipe for this candy, I have not been able to create a *turrón* that measures up to the imported candy.

Spanish Cheese

UNTIL recently, Spanish cheeses were rarely available in the United States. But as interest in cheese in general increases and Americans search for new and exciting tastes, a small but growing market for the great cheese of Spain has developed. Spanish cheese is unlike any other imported cheese; the raw product may be the same—goat, sheep or cow's milk—but the taste is distinctly Spanish. I have every confidence that the American consumer will realize the undeniable merits of Spanish cheese, just as we have recognized the superb quality of Spanish wines, and demand the authentic product. If your cheese store does not yet have any of the dozen or so varieties now imported from Spain, they may order them through De Choix Specialty Foods, Woodside, New York.

I offer the following cheese descriptions for those of you buying here and also for those who may wish to sample cheese while traveling in Spain and perhaps bring some home (it is perfectly acceptable under American customs regulations to bring back cheese from Spain). In Spain cheese is generally bought at delicatessen-type stores called *mantequerías* or *tiendas de ultramarinos*. And if you wish to picnic, these stores can also provide a large selection of cold cuts (see the introduction to the sausage section of this book for specific types and names), olives, breads and canned goods.

Although every region of Spain has its own kind of cheese, the following are some of the most popular:

Queso Manchego, sheep's-milk cheese from the central plains of La Mancha, is perhaps the cheese most widely available in Spain. It runs the range from semi-soft and mild to hard and sharp, depending on how long it has been cured. One delicious variety is cured for several months in olive oil. Spaniards love Queso Manchego as an appetizer with *chorizo* sausage or cured ham. Imported Italian "table cheese" can sometimes be similar.
Queso Cabrales is a wonderful, blue-streaked cow's-milk cheese, aged in the mountain caves of Asturias and wrapped in tree leaves. It is strong but not bitter, smoother, and less biting than a French Roquefort.
Queso del Roncal is produced in the Spanish Pyrenees from cow and sheep milk. It has the consistency of a medium-hard Parmesan but is milder and smoother than the Italian cheese. It is similar to Queso Manchego.
Queso de Mahón comes from the island of Menorca and is a semi-soft, cow's-milk cheese with an unusual and unexpectedly strong taste—a little like a Gouda.

*Personal preference

Queso de Idiazábal is a smoked sheep's-milk cheese from the Basque country and bought in small balls. There are two types: fresh, a soft cheese with a smoky aftertaste, and cured, lightly smoked and firm.

Queso Tetilla, cow's-milk cheese, so named because of its resemblance to a woman's breast, is a Galician cheese, creamy but never bland, with a lingering pungency. It is a cheese that pleases more with every tasting. A good-quality Monterey Jack cheese has a similar creamy consistency but lacks the character of Tetilla cheese.

Queso de San Simón from Galicia is a cow's-milk cheese, pear shaped, heavily smoked, and medium-cured, with a slight herbal flavor.

Queso de Burgos is a mild, pleasantly flavored cheese of sheep's milk, produced in and around the city of the same name. It is a fresh cheese, best eaten within a few days after it is made. Queso de Burgos is often served for dessert, sometimes with a topping of walnuts and honey. A fresh mozzarella has a similar texture and flavor.

Queso de Villalón is a fresh, mild, sheep's-milk cheese from Valladolid, somewhat like Queso de Burgos. It is shaped like an animal hoof—thus its other name, *Pata de Mulo* (mule's hoof).

Restaurants Mentioned in
The Foods and Wines of Spain

Andalucía (southern Spain)
  Bar Lo Güeno, Málaga
  El Anteojo, Cádiz
  El Burladero, Sevilla
  El Caballo Rojo, Córdoba
  El Faro, Cádiz
  Parador de Gibralfaro, Málaga

Aragón (northeastern Spain)
  Edelweiss, Torla

Asturias (northwestern Spain)
  Casa Fermín, Oviedo

Balearic Islands
  Casa Burdó, Fornells (Menorca)

Basque Country (northeastern Spain)
  Casa Cámara, Pasajes de San Juan
  Casa Nicolasa, San Sebastián

Castilla (central Spain)
  Café Gijón, Madrid
  Casa Botín, Madrid
  Casa Florencio, Aranda del Duero
  Casa Paco, Madrid
  Cerveceria Santa Bárbara, Madrid
  Espartero, Madrid
  Hostal de San Marcos, León
  Lhardy, Madrid
  Los Caracoles, Madrid
  Malacatin, Madrid
  Mallorca, Madrid
  Mesón de Cándido, Segovia
  Mesón de Don Pedro, Madrid
  Posada de Javier, Torrecaballeros

Cataluña (northeastern Spain)
  Agut d'Avignón, Barcelona
  Casa Irene, Artiés
  Los Caracoles, Barcelona

Restaurante Sant Climent,
  Sol-Ric, Tarragona

Extremadura (west-central Spain)
  Parador Nacional Vía de la
    Plata, Mérida

Galicia (northwestern Spain)
  Bar Coruña, Santiago de
    Compostela
  Duna-2, La Coruña
  Hostal de los Reyes Católicos,
    Santiago de Compostela
  Viuda de Alfredín, La Coruña

Huesca (northeastern Spain)
  El Galán, Santa María

Levante (southeastern Spain)
  El Pegolí, Denia
  Els Capellans, Elche
  La Pepica, Valencia
  Merendero La Plana, Jávea
  Racó de l'Olla, El Palmar
    (Valencia)
  Rincón de Pepe, Murcia

Navarra (northeastern Spain)
  Las Pocholas, Pamplona

Rioja (northeastern Spain)
  Beethoven, Haro
  Mesón Terete, Haro
  Parador Santo Domingo de la
    Calzada, Santo Domingo de la
    Calzada

New York City
  Café San Martín
  Mesón Botín
  Rincón de España

Marketing Sources

Spanish Foods and Cooking Equipment

CONSULT your local yellow pages under "Grocers-Retail" for more stores carrying Spanish products. Also, many supermarkets around the country, especially in neighborhoods where there is a demand, carry a line of Spanish products, usually those made under the Goya brand name.

ANN ARBOR

*Zingerman's
422 Detroit Street
Ann Arbor, Michigan 48104
(313) 769-2097
A great selection of quality
Spanish food imports.

ATLANTA

*Diaz Market
106 6 Street, NE
Atlanta, Georgia 30308
(404) 872-0928
Several other locations also in
Atlanta.

CHICAGO

*Casa Esteiro
2719 West Division
Chicago, Illinois 60622
(312) 252-5432
Imported Spanish cheeses in
addition to the usual Spanish
products.

International Food Shop
1135 West Belmont Avenue
Chicago, Illinois 60657
(312) 525-7838

La Casa del Pueblo
1810 South Blue Island Avenue
Chicago, Illinois 60608
(312) 421-4640

Supermercado Gutierrez
1628 West Montrose Avenue
Chicago, Illinois 60613
(312) 271-7741

*El Original Supermercado
Cardenas*
3922 North Sheridan Road
Chicago, Illinois 60613
(312) 525-5610

CLEVELAND

Spanish American Food Market
7001 Wade Park Avenue
Cleveland, Ohio 44103
(216) 432-2720

DALLAS

Mendez Grocery
3725 McKinney Avenue
Dallas, Texas 75204
(214) 521-5451

DETROIT

Moreno's Market
425 Puritan Street
Detroit, Michigan 48203
(313) 554-1168

La Fiesta Market
3438 Bagley Street
Detroit, Michigan 48216
(313) 554-1168

*Most complete selection of food and cooking equipment

FORT LAUDERDALE

*La Aurora Super Market
341 SW 40 Avenue
Fort Lauderdale, Florida 33317
(305) 583-9733

HARTFORD

La Placita del Pueblo
546 Park Street
Hartford, Connecticut 06101
(203) 246-1825

HOUSTON

Fiesta Mart
5600 Mykawa Road
Houston, Texas 77037
(713) 644-1611

LOS ANGELES

La Raza Mercado
716 North Virgil Avenue
Los Angeles, California 90029
(213) 663-5882

El Mercado Grocery
3425 East First Avenue
Los Angeles, California 90063
(213) 269-2269

MIAMI

Ayestaran Supermarket
700 SW 27 Avenue
Miami, Florida 33135
(305) 642-3539

MILWAUKEE

Elrey
1023 S. 16 Street
Milwaukee, Wisconsin 53204
(414) 643-1640

El Paraiso Grocery
1407 S. 7 Street
Milwaukee, Wisconsin 53204
(414) 643-4949

NEWARK

Caridad del Cobre
115 Roseville Avenue
Newark, New Jersey 07107
(201) 482-1827

NEW ORLEANS

Latin Super Market
1800 North Broad Street
New Orleans, Louisiana 70119
(504) 943-1988

NEW YORK

Dean & Deluca
560 Broadway
New York, New York 10012
(212) 431-1691
Fine Spanish foods and cooking
equipment. Mail order.

Paprikas Weiss
1546 Second Avenue
New York, New York 10028
(212) 288-6117
Mail order.

Iron Gate Products
424 West 54 Street
New York, New York 10019
(212) 757-2670
A variety of game, fresh and frozen,
including quail, partridge,
pheasant, rabbit, and wild duck.
Mail order.

*Most complete selection of food and cooking equipment

NEW YORK (cont'd)

España Specialties
41–01 Broadway
Astoria, New York 11103
(718) 932-9335

Ines Grocery
269 Willis Avenue
Mineola, New York 11501
(516) 746-6637
Fresh rabbit and frozen quail in
addition to the usual Spanish
products.

PHILADELPHIA

El Botecito
401 West Cumberland Street
Philadelphia, Pennsylvania 19133
(215) 634-8772

PITTSBURGH

Ou's International
707 Penn Avenue
Pittsburgh, Pennsylvania 15221
(412) 731-8810

PORTLAND

*Becerra Elda
108 NE 28 Avenue
Portland, Oregon 97232
(503) 233-6830

SAN FRANCISCO

*Casa Lucas Market
2934 24 Street
San Francisco, California 94110
(415) 826-4334

WASHINGTON, D.C.

Casa Peña
1638 17 Street, NW
Washington, D.C. 20009
(202) 462-2222

Eastern Market
400 East Capitol Street
Washington, D.C. 20003
(202) 547-7259
A source for game

Spanish Wine

The Wine Gallery
576 Avenue of the Americas
New York, New York 10011
(212) 242-2719

Crossroads Wine and Liquors
55 West 14 Street
New York, New York 10011
(212) 924-3060

Morrell & Company
535 Madison Avenue
New York, New York 10022
(212) 688-9370

Zachys
16 East Parkway
Scarsdale, New York 10583
(914) 723-0241

*Most complete selection of food and cooking equipment

Index

A NOTE ABOUT THE AUTHOR

PENELOPE CASAS was born in New York City, was graduated from Vassar College with a magna cum laude in Spanish literature, studied at the University of Madrid, and for a time taught Spanish literature and language in New York. She lived in Spain from 1965 to 1968 and since then she and her doctor husband, who was born in Spain, return there several times each year.

Penelope Casas has written about Spanish food and travel in Spain for *The New York Times, Gourmet, Connoisseur,* and *Condé Nast Traveler.* She teaches courses on Spain at New York University, where she is an Adjunct Professor, and has been awarded by the Spanish government the Spanish National Prize of Gastronomy, the Medal of Touristic Merit, and was named Dame of the Order of Civil Merit. She lives in New York with her husband and leads tours to Spain each year.

A NOTE ON THE TYPE

THE TEXT of this book was set in a film version of Bembo, the well-known monotype face. The original cutting of Bembo was made by Francesco Griffo of Bologna only a few years after Columbus discovered America. It was named for Pietro Bembo, the celebrated Renaissance writer and humanist scholar who was made a cardinal and served as secretary to Pope Leo X.

Sturdy, well balanced, and finely proportioned, Bembo is a face of rare beauty. It is, at the same time, extremely legible in all of its sizes.

Composed by Superior Printing, Champaign, Illinois.
Printed and bound by the Murray Printing Company,
Westford, Massachusetts.
Endpapers, pre-printed covers, and jackets printed by
Phillips Offset, Mamaroneck, New York.
Typography and binding design by Virginia Tan.

Mar Cantábrico
Asturias
La Coruña
Oviedo
Galicia
Santiago
León
Castilla
Atlántico
Salamanca
Segovi
Toledo
Cáceres
Extremadura
Córd
Andalucía
Sevilla
Jerez
Málaga
Islas
Canarias
Cádiz